Oct 2012

Thanks for your support of American Technion Society.

Best wishes,

[signature]

"The scope, brilliance, and power of this book makes it essential reading for everyone interested in understanding the major global challenges facing the United States, as well as the Jewish people and Israel in the twenty-first century, and how to meet them successfully. As Israel's major ally, Stuart Eizenstat compellingly makes the case that a strong America is an indispensable ingredient to a more secure Israel."—**Former Vice President Walter Mondale**

"In bold strokes, combined with meticulous knowledge of politics, economics, and technological innovations, [Eizenstat] paints the major challenges ahead, offering sober, wise, and measured advice, deeply anchored in his awareness of world trends as well as major Jewish concerns."—**Shlomo Avineri**, The Hebrew University of Jerusalem, former director-general of Israel's Foreign Ministry

"[Eizenstat's] book is a balanced, insightful, and sober but is ultimately optimistic assessment of the Jewish future in the face of a rapidly changing world. This book is an effective response to the doomsayers as well as to those who see smooth sailing ahead. It should serve as a useful guide for discussions about the Jewish future for years to come."—**Abraham Foxman**, national director, Anti-Defamation League

"This book illustrates what can be accomplished when the keen mind of the intellectual and the rich perspective of the practitioner are put together in order to reflect on the state of the Jewish people and to offer thought and advice on the challenges presented to them by the new world order. It is mandatory reading for Jews and Israelis who must adapt old policies and institutions to new conditions and for non-Jews who want to understand the concern of an unusually successful yet vulnerable people."—**Itamar Rabinovich**, Tel Aviv University, New York University, and Brookings Institution; former Israeli Ambassador to Washington and former president of Tel Aviv University

"An impressive grasp of the issues, powerfully and masterfully argued, this book should be required reading."—**Jehuda Reinharz**, president, Mandel Foundation and president emeritus, Brandeis University

"The fate of the Jews has always been influenced by their interaction with the global and regional environments. What will be the fate of the Jewish people and the Jewish state in the twenty-first century? Stuart Eizenstat's masterful, horizons broadening, and deeply thoughtful analysis of the global forces impacting on Western civilizations and the Jewish future is an eye opener for anyone interested in the fate of the Jewish people and Israel, and is an invitation for innovative action to those who wish to impact on the Jewish fate in the twenty-first century.—**Sallai Meridor**, former Israeli Ambassador to the United States

THE FUTURE OF THE JEWS

THE FUTURE OF THE JEWS

How Global Forces Are Impacting the Jewish People, Israel, and Its Relationship with the United States

Stuart E. Eizenstat

ROWMAN & LITTLEFIELD PUBLISHERS, INC.

Lanham • Boulder • New York • Toronto • Plymouth, UK

Published by Rowman & Littlefield Publishers, Inc.
A wholly owned subsidiary of The Rowman & Littlefield Publishing Group, Inc.
4501 Forbes Boulevard, Suite 200, Lanham, Maryland 20706
http://www.rowmanlittlefield.com

10 Thornbury Road, Plymouth PL6 7PP, United Kingdom

British Library Cataloguing in Publication Information Available

Library of Congress Cataloging-in-Publication Data

Eizenstat, Stuart.
  The future of the Jews : how global forces are impacting the Jewish people, Israel, and its relationship with the United States / Stuart Eizenstat.
    p. cm.
  Includes index.
  ISBN 978-1-4422-1627-3 (cloth : alk. paper) — ISBN 978-1-4422-1628-0 (paper : alk. paper) — ISBN 978-1-4422-1629-7 (ebook)
  1. Eizenstat, Stuart—Political and social views. 2. Jews—United States—Politics and government. 3. Jews—United States—Attitudes toward Israel. 4. United States—Foreign relations—Israel. 5. Israel—Foreign relations—United States. 6. Israel and the diaspora. I. Title.
  E184.36.P64E37 2012
  973'.04924—dc23

                                                                    2012047880

♾™ The paper used in this publication meets the minimum requirements of American National Standard for Information Sciences—Permanence of Paper for Printed Library Materials, ANSI/NISO Z39.48-1992.

Printed in the United States of America

To my wife, Fran, my inspiration for over four decades,
who embodies the best of American and Jewish values in a
lifetime of service to both the Jewish and general communities.

Contents

Foreword

Sir Martin Gilbert

STUART EIZENSTAT IS A MAN OF remarkable abilities and achievements. A public servant of distinction, he has made an impact in many branches of administration and international relations. At this testing time for the world, his voice is worth listening to. This book brings that voice to a wide public.

At the center of this thoughtful, and in many ways provocative, book is the Jewish world and the State of Israel—the place of the Jews and Israel in the world—and Israel's internal dynamic: its relations with the Palestinians whose land it occupies, and with the Arab nations around it, and its place in the wider world of economic challenges, global terrorism, and the aspirations of fundamentalist Islam. Stuart Eizenstat stresses the impact of two outside forces—he calls them "global forces of the twenty-first century"—on the Jewish Diaspora. One is globalization, which he sees as generally positive. The other is demography, where he sees considerable danger ahead for the Jewish world. Part of the dwindling Jewish numbers worldwide, he points out, is a direct consequence of the successful integration of Jewish communities in most countries and the continual increase in the rates of intermarriage, now 50 percent in the United States and 45 percent in Argentina. "Ironically," he writes, "at this very hour of our success, many Jews have chosen to abandon their identity. At the very time in history when Diaspora Jews can openly and proudly assert their Jewishness in countries . . . where the rule of law fully protects Jews and others in their religious and cultural expressions, too few are willing to do so." Wise words.

Stuart Eizenstat examines in detail the impact of globalization and demography on both the Jewish people worldwide and on Israel. He also looks at the impact on Israel of the growth of Muslim communities in Europe, looking at the example of

France, where there are half a million Jews and four million Muslims, and noting that the street demonstrations there of young Muslims angry at their alienation from French society are "replete with anti-Israel and anti-Semitic expletives." The only logical assessment that he can see with regard to European policy toward Israel—a subject of concern to Jews worldwide—is that it will begin to reflect "the impact of the emergent political force of European Muslims."

For the Jewish world and for Israel, the United States is of crucial importance. What is to be the role of the United States in the world, as the world lurches from one crisis to another, faces global economic challenges, and has to engage with a Middle East in uncertain transition, Stuart Eizenstat asks. He is in no doubt of the answer. "The U.S. must remain directly engaged," he writes, on every front in which the radical rejectionists and jihadists and pro-Western elements confront each other, "but must do so with discernment." He fears that one result of the Iraq War that began in 2003 is that when the United States leaves Iraq, Iran will be the dominant force in the region, and that the Iranian and Iraq Shiite populations will make common cause.

For Stuart Eizenstat, such a development will be part of the onward march of militant Islam. He saw this perspective through his experience as the cochair in 2004 of a commission—set up by the Center for Global Development—on weak states and U.S. national security. The world has become as dangerous a place as it has ever been, with the terrorist dimension making outdated the former confrontations of armies facing each other on the field of battle.

There is much food for thought in these pages. Those who, like Stuart Eizenstat, see Israel as an outpost of Western values and aspirations in the Middle East, will read his diagnosis with close attention. He is concerned with the impact on Israel of potential failed states, whether Lebanon or Syria at some future time, or a more distant Somalia whose pirates could have a devastating impact on Israel's sea-borne oil imports, or a country like Sudan, whose refugees—hitherto unwelcome in Egypt—have found a safe haven in Israel, a country whose historic experiences make it unwilling to turn people away.

The instability in Africa, Stuart Eizenstat warns, and even the "lawless tri-border region between Brazil, Argentina, and Paraguay" could help terrorism—now a global phenomenon—funnel raw materials and other assets back to the Middle East. Reflecting something that the West would ignore at its peril, he notes: "The rise of violent, jihadist Islamic groups also depends heavily on the sanctuary of failed or failing states unwilling or unable to control their activities."

This book has many lessons for our time and disturbing thoughts for the years ahead. Iran, Russia, and China are among the countries of which he writes with perceptive foresight. And looming above the problems of individual states are the overarching problems of the continuing reliance of industrialized nations on the Arab oil producers, the global energy problems, the crises facing the global economy, the imminent massive increase in the global population, the global outreach of Islamic terrorism, and—of immense importance in seeking answers to all the pressing problems—the changing demographic realities, whereby, in the United States, the probability of a non-Caucasian, largely Hispanic majority will impact on every aspect of United States policy, not least, Stuart Eizenstat points out, its relationship with Israel and the demands of a world in which, by 2050, 90 percent of the estimated population of ten billion will be "outside that part of the world where Israel has its historically closest contacts."

Of immediate current concern is Stuart Eizenstat's view that, even with "a healthy demographic increase," Israeli Jews will, in his words, "still be an increasingly smaller percentage of the world's population, and—more telling—of the Israeli Arab and Palestinian populations." This, he warns, places a premium on reaching a peace agreement, so that Israel can maintain a Jewish majority. This is an ongoing debate in which Stuart Eizenstat's thoughts, based on his devotion to Judaism and to the Jewish state, and his statesmanlike sense of the realities of international affairs, will make a significant contribution. All those interested in the future of Israel, including Israel's leaders, should read this book with close attention.

On a more optimistic note, in examining the current turmoil in the Arab Muslim world, Stuart Eizenstat concludes that both for the Jewish world and for the United States the upheavals in early 2011 "were not ideological or radical revolutions" but popular movements that "wanted the same democracy enjoyed in the West," a democracy they saw and were connected to by their cell phones and computers. It was the social media, he writes, "particularly Facebook, that was the spark that lit the fire, and enables young people without one dominant leader to coalesce and make common cause on the streets of Tunis, Cairo, Amman, and Sana." For Stuart Eizenstat, a man of wide experience far from home, who has traveled widely in the Arab world since the Carter era in which he served the president, during the Clinton administration and more recently in his private capacity, these are encouraging words.

Sir Martin Gilbert, CBE, PC, is a British historian, the official biographer of Sir Winston Churchill, and the author of over eighty books, including works on Jewish history and the Holocaust.

Acknowledgments

I AM GRATEFUL TO Rowman & Littlefield Publishing Group for their confidence in my book and for the able assistance of Jonathan Sisk, senior executive editor for American government and politics; Elaine McGarraugh, production editor; and Patricia MacDonald, copyeditor.

Avinoam Bar-Yosef, president of the Jewish People Policy Institute (JPPI), whose board I co-chair, asked me to prepare a paper in 2009 on the major forces affecting the Jewish people in the Diaspora and the State of Israel. Because most of those also impact directly on the United States, Israel's major ally, I also added that dimension. It was presented at that year's presidents' conference in Jerusalem under the auspices of President Shimon Peres. At Avinoam's suggestion, I converted it into a book, *Global Forces of the 21st Century: Their Impact on World Jewry, Israel and the United States*, which JPPI published and has distributed to Israeli government and academic leaders and to selected officials of Jewish organizations around the world. Avinoam's support and encouragement were essential throughout.

This book published by Rowman & Littlefield is aimed at a more general audience. It identifies a number of global trends that especially impact the Jewish world: the shift of power and influence away from the United States and the Western democracies to the emerging nations of the East and South; the integration of a world powered by digital technology; the battle between moderates and radicals over the direction of the Muslim world, dramatized by the 2011 Arab Spring revolutions; new security threats from nuclear proliferation, cyberwarfare, and environmental, energy, and demographic developments; a new form of anti-Semitism aimed at undermining Israel's legitimacy; and America's evolving relationship with Israel, which is central to Israel's security. Adam Smith, a brilliant young attorney who was then an associate at my law firm, Covington & Burling, was indispensible during much of the writing of my paper and book. Already the author of two books, Adam provided ideas, research, and editing. He now holds a senior position in the U.S. Treasury Department and is sure to make major contributions through public service in the decades ahead. I am grateful for the time, energy, and talent he brought to my project, from start to finish.

At Covington & Burling, my longtime assistant of over thirty years, Carolyn Keene, and my secretary, Pat Adams, were also helpful in many ways in the preparation of this book.

Lawrence Malkin, a former foreign correspondent for *Time* magazine and a respected author and editor, offered initial and final oversight of my manuscript. I am grateful for the same talent and sharp insight that he brought to the editing of my book *Imperfect Justice: Looted Assets, Slave Labor and the Unfinished Business of World War II* (Public Affairs, 2003), about my negotiations during the Clinton administration on behalf of Holocaust survivors and families of victims, as well as other victims of Nazi oppression, non-Jewish and Jewish.

Rami Tali of Yedoth Books and an associate of JPPI served as the principal editor of the JPPI book but also supplied ideas, challenged assumptions, and sharpened my thinking about many subjects; he also proved invaluable with his encyclopedic knowledge of Israeli political history. Barry Geltman of JPPI provided thoughtful copyediting.

Ronald Goldfarb, my agent for *Imperfect Justice*, played the same professional role in this book with his usual high standard of excellence.

My wife, Fran, my partner for forty-four years of marriage, sustained me as I wrote these books, while I was maintaining an active law practice in international trade and finance, serving on a variety of corporate and nonprofit boards, and assuming my family responsibilities. More broadly, she has been my inspiration over the decades in strengthening my Jewish identity while I was acting as a public servant of the United States government and engaging in a range of other public activities. If the measure of successful Jewish parents is fostering strong Jewish identities among their children, then the fact that my son Jay and daughter-in-law Jessica and my son Brian and daughter-in-law Erin are raising a total of seven of our grandchildren (Menachem, Bracha, Eli Kalman, Michal, and Yitzchok and Julia Mae and Caroline) committed to the Jewish religion and culture owes more to Fran than to anyone. Her courage and wisdom are a source of strength to me and to all of our family and friends.

Stuart E. Eizenstat
Washington, D.C.
2012

Introduction

WE LIVE IN AN ERA OF astonishing change that is taking place in more fields of human endeavor and at a rate never before witnessed in history. The traditional moorings for all of us are shifting in the family, the community, and the way we do our jobs. Among nations, these seismic changes present unprecedented global challenges, but they have a special impact on world Jewry and Israel, and on the United States, the country with the largest Jewish Diaspora and Israel's only reliable ally.

With the end of the Cold War came the end of a bipolar world in which the United States and its allies confronted the Soviet Union and the Communist nations. Now we live in a multipolar world with economic power and global influence shifting from the United States and Europe to the nations of the East and South, especially China, India, and Brazil, with very small Jewish communities and no historical or emotional connection to the modern State of Israel. Moreover, to satisfy their growing energy demands they are deepening their strategic relationships with the Arab world, the Persian Gulf states, and Israel's sworn enemy, Iran. New global institutions such as the Group of Twenty (G20) have been created to provide a greater voice for the emerging nations, diluting the influence of the Western powers.

A new era of globalization powered by digital technology now integrates nations and peoples in mutual dependence, changing the world as profoundly as the printing press did half a millennium ago. While globalization has empowered individuals to assert themselves, as they are doing in the Middle East in the Arab Spring and its aftermath, private multinational corporations and environmental, human rights, and prodemocracy nongovernmental organizations reach across borders to influence governments. But there is also a dark side to the globalized world: The speed of communication and ease of transport provide new tools for terrorist groups, international criminal gangs, and those who are frustrated by the new, interconnected world and seek to destabilize it. Yet on balance, globalization is an enormous advantage for the Jewish people, Israel, and the U.S., by creating a more interdependent, interwined world for those nations and people who have the education, creativity, and capacity to take full advantage of the technology revolution that is powering globalization.

Islamic extremism plays on this frustration, and adds a religious jihad element, to animate terrorist groups challenging the very foundations of the modern state. Their attack on modernism reflects as much a deadly internal struggle for the allegiance of more than 1.5 billion Muslims, the vast majority of whom seek prosperity and security, as it does a supposed war of civilizations between a radical version of Islam and the West, including Israel. Just as the Cold War provided a clear but oversimplified division between the free world and the Communist world, so too since the Iranian Revolution has a rough division emerged within the Muslim world between Iran and its radical terrorist allies and pro-Western moderate Arab countries who took a more benign view of Israel under American pressure. Confronting these cataclysms in the Muslim world is one of this century's greatest challenges to the West. At the same time it poses a unique challenge to the Jewish people and the State of Israel.

The balance among these forces has long rested on a sword's edge but now is complicated by the upheavals of the Arab Spring. The two closest Arab allies of the United States—Egypt and Jordan, which are also the only two Arab nations that have formally made peace with Israel—faced popular revolutions from their own citizens in 2011 and struggled to develop new forms of governance. In a breathless period of months, pro-American, antiradical, autocratic leaders who had been in power for decades fell like a stack of dominos in Tunisia (Zine El Abidine Ben Ali, twenty-three years), Egypt (Hosni Mubarak, thirty years), and Yemen (Ali Abdullah Saleh, thirty-three-years); the rule of the longest-reigning dictator in the world, Libya's Muammar el-Qaddafi, in power for forty-four years, came to an end with his violent death, after a revolution aided by NATO forces and the U.S. and supported by the Arab League.

Bahrain, the site of the U.S. Fifth Fleet, was shaken to its roots by a revolt by the majority Shiite population protesting long-standing exclusion by the Sunni-based monarchy, which dates back to 1783, leading Saudi Arabia to send in troops to stabilize the uprising on its border.

The regime of Syria's president Bashar al-Assad, heir to the decades-long dictatorship of his father, Hafez al-Assad, a close ally of Iran and Hezbollah and Israel's enemy, is threatened as never before and likely to end by demonstrations and international sanctions, with Turkey and the Arab League calling on him for immediate democratic reforms, and most recently, as he has ignored their recommendations, for his resignation after forty years of brutal rule by the al-Assad dynasty.

The wiser monarchs, King Abdullah II of Jordan and King Mohammed VI of Morocco, have instituted democratic reforms, leading in Morocco's case to the election of a moderate Islamic government in what had been a secular state, which together with their respect among the public have enabled them to stay in power. At the same time, King Abdullah of Saudi Arabia has maintained the stability of the House of Saud by massive infusions of cash to improve the life of his subjects and by educational and limited democratic reforms.

These unprecedented Arab upheavals are driven by a huge demographic bulge of youth dissatisfied with autocratic and corrupt rulers and demanding more freedom, personal empowerment, and economic opportunity, as well as less of what they see as Western domination. These revolutions are complicated by splits between Sunnis and Shiites in some countries. But all the initial leaders of the Arab revolutions have employed the social media of the Internet to rally support over the heads of their own governments. Whatever the outcome, it will affect the balance within the Muslim world, reducing the attraction of radicalism in some places but intensifying it in others.

While democratic outcomes may provide the Arab masses a voice long denied to them, they are less invested than their traditional leadership in peace with Israel or partnership with the West. What began as an Arab Spring, whose revolutions were spearheaded by the Facebook generation, high-tech and savvy young, secular democratic idealists, has been transformed into an Islamic winter, as well-organized Islamic forces, long suppressed and now able to compete in free elections, have won early victories in parliamentary elections in Tunisia, Egypt, and Morocco, sidelining the weaker secular and democratic forces. Going back to the 2006 elections in the Palestinian territories, in which Hamas overwhelmed the more moderate, secular Fatah Party, all of the postrevolution elections in 2011 have gone to the newly empowered Islamic parties, some more moderate, such as the Ennahda Party in Tunisia and the Islamic Justice and Development Party in Morocco, others more fundamentalist, such as Egypt's Muslim Brotherhood, and the even more radical Salafists.

The governments that emerge will be internally more Islamic and externally cooler toward the West, less cooperative with Israel, and more assertive in pressing the Palestinian cause. But none is likely to follow the course of Iran after the 1979 revolution, which I witnessed from the Carter White House, and try to create a radical, theocratic regime, and will be judged by their newly restive populations on how they create jobs and economic opportunity and deliver public services.

At the same time nontraditional security threats have arisen: cyberattacks on both governments and major multinational corporations; the spread of nuclear weapons technology to rogue states such as North Korea and Iran; the century's greatest challenges to the human environment (global warming and a looming water crisis with particular impacts on the Middle East and Israel); and continuing population growth in the explosion from 1 to 6 billion people over the past century (seven billion today) and likely more than 10 billion by the end of this one. But the population of world Jewry has stagnated.

Inside the Jewish world, a paradigm shift has taken place: The center of gravity has shifted from Europe, where it existed for a millennium, until the Holocaust, to the United States, and now, almost unrecognized, it has shifted again in the twenty-first century to the State of Israel, where since 2006 more Jews live than in any other country. For six decades since the founding of Israel as a state, the Jewish Diaspora has given material, moral, and political support, often unstintingly. Now that Israel is the stronger of the two parties the relationship is changing, and Israel needs to help strengthen the Diaspora at a time of massive assimilation and less focus by too many on Judaism and the Jewish state.

For the Jewish people as a whole, this second decade of the twenty-first century is a genuine golden age, as Jews are in the strongest, most secure position in history. This is all the more remarkable for the depth of the tragedy in the twentieth century, the most murderous in history, and not only for the Jewish people, who lost 6 million to the disciplined and murderous Nazi regime. More than 65 million people were killed in the century's two world wars, quite apart from tens of millions more dead in famine, civil strife, revolution, genocide, and sheer brutality in the Russian Revolution and its Stalinist aftermath, in China during the Cultural Revolution, in the killing fields of Cambodia, and in the murderous tribal conflicts in Africa.

As for the Jews, there now are only 13 million in the world, 4 million fewer than in 1939, before the Holocaust. The losses are counted beyond numbers, with the tragic demise of the flower of European Jewish scholarship; religious, financial, scientific, and business leadership; and the culture and traditions of millions of ordinary men and women, along with the confiscation of their homes, businesses, places of worship, schools, community centers, even cemeteries, most of which have not been returned to this day.

Yet, from this catastrophe a modern miracle has occurred. In the United States, home to the largest Diaspora community, Jewish success is nothing short of remarkable: Quotas restricting the access of Jews to higher education and the professions have long been abandoned. Today a remarkable 85 percent of American Jewish youngsters attend college, twice the national average. Jews are disproportionately represented at leadership levels in academia, business, finance, and politics. Forty-four members of the U.S. Congress that concluded in 2010 were Jewish; at more than 10 percent, Jewish representation was more than four times the proportion of Jews in the population itself. And three of the nine U.S. Supreme Court justices and the chairman of the Federal Reserve Bank are Jewish. In 2004, *Fortune* magazine reported that nearly 10 percent of the CEOs of the nation's leading one hundred companies were Jewish. Similar success has been enjoyed by Jews in most European countries, Canada, Australia, and Latin America. Jews make up barely two-tenths of 1 percent of the world's population but represent 54 percent of world chess champions, 27 percent of Nobel physics laureates, and 31 percent of Nobel laureates in medicine. There is hardly a field of endeavor in science, the arts, medicine, law, literature, government, and finance in which Jews are not disproportionately prominent.

Jews in Israel have achieved something no other people in recorded history have accomplished: the return to an ancient homeland after two millennia of exile through the creation of a sovereign state that has successfully absorbed waves of refugees from many cultures. Israel is a vibrant democracy with a free press and the right of assembly for hundreds of thousands to protest economic injustice as they see it. The nation has one of the world's strongest and most respected military forces, composed overwhelmingly of citizen-soldiers. It has grown at a faster pace than almost every other country that gained independence after World War II and is a world leader in science and technology that attracts investment from leading multinationals.

There are clouds on the horizon of the Jewish world, however. In the Diaspora, success has come with a price. While it has encouraged an engaged core to assert their Jewishness in manifold ways, an equally large segment is assimilating, disaffiliating from Jewish life and melting into the general society, ironically at a time of maximum appreciation for Jewish culture and religious practice. And as a whole, the Jewish Diaspora is declining in population.

At the same time, a new form of anti-Semitism has arisen, linking Jews worldwide to Israeli political actions over which they have no control and attacking Israel's legitimacy with increasing intensity far beyond the long-standing refusal of most Muslims to recognize Israel.

It is an illusion to think these unacceptable attacks on Israel's legitimacy have no connection with the internal politics of Israel itself, but Israel cannot be primarily blamed for the efforts by its antagonists to delegitimize the very concept of a state for the Jews, which the United Nations recognized explicitly at Israel's rebirth as a modern state. Still the internal divisions in Israel go beyond settlement policies of successive Israeli governments and involve deep divisions within Israeli society over the evolution of the Jewish state. Over six decades after its founding, there is no consensus within Israel on fundamental questions about its permanent borders, its relationships with its own Israeli Arab citizens, and the nature of the state to which Israel's Palestinian neighbors, living under Israeli control since 1967, aspire.

One vision is propounded by assertive nationalists, many Israeli religious leaders, and security-minded secularists who seek permanent control over the Palestinian territories they call Judea and Samaria. A competing Israeli vision, while despairing of the short-term possibilities of peace with the Palestinians or gaining broad acceptance in the Arab world, warns that incorporating the West Bank would mean absorbing the Palestinian population into Israel and threatening the very basis of a democratic Jewish state.

Still, it is from a position of strength that Jews in Israel and the Diaspora confront the daunting global challenges of the twenty-first century. For the first time in two millennia, Jews are no longer flotsam and jetsam, tossed about by great waves they cannot control; they are no longer isolated from the family of nations, nor subject to the caprice of despotic rulers or violence from anti-Jewish peoples.

Most of today's global forces affect not only a much stronger Israel and Diaspora but also much of the world. Virtually every major challenge facing Israel and the Jewish world also threatens Western nations, new emerging powers, and moderate Arab nations.

If there is one step that would do the most to help cope with many of the ferocious forces of this century, it is establishing a secure, durable peace with Israel's Palestinian neighbors. Israel cannot make peace itself and still faces hostility from parts of the Palestinian population and others in the Arab world. But too many Israelis and Diaspora Jewish leaders view the status quo as acceptable because Israel's economy is strong, although its fruits have been unequally divided and, thankfully, there is virtually no terrorism inside Israel.

The dividends of peace are too often forgotten. If better recognized, they could embolden Israelis to take the tough compromises necessary for peace when there is a willing Palestinian side. Peace would make it easier for emerging new powers and the new democratic forces arising in the Arab Middle East to develop closer ties with Israel; accelerate Israel's acceptance in a globalized world; strengthen pro-Western, modernizing Arab states; and weaken the appeal of radical Islamic states and terrorist groups. Peace would enhance Jewish identity in the Diaspora; serve as a strong antidote to the effort to undermine Israel's legitimacy; and help ensure a durable, democratic state with a Jewish majority.

The achievement of peace with the Palestinians hardly rests on Israel's shoulders alone. It requires a Palestinian leadership willing and able to make the difficult compromises that seem even more unlikely with the alliance between a reformed Fatah and a still intransigent Hamas. But Israel, in word and deed, must nevertheless do its utmost to accelerate the peace process and to be seen by the world as willing to accept the hard choices with all the risks they entail. Let the burden of failure, if that is the result, rest clearly with the Palestinians. At a minimum, Israel should take no action that would further complicate the achievement of a just solution, with a Jewish state and an Arab state living at peace with each other in secure, internationally recognized borders.

And yet, with all the challenges facing Israel and the Jewish people, there is every reason for optimism, with a strong, independent, sovereign Jewish state for the first time in two millennia capable of defending itself; a Jewish Diaspora more integrated, accepted, and fully taking advantage of unparalleled opportunities in their own countries, most particularly in the United States and Europe; and most of the threats facing them being addressed by other countries, as well.

The Jewish people, small in number and certainly to be an increasingly small percentage of a growing world population, have survived and thrived, while the empires that threatened them, from the Assyrians, Greeks, and Romans to the Czarist Russians and Nazis, have vanished. Jews will have to run faster, be more creative, and become even more adaptable in the twenty-first century. But that is not a novelty; it is these attributes, together with religious beliefs, ethical values, and an enduring sense of peoplehood, that have allowed Jews to overcome every adversity, despite grievous costs. The challenges of the twenty-first century are different from, but no greater than, those of the past. And Jews are in a better position to address them than ever before, since Abraham went forth at God's direction from Ur of the Chaldees to create a new people in a new land and to begin an unbroken history of 3,500 years, guided by divinely inspired scriptures.

1

The Historic Shift of Power from the West to the Emerging Nations of the East and South: A New Multipolar World

WE ARE WITNESSING THE geopolitical equivalent of the movement of the earth's tectonic plates. One force shaping the twenty-first-century world is the dramatic shift in power from the developed democracies in North America and Europe to emerging nations in Asia and Latin America; from nations with a historic relationship to the Jewish people and, in the case of the United States, Israel's major ally, to nations with little sensitivity to Jewish history, tiny Jewish communities, and ties with states often at odds with Israel and the United States.

During the Cold War, despite the manifest dangers of the historic competition between the U.S. and its NATO allies and the Soviet Union and its captives, the Eastern Bloc states, there had been a certainty about the world, with most global issues put into that context. The State of Israel unequivocally sided with the democratic West. Though American and Israeli policy makers did not see eye to eye on every issue, Israel at the behest of the U.S. acted as a bulwark against Soviet expansion in the Middle East. During just two decades following the fall of the Berlin Wall and the implosion of the Soviet Union, the world has changed profoundly.

For a few brief years, there was a shining period when the U.S. was left as the world's sole superpower, and many felt the world would bask in a benign *Pax Americana*, moving benignly in the direction of democracy, free markets, tolerance, stability, prosperity, and peace. Francis Fukuyama famously declared it "the end of history" in his 1989 essay, in which we were at the "end point of mankind's ideological evolution and the universalization of Western liberal democracy as the final form of human government."[1] But this brave new world lasted less than a decade. Instead fierce forces of nationalism, tribalism, and radicalism that had been suppressed during the Cold War were unleashed, pushing the U.S.

and the world community, along with Israel and the Jewish people, in new directions that altered fundamental political and economic relationships. Horrific African genocides in Rwanda, Sudan, and Congo; the rise of Islamic terrorism; the brutal Balkan Wars; and the rise of competing global powers all mocked the hope for a more tranquil world. It will take all the historical resilience, creativity, and determination of the U.S., Israel, and the Jewish people to adapt.

While the twentieth century was the Atlantic century dominated by the United States and Europe, the twenty-first century will be the Asian and Pacific century. A new global order is quickly rising, moving the axis of economic, political, and military power from the U.S. and its European allies across the Pacific to China and India. By 2020, Asia will become the world's largest market—almost twice the size of the United States and producing three-fifths of the world's output. This shift is, of course, more complicated than a simple geographic movement, and other non-Asian states, such as Brazil, will play a large role in the birth of the new global order.

The twenty-first century is already witnessing the movement of several emerging powers, only recently struggling developing nations, insisting on taking their place on the world stage, along with the established democratic industrial powers—the U.S. and its Western allies—creating a multipolar, more complex world with many new centers of power, or a "nonpolar world" in the words of Richard Haass, president of the Council on Foreign Relations.

In November 2008, a joint assessment by the sixteen U.S. intelligence agencies entitled *Global Trends 2025: A Transformed World*, noted that the shift of economic power from the West to the East was "without precedent in modern history." The report forecast that within fifteen years a global multipolar system will have emerged, made manifest by a "diminished gap between the United States and everybody else. . . . The unipolar moment is over."[2] The trends are clear: The economic, political, and diplomatic power of the chief supporter of Israel and the Jewish people since 1948, the United States, is being challenged as never before since the U.S. emerged victorious from World War II as the world's dominant superpower.

In the post–Cold War world a variety of actors—emerging states, multinational corporations, nongovernmental organizations (NGOs), terrorist groups—exercise power for good and ill and in so doing vastly complicate global governance.[3] The new world order risks becoming a new world disorder, unless a strong U.S. continues to act as a ballast to provide coherence and balance to these conflicting forces and multiple power centers. No other country or entity can play that essential role. It is historically unprecedented for so many previously underdeveloped countries to move up the economic ladder so quickly and demand a major role in global governance. In the past, one world power often contended for power with another until a major event transpired, such as the Battle of Trafalgar that confirmed British ascendancy by the decisive defeat in

1805 of the combined Spanish and French fleets. This is not the world of today. Now there are a number of emerging powers, each eager to assert themselves on the world stage, foremost China.

Changing models and new leadership are appearing across every field of endeavor, from high finance to high technology to leisure. Depending on market fluctuations, the world's richest man is a Mexican—Carlos Slim, the son of a Lebanese immigrant, Latin America's largest telecommunications entrepreneur, and the largest single investor in the New York Times Company. The world's largest casino and gambling center no longer is in Las Vegas, but in Macau, owned by American Jewish philanthropist Sheldon Adelson; the world's largest Ferris wheel is in Singapore; the largest man-made structure in the world is in Qatar, the Ras Laffen natural gas plant that opened in 2010;[4] and the world's tallest building is not in a historical home of the skyscraper, New York City or Chicago, but in Dubai, which opened its new skyscraper, Burj Khalifa, in the same year.

The "space race" no longer solely pits the superpowers against one another; the U.S. and Russia jointly man the international space station, along with Japan, and the U.S. now relies on antiquated Russian spacecraft to reach the station, with the end of the U.S. space shuttle program in 2011. Space agencies are at work from Iran to Malaysia, Argentina to Pakistan. China, India, and other developing countries are increasingly the homes of the world's fastest supercomputers. As of November 2008 sixteen of the five hundred fastest were located in China and eight in India, a one-third increase in one year. As for broadband, the intellectual infrastructure of the future, coverage of subscribers in emerging countries is reckoned to have doubled to 54 percent by the end of 2011.[5]

Global energy demand will increase 40 percent over the next twenty years, almost all from the developing and emerging nations as they buy more cars, electric appliances, and consumer goods that the developed world has taken for granted.[6] By 2030, to satisfy this new demand, the world must bring on new production that is four times what Saudi Arabia, the largest oil producer, pumps daily.[7]

Population trends accentuate this new global order. The populations of the industrial nations are aging and in some countries falling; those of the developing and emerging nations are young and booming. Today, the Middle East, North Africa, and Asia have 30 percent of the world population; within 25 years they will have 50 percent, with six out of every ten people in the Arab Middle East under 30 years of age. With less open immigration than the U.S., where the bulk of population growth is among immigrants, European birthrates are plummeting, imposing an unsustainable burden on the smaller percentage of young workers to support retirement and social benefits—one of the underlying reasons for the European financial crisis.

In recent years, developing nations have begun to account for nearly half of all global output, compared to only a third as recently as 1990. In the mid-1970s, when key industrial countries created the Group of Seven (U.S., UK, Germany, France, Italy, Canada, and Japan) to oversee the world economy, they accounted for 62 percent of the world total gross domestic product (GDP). In 2012, the G7 share of world GDP will be below 50 percent for the first time, and it will continue to decline.[8] As early as 2014, the output of emerging countries for the first time is projected to surpass that of the entire developed world.[9] And of the $20 trillion in global output in 2020, 39 percent will come from China, India, and Latin America, compared with 21 percent from the U.S., and only 16 percent from Europe.

As these states amass economic power they will also accrue political power. As Walter Russell Mead noted in his recent book, *God and Gold: Britain, America, and the Making of the Modern World*,[10] economic and political power are two sides of the same coin. Or, as President Obama noted in his 2010 National Security Strategy, "At no time in human history has a nation of diminished economic vitality maintained its military and political primacy."[11]

Since the Dutch invented modern capitalism in the seventeenth century, global powers have thrived by combining economic and military forces. This combination exported free-market economic and democratic political systems from the U.S. and Europe around the world. The West is now reaping what it has sown. The Anglo-American liberal democratic and free-market system has influenced, and empowered, these developing states. As they become more confident, they have viewed the Anglo-American tradition à la carte, selecting and refusing various aspects. In the early 1990s, a democratic India was compelled to open its economy to the outside world and unshackle its markets. Meanwhile, Beijing adopted its own version of a market economy, with heavy state involvement, and largely abandoned Communist economic theory, but it remains committed to the single-party rule by the Politburo and a form of state-dominated capitalism through thousands of state-controlled and favored corporations.

It is easy to be carried away by the changing nature and locus of power and the growth of the emerging giants. Former World Bank president James Wolfensohn, in a 2009 speech to the Jerusalem Conference sponsored by Israeli president Shimon Peres, issued a cautionary warning. With all the focus on the staggering rise in influence of several key emerging powers, the very growth of the emerging world could portend instability writ large, because of both the scope and unevenness of the changes. Even as some emerging countries have successfully created wealth and modern living standards almost overnight, many nations have proven stubbornly resistant to development, including many of Israel's neighbors in the Middle East. Some are failing or weak states that have become sanctuaries for terrorist groups. But most are simply dirt poor. One-sixth of the world—or one billion people—have no clean drinking water; and three billion, almost half our world's population, lack adequate sanitation. One-quarter of the population of these poor countries live on less than $1.25 per day, and these poor countries are the most cruelly vulnerable to the impact of climate change and water shortages.[12]

As Wolfensohn noted, electricity is crucial for economic development. But some 20 percent of the world's population are so poor they have no access, and another billion have only an intermittent supply, the vast majority in rural areas, mainly in South Asia and Africa. The United Nations estimates that it would cost over $35 billion annually during the next twenty years to give everyone in the world the electricity necessary for a better life. This requires creative approaches such as using biomass in rural villages for microgrids to fill the gap.[13] Not only the U.S. but Israel too could gain the respect and gratitude of the developing world by helping them adopt such technologies.

While the continuation of vast inequalities and the depths of poverty will play important roles in the new twenty-first-century global order, the most important challenges will come from those emerging states that have made incredible strides in a short period of time to amass wealth, create middle classes, and develop workable educational, corporate, industrial, and physical infrastructures. Chief among these states are the BRIC countries—the acronym coined by Goldman Sachs' chief economist, Jim O'Neill, to describe the major emerging countries: Brazil, Russia, India, and China. Today, the BRIC nations and other emerging countries represent almost 50 percent of global GDP, 40 percent of world exports, and 65 percent of foreign exchange holdings—roughly equal to the combined economic positions of the United States and the European Union (EU) countries. Their foreign reserves of some $3 trillion are triple what they held only seven years ago.

The Rise of China

The rapid rise of China as a world-class economic power and major political force is the most important story of the early years of the twenty-first century, and it is nothing short of astounding. The most critical bilateral relationship in this new century will be between the U.S. and China; the course it takes will shape the new global order, with major impacts on Israel and the Jewish world.

The Middle Kingdom—the world's center of wealth and power a millennium ago when Europe was just emerging from the Dark Ages—had declined to a largely feudal society under foreign occupation during World War II and was impoverished by the brutal Communist rule and Cultural Revolution of Mao Zedong. Yet within thirty years after the market-based reforms of Deng Xiaoping in 1979, China by the start of the twenty-first century became a world-class power. I remember vividly Deng's visit to the White House after President Jimmy Carter's historic restoration of full diplomatic relations with China. A diminutive man who had survived his opposition to Mao Zedong and his catastrophic Cultural Revolution, Deng held the future of one billion Chinese in his hands. In the Cabinet Room meeting with President Carter, in which I participated, he asked that China be extended "most-favored nation" trading status, which the Soviet Union had been denied under the 1974 Jackson-Vanik amendment because of its restriction on Soviet Jewish emigration. Impishly, Deng told President Carter that he had studied Jackson-Vanik and that China had no limit on its emigration. He pushed a pad and pencil over to President Carter and asked the president to fill in the number of Chinese the U.S. would like to receive each year—2 million, even 20 million!

Napoleon is reputed to have warned the world to let China slumber because it would make the world tremble when it awoke—and so it has. A 2005 U.S. National Intelligence Council report compared China's emergence as a great power in the twenty-first century to Germany's in the nineteenth century and America's in the twentieth.

The Chinese leadership has a clear strategic plan to become the dominant power in the twenty-first century, as well as the discipline and autocratic system to sustain a ruthless drive toward that goal. 2008 was a landmark year for China, not simply for hosting the Olympic Games as its "coming out" party as a world power, but because, with 20 percent of the world's population, China became the third-largest economy in the world, leaping ahead of Germany. Only four years before, China was the fifth-largest economy. In 2010 China surpassed Japan, America's closest Asian ally, as the world's number two economy.

China is likely to have the largest economy in the world by midcentury, and perhaps sooner. Measured by what a dollar can purchase in China—purchasing-power parity—the International Monetary Fund (IMF) predicts that China will be the largest economy in 2016. And Daiwa Securities predicts that, by the end of this decade, on a GDP per person basis, Shanghai will almost equal the average for America in 2009.[14]

Its total output has increased by an average of almost 10 percent annually for the past thirty years, and its middle class is already larger than the entire population of the United States.[15] The Chinese people have a palpable feeling of optimism for the future, the most optimistic of some dozen countries surveyed in 2008 by the Pew Center. Support for their government stood at 86 percent, while only 23 percent of Americans expressed similar optimism. China already leads the world in a number of significant economic indicators—the largest foreign trade surplus and foreign currency reserves; the fastest supercomputer; the most cell phone users (400 million); the largest initial public offering for one of its state-owned companies seeking private capital; the largest steel producer;[16] the largest manufacturer of cars, surpassing Japan;[17] and the largest exporter of manufactured goods, surpassing Germany in 2010. It has also become a leader in some surprising products, passing Italy as the largest producer of violins, with almost three-quarters of the world market.[18]

Of course these rankings arise in part from the sheer size of the country—140 cities with a population of over one million, compared to 35 throughout all of Europe and less than a dozen in the U.S. By 2025, China will have more than two hundred cities with a population of over two million. In this period, the country will build 170 mass transit systems and five thousand skyscrapers, equivalent to ten New York Cities.[19]

But size alone does not account for its galloping race to the top. Beijing is also developing a modern infrastructure—an average of 10,000 new bridges built annually during the past fifteen years and 7,000 kilometers (4,350 miles) of track for fast trains. In addition to physical infrastructure, China is investing in the human capital critical to success in the twenty-first century. Since 1998, the number of college-educated people in China has doubled and the number of college students has risen fivefold. In 2011 Shenzhen University graduated more engineers than all the American universities put together.[20] China's growth in research has been the strongest of any country; it now is the second-largest producer of scientific papers and is on a course to overtake the U.S. by 2020.[21]

In order to feed its frenetic growth, China consumes half of the world's cement, half of the world's pork, and over a quarter of its aluminum. China owns 21 percent of the world's refrigerators and 29 percent of its computers.[22] Since 2000, China has consumed more than 80 percent of the increase in the world's copper supply. Even in trash, China is becoming the world's leader, with global impact, because its generally weak standards for incinerators outside larger cities such as Beijing and Shanghai mean they release high levels of dioxin that can travel long distances. By the end of 2009, China earned the dubious distinction of being the world's leading emitter of greenhouse gases, surpassing the U.S. China builds a staggering one coal-fired power plant a week and is the world's leading coal producer.[23] Yet it is also the world's top producer of green energy—wind turbines and solar panels.

China now consumes 10 percent of the world's oil and will be the largest consumer of oil well before midcentury. Its voracious need for imported oil to power its economy is troubling news for Israel. Already, 12 percent of China's oil is imported from Iran, and notwithstanding UN sanctions, it is planning to invest billions of dollars in Iran's oil and gas fields and deepening its ties to other Middle Eastern oil producers. This is one of the reasons China exacted a price for supporting a fourth round of UN sanctions against Iran in 2010, diluting them and refusing to add unilateral sanctions like the U.S. and the EU adopted.

This industrial expansion, and its accumulation of dollars and euros in payment for its exports, rather than spending them domestically, has allowed China to amass colossal foreign reserves and deploy them to its economic and political advantage—from $166 billion in 2000 to $2.2 trillion in 2009, while U.S. reserves barely grew from $31 to $47 billion, an imbalance mainly arising from a massive

U.S. trade deficit with China. At a time when American and European banks were enfeebled from the financial crisis, Chinese state-owned banks stepped in during 2009 and invested more than $1.5 trillion around the world. They accrued $6 trillion in outstanding loans, second only to U.S. banks, whose outstanding loans shrank by 7 percent to $6.7 trillion.[24]

Chinese foreign investments have also matured, moving from passive, portfolio participants to active, engaged directors. More than 190 funds are now denominated in Chinese currency, worth more than $30 billion in combined capital.[25] China is already the largest investor in Africa, where 750,000 Chinese workers are extracting natural resources for its growth machine. Chinese state-controlled companies and sovereign wealth funds are increasingly looking to the U.S. for investments, already taking minority shares in large American financial institutions such as Blackstone. Its telecommunications giant, Huawei, is stretching its tentacles around the world and seeking acquisitions in the U.S. despite American security barriers.

In 2010, China began turning its attention to Europe. Already in the spring of 2010, Europe supplanted the U.S. as China's largest trading partner. It is using its foreign currency reserves to buy assets cheaply in Europe after the global financial crisis as well as stockpiling goodwill along with the government debt of Greece, Spain, and Portugal as Western investors fled. Prime Minister Wen Jiabao reminded Europeans of this during a 2010 visit, and in hard-pressed Greece, where China is remodeling the port of Piraeus as a staging post for its European exports, its minister of state proclaimed, "The support of our Chinese friends is fortunate for us." These investments, like those in Africa, have political as well as economic ramifications in increasing China's global influence. There is a strategic motive: China hopes its help to Europe at a critical time will lead Europe to support its position on a range of issues, such as reducing U.S. pressure to raise the value of its currency and treating it as a market economy to make Chinese products more resistant to European anti-dumping remedies.[26]

It is in Asia, however, that China's increasing dominance is most evident. In 2009, the U.S. accounted for 13.6 percent of China's total trade, almost identical to its trade with the ten countries of the Association of Southeast Asian Nations (ASEAN). But the center of gravity is moving. Since 2003, there has been a twentyfold increase in trade between the ASEAN countries and China, and China has now replaced the U.S. as their largest trading partner. China is also beginning to use its wealth strategically, signing a free trade agreement with the ASEAN nations of Southeast Asia,[27] opening negotiations for a historic free trade agreement with Taiwan,[28] and planning to negotiate free trade agreements with America's major Asian allies, Japan and South Korea.

Its growing Asian footprint even reaches Australia and New Zealand, the other members of one of the United States' most long-standing mutual defense pacts,

ANZUS, home to vibrant Jewish communities—100,000 and 10,000 respectively—and historically aligned with America's and Israel's interests. China has displaced the U.S. as Australia's largest trading partner and its largest buyer of its government debt. Australia has become a major destination for Chinese tourists and home to 120,000 Chinese students studying in Australia's colleges and universities.[29] China will soon also be the top trading partner of New Zealand, a phenomenon that New Zealand's ambassador to the U.S. Mike Moore told me will be unique for his country. For the first time in New Zealand's history its major trading partner will not be its major security partner.

China also used its economic clout for diplomatic benefit by opening an 1,140-mile pipeline in 2009, across three Central Asian nations, bringing gas from Turkmenistan to Xinjiang in the west of the country. This is the first major export corridor for Central Asia's natural gas that does not go through the Russian pipeline system. This broke Russia's pipeline monopoly, a move that has so far eluded U.S. companies and European nations, some of which are so dependent to have become subject to Russian political influence. China succeeded, in part, because it did not tie its energy ventures to demands for democratic change or access to military bases.[30]

China is closing its technology gap with the West, in part by conditioning investment by American and European companies on a transfer of technology to Chinese firms, and in part by sophisticated computer hacking of Western high-tech companies. China has overtaken the U.S. as the country with the largest number of Internet users, more than tripling in three years to 338 million in 2009 and by 30 to 40 percent annually.[31] China Telecom gains 15 million new mobile phone subscribers each month, and U.S. high-tech companies such as HP and Apple no longer exclusively supply the designs for new products. China and other Asian countries are moving to increase their control over the development of personal computers, smart phones, and websites. Investment arms of Chinese companies, such as DFJ DragonFund China, are investing in high-tech companies in both China and the U.S., creating a network in America's Silicon Valley, filling a capital gap caused by the financial woes of U.S. banks and venture capital funds. This is giving China access to the latest developments in computer chips, software, and other U.S. technology. Decades ago the U.S. lost electronics manufacturing to offshore facilities, leaving at least the high-value electronic design jobs in America. Now, many of these may also be lost.

Despite its nominal attachment to Communism, Red China is now an emerging "green China." In response to demands from China's growing middle class for a cleaner environment, and to reduce its own dependence on foreign oil, China is going green and has made it a national priority to be the number one country in developing renewable energy sources.[32] China's goal by 2020 is for wind, solar, and biomass energy to represent 8 percent of electricity generation, with coal still supplying two-thirds of capacity and nuclear and hydroelectric power the rest. The Chinese government spent $45 billion in 2009 alone to upgrade its electricity grid, with government mandates to produce more renewable energy as well as subsidies to Chinese citizens to install solar water heaters and panels. China has a built-in advantage in the renewable energy areas because its huge internal market for electricity rises by 15 percent annually as power reaches rural villages and farms, aided by cheap labor costs and state-supported low-interest loans, just as in the United States during the 1930s. The International Energy Agency (IEA) estimates China will need to add nearly nine times as much electricity-generating capacity as the United Sates. Already, China is on track to surpass the U.S. by 2012 in total power generation.

China is attempting to enter the next phase of its growth with a sustainable economic strategy. Beijing has begun discouraging foreign investment in low-wage, low-value products and is content for such work to migrate to even lower-wage countries in Asia, such as Vietnam, while China seeks higher value-added investment. Beijing is also updating its antiquated legal system. In 2008, the government enacted a modern labor relations law, designed more on the European than the American model, providing labor unions and workers more bargaining power and protection. This will lead to higher wages in China, although they will still be a fraction of those in the U.S., Europe, and Japan.

Chinese companies are extending their tentacles around the world. By 2020, Chinese businesses are projected to spend more than $1 trillion in buying up assets outside China, especially in natural resources in Africa, to stoke their industrial growth. In the U.S. alone, despite congressional opposition to high-profile Chinese takeovers, such as CNOOC's effort to acquire Unocal, an American energy company, Chinese investment is doubling every year. China has a business presence in thirty-five of the fifty U.S. states, with a particular emphasis on industrial machinery and real estate. By the end of 2009, the total amount of Chinese offshore investments already stood at $230 billion, and their purchases of short-term financial assets, such as Treasury bonds, were far above direct investment, standing at over $1 trillion. But the resistance to investment in the U.S. comes from concerns not only about acquiring technology that can be put to military use but also that the top executives of many of China's state-owned companies are beholden to the Communist Party.[33]

"Soft" Chinese Power?

Chinese president Hu first publicly talked about "soft power" in 2007, recognizing it was of growing significance in what he called "competition in overall national strength," so China, he asserted, must "enhance culture as part of the soft power of our country."[34] China has opened dozens of Confucius Institutes (modeled on the British Council and Alliance Française) to promote Chinese language, training, and culture. Beijing is also spending over $6.5 billion in a global strategy to create companies to challenge Western global media firms. There are other signs of rising Chinese influence: While most foreign language study has dropped in the U.S., it has risen for Chinese. About 1,600 American public and private schools teach Chinese compared to 300 a decade ago. As part of a concerted Chinese strategy, the Chinese government is sending teachers to schools all over the world and paying part of their salaries. Since 2006, more than 325 Chinese "guest teachers" have worked in the U.S.[35]

China wields its political clout in the United States; Beijing spends at least $4 million annually to hire some of Washington's best law firms to represent its interests on trade, human rights, and Taiwan. The results have been impressive. While ten years ago, the U.S. Congress accused China Ocean Shipping Company of being a front for espionage and blocked its plans to expand its Long Beach, California, terminal in 2009, Congress welcomed China's efforts to rescue Boston's ports and create thousands of jobs when a European shipping line moved out.[36]

China is also playing a constructive role in UN peacekeeping missions, using its growing military might to project an image of a benign power. Some 2,150 Chinese military and police personnel are deployed in ten countries on UN missions. However, China has often played both sides of local politics in order to secure its own economic and political advantage. After providing missiles and advanced weaponry to the military in Sudan, a country that supplies oil to China, but which committed mass atrocities in Darfur, China sent 800 troops on a UN peacekeeping mission to Sudan.[37]

Still, China is careful to keep its disagreements with the U.S. within bounds and not be openly provocative. While it strongly objected to the Obama administration's 2010 sale of weapons to Taiwan and threatened to stop a variety of cooperative military efforts, by the time President Hu came to Washington in April 2010 for the Nuclear Safety Summit, the issue was barely raised, and the military talks resumed in 2011.

Is China Playing by the Rules?

China has developed a model of economic and political governance never seen in modern times and which the Chinese leadership is touting to the world as the solution to the challenges of the twenty-first-century economy. It offers neither the discredited Soviet model nor the democratic, free-market capitalist model of the U.S. and Europe, which China holds in disdain. It combines political autocracy with Communist Party dominance of all instruments of civilian and military power, as well as tight controls over news and information—with a state-dominated capitalist system and heavy doses of old-fashioned mercantilism subsidizing Chinese companies to pile up wealth from other nations. The Chinese economy is dominated by over 120 state-owned corporations (SOEs) directly controlled by the central government in Beijing and thousands of others by provincial and local governments, all mandated to achieve a profit and aggressively compete for business around the world, backed by billions of dollars of low-interest, subsidized loans from state-owned banks, with access to land at below-market rates.

While between 1999 and 2009 many SOEs were closed or sold and the state's share of industrial output dropped in half, from just less than 50 percent to 27 percent, in the last several years there has been a revival in SOEs. The state has defined whole sectors as "strategic" that must be controlled only by "national champions," pushing out their own private enterprises and restricting competing foreign investment. In the 2010 Fortune 500 list of the world's largest companies, almost every one of the forty-two mainland China firms on the list were SOEs, and on China's own top 500 list spanning seventy-five sectors, not one private firm is listed in twenty-nine of those sectors, and seventy-five of the hundred biggest publicly traded firms were government dominated.[38]

Though over time I believe China will increasingly play by global rules like those set by the World Trade Organization (WTO), Beijing is certainly not always doing so now. Instead, it is rewriting the global rulebook to favor its own companies in huge government procurement programs in violation of the WTO Government Procurement Act—which they have never signed. Their foreign aid is tied to Chinese purchases, a practice now banned by the Organisation for Economic Co-operation and Development (OECD)—to which China does not belong—and offers huge state-subsidized loans and grants from dollars earned in exporting to the U.S. to lock up natural resources in Africa and Asia, regardless of the character of any local regime.[39]

An example of the negative impact China enjoys by playing by its own rules is the 2011 bankruptcy of three American solar power companies and a fourth that halted production, representing almost one-fifth of the total solar panel manufacturing capacity in the U.S. While they maintained a technological edge over their Chinese competitors, the U.S. government and the American solar industry allege that low-cost loans from state-owned banks in Beijing, cheap land from government, and low labor costs were too much for the American companies. China has gone in just a few years from a minor to a dominant player in the production of what will be an increasingly important source of electricity the world over in the years ahead.[40]

As if these unfair advantages were not enough, China maintains an undervalued currency to make its exports cheaper and to dominate world markets, in the process building up trillions of dollars of foreign reserves at the expense of domestic consumption. While favoring its own home-grown intellectual property (IP), China does not respect the protection of IP foreign firms, ripping off foreign music, movies, and software and often forcing technology transfer to its SOEs as a condition of investing in the country.

China also has no antibribery laws and, unlike the major democracies including Israel, is not a party to the antibribery convention of the OECD (which I helped negotiate during the Clinton administration).

China accepts all the advantages of economic development while pleading it is still a poor country, unable to shoulder global responsibilities consistent with its size and power. China's opposition to the Doha trade agreement and to accepting binding reductions in its greenhouse gas emissions in the Kyoto Protocol (in which I was the lead negotiator for the U.S. government and bore the brunt of China's furious attack on the West for attempting to limit their emissions, even as we were accepting reductions) further demonstrates that the Chinese are as yet unwilling to accept responsibilities commensurate with its new economic power.[41] Yet, there is a gradual reckoning on China's part. At the 2011 Durban Conference on global warming, China agreed to general language about binding restrictions on greenhouse gas emissions, and in its most recent five-year plan, promulgated in 2011, China has built in a significant reduction in the level of emissions per unit of GDP growth.

The desire for stability and order is so great, the pride of the Chinese people in "the new China" so intense, the antipathy to still-remembered Western and foreign rule so raw, and the deference to authority so central to the Chinese psyche that for the foreseeable future China will be able to do what I once thought impossible: become integrated into the global economy while maintaining Communist Party political autocracy. There is more personal, if not political, freedom in China today. People can travel freely, for example. Western newspapers are available in major tourist hotels. There is the beginning of village democracy, and demonstrators regularly take to the streets to demand better working conditions and the end of local Communist Party corruption, and with some effect. But broad democratic political freedoms are no greater than they were ten years ago and are not likely to be greater ten years from now. As long as Chinese leaders can deliver economic benefits to the people, it is unlikely that any real challenge to the ultimate authority of the Communist Party will emerge in the foreseeable future.

As China's recovery from the great global recession of 2008–2009 far outpaced that of the West, it provided other developing countries with an alternative political mode: what *The Economist* magazine called a "Beijing consensus," extolling the virtues of decisive authoritarianism over what they describe as shilly-shallying democratic debate, competing with the "Washington consensus" of free-market democratic capitalism that has been the dominant global model since the end of World War II, even more so after the implosion of Communism ended the Cold War.[42] With the partisan polarization in Washington hamstringing the capacity of the U.S. to meet its major economic challenges, even over what should have been the simple act of raising the U.S. debt limit in 2011, leading to the downgrade of America's long-held AAA debt rating, it has given China bragging rights that its autocratic governing model is best for the twenty-first century, a disastrous outcome if it persists.

China's Weaknesses

For all of its startling accomplishments, China should not be viewed as an unstoppable juggernaut. Serious weaknesses will prevent it from being a fully equal to the United States for decades to come, although the gaps will continue to narrow. For one thing, China's double-digit growth rates will slow down. Its latest five-year plan calls for growth to slow from double-digit rates to 7 to 8 percent a year.[43] China's long-booming economy is slowing down appreciably, and one of its own senior economists, Yu Bin, said clearly at the end of 2011 that "China is nearing the end of the period of high economic growth" and would have less than 9 percent growth in 2012, followed by 7 to 8 percent through 2017, as its five-year plan calls for. Yu noted that "China had been growing at high speed for three decades," but now "China's fundamentals are changing, including demography and the demand and supply of labor."[44]

Its one-child policy has slowed population growth, will reduce the size of the labor force and the number of young workers who helped fuel double-digit growth, and will increase the percentage of people dependent on the government relative to the number of its workers. Selective abortions of female fetuses will intensify the gender imbalance and give rise to social problems that are already apparent in the mass of young, unmarried men.[45] Chinese government figures underscore this dramatic gender gap, with 188 male newborns compared to only 100 females.[46]

It is little recognized that beginning in 2000, China officially became an "old" country, with 10 percent of its population (130 million people) over 60 years of age, growing to 342 million in 2030, larger than the current population of the U.S. Its population will peak in 2030 at 1.46 billion and then begin to slowly decline.[47] China's latest census, taken in 2010 and released the next year, indicated that China had 1.34 billion people, a roughly 6 percent increase since 2000. China's share of the population under fifteen years of age dropped by over 6 percent from the 2000 census, while those over sixty years old increased almost 3 percent.[48] Even now, from 1995 to 2008 its primary school enrollment dropped precipitously, from 25 million to under 17 million, and in the next decade their twenty- to twenty-four-year-old population will decrease by half.[49]

Slower growth presents grave challenges for the new leadership team that will come into power in 2012. Stability is the watchword of the Communist Party leadership; as President Hu Jintao put it, "without stability nothing can be accomplished."[50] But China is seeing growing instability, aimed not at changing the prevailing one-party autocratic system but at making it more accountable.

There is an unprecedented amount of labor unrest, particularly in Guangdong Province, the country's main export base,[51] but also at Honda plants, with suicides at Foxconn Technology, the world's largest contract electronics supplier. Chinese workers are demanding, and in many cases receiving, higher wages, better working conditions, and more rights.[52] The 2010 International Labor Organization report showed that Chinese wages in the manufacturing sector have risen by over 14 percent a year since 1987.[53] This is forcing China to abandon its market share in lower-value products such as textiles and to move up the value chain of products. I have heard CEOs say they are moving plants either to lower-cost countries in Asia, such as Vietnam, or even back to the U.S., where stagnant wages and proximity to the huge American consumer base make it competitive to be in the United States.

Moreover, there have been thousands of demonstrations—in 2010 as many as 180,000 strikes, sit-ins, rallies, and violent confrontations—by local citizens against corruption and cronyism of Communist Party officials; poor environmental conditions; police brutality; seizure of farm land; and mass evictions, with a pittance of compensation, of industrial, residential, and commercial facilities, which enhance the status of local Communist Party operatives to their superiors in Beijing. In Wukan, for example, a small town in southern China, villagers openly chased away government officials, took up homemade weapons, and set up road blockades to protest land seizures, calling for democratic elections to replace Communist Party village officials. The government responded by arresting five of the leaders, two of whom died in captivity. At the same time, the government negotiated with village representatives chosen by the villagers to address their concerns.[54]

In addition, China has restive ethnic populations in Tibet and in the western desert region of Xinjiang. While they are a small percentage of China's population, the Muslim Uyghurs live in one-sixth of China's landmass. Including Tibet and the Tibetan populations that abut Tibet, some 40 percent of China's territory has significant strife. China's predictable reaction has been suppression. They have not dealt with the underlying concerns of either the Tibetans or the Uyghurs and accuse the latter of connections to al-Qaeda on the basis that some were imprisoned by the U.S. at Guantanamo.

Another challenge is the increasing demand of its people for more information as well as more governmental accountability at every level. At one and the same time, China has the largest number of Internet users in the world and the most sophisticated system of Internet censorship, nicknamed the Great Firewall.[55] Most recently, China added another layer of web surveillance by requiring new website users to log on under their true identities, rather than anonymously, to comment on news events. Government censors have shut down thousands of websites for spreading what they call "harmful information" and have blocked access to popular social network sites.

Most recently, the Chinese government further tightened censorship with the creation of Bureau Nine, a new department charged solely to police social networking sites.[56] But twenty-first-century communications limit the effectiveness of Chinese censorship. With the Uyghurs, for example, photographs appeared online after the ethnic battles with the Han in Xinjiang (moved there by the government over the years to ensure a Han majority, China's dominant ethnic group), showing piles of dead bodies on websites that the government censors were unable to delete. A call for protests spread around websites and on QQ, China's most popular instant messaging program, notwithstanding the government's efforts to block it. And a group of retired former senior Communist officials have called for an end to censorship.[57]

Microblogging sites are now used by millions of Chinese to obtain real-time, uncensored news. There has been a recent surge in use of Weibo, one of the most popular, a private social networking microblogging site used by more than 200,000 Chinese citizens, a combination of Twitter and Facebook, both of which are banned. Just as the government has cracked down on traditional media to ensure they follow the party line, so too they are threatening Internet users of these sites, and with some success. The minister of the State Council Internet Office warned that "the Internet should not be used to jeopardize the national or public interest."[58]

Responding to the Internet's role in catalyzing revolution in the Arab world, China instituted a further crackdown: hotels, restaurants, bars, and bookstores are now required to install expensive web-monitoring software, forcing many to simply stop offering Internet access at all. Those Chinese young people who expect to be able to do what Westerners can do at Starbucks, for example, which is to have free Wi-Fi service with their drinks, will be sorely disappointed. When added to the existing blockage of websites such as Facebook, Twitter, and YouTube; the difficulty of establishing individual websites; and the filters of Internet sites for key topics and words that the Chinese government believes undermines their central authority,[59] China is aggressively restricting access to information, but at the risk of alienating its citizens, undermining its global credibility, and impairing its capacity to innovate, a key requirement for dominance in the twenty-first century.

An additional challenge arises from China's membership in the World Trade Organization. A recent decision struck down the limits the Chinese government has imposed on the distribution of movies, songs, and imported books, which had to be handled by state-controlled companies, opening China further to foreign information, whetting the appetite of its population for even more information.[60]

Finally, it is important to put China's power in context. Its huge economy masks its relative poverty. On a per capita basis, its wealth is a tiny fraction of America's and stands in the bottom half of the countries of the world; it has one of the largest numbers of poor people (over 300 million) of the entire globe.[61]

Looking at China and India together, never before have two nations been so powerful in aggregate income but so poor on an individual basis. China and India both are expected to act as great powers but are poor countries by many measures.[62]

China now has the second-largest economy in the world but ranks 133rd in per capita income, while India is the fifth-largest economy in the world but ranks 167th per person. Together they have $11.3 trillion worth of economic power, but divided by their massive populations, that impressive figure comes to only $4,500 per person.

At the height of the British Empire at the outbreak of World War I, Britain controlled 45 percent of the world's foreign direct investment. America reached its peak of 50 percent in 1967. By contrast, China accounts for only 6 percent of the world's share. And there are reasons not to fear that despite their huge pool of funds, China will buy up the world. Chinese companies are "limited by lack of management depth to run worldwide enterprises, cultural barriers and political resistance to takeovers by state-controlled firms, with their embedded Communist Party and government officials and opaque governance."[63]

To maintain the dominance of the Communist Party, China's leaders must focus on creating jobs for their people rather than on foreign adventures. Its export model for growth will begin to change as China's growing middle class demands more products at home and as pressures grow from the U.S., the EU, and its Asian neighbors for a more realistic level for China's currency. Moreover, the government and the society must contend with massive movements of people from rural to urban China (undertaken in large measure as a device to alleviate poverty). In the first two decades of this century, some 300 million people will move from rural to urban areas, a number equal to the entire U.S. population, swelling the population of urban China from 500 million to 830 million people. From 1980 to 2011, China's urban dwellers grew from one-fifth of the country's population to one-half, marking the first time in its history that the urban and rural populations were essentially equal,[64] and in order to maintain its economic dynamism and political stability, China will have to continue to persuade its rural population to move to its cities to fill jobs as its workforce grows older.[65] This is more than enough to keep China's autocratic leaders focused on domestic tasks rather than foreign adventures.

The global economic crisis exposed the weak link in absorbing this huge bulge by creating the worst unemployment crisis since economic reforms began three decades ago. From the middle of 2008 to the first quarter of 2009, an estimated 20 million Chinese workers lost their jobs after they migrated from the countryside, as plants shut down or drastically restricted production. The new city dwellers cannot easily return to their rural farm plots, which in many cases have been sold to developers for shopping malls, apartment buildings, and office buildings that increasingly dot the countryside. City and provincial governments were handing out food coupons and distributing essentials such as vegetable oil. Charitable endeavors sprang up to provide soup kitchens. The crisis forced the hand of the government to create a universal safety net, including unemployment insurance, for the first time.[66]

Another check on China's rising power comes from its own Asian neighbors, who fear China's rising power, providing the U.S. the opportunity to solidify its standing in the region. China has aggressively asserted a national security interest in contested islands in the East China Sea with Japan and refused to export rare earth minerals to Japan, crucial for computer and industrial products. China has harassed Vietnamese fishermen and oil exploration teams in the South China Sea and claimed all of its one million square miles as its territory.[67]

China's flexing its new military might has led to reactions by Beijing's smaller Asian neighbors. Vietnam is buying half a dozen submarines from Russia to form the largest undersea fleet in Southeast Asia. Malaysia also took delivery in 2009 of its first submarine, and even tiny Singapore has purchased two submarines from Sweden. The father of modern Singapore, Lee Kuan Yew, called on the U.S. to maintain its presence in Asia and warned: "U.S. core interest requires that it remains the superior power in the Pacific. To give up this position would diminish America's role throughout the world."[68] This is one of the key reasons the United States has strengthened its military capabilities in the Pacific—now no longer "an American lake."

The Obama administration has taken advantage of the nervousness of many of China's neighbors by the most aggressive courting of Asian countries since the end of World War II. The November 2011 Asia-Pacific Economic Cooperation (APEC) summit in Honolulu marked a turning point in U.S. diplomatic history, signaling that security in Asia, rather than Europe, would be the prime focus of American foreign policy and that the United States was a Pacific as well as Atlantic power. The summit helped ensure Asian nations that despite the distractions of the Middle East and the European financial crisis, the U.S. was reasserting itself in China's backyard.[69]

President Obama announced a framework agreement for a new Trans-Pacific Partnership (TPP) free trade agreement between the U.S. and key Asian countries and, together with Secretary of State Hillary Clinton, sent clear signals to China that the peaceful resolution of China's territorial claims in the South China Sea was in America's security interests. The president called on China, as its power grows, to "play by the rules,"[70] causing tension at the summit. Immediately following APEC, the president signed a new security agreement with Australia, which will establish a permanent base for American soldiers, to further offset China's military might in Asia.

Beijing has also shown increased stridency over its long-disputed claims to the Indian state of Arunachal Pradesh, near Tibet, and has pressed Nepal to accept

Chinese assistance in policing isolated regions on its northern border and closing the Himalayan passages through which Tibetans had long made surreptitious trips from China to visit the Dalai Lama in his exile in India. Nepal, long closely tied to India, now seeks closer ties with China, with whom trade has quadrupled since 2003, and has asked China to extend rail service into the Himalayas to the Nepalese border. This is an alarming development for New Delhi, which shares a long and porous border with Nepal.[71] Beijing is building ports in Pakistan and Sri Lanka that, although for commercial purposes, could be turned to military use.[72]

As a result, India, a traditional rival of China, is developing a strategic partnership with the U.S., including a nuclear energy treaty negotiated during the Bush administration and a major agreement to buy American military transport aircraft and jet fighters, signed during President Obama's November 2010 state visit. Vietnam, America's bitter enemy and China's ally during the Vietnam War, now seeks a closer partnership with the U.S. Visits by Secretary of State Clinton and then Secretary of Defense Gates have led to the first security dialogue: U.S. naval vessels have visited Vietnam and Vietnamese officers are studying at U.S. military academies. Both countries are negotiating a civilian nuclear technology agreement that would reduce Vietnam's dependence on Chinese electricity. Singapore and South Korea have joined with Japan and Vietnam to affirm their desire for American security. Most encouraging, Japan and India are discussing a "circle of democracy" of trade and security agreements, with the democracies in Asia as a counterweight to China.[73]

But sound U.S. policy toward China also involves even deeper engagement at every level. In 2010, the U.S. exported $20 billion of badly needed soy to China for its livestock, essential to meet its rising meat consumption, three times the level of a decade ago.[74] In a 2011 visit by Vice President Joe Biden to Vice President Xi Jinping, each recognized the importance of a shared relationship, with Xi stating that "under the new circumstances, China and the United States share even broader common interests and co-shoulder more common responsibilities."[75] And importantly, military ties are being enhanced, with the then chairman of the Joint Chiefs of Staff, Admiral Mike Mullen, exchanging visits with his Chinese counterpart in 2011 and with joint exercises in areas such as counterpiracy in the Gulf of Aden.[76]

All this should put U.S. relations with China into a broader and less fearful context. While an emerging giant, China nevertheless is still "emerging." It is a regional power, with no formal military alliance, compared to more than fifty for the U.S., a perceived need for better military and diplomatic relations with America,[77] and global ambitions; those ambitions, fueled by staggering progress, make China unique and will certainly lead it to assume an ever-larger place on the international stage.

India

With so much global attention paid to China, India has quietly but forcefully moved to the forefront of emerging economies. Within twenty-five years, India will be the most populous nation in the world. While economic growth rates have lagged behind China's, India has compiled a robust average annual growth of nearly 7 percent since 2000 and achieved a historic transition: For the first time, in 2010, its agricultural sector accounted for a smaller share of its GDP than industry and services.[78]

India has become the "back office" for the global economy, hosting call centers and computerized responses for multinational companies the world over. India excels in software engineers, and the Indian state of Bangalore has become a high-tech hot spot. Indian companies such as Tata and CMC are world class. Like other developing nations in Asia, India has leaped over the telephone landline generation directly to mobile phones and is adding 15 million new subscriptions every month,[79] with a total now of nearly half a billion users, connecting rural villages in India to the world. Like China, India is seeking to be a leader in renewable energy, with one of the most ambitious solar programs in the world: Delhi's goal is 20,000 megawatts of installed solar energy by 2020.[80]

Indian growth presents fewer challenges than China's to the United States and the West. Its growth has come largely on the back of technology and its much-heralded outsourcing business, which accounts for as much as 5 percent of its economy. India produces more software engineers than any country in the world. But it is not just high technology that has vaulted India ahead. Four of the eight richest people in the world are Indian born, with steel tycoon Lakshmi Mittal leading the list, followed by leaders in the petrochemical, telecommunications, and real estate industries, all of which are spreading investments abroad. Two of the most redoubtable English automobile brands—Jaguar and Land Rover—were bought by Mumbai-based Tata Motors.

India's space agency, ISRO, has become a leader in satellite deployment, giving the country four dedicated communications satellites and eight remote sensing satellites, almost as many as the U.S. By 2015, India plans its first manned space mission.[81] India is also second only to the United States as a site for the world's generic pharmaceutical manufacturing.

India also has played the role of the poor developing country when it suits its aims, joining China in blocking completion of the WTO's Doha Round by trying to protect its farmers from global competition, and preventing developing countries from making any significant contribution to reducing greenhouse gasses at the Kyoto negotiations in 1997. At Kyoto, I found the Indian delegation as profoundly opposed as China to any contributions from the developing world to the global warming challenge, playing to the anti-Western attitudes of the G77 developing countries.

India is also following China's restrictive rules against foreign investment in the telecommunications area, favoring local intellectual property and making it more difficult for foreign corporations to compete on a level playing field.

Like China, India is translating its growing economic power into military strength. The country so closely associated with the Gandhian tradition of non-violence is an increasingly important military power but one that often supports the American view in Asia and serves as a counterweight to China and Russia. In the past, its military focused on its two neighbors—Pakistan and China, with whom it has fought several wars. During the Cold War, India was nominally neutral but titled toward the Soviet Union as its principal supplier of arms and an ideological model for rapid, government-directed industrialization. Now India and the U.S., closer both in ideology and arms, have created a strategic orbit and in the past seven years held some fifty joint military exercises.[82]

India is spending as much as $40 billion annually on military modernization during the next five years, much of that on weapons for potential use far beyond its borders, including airborne tankers that can fly as far as Alaska, C-130 transport planes, nuclear submarines, and aircraft carriers that can protect its sea lanes and political interests in the Indian Ocean and beyond. Rahul Gandhi, heir to the Nehru political dynasty, who was educated at Harvard rather than England like his father and grandfather, put it pithily by declaring it was time for his country to "stop worrying about how the world will impact [India] and . . . step out and worry about how [India] will impact the world."[83]

The clearest example of India's geostrategic ambitions came in the wake of its first testing of an atomic bomb in 1998, when it exploded the device but refused to sign the Nuclear Non-Proliferation Treaty (NPT) and subject itself to international inspection. This was shortly followed by Pakistan doing the same, in retaliation. I was scheduled to visit India as under secretary of state to prepare the ground for a visit by President Clinton, but my trip was canceled, and instead, the U.S. imposed sanctions required by U.S. law. It is a demonstration of how dramatically U.S. relations with India have improved and how much Delhi's influence has increased that in 2008, far from continuing sanctions, the U.S. and India embarked on a historic Nuclear Cooperation Treaty to share nuclear technology and nuclear fuel, even though, like Israel, it has never signed the NPT.

A 2009 trip to India by Secretary of State Hillary Rodham Clinton provided further evidence of how much the relationship has changed. The victory of the Congress Party in that year's elections and the continuing decline of the Indian Communist Party led to the creation of a strategic dialogue including more than just government officials, bringing in business leaders, social activists, academics, leaders of charitable foundations, educators, and entrepreneurs.[84] India allowed U.S. defense companies to compete for the sale of fighter jets worth some $10 billion; has identified two sites for potential U.S.-made nuclear reactors; and signed an agreement permitting U.S. parts on Indian satellite launch vehicles.[85]

And President Obama publicly supported India's bid to have a permanent seat on the UN Security Council, a strategic gesture he did not extend to Brazil during his state visit in 2011.

India, on the other hand, although an open, vibrant democracy, is in some respects a more inhospitable place for foreign corporations than China because of a stifling bureaucracy, excessive red tape, and endemic corruption, dramatized by Anna Hazare's famous hunger strike to pressure the Indian Congress to fight graft by creating an independent anticorruption agency to oversee public officials and bureaucrats.[86]

Brazil

Outside of Asia, Brazil is the other key emerging power of the twenty-first century. For years, pundits reveled in the often-repeated wry remark that "Brazil is the country of the future—and always will be." But the future now has come to Brazil, and the world is paying attention. With skillful political leadership of a diversified economy by the former union official Lula da Silva, who recently completed two highly successful terms as president, and a continuation of his policies if not his charismatic tactics by his chosen successor, and former chief of staff, Dilma Rousseff, Brazil is now the seventh-largest economy in the world and well on its way to becoming the fifth-largest economy during this decade, overtaking Britain and France.

Brazil has a vast land mass equivalent to the size of the continental United States; a large population, with Sao Paulo's 12 million people making it one of the largest cities on the planet; and enormous and varied natural resources, including newly discovered huge hydrocarbon reserves off the coast. With $20 billion in investments throughout Latin America, Brazil will eventually supplant the United States as the continent's largest foreign investor and already has done so in Argentina. Petrobras, the Brazilian state-owned energy company, is the largest corporation in Latin America.

The shift of influence is evidenced by the first foreign visit of Colombian president Santos—to Brazil and not the United States even though Washington is the largest source of Colombian military and foreign assistance. In a remarkable turnabout, Brazil has become one of the largest creditors of the U.S., which in past decades helped put together debt relief packages for Brazil, in one of which I was involved as under secretary of state in the Clinton administration.

A nation of 190 million, Brazil is finally reaching its economic potential. It has the opportunity to be not just a regional but an international power, despite limited military projection and no nuclear weapons. Brazil has no conflicts with any of the ten countries on its borders, no hostile insurgents or ethnic and religious conflicts, and it treats foreign investors with respect. In the past ten years,

31 million Brazilians have moved into the middle class and 20 million out of poverty. Its foreign reserves have leaped from $38 billion to $240 billion. During Lula's presidency, Brazil went from needing a record $30 billion bailout from the IMF to lending $5 billion to the IMF. Equally telling, in December 2011, when IMF president Christine LaGarde sought additional contributions to assist Europe in its sovereign debt crisis, she came to Brazil, which was proud to help the enfeebled eurozone.

Brazil's economy also shows few of the vulnerabilities of other emerging powers, escaping the worst of the global downturn. It is a world leader in mining, and its newly privatized Vale Corporation is the world's largest exporter of iron ore. Brazil's industrial base ranges from high technology to manufacturing, with massive potential to expand a booming agricultural sector and a tremendous pool of untapped natural resources. It has become a world leader in the production of soybeans, corn, sugarcane, cotton, and tropical fruits. The Brazilian company JBS will soon become the world's largest meat producer.

Aided in part by record foreign direct investments and Lula's antipoverty programs, Brazil has markedly shrunk its income inequalities. At the same time, since the 1990s its central bank was granted the independence central banks have in developed nations, with a mission to keep inflation low and to regulate banks to avoid excessive risks. Its banks did not suffer the same fate as America's during the financial crisis. Brazil has privatized many of its state-controlled companies and opened its economy to foreign trade and investment, although it still maintains protectionist tariffs and import fees.

Petrobras shocked the oil world in November 2008 when it announced that its Tupi deepwater field offshore of Rio de Janeiro could hold up to eight billion barrels of oil, with much more likely to be discovered. But unlike Russia, Brazil is in little danger of degenerating into another underperforming petro-state, addicted to easy oil revenues without diversification. Brazil's economy is diversified, and its growth is also based on foresight that is likely to pay off if good governance continues. During the oil crisis of the 1970s, it used its massive sugarcane resources to create an alternative fuel: ethanol. By the mid-1980s almost every new car sold in Brazil ran on it, and today, ethanol makes up 40 percent of the nation's fuel.

Brazil has also begun to act more aggressively to combat global environmental issues. Because of the vast denuding of its Amazon rain forests, Brazil is one of the top five emitters of greenhouse gases, but it has recently become more protective, relying on world-class satellite telemetry and on-the-ground monitoring programs to protect this vital asset. It has recently pledged to reduce its rate of deforestation by 50 percent by 2020.

It was no accident that Lula was one of the first foreign leaders received by President Obama in early 2009 and that he returned to Brazil in 2011 to meet with President Rousseff. But even with the outreach by the Obama administration, Brazil, like the other BRIC countries, continues to take a more independent foreign policy from the U.S. to enhance its diplomatic position. Like other emerging powers, Brazil is intent on carving out its own distinctive foreign policy, as the premier regional power in Latin America. It took a different approach from the U.S. in dealing with Iran's nuclear threat, to Israel's disadvantage.[87] With much of Latin America tilting leftward, and Bolivia, Ecuador, Nicaragua, and El Salvador electing leftist governments, Brazil is the key to a stable, prosperous, democratic, and moderate Latin America.

Its foreign policy has come with a "Brazilian twist," as Brasilia sought to anoint itself as the leader of regional South American integration. In 2010, Brazil validated the BRIC concept by hosting a meeting of the four leaders plus South Africa, that continent's emerging power. It rejected a U.S.-led Free Trade Area of the Americas in favor of the Mercosur free trade area, the trading bloc composed of Brazil, Argentina, Paraguay, and Uruguay.

Moreover, at the tail end of the Bush administration, Lula hosted a conference of Latin countries, showing its new military and political influence by inviting all South American countries to a regional conference, including Cuba and excluding the U.S.—a double poke in the eye to the departing President Bush. The conference became a forum to attack the U.S. for the global financial crisis—created, as Lula bluntly put it, by "men with blue eyes."[88] This underscored both the increased ambitions of Brazil and the diminished influence of the U.S. in its own hemisphere: A key ally created a platform for anti-American countries such as Venezuela, Bolivia, Cuba, and Ecuador to take on the U.S., with no defenders. Brazil has increased its diplomatic corps by almost 50 percent in the past five years, even opening an embassy in North Korea.

In 2009 Brazil hosted Iranian president Mahmoud Ahmadinejad, only a short time after democratic demonstrations against his fraudulent reelection. Yet, during his visit to Brasilia, not a word was raised about the elections by Lula, a champion of a democratic Brazil, nor against the brutal suppression of the Green Movement or Iran's nuclear program, despite Brazil's own example of abandoning its efforts to build nuclear weapons. The clear message to Washington was that Brazil will deal with whomever, whenever, and however it wants.

This was demonstrated again in 2010, when Brazil joined Turkey in reaching a compromise with Iran on its uranium enrichment program on terms highly favorable to Iran, undermining American efforts to rally support for a tough set of UN Security Council sanctions, and then voted against sanctions to which even Russia and China agreed.

In December 2010, Brazil, along with Uruguay, became the first country unilaterally to recognize a Palestinian state based on the pre-1967 borders.[89] But Brazil has been keen to maintain proper relations with Israel and has a small but influential Jewish community of less than 100,000, making it the tenth-largest Diaspora community, about half the size of Argentina's. Israel, world Jewry, and the U.S. have a great stake in Brazil's remaining a pro-Western country rather than a party to Latin America's anti-Western, anti-Israel bloc headed by Venezuela's president Hugo Chavez.

Russia

Russia is the fourth BRIC power to be reckoned with in the decades ahead. But it is the only "old" power, misplaced as a rising power in contrast to the other BRIC countries, and is greatly in want of economic and political reforms. President Dmitry Medvedev bluntly declared that his country's economy was "chronically backward," with "chronic corruption" eating away at its potential.[90] It has failed to diversify its economy and suffers from growing authoritarianism, with political opponents and independent journalists commonly jailed, harassed, or even killed.

However, with massive nuclear armaments, a large standing army, enormous energy reserves, a geography that spans eleven time zones, and a continued desire to dominate the former states of the Soviet Union, Russia remains a major world force. Under former (and recently re-elected) President Vladimir Putin's and current prime minister Vladimir Putin's leadership it has engaged in serious efforts to regain its old power and prestige.

Regardless of Russia's declining power relative to key emerging countries, its development over the coming decades is crucial to world Jewry and Israel. There remain more than 250,000 Jews, the sixth-largest Diaspora community in the world; there are some one million Russian *olim* in Israel, many of whom retain ties to Russia; and Russia's participation in the Quartet (U.S., UN, European Union, and Russia) gives it a role in the Middle East peace process.

As Sir Richard Dearlove, the former head of British foreign intelligence, succinctly put it,[91] Russia was an empire for four hundred years, an "ideological warrior" for Communism for seventy years, and a military superpower for forty years. During this entire sweep of history it oppressed and suppressed its huge Jewish population, with periodic pogroms, and forced its huge Jewish community to live in the Pale of Settlement. One of the most abused and influential anti-Semitic pieces of literature in history, *The Protocols of the Elders of Zion*, supported by the Nazis to justify their murder of European Jewry and still used to this day in many Muslim countries, emanated in 1903 as a fraudulent text from the Czar's secret police, setting forth a false Jewish plan to achieve world domination.

The 1917 Communist Revolution was led by many nominal Jews, such as Leon Trotsky. Initially, it liberated Jews as individuals, even as it suppressed Judaism, along with other religions. But the endemic anti-Semitism returned with Stalin's Doctors' Plot. With the Molotov-Ribbentrop Pact, Stalin and Hitler divided Poland and the Baltic states, bringing hundreds of thousands of Jews into the Soviet orbit. Although the Red Army liberated Auschwitz, and the Soviet Union served as a refuge for Jews fleeing the Nazi invasion of Russia, it also stood by passively when Adolf Eichmann was leading the 1944 destruction of Hungarian Jewry.

After World War II, the Soviet Union refused to allow the emigration of its large Jewish community, leading Congress to pass the 1974 Jackson-Vanik amendment denying the Soviet Union trade benefits. In the Carter White House, I was involved in a decision urged upon us by Congressman Charles Vanik to consider waiving the application of the amendment he coauthored, when the Soviet Union permitted the emigration of 50,000 Jews in 1979. But Senator Henry "Scoop" Jackson's strong opposition ended the effort.

One of the great rallying cries of American Jewry and "peoplehood events" was the cause of liberating Soviet Jews. Unlike the silence of much of the American Jewish leadership about the evolving Holocaust during World War II, on Freedom Sunday, December 6, 1987, 250,000 American Jews marched on the National Mall in Washington, including my wife Fran and me. Signs were posted in front of congregations around the country, calling for the Soviet Union to "Let Our People Go," evoking Moses' plea to the Egyptian pharaoh three millennia before.

Only as the Soviet empire began to erode and finally implode was free emigration of Russian Jews permitted. Eventually, one million went to Israel, profoundly changing the economic, political, and demographic future of the Jewish state. Today around 20 percent of the population of the State of Israel is of recent Russian origin, from the great emigration beginning in the late 1970s and accelerating after the implosion of Communism in the late 1980s. The stunning economic rise of Israel as a high-tech leader in the world has been aided by Russian immigration.

I vividly remember participating in a debate in Jerusalem over 20 years ago about the likely impact of the Russian *olim*; the predominant view was that they would be an unaffordable burden on the state. Far from it, the Russian immigrants were generally well educated and ready to work hard in a country that permitted them to reach their own level of achievement, something they had been denied in the Soviet Union. It was joked that if any Russian immigrants came off the plane at Ben-Gurion Airport without a violin, it was because they played the piano. What they really brought was their brains, their determination to make a better life for themselves and their families than they could in the Soviet Union, and a desire to have a genuine free market in which to operate, not the semi-socialist Israeli model of Israel's first decades, which was a pale shadow of the inefficient system they left behind.

Politically, Russian *olim* have helped transform Israel from a center-left to a center-right country. As a group they have brought a decidedly hawkish attitude to their new land, deeply suspicious of Israel's Palestinian neighbors and Israeli Arabs. Epitomizing the impact of Russian émigrés is Avigdor Lieberman, the founder of the Yisrael Beiteinu (Israel Is Our Home) Party and foreign minister in the second Netanyahu government. Lieberman's conservative philosophy and hawkish attitudes toward both Palestinians and Israeli Arabs (whom he wants to be required to sign a loyalty oath to the Jewish state or move to a new Palestinian state) led French president Nicolas Sarkozy to compare him to the notorious leader of the French far right, Jean-Marie le Pen.[92] Martin Peretz, former editor of *The New Republic* and an ardent supporter of Israel, has called Lieberman a "neo-fascist . . . [and] a certified gangster."[93]

This is an unfair exaggeration. But the rough brand of Soviet politics he knew from his early days in his Moldovan birthplace clearly has had an impact on him and many other Russian *olim*. It was Lieberman who rejected an agreement Prime Minister Netanyahu had accepted, reached between Israel's representative and Turkey's to the UN panel reviewing Israel's actions in 2010 in boarding the Turkish ship trying to break the Israeli naval blockade of Gaza. The Israeli decision led to Turkey's withdrawing its ambassador to Israel in 2011.

Moscow's decision to limit its reflexive support for Arabs has had major geopolitical impacts on Israel and the Middle East. One commentator noted that the Oslo peace process was made possible, in part, by the combination of Russian emigration to Israel and the end of Soviet support for the Arabs. With the ascendancy of President Putin, a new direction was set, neither pro-Western nor a full return to the old Soviet days. Putin has been an enormously popular political leader because he has produced what the Russian public desired: stability, order, prosperity, and the return of Russia as a major player on the world stage. Quite simply, Putin delivered, thanks to Russia's oil and gas wealth. During his years as president from 2000 to 2008, GDP growth averaged 11.2 percent per annum; a genuine middle class emerged; and Russia not only paid off its IMF debt from the 1998 financial crisis ahead of schedule but also enjoyed a budget surplus and over $500 billion in foreign currency reserves.

But Putin also created an autocracy with only a thin veneer of a democracy and centralized political power in the Kremlin. This provided a twist that particularly disadvantaged the wealthy oligarchs, many of whom were either overtly Jewish or had Jewish roots, such as Mikhail Khodorkovsky, whose Yukos oil company was confiscated as he was imprisoned, along with his partner Platon Lebedev. Several were leaders of the Russian Jewish community, such as Leonid Nevzlin, who was forced to flee to Israel where he has become a leading philanthropist. Just as their imprisonment was about to expire, another set of ludicrous charges, this time for alleged tax fraud, was brought, and both Khodorkovsky and Lebedev were convicted and sentenced to serve until 2017. Putin knew that attacking them would be popular with the Russian public, not only because of anger at their wealth but also because of their Jewish backgrounds.

Still, it would be inaccurate to brand Putin an anti-Semite. He has developed a close relationship with the Chabad Lubavitch rabbi Berel Lazar, on whom he has bestowed an Order of Friendship, and provided support for a Lubavitch school and community center. Russian Jews are free to practice their religion as never before in Russia's sordid history toward its Jewish citizens, which included mandatory twenty-five-year military service and forcible taking of young Jewish boys as teenagers for a preparatory period, under Tsar Nicholas I (1825–1855), separating them from parents they often never saw again.[94]

Just as Putin has tried to consolidate domestic political power in his hands, his goal abroad has been to restore Russia's power and prestige after the loss of the Soviet Empire, its prestige, and its military and political influence. Russia remains a mammoth nation geographically, but its loss of its vassal states in Eastern Europe and its own republics, especially Ukraine, Belarus, and Georgia, which were all integral parts of the USSR, is deeply offensive to Putin and much of the Russian public. He has stated that the demise of the Soviet Union was one of the darkest hours in Russian history.

Putin has sharply dismissed any suggestion that Russia still has progress to be made. His speech at the 2009 World Economic Forum in Davos was confident and disdainful of the U.S. I saw him bristle with indignation when Michael Dell, the founder of Dell computers, asked how the American IT industry could help Russia's development. Putin's response was "We do not need your help; we are not a developing nation; save your help for them." Putin's disdain was evident following the 2011 debt limit debacle, calling the U.S. "parasites."

For almost all of Putin's time in office, growth masked an economy heavily (and unsustainably) dependent on oil and gas exports, with half of its government budget coming from energy-related taxes. The sudden decline in commodity prices in late 2008 greatly reduced overall Russian growth rates, with projected future rates also suffering, and few countries were harder hit by the Great Recession.

Still, Russia is guaranteed a place of importance by its status as the second-largest oil producer in the world after Saudi Arabia. And whenever oil prices run up in response to upheavals in the Middle East, Russia is a direct beneficiary. As the provider of one-quarter of Europe's natural gas, Russia is essential to Europe and vice versa. Putin is using "pipeline diplomacy" to lever Russia's energy resources into recapturing political influence. The country is building a series of pipelines, the North Stream and South Stream from Central Asia through Russia, bypassing Ukraine, and further enhancing its energy chokehold over Europe. Under Putin's guidance, Russia has also used its oil and gas weapon to try to reassert its control over the "near abroad," its neighboring countries Georgia, Belarus, and Ukraine, with its periodic shutoff of gas flows, often in the middle of winter. And Russia will contribute to the IMF's fund for Europe, a dramatic turnaround from the 1998 IMF bailout to Russia, after it defaulted on its international debts during the Clinton administration.

The Georgian clashes of August 2008 were the most brutal example of Russia's new assertiveness. Russia used Georgia's actions to assert authority over its restive territories of South Ossetia and Abkhazia, to insert its military forces deep into the heart of Georgia, and to effectively remove the territories from Georgian government control. Russia went as far as to recognize the independence of the two regions, and President Medvedev said that he no longer recognized Mikhail Saakashvili, Georgia's elected president, as the president of Georgia, calling him a "political corpse."[95]

Russia's political influence is also demonstrated by the increased dependence of Germany, America's strongest continental ally, on Russian gas. On issues such as NATO expansion Berlin is deferential to Russian concerns. During the administration of George W. Bush, Germany played a leading role in blocking the American-led effort to designate Georgia and Ukraine official candidates for eventual NATO membership. Following Russia's invasion of Georgia and its still incomplete withdrawal, there was barely a whimper of threatened sanctions against Russia for violating a basic tenet of the post–Cold War era, namely that European borders should not be changed by force, in part because of German and broader European dependence on Russian natural gas. Russia's energy power gave it political clout. NATO had warned there would be "no business as usual" with Russia until it agreed to pull its troops back to their previous position and to cancel the recognition of the independence of South Ossetia and Abkhazia. Russia fulfilled neither condition, but Western resolve crumbled, with NATO secretary general Jaap de Hoop Scheffer explaining that Russia was such an important factor in geopolitical terms that there was no alternative for NATO than to reengage Russia.[96]

Germany is a key example of the growing symbiosis between Russia and several large countries. Germany needs Russian natural resources, but Russia needs Germany's capital investment and technical expertise. As a result, German companies have invested heavily in Russia. The bright side of this exchange is that the economies of two erstwhile bitter enemies are becoming increasingly intertwined. Since the Holocaust, Germany has been the most sympathetic European country to Israel. But there is as much chance that Germany will slowly drift into Russia's policy orbit as there is that Russia will become more closely integrated with the West through its deepening relationship with Germany.[97]

Which direction this relationship takes will be important for Israel's relationship with both Germany and Russia. For the foreseeable future, Moscow will not just be active in its near abroad but will also become involved in the U.S.-Venezuelan competition. It accepted a Caracas invitation to visit the Caribbean with nuclear vessels in late 2008. Russian companies are also exploring potential oil fields in Venezuela, as well as in Venezuela's allies Ecuador, Bolivia, and Cuba. More recently, Moscow went as far as to publicly discuss the permanent positioning in Venezuela or Cuba of bombers capable of carrying a nuclear payload, a clear "red line" for the United States after the settlement of the Cuban Missile Crisis almost fifty years ago. And, during a state visit to Russia, the Kremlin discussed a nuclear energy deal with Chavez.

Though Russia's actions in the Middle East have a direct impact on Israel, it is important not to exaggerate. Russia is not returning to a Soviet Cold War strategy of diplomatic isolation and playing the Arab card at every turn. Under Putin's direction, Russia has charted an independent course, with a tilt toward the Arab cause, while still maintaining proper relations with Israel.[98] For example, it deviated from Quartet policy by dealing with Hamas, considered a terrorist group by the U.S. and the EU, although in general it has supported Quartet policies. Russia, along with China, blocked UN Security Council condemnation of Syrian President Bashar al-Assad's brutal suppression of the opposition, in part because Syria is a major purchaser of Russian armaments, in part to strike a different posture from the U.S.

Russia has taken a firm stand against a nuclear-armed Iran and has creatively offered to reprocess nuclear fuel from Iranian reactors to ensure Iran does not create weapons-grade uranium. It has supported four sets of UN sanctions against Iran for its failure to abide by UN resolutions on its enrichment of uranium, though only after working with China to dilute their effectiveness. And it has opposed another round of UN sanctions following the 2011 UN International Atomic Energy Agency's bold report that Iran's nuclear program left little doubt it was seeking a nuclear weapon.

But Russia has been careful to keep its relationship with Iran intact by proceeding with construction of a civilian nuclear reactor for Iran at Bushehr. Although this undercuts American efforts to isolate Iran, the deal complies with the terms of the Nuclear Non-Proliferation Treaty, since Russia controls the nuclear fuel and can effectively prevent Iran from upgrading it to weapons-level status.

Russia has many points of leverage that allow it to continue its independent course. It could cease cooperation with the U.S. and the West on nuclear nonproliferation and counterterrorism; it could reverse its agreement to allow nonlethal NATO supplies to pass through its territory en route to Afghanistan; it could frustrate UN efforts in a range of areas, not only with Iran but in vetoing sanctions against states such as Zimbabwe, Sudan, and Syria; and it can manipulate oil and gas supplies in cooperation with OPEC. But it has not yet taken these actions and is unlikely to do so.

Russian Vulnerabilities

Russia also has a demographic crisis that will limit its influence despite its petro-power. Its population will continue to decline, precipitously so in the next fifty years, when its population is likely to be only half of today's. It suffers under a staggeringly low average lifespan—the average lifespan of a Russian male is less than sixty years, the lowest in the industrial world. A fundamental failing of the post-Soviet period has been its inability to diversify its economy and reinvest its energy wealth in new industries. President Medvedev has issued dire warnings about the need for Russian economic reforms, with little to show for it. Revenues from oil and gas exports represent some 60 percent of the Russian budget,[99] and Russia suffers from the same disease that afflicts so many countries rich in natural resources. After the global economic recession led to a collapse of oil prices, Russia's fledgling stock market imploded and market capitalization was halved.

After the chaotic but vigorous democracy of the Boris Yeltsin years, order has come at the expense of free expression. Nationalist forces hold sway. Political opponents have been jailed. Independent journalists have been harassed or killed. Russia is one of the most dangerous countries in the world to be an independent, outspoken, investigative journalist. Russian journalists who uncover and publicize the rampant graft and corruption in Russia are warned, harassed, and then beaten or killed, along with human rights activists and opposition politicians, with only perfunctory police investigations and no arrests. The Kremlin has sharply restricted the activities of international human rights groups such as Amnesty International, Human Rights Watch, and Freedom House, who have criticized Russia's suppression of speech and the press, as well as educational institutions such as the British Council.

The rule of law is often invisible, with a court system under Kremlin control, and jury trials were eliminated in 2009 for "crimes against the state," as demonstrated by the politically motivated convictions of Khodorkovsky and others who seemed politically threatening to the Kremlin. But this breakdown of the rule of law will impede the foreign investment necessary to diversify their heavily energy-dependent nation.[100]

Dealing with the New Russian Bear

How to deal with a Moscow bent on re-creating its former superpower status, even without the ability to do so? It remains critical for both the U.S. and Israel to maintain open communications with the Russian leadership. Prime Minister Netanyahu's personal intervention with Putin and Medvedev bore fruit in forestalling the sale of sophisticated S-300 Russian anti-missile defense systems to Iran in 2010, depriving Iran of a weapon to repel an Israeli military strike against its nuclear facilities. This decision will create more breathing space for Israel if it feels it must act militarily to prevent Iran from acquiring a nuclear weapon.

In late 2011, the Obama administration sharpened its tone in light of the Russian parliamentary elections widely viewed in the West as fraudulent, angering Putin. Israel can ill afford to take such a confrontational stance, but it does little for Israel's international standing when Foreign Minister Lieberman goes to Moscow to openly support the fairness of the elections.

As with so many other issues, Israel and world Jewry must look to the U.S. to set a course that is at once firm on vital issues to American and Western security but likewise sensitive to Russian concerns. There is a U.S. security interest, shared by Israel, in a cooperative Russia, embedded in international organizations and playing by accepted international rules. The U.S. does not have the leverage from the international economic relationship with Russia that Washington is developing with China. U.S. trade with Russia is at an annual level of only $36 billion, around 1 percent of total American trade, while U.S. trade with China amounts to 12 percent of its total. But the U.S. is far from powerless in dealing with Russia.

The Obama administration sought from its earliest days a less contentious relationship with Russia than the Bush administration in part to enlist Russian support in curbing Iran's nuclear appetite. A new arms control agreement was ratified by the U.S. Senate in 2010, which Russia badly wanted.

The U.S. must remain firm on core principles but flexible where possible. Washington should not give Russia an implicit veto over Ukrainian and Georgian membership to NATO, but neither state is ready for membership, making the immediate prospect of their joining moot. Likewise, there was an unnecessarily provocative character to the Bush administration's decision to place an antimissile system aimed at Iran in Poland and the Czech Republic, on Russia's doorstep. The system has not even been tested, and construction had not been planned to even begin until early 2010. The Obama administration's 2009 announcement that it would cancel the deployment in favor of a ship-based system that could be placed closer to Iran was well received in Moscow and is more helpful to Israel.[101]

The world in general and the Jewish world in particular have a great stake in how Russia develops in the next ten years and whether it will become more confrontational or more cooperative with the U.S. and the West. It is crucial to embed Russia into global institutions where it must observe international rules. That is why it is important that Russia's long-delayed accession to the WTO be accelerated, along with most-favored nation treatment, at the end of the process. Lifting the 1974 Jackson-Vanik trade restrictions on Russia is long overdue, and I say this as someone who had a role in the Carter White House in trying to use it as a lever to encourage Jewish emigration. But neither should Russia receive a totally free pass to WTO support, as Congress should insist that the administration press Russia on adherence to the rule of law, and protection of American investors in Russia, and regularly report to Congress on the results.

The U.S. should encourage engagement with Moscow by focusing on areas of mutual interest, such as arms control and Russian participation in international organizations, such as the Organisation for Economic Co-operation and Development (OECD), which Israel recently joined, but on terms that other member countries meet. The U.S. should also use institutions in which Russia is already a member—the Council of Europe, the Asia-Pacific Economic Cooperation forum (APEC), the Association of Southeast Asian Nations (ASEAN), and the NATO-Russia Council—to encourage constructive, nonbelligerent behavior.[102]

The Obama administration has found the right balance in the relationship of the West to Russia. Putin craves Russia's return to the world stage as a key country to deal with the world's problems. To the extent it acts contrary to acceptable international norms, Russia should be challenged directly.

But the biggest lever available to the U.S. and the West is to reduce its dependence on imported oil and gas and to "dramatically lower oil prices, which would force the country to integrate or stagnate."[103] Strobe Talbott, a former deputy secretary of state with whom I served in the Clinton administration, and a foremost Russian expert, has it right. He notes that as oil prices fall, Russia faces a choice: Either become more truculent or become more globally engaged. But as alternative energy sources become more available, its petro-power will sink. Already it lacks the budget resources to support its large standing army and to properly provide it with modern armaments.

Putin's Russia is not immune to the stirrings of the Arab Spring. Even with clear election manipulation, his United Russia party got only 50 percent of the vote for seats in the Russian Duma in the winter 2011 elections, down from two-thirds control. Tens of thousands of Russians took to the streets to demand new free and fair elections. The chairman of United Russia, Boris Gryzlov, the highest-ranking official in the party after Prime Minister Putin, and his close ally, resigned as speaker of the parliament, in a bow to public pressure, and nearly half the parliamentary committees were given to opposition parties, where United Russia members previously controlled almost all of them.[104] While Putin has been re-elected president once again in 2012, his absolute authority over an autocratic government has been diminished.[105] Street demonstrations, never imaginable in the size and tenacity, protested his deal to switch positions with then President Medvedev, with Putin again running for president, after serving for four years as Medevev's prime minister, following his previous eight as president, and Medvedev becoming Putin's prime minister.

Russia will nevertheless remain a force to reckon with in decades ahead. Hopefully, its behavior will increasingly follow global norms, the more deeply Russia can be embedded in international institutions, such as the Middle East Quartet; the more dialogue NATO can have with Russia; the more economic reform it can muster to broaden its economy beyond energy; the more it can be integrated into the global economy through the G20 and the WTO; and the more it recognizes a relationship between its political actions and its economic well-being.

What Winston Churchill said about Russia in 1939 is true today: "I cannot forecast to you the action of Russia. It is a riddle wrapped in a mystery inside an enigma; but perhaps there is a key. That key is Russian national interest."[106] Russia will not become a mirror image of a Western democracy. But over time, its national interests and those of the U.S., the West, and Israel will hopefully increasingly converge.

Other Rising States

While the BRICs are the most impressive challengers to U.S. power, many countries are challenging the U.S. in special areas and "punch above their weight."[107] Tiny Singapore, with a population even smaller than Israel's, is the ninth-largest trading partner of the U.S. South Korea has become a global economic and manufacturing powerhouse. It is Asia's fourth-largest economy and the twelfth biggest in the world. Samsung, one of its flagship global companies, is manufacturing TVs, cell phones, and DVD players for consumers worldwide. Its elevated status was underscored by the new U.S.-South Korea Free Trade Agreement, negotiated by the Bush and Obama administrations and finally ratified by the U.S. Senate in 2011. The new Asian Tiger economies, including Thailand, Cambodia, Indonesia, and, most recently, a reforming Vietnam, have been growing by some 8 percent a year for the past decade.[108] All are attractive places for Western investment, with stable governments, low labor costs, and highly educated and youthful work forces with a strong work ethic.[109] They are increasingly producing the lower-skill products the Chinese have abandoned, as their wage levels have risen.

Turkey

Turkey's economy is booming. As a nation that bridges the European and Muslim worlds geographically, culturally, and politically, Turkey has one of the healthiest economies compared to the twenty-seven nations of the European Union or the Muslim Middle East. Even though its efforts to join the EU remain stymied, the economic and political reforms the Erdogan government has instituted to qualify for membership has made it an increasingly attractive place for foreign investment. However disappointing its foreign policy is toward Iran and Israel, cold-shouldering its longtime partner, now withdrawing its ambassador to Israel in the wake of the UN report on the Gaza flotilla episode with Israel,[110] and tilting toward its former rival Iran, Turkey has joined the global economy and is an economic force to be reckoned with.

Turkey may be the best model for the new governments in the Middle East arising out of the 2011 upheavals, with a free-market economy, a generally free though increasingly restricted press, an independent judiciary, and a moderate brand of Islam, along with its continued NATO membership and an interest in joining the European Union. Turkey clearly wants to play a bigger role on the world stage, not always to America's liking or Israel's. It sees itself as a bridge between the West and the Muslim world. Turkey was unhelpful in the effort by the U.S. to impose stricter sanctions on Iran's nuclear program, and it has warmed up relations with Iran as it has cooled them down with Israel. Yet, having accepted thousands of Syrian refugees who have fled from President Assad's brutal crackdown, Turkey has taken a firm line against continued violence and has sharply criticized Assad.

Turkey can only drift so far from the U.S. as a NATO ally. It agreed to permit a U.S. anti-missile system on its soil, aimed clearly at Iran.

Oil states have also seen a change in fortunes, which are bound to seesaw with oil prices volatile in an uncertain world economy. But the boom that ended in 2008 and began again in 2011 with the Arab Spring created a staggering transfer of wealth from the West to oil-producing countries in the Persian Gulf and in Latin America. This has provided funds not just for a regional arms race but also for the development of indigenous financial and economic engines, with international banks, law firms, consultancies, and other service providers, along with a handful of major American universities and museums, establishing major footholds in the Gulf region. Sovereign wealth funds have been widely investing in major American and European financial institutions and helped bail out Britain's Barclays Bank, just as a Saudi sheik injected capital into Citicorp.

The Reality of the New Economic and Political Order

The United States and its European allies, along with Japan, have come to realize a new global economic order is forming, that the reshaping will accelerate in the coming decades, and that the institutions created to guide the global economy since the end of World War II must be fundamentally reordered to take into account the weight of the emerging powers. In 1975, a group of six industrial democracies, France, Germany, Italy, Japan, the United Kingdom, and the United States, came together. Canada was added the next year, and the G7 finance ministers met regularly to guide the global economy. After the fall of Communism, the G8 heads of state met with Russia. This was hardly presumptuous because in the 1970s, the G7 countries controlled almost two-thirds of global GDP. Even now, the G7 nations make up 50 percent of nominal global GDP (39 percent when viewed from a purchasing power perspective). As recently as the year 2000, the G7's collective GDP was twice as large as the world's largest emerging markets, sometimes called the E7 (China, India, Brazil, Mexico, Russia, Indonesia, and Turkey). But by 2010, the gap had shrunk to 35 percent, and in 2011 PricewaterhouseCoopers estimated that by 2019 the combined GDP of the E7 will match the G7, and by 2032, the emerging economies will overtake the developed democracies in total GDP.[111]

These trends led President George W. Bush in the last year of his administration to take the lead in creating the G20, a group of twenty countries, to supplant the G7, for the first time giving the major emerging nations a role in the management of the global economy. In addition, the voting power determined by the quotas for contributions to the International Monetary Fund and the World Bank has been shifted from European countries toward China, India, and other rising powers.

If the United States is struggling to maintain global supremacy in the midst of a profound economic downturn, in the face of surging growth from the BRIC countries and other emerging powers, America's closest allies, Japan and the 27 nations of the European Union, particularly the 17 Western European nations who compose the Eurozone, are slipping badly.

Japan

Japan's rise from the ashes of destruction and defeat following World War II, being the only nation to experience a nuclear weapons attack, was nothing short of astonishing. By the 1970s, Japan had become the second-largest economy in the world, next to the U.S., with world-class companies such as Toyota, Honda, Hitachi, and Sony establishing their excellence around the globe in automobiles, electronics, and industrial products. There was a fear in the 1970s and 1980s that "Japan, Inc.," describing the close relationship between Japan's government and huge corporations, would literally buy up America's crown jewels—CBS and Rockefeller Center, for example.

While Japan's foreign policy has been largely passive and its military power is carefully muted, the U.S. has few more reliable allies and buffers to China, and Israel has few closer friends than Japan. In 1952, Japan recognized Israel, and there have been periodic high-level visits, in contrast, for example, to India, including Prime Minister Junichiro Koizumi in 2001, and a succession of foreign minister–level visits on both sides from 2007 to 2010. In 2008, Ehud Olmert became the first Israeli prime minister to visit Japan. There are also lively scientific exchanges, and in 1988 the prestigious Japan Prize was awarded to former Israeli president Ephraim Katzir. Israel exports over $500 million of machinery, electronics, and medical equipment to Japan, which in turn exports $1.1 billion of automobiles, electrical equipment, machinery, and chemical products to Israel.[112]

This is what makes Japan's slow, inexorable economic decline so frustrating. China has now overtaken Japan as the world's second-largest economy. In the late 1980s, a combination of high land values, exceptionally low interest rates, massive borrowing, and speculation by Japanese corporations and banks created an asset bubble that burst. It was joked that the value of land under the Royal Palace was worth more than the state of California. The bursting of this asset bubble caused a stock market crash, a debt and banking crisis as loans turned sour, and the need for massive government bailouts of what Michael Schuman of *Time* magazine called "zombie firms," too big to fail, but too debt ridden to survive—not unlike the U.S. response to the bursting of the housing bubble and its consequences in 2008.[113]

What followed has been widely called Japan's "lost decade" during the 1990s, with deflation and stagnant growth. While there has been some improvement, growth continued to stagnate from 2001 to 2010, and Japan's debt levels are approaching 200 percent of its GDP, more than even Greece's and more than twice the levels of the U.S., the UK, and Germany (although most is owed to its own citizens, and only around 10 percent is held by foreign investors).[114] Japan's political leadership is uninspiring and is heavily dominated by a career bureaucracy with little creativity.

Japan's problems are deeply aggravated by a demographic problem of enormous proportions. Japan has one of the lowest birthrates in the world—only an average of 1.3 children per mother compared to an average of 2.1 needed simply to keep even—and an aging society. So Japan, with a population today of over 125 million people, is forecast to have between only 90 to 100 million by midcentury.[115] By 2050, its percentage of people over sixty-five years of age will rise by nearly 40 percent, and 70 percent of its government spending will be consumed by debt payments and social security spending.[116] This is a prescription for national disaster, a drop in growth and tax revenues to sustain an aging population, and a certain diminution of global influence,[117] all to the detriment of the U.S. and Israel, as well as to the Japanese people.

Still, Japan's slide will be gradual. Its unemployment rate is half that of the U.S. and Europe, it has formidable assets, and it remains a great country. Israel would be well advised to deepen its relationship with Japan at all levels.

Europe

Nothing better exemplifies the shift of power from West to East and South than the current sovereign debt crisis in the seventeen countries of the eurozone, which use the euro as their single currency and are the core economies of the twenty-seven-nation European Union (EU). Already buffeted by the Great Recession, like the U.S., the financial trauma of Greece, only 2 percent of the GDP of the EU and a member of the eurozone, beginning in late 2009, has nearly brought the eurozone to its knees and is one of the greatest threats to the fragile economic recovery in the U.S. Because other countries in the eurozone, such as Italy, the EU's third-largest economy, Ireland, Spain, and Portugal had built up large debts, much of it held by European banks, the sovereign debt crisis became a European banking crisis, as well.

The euro was to be the crowning achievement of the single market, which even without the common currency had made it virtually as easy to ship goods between the twenty-seven members of the EU as between the fifty states of the United States. The euro was born on January 1, 1999, after years of planning and formally launched in the marketplace on January 1, 2002. It met with initial success, becoming one of the major reserve currencies of the world and being stronger in the global financial marketplace than the dollar.

But the euro had fundamental flaws, which the Great Recession and the excessive buildup of debt by key members brought to light, with disastrous impact. The European Central Bank (ECB), which was charged with administering the euro, had a limited charter that entitled it only to focus on price stability, not to serve as a genuine central bank, like the U.S. Federal Reserve, serving as a "lender of last resort" to its member nations. Therefore, when markets drove prices sky high for sovereign debt borrowing by some of the weaker member states, the ECB did not stand behind that debt to ensure investors against default or taking a "haircut," like the investors in Greek debt were forced to assume. Instead a number of other cumbersome devices, such as the European Financial Stability Facility and an IMF emergency fund, were used to try to assure international investors.

A second flaw in the euro was that its seventeen members maintained control over their own budgets and fiscal policies. While they were technically bound to follow the so-called Maastricht criteria to ensure their annual deficits did not exceed 3 percent of their GDP and that their accumulated debt did not exceed 60 percent of their GDP, these were honored in the breach, with no effective enforcement mechanism. Third, countries such as Greece were permitted into the eurozone without effective policing by central EU institutions to ensure their budget numbers were accurate—and they were not. And closely related, countries with highly different stages of development and historical practices were placed under one monetary umbrella, with a common fiscal policy.

Led by Germany's chancellor Angela Merkel, a December 2011 new fiscal pact was agreed to by the seventeen eurozone countries, which, if approved by each parliament, will provide penalties if member states violate the ironclad rules laid down by Germany, by far the EU's strongest economy. It is uncertain if this new treaty will ever be enacted and, if so, whether it will succeed in removing the basic flaws.

It is too late to avoid an almost certain recession in 2012 in the EU. The austerity measures to reduce the deficits and debts will ensure short-term pain and slower growth.

The EU countries had an unemployment rate from 2001 to 2005 of 8.5 percent, considerably higher than the U.S., but from 2005 to the first quarter of 2008, when the Great Recession hit, unemployment had dropped to 6.7 percent. By October 2011, the U.S. had only a slightly lower unemployment rate (9.0 percent) than the EU twenty-seven (9.8 percent). But this masks an EU growth rate that has been considerably lower than America's since the year 2000.[118]

And the EU growth trajectory, because of the euro crisis and less dynamic, more rigid economies than that in the U.S., has a broader problem: demographics. While not as severe as Japan's, European nations are aging, with low birthrates (an average of 1.5 children per family), particularly in Central and Eastern European nations, and a costly social welfare structure they cannot afford to support with their low economic growth rates and the high costs of supporting an aging population. A century ago, Europe (including Russia and Turkey) had

25 percent of the world's population. Now only 12 percent of the world's population lives on the European Continent, and it is projected that by 2050, only about 7 percent of the global population will be European.[119]

Ironically, the effort to save the euro, which was designed to unite the EU, has caused great internal tensions and resentment toward Germany's dominating hand. This is a sad development because the European Union is a great and largely successful experiment in shared sovereignty, and increasingly common foreign policy binding together nations that had been at war with each other for centuries in commerce and trade.

Both the U.S. and Israel have a great deal at stake in Europe's future. The European nations remain America's major allies in NATO and the EU. It is more complicated for Israel. The EU nations have been highly critical of Israel's military actions in Lebanon and Gaza, its blockade of Gaza, and its settlement policy, which the EU believes violates international law, and are more sympathetic to the Palestinian cause than the U.S. The EU position on the Middle East peace process is a two-state solution in which Israel will go back to its pre-1967 borders, with land swaps, and Jerusalem will be divided as the capital of Israel and a Palestinian state. The European Court of Justice agreed in 2010 with a petition from Germany that Israeli goods produced in the occupied Palestinian territories should be boycotted.

And yet, Europe, not the U.S., is Israel's major trading partner, with over 20 billion euros of trade in 2009. The EU delegation to Israel states that the EU and Israel "share a long common history marked by growing interdependence and cooperation. Both share the same values of democracy, respect for freedom and the rule of law and are committed to an open international economic system based upon market principles."[120] This is not merely rhetoric. Israel is the first non-European country to be part of the EU's program for research and development due to Israel's high level of scientific and research capability, and it has special agreements with Israel on scientific and technical cooperation, agricultural trade, good laboratory practices, and telecommunications operations. Starting in 2004, Israel has been a partner in the EU's Galileo program for developing a global satellite system. Israel is considered a "preferred partner" of the EU for trade, and the formal EU-Israel Association Agreement of 2000 has established the legal basis for their relationship and participation in the Euro-Mediterranean agreement.[121]

With generally friendly leaders in France, Germany, Italy, and the UK, the EU has taken a strong position supporting tough sanctions against Iran for its nuclear program. If Europe goes into an economic swoon from its euro crisis, it will be to the detriment of Israel and the U.S.

The shift in power is not only economic but diplomatic as well. America's standing in the world took a beating during the Bush administration, largely due to a series of unilateral actions, ranging from the invasion of Iraq to rejecting the threat of climate change. Despite this, some of the criticism of the Bush administration's unilateralism is unfair. It played a crucial role in the 2003 Middle East Road Map, endorsed by the Israelis, the Palestinians, and much of the Arab world. And in his second term, President Bush launched a number of laudable international initiatives in AIDS prevention, poverty reduction, and foreign assistance reforms. But these never erased the damage from Iraq among America's friends abroad.

When Israel's principal ally is held in such low esteem, there are serious implications, the most critical regarding Iran. Europe, China, and Russia had been less willing to pressure Iran on its nuclear programs during the Bush years, partly because they have had little desire to be seen working alongside the United States, although they eventually went along with three sets of diluted sanctions. President Obama has helped turn around any of the negative perceptions of the U.S.; has established more positive relations with Russia, including a new arms control treaty; has begun to repair relations with moderate Muslim countries; and has won support by the UN Security Council and the European Union for stiff penalties against Iran.

The Great Recession of 2008–2009 proved a watershed event exposing American weaknesses: a crumbling infrastructure and an educational system that, within a few decades, has declined from first to twelfth in the percentage of college graduates and that has produced math and reading scores for young American students near the bottom rung of industrialized countries.[122] Incomes have stagnated for the vast majority of Americans for almost two decades, and median family incomes were 5 percent lower in 2009 than a decade before. There has been a significant rise in the number of Americans in poverty to 44 million people, including one in five children, and a growing gap in income between the superwealthy and the rest of the population. The U.S. ranks thirty-first among the OECD's thirty-four industrialized countries in income inequality. This is a source of public anger as America's banks necessarily had to be bailed out by taxpayers' money to avoid a global financial crisis, while average Americans saw their home values and jobs go up in smoke, and it is a major factor in the rise of the conservative Tea Party movement in the 2010 midterm elections, and on the other side of the political spectrum, the Occupy Wall Street movement.

The debilitating 2011 battle over raising the debt limit, and the inability of the government to reverse the Great Recession into a great recovery, has led to a profound decline in the trust of the American people in their government's capacity to meet major challenges on a scale not seen since the Great Depression of the 1930s.[123]

A staggering 25 million Americans cannot find full-time employment, while the burst in the housing bubble cut home values by some 30 percent; one in seven Americans has a mortgage worth more than the home. For minorities the picture is even bleaker, as the wealth of Hispanic Americans has declined by 60 percent and that of African Americans and Asian Americans by 50 percent since the Great Recession began in late 2008. The investment banking industry, which financed America's industrial growth to world leadership and survived the Civil War and two world wars, collapsed overnight. The U.S. deficit ballooned to over 12 percent of GDP, and federal debt doubled, with three straight years of $1 trillion budget deficits through 2012.

America's ability to continue to be a global leader, so critical to Israel and world Jewry, has been impacted by the economic crisis. Soaring health care costs and government commitments to retirement support of post–World War II baby boomers, together with the economic costs of dealing with the recession of 2008–2009, will force a rise in taxes or severe cuts in government services, including foreign assistance, or both.

Former comptroller general of the United States David Walker believes that the U.S. has "no more than five years" to "stave off financial ruin."[124] The fifty states face funding gaps of between $1 trillion and $3 trillion to cover soaring pension, health care, and life insurance benefits for their public employees. This has created a vicious cycle in which the U.S. has become ever more reliant on foreign governments to fund U.S. government operations. U.S. government debt, much of it now held by China and other foreign investors, will equal 77 percent of total U.S. output by 2020, up from 49 percent today. This would be the highest since just after World War II, but then most of the U.S. government debt was held by American, not foreign, institutions.

The U.S. is in a new economic and political era, in which China has become a principal banker. The old joke that when you owe the bank $1,000 the problem is yours, but when you owe them $1 million the problem is the bank's may be true in the case of the $1 trillion-plus in U.S. public debt held by China. This has the political impact of shifting the terms of debate. Great global power and great debt cannot coexist for long, leading some, such as Larry Summers, the former chief economic adviser to President Obama and my boss as treasury secretary to President Clinton, to ask, "How long can the world's biggest borrower remain the world's biggest power?"[125]

The trends are clear: American power has reached an inflection point. For its entire history, the U.S. has been a rising power, not initially the most powerful of states, but always with an upward trajectory compared to other nations. This is no longer the case.

America's lead has been cut, its margin for maneuver and its influence have been shaved by the emerging powers. For the foreseeable future, America will remain the most important power, a creative and resilient country to provide stability to an unstable world. But it is no longer the sufficient power. If seventy years ago *Time* magazine's Henry Luce could describe his era as "the American century," few would give this title to the twenty-first century. The United States is increasingly dependent on other new indispensable powers, such as China, Brazil, and India, to make progress on issues from global warming and Iranian nuclear ambitions to global economic growth. The recent upheavals in the Middle East have also demonstrated the limits of American power.

America's economic success is essential to support a world-class military, to restore America's competitiveness, and to rebuild the shattered confidence of the American people about their future. But it is also important to blunt the rise of what Ian Bremmer, the president of the Eurasia Group, calls "state capitalism,"[126] the Chinese system in which the state functions as the leading economic actor, owning and controlling large parts of the economy, with a large group of private companies that are "government-favored" with privileged status in domestic economies and support for exports. Outside China, such companies included Israel's Tnuva, which produces meat and dairy products. But Tnuva was found to be a monopoly by the Israel Antitrust Authority and subject to greater government regulation of its pricing to protect the public, something that would be unimaginable for China's state-controlled companies.

One of the major results of the Great Recession stretches far past the shores of the United States: the challenge to the so-called Washington Consensus of democratic governance, considerable self-regulation, spending restraint, and free trade. The ideology was dispersed via the World Bank and the IMF, which made funds available on the condition that governments adopt these policies, which for a time became the norm for economic stewardship in other countries and helped lift more than 400 million people from poverty

Israel joined the consensus as well and maintained it. In the early 1980s its economy was flagging, weighed down by heavy state intervention, high inflation, foreign exchange controls, decades of spending for defense, and the initial costs of absorbing new immigrants. In 1984 Secretary of State George Shultz created the American-Israeli Joint Economic Development Group, which pressed Israel to adopt key aspects of the Washington Consensus including budget cuts, tighter control of the money supply, and devaluation of the shekel.

Israel has been blessed with a succession of enlightened central bank governors, now Stanley Fischer, who helped Israel steer clear of the worst of the global financial crisis and Great Recession. But it was Jacob Frenkel, as governor from 1991 to 2000, who successfully tackled Israel's endemic inflation, liberalized Israel's financial markets, removed foreign currency controls, and integrated Israel's economy into the global financial system.

During the Clinton administration, I chaired the U.S. side of this joint group, once bringing in a then little-known economist from Princeton, Ben Bernanke (now chairman of the Federal Reserve), an American Jew with an interest in the Israeli economy; he was willing to spare several days to travel to Israel. Since then, successive Israeli governments have maintained the outlines of this policy with Prime Minister Netanyahu, during his terms as both finance and prime minister, an especially willing champion.

Today, the Washington Consensus lies in tatters, largely because the U.S. government failed to practice the principles it preached to countries abroad. It began to unravel with the Asian financial crisis in 1997–1998, with great resentment at the tough conditions imposed by the U.S.-led rescue effort, managed through the IMF. Another blow occurred after the Enron scandal when the company collapsed like a house of cards because of crooked accounting; the passage of the Sarbanes-Oxley legislation marked the beginning of the end of laissez-faire in financial markets. It was finally done in by the Great Recession, the result of too much borrowing by consumers; too little regulation of Wall Street's mortgage-backed securities, which plummeted in value as a historic housing bubble burst; and soaring government debt from three large Bush administration tax cuts, two unfunded wars, and an expensive drug benefit for senior citizens as well as the costs of dealing with the Great Recession.

Contrary to its own Washington Consensus orthodoxy, to avoid a great depression, the U.S. government became the nation's single largest investor, taking key stakes in everything from General Motors and Chrysler in auto manufacturing to financial service firms on the brink of meltdown and housing finance guarantors Fannie Mae and Freddie Mac. From here on, Washington's lectures to other countries about sound economic policy will be met with extreme skepticism until the U.S. gets its economic house in order.

But the embattled Washington Consensus must not be replaced by a new Beijing Consensus of an authoritarian political structure and state-managed and -subsidized capitalism. To avoid this, the U.S. must show it is willing to live by tenets of the consensus it preached to other nations, including sound fiscal policy to tackle mammoth deficits and debt; and to continue championing free markets while adding a corrective of stronger financial regulation, tackling income inequalities, and investing in the things that made America great— superior education, science and technology, and modern infrastructure.

Even before the global recession, there were rising complaints that globalization, as championed by the U.S., was not delivering benefits to all sectors of society. Asian countries were starting to lecture the West in general, and the U.S. in particular, about what the *Financial Times* called "its casino capitalism and its credit-fueled, asset bubble growth model."[127] China and Japan, the biggest foreign holders of U.S. debt, have in effect bankrolled America's spending binge. Eisuke Sakakibara, a former Japanese financial official, proclaimed that Asian countries "want the satisfaction of being able to tell the West where it went wrong . . . the American jig is over."[128]

For Asia, the Great Recession has reinforced the correctness of its model of investing in education and infrastructure, moderate borrowing, and prudent currency management, the very policies the Clinton administration urged on Asia in the wake of its financial crisis in 1997–1998. But at the same time, the crisis has shown Asia that it cannot grow independently. Its future as an export-oriented region continues to tie in directly to the health of the countries that purchase their products in Europe and especially the United States.

There are broader grounds for believing that the American capitalism model will again become a beacon for the world, including the creative capacity of the U.S. to reinvent itself under crisis, particularly if the polarized U.S. government can find the political will to meet the challenges of the twenty-first century. Already, there are flickers of hope that a new, twenty-first-century American economic model is arising, which could have a transformative impact. It is being led by large multinational American companies, not the U.S. government. Neville Isdell, former chairman and CEO of the Coca-Cola Company, has called it "connected capitalism." Michael Porter, a professor at the Harvard Business School, and Mark Kramer at Harvard's Kennedy School described it as "shared value" in a seminal article in _Harvard Business Review._[129]

The essence is that at a time when Porter and Kramer correctly see that the "capitalist system is under siege," American corporations should move beyond philanthropy and "corporate social responsibility" to create a new business model that combines making a profit with helping solve major challenges facing the world, "creating economic value in a way that also creates value for society by addressing its needs and challenges," and adopting practices that "enhance the competitiveness of a company while simultaneously advancing the economic and social conditions in the communities in which it operates," often by partnering with NGOs and government. This is not a pipe dream. Walmart, the world's largest retailer, has embedded social values such as reducing greenhouse gas emissions into their business model, building white-roofed buildings and insisting that their chain of suppliers adopt climate-friendly policies as a condition of doing business.

Under the leadership of Muhtar Kent, chairman and CEO of Coca-Cola, this new brand of capitalism is being implemented around the world in a variety of projects. Coca-Cola announced in 2010 a ten-year global initiative to empower women in their extended systems to break down barriers to growing their businesses. In Uganda and Kenya the company created Project Nurture in partnership with the Bill & Melinda Gates Foundation and TechnoServe; the idea is to enable more than 50,000 small fruit farmers to double their incomes by 2012 by providing mango and passion fruit for locally produced juices in the Coca-Cola portfolio, while receiving training to improve quality and gain access to credit and business skills. A similar initiative, Project Hope, was begun in Haiti after the devastating earthquakes and makes a new mango juice drink that is helping 25,000 Haitian farmers. More than 3,000 micro distribution centers have been created in Africa, employing more than 13,500 people, to deliver Coca-Cola products to areas in East and West Africa that are inaccessible through the company's trucks.[130]

Major companies from GE and Google to IBM, Nestle, and Unilever have joined Walmart and Coca-Cola with their own innovative programs. While this concept is still in its infancy, it underscores the recognition by major Western corporations that consumers are demanding higher standards and that by doing good for society, they can do well for their shareholders, enhancing the value of their brands.

The U.S. Edge: Innovation, Democracy, and Military Might

The relationship between the BRIC nations and other emerging powers and the U.S. in the new world order, in the wake of the Great Recession, will speak volumes about the course a globalized world will take, either toward more stability or more confrontation. When she served as U.S. secretary of state, Madeleine Albright described America as the "indispensable" nation. China is fast approaching a similar stature. If there are no major world issues that can be solved without the leadership of the United States, there are few that do not require Chinese cooperation.

With all its tensions, the bilateral relationship between China and the U.S. is vastly different from the hostile U.S.-Soviet standoff of the Cold War years. China is a political, economic, and military rival and often plays by its own rules on trade, government procurement, natural resource contracts, intellectual property protection, the Internet, corporate hacking to acquire technologies, and currency policy.

But Beijing, unlike Moscow in the years of Soviet confrontation, is neither friend nor foe. China is at one and the same time the biggest foreign creditor and yet deeply dependent on American prosperity for its own well-being; a military competitor in Asia and yet the location for tens of billions of investment dollars in manufacturing plants and research facilities for virtually every major American corporation; a rival and yet a necessary partner in dealing with nuclear threats in Iran and North Korea; possessing a competing political and economic governance model for the twenty-first century, yet a country in which millions of its students annually learn English, and a growing number of American students learn Chinese and study there; a country with a starkly different cultural history, but one that invited Reynold Levy, the president of Lincoln Center, and a consulting team of colleagues to advise the city of Tianjin on the creation of a new performing arts center and to train Chinese administrators.

The U.S. and China have an increasingly intertwined set of interests, uncomfortably bound together like conjoined twins. The U.S. is a major destination for Chinese exports, American companies have large investments there, and at the same time, the U.S. relies on China to purchase its debt, thus serving as its international banker. When faced with a choice between Iran and the U.S. over UN sanctions, China grudgingly followed the U.S. lead, though watering down its impact. As China and the U.S. deepen and broaden their relationship, leading as I believe it will to a more responsible China with a greater stake in the world's prosperity and security, it will benefit the entire world order, including Israel and the Jewish world.

The leaders of China and the U.S. recognize this. During the Bush administration, an economic dialogue was initiated, led by then secretary of the treasury Henry Paulson, which President Obama broadened into a strategic and economic dialogue with the secretaries of state and treasury. In 2011, they reached what officials called a "milestone" agreement for comprehensive economic cooperation, regular meetings of top military leaders, an opening of China's financial sector to more foreign and American services, and development of common rules on export credits, which China often uses unfairly.[131]

This agreement, even if fully implemented, hardly ends all tensions. China is openly threatening the supremacy of the dollar, which allows the U.S. to borrow at lower rates, run large budget deficits, and print money during times of economic crisis. Instead, China is moving to place its reserves in a basket of currencies, including the euro. In an early signal of China's growing impatience with its huge dollar reserves, its leaders called for the dollar to be replaced by a new international currency reserve controlled by the IMF.[132] While there were political motives behind this, and the idea of one global currency is unrealistic given the divergence of fiscal policies, the proposals are a warning sign.

During U.S. Treasury Secretary Geithner's 2010 visit to China, he was forced into an unprecedented public declaration that the U.S. would make good on its debts,[133] just as Vice President Biden's summer 2011 trip to Beijing was intended to convince China the U.S. remained a good credit risk for its reserves, following the downgrade of America's AAA debt rating, in the wake of the debt crisis fiasco of 2011.

China is slowly but surely building up its currency as an alternative to the dollar-based global economy.[134] This could mean that Asian countries could be borrowing in yuan just as Europeans borrow in their own regional currency.[135] The difference between the euro and the yuan is that the latter would be backed not only by China's wealth but also by its government—a two-edged sword offering China advantages as a lender. In 2009, for the first time, Beijing authorized international companies to issue securities in yuan. Through the sale of yuan-denominated bonds to foreign investors, the market will establish a benchmark on yields and raise China's global financial profile. Meanwhile Beijing is in the process of establishing conditions for Chinese exporters to settle contracts in yuan rather than U.S. dollars, and other Asian countries are also moving in that direction.[136]

If the eighteenth and nineteenth centuries were dominated by the British pound and its vast empire, and the twentieth century by the U.S. and the American dollar, will the twenty-first century become the Asian century, dominated by the Chinese yuan? This is unlikely for the next several decades, since it will take more time to liberalize the tightly controlled Chinese currency so it can serve as a global benchmark.[137] China would have to ease restrictions on financial flows in and out of the country; make its currency fully convertible; deepen its financial structure to allow full foreign participation; and make its bond markets more liquid. Each of these steps faces internal political constraints, as China is only inching toward the openness that the world requires. But there can be little doubt that by midcentury, the yuan will be one of the world's reserve currencies along with the American dollar and the European euro.

The twenty-first century will see a battle between competing Chinese and Western models of governance. The collapse of the Soviet Union has not ushered in the worldwide rush to democracy for which many had hoped. While there has been a growth of democratic countries since the end of the Cold War, the Freedom House 2010 democracy report, "Freedom in the World 2010: Global Erosion of Freedom," found that democracy, human rights, and liberty have actually retreated around the world for the fourth consecutive year, the longest period of decline since the organization began issuing its annual reports almost four decades ago. Hopefully, the Arab Spring of 2011 will create new momentum for democracy. But for many autocratic leaders intent on keeping power, China may seem to demonstrate the advantages of maintaining tight political control without sacrificing economic growth.

Many of Africa's poorest countries see China as the partnership model, with aid provided on a "no questions asked" basis, leaving their recipients unconcerned about improving political freedom and human rights.[138] I strongly believe that democratic governance is the best path to cope with twenty-first-century global forces, which require individual creativity, protection of intellectual property, the freedom to explore and exchange new ideas, and the ability of citizens to hold their governments accountable for transparent, noncorrupt decisions. These are all deficiencies of the Chinese model and Western strengths. It is not coincidental that the major discoveries of our time are almost all from individuals in Western nations, most from the U.S., and implemented by Western corporations—the automobile, airplane, telegraph, telephone, phonograph, computer, software operating systems, semiconductor chips, the Internet, social media, pasteurized products, vaccines, and medical breakthroughs to name only a few.

In fact, Israel stands as an example in the post–Great Recession world of how a free-market economy can flourish, relying on entrepreneurial activity, an educated public, and high-tech research—and sound regulation by incorruptible officials at the nation's central bank who, by law, have the primary responsibility for managing the economy. And when the relationship between economic efficiency and social justice is tipped out of balance, the 2011 public outcry has provided a safety valve and possible corrective, which do not exist in autocratic systems.

Transparency International found that democracy is the least corrupt form of government, with all but two of the thirty least corrupt, most honest countries being democracies. Autocratic governments breed endemic corruption, which exists from China to the Arab Middle East, and corruption is a key barrier to sustainable, broadly shared prosperity. There is no evidence that an autocracy's growth is faster than a democracy's; indeed, on average, democracies grow faster and are more innovative. A "climate of freedom" is the best environment for the twenty-first-century knowledge-based economy.

Every country in the top twenty-five of the Global Innovation Index, including Israel, is a democracy, with the exceptions of the more restrictive Singapore and Hong Kong touting their "Asian values" of hierarchy and stability. Can China really become a creator rather than imitator of innovation and creativity when it blocks search engines such as Google and restricts social media that connect their population to the world of ideas outside their boundaries? The answer is no. Nor are autocracies more stable than democracies. The accountability of democracies produces more public support.

But to show a doubting world the value of democracy, the great democracies of North America and Europe must show they can create jobs and growth and govern successfully.[139]

The Military Exception and "Hard Power"

The BRIC countries are using their new wealth to develop military capabilities commensurate with their economic standing and have embarked on ambitious military programs, China in particular.

China has undertaken a rapid and massive military modernization program—far beyond its need for self-defense or dealing with Taiwan. China is wielding its new power to try to alter geopolitical realities in its own neighborhood and now has the world's second-largest military budget after the United States. While China remains a generation behind the U.S. in military technology, it is fast closing the gap. According to the U.S. commander in the Pacific, Admiral Robert Willard, China has developed an operational capability to launch a new land-based, antiship ballistic missile, which can both intimidate its Asian neighbors and target U.S. aircraft carriers in the region. The U.S. Navy operates in what China calls its "near seas" and has naval bases there.[140] Because China has not joined the U.S. and Russia in signing the Intermediate-Range Nuclear Forces Treaty (INF), it can increase its ballistic missiles without limitation. Then-secretary of defense Robert Gates speculated that if China has a highly accurate ballistic missile that "can take out a carrier at hundreds of miles of range and therefore in Asia puts us back behind the second island chain, how then do you use carriers differently in the future?"[141]

Military experts have consistently underestimated China's growing military capability. During Secretary Gates's visit, the Chinese military conspicuously publicized a new long-range radar-evading stealth bomber, which will be operational in 2018, far earlier and more sophisticated than expected. Its 160 nuclear warheads, still a fraction of the number the U.S. possesses, have now been placed in better-protected mobile launchers and submarines.[142] While there remains a gap with the U.S., many experts believe China by 2020 will have equivalent military firepower to the U.S. in their Asia region, although not worldwide.

While its growing military capability is clear, China's defense budget is opaque, and its intentions are unknown,[143] as is the chain of civilian command. Add to this China's professed military goal that cyberwarfare is "integral to advancing information superiority and an effective means for countering a strategic foe," and it is understandable why a senior Pentagon official, in commenting on a 2011 report on China's military, called China's arms buildup "potentially destabilizing."[144]

China is not alone. Each of the major emerging powers is devoting a growing share of spending to defense—10 percent annual increases in Brazil and a doubling of spending by Russia and India in the latter part of the last decade. These resources go into local production, often with impressive results. Brazil's aerospace industry, led by Embraer, provides transport aircraft to its air force. In India, cooperation agreements with foreign suppliers have led to hybrid aircraft, such as the Russo-Indian S-30 fighter produced by India's Hindustan Aeronautics. But India wants to increase local production of its military equipment from 30 to 70 percent of its needs. Russia, once second only to the U.S., has been working to modernize an industry that fell apart after the fall of the Soviet Union.

Military doctrine in all four BRIC countries has also undergone a radical shift. The Chinese have been most explicit, proclaiming that the People's Liberation Army had reached a "historic turning point" by playing a role in the international security order. For the first time, its ships joined in antipiracy patrols on its trade routes off the Horn of Africa. The Indian defense establishment has made it an explicit goal to become a continental force, rather than one operating only on its own subcontinent, and has followed up by opening its first foreign air base, in Tajikistan, in Central Asia. Brazil has been less explicit about its military force projection goals but is positioning itself to project military power throughout Latin America, by declaring a goal of acquiring in-flight refueling aircraft and offshore naval vessels with a range of 6,000 nautical miles.

While huge U.S. budget deficits impose long-term constraints on the projection of American military power, the American military has shown itself to be the best-trained, best-equipped, hardest-fighting, and most technologically competent force in the world, as demonstrated by its military prowess in the rough terrain of Iraq and Afghanistan as well as its special forces exploits in severely disrupting al-Qaeda's central network, and it will remain so for the foreseeable future. Present investments in defense capability remain staggering. U.S. annual defense spending is more than twice that of all other NATO members combined, more than the next fifteen largest military budgets put together, and from five to seven times China's estimated defense expenditures. (China's published military budget for 2011 is $91.5 billion, but the Pentagon estimates it far higher, at over $150 billion. By comparison, the base U.S. defense budget is $553 billion, with another $118 billion for the wars in Iraq and Afghanistan, for a total of $671 billion.)

The U.S. remains the only nation with effective, truly global force projection by air, land, and sea, most recently demonstrated by the audacious attack on Osama bin Laden's compound with unparalleled electronic and intelligence support. No country can come close to matching this triad of worldwide capabilities. Over 350,000 American military personnel are deployed in more than 150 countries, far exceeding any other nation. It is this global reach, along with substantial arms sales and training for the militaries of scores of nations, that provides important leverage of great value to Israel. For example, in postrevolutionary Egypt, the close relationship the U.S. has with the Egyptian military provides important leverage to maintain a modicum of bilateral Egyptian-Israeli relationships, and the huge arms sales to Saudi Arabia and the Gulf states helps them serve as a counterweight to Iran, to Israel's benefit.

While its military expenditures have rapidly increased and it is the strongest regional military force among Asian countries, China does not have a global capacity to project its military power. It is the only one of the five permanent members of the UN Security Council without an operational aircraft carrier. China only began sea trials in the summer of 2011, when Taiwan publicly displayed a new advanced missile it described as an "aircraft carrier killer."[145] Military experts believe China is years away from having a full carrier group with the capacity to launch and land fighter jets. By contrast, the U.S. Navy has eleven carrier strike groups, consisting of aircraft carriers, guided missile carriers, antiaircraft war ships, and antisubmarine destroyers. No other state has even one such group.

The disparity between the BRIC's growing economic competitiveness and their military noncompetitiveness when matched against the U.S. is a result of several factors. They are building from a low starting point, while the U.S. has steadily increased defense spending since the 1960s.

Russia's military is in a very poor state. Its defense minister made the astonishing admission in 2009 that only 10 percent of all weapons and equipment were up to modern standards. Russia's larger goal is to reshape its mass-mobilization army into small and more specialized forces suited to local or regional conflicts to support its more restricted foreign policy objectives.

Despite sometimes bellicose statements, particularly from China, all BRIC countries remain largely focused on regional security. A large part of Brazil's spending reflects its desire to keep up with Venezuela as well as improve its domestic security, especially in the Amazon region. India's defense acquisitions, including sophisticated radar from Israel Aircraft Industries, have been deployed to monitor its porous borders with Bangladesh, China, and Pakistan and to protect Kashmir against Pakistani threats.

Much military hardware in the BRIC nations is not equal to the U.S., with its advanced technology, and some BRICs are keen to bring foreign technology to bear by forging agreements with foreign suppliers, not always with success. In India, the navy has been working with French industry to produce six Scorpion-class submarines, but integrating local production with Western technology has delayed delivery for six years. And Russia has suffered the embarrassment of having to purchase French-made ships for its navy.

It is in the interests of Israel and Jews around the world for the U.S. to maintain its ability to project military force worldwide, which remains one of America's greatest advantages to compensate for a shrinking economic edge. But the defense establishment must ultimately rest on a strong economy, so overcoming America's economic and budget woes is of paramount importance in continuing to enjoy a wide lead in the military sphere. To get America's resulting huge and unsustainable budget deficits under control will require defense cuts of at least $400 billion over the next ten years. The more cuts, the more it threatens one of America's greatest assets in the twenty-first century.

It is hard to overestimate the impact the shifting balance of power will have on world Jewry and Israel. The rise of the United States as a world power after World War II had a profoundly positive impact on global stability, prosperity, and freedom as well as on Jews and Israel. This enabled the U.S. to take the lead in recognizing the Jewish state at the United Nations from the outset. There have been periods of disagreement between the U.S. government and the State of Israel, some more significant than others. But the U.S., and the U.S. alone, has been the prime source of support for the State of Israel, in vetoing anti-Israel resolutions in the UN Security Council; in providing massive, unprecedented economic and military assistance; and, more recently, in helping to fund and design Israel's antimissile systems. The United States government during the Carter and Reagan administrations pressured the Soviet Union to open the gates for Soviet Jewish immigration to Israel and the rest of the world.

More broadly, after the end of World War II, the United States was the ballast for maintaining world order through a stable world currency, international security, and an open market for goods in world trade. This provided an American umbrella of protection that was an essential for Israel's security as a nation. The active efforts of the American Jewish community in support of a strong U.S.-Israel relationship created a triangular relationship unlike any before in Jewish history. Other than Americans themselves, no people or nation has more at stake in the continued strength and world leadership of the United States than the Jewish people and Israel.

While the global edge the U.S. enjoyed immediately after the end of the Cold War has eroded, it is important to keep American power in context. The U.S. is not the declining Spanish Empire of the seventeenth century, nor the British Empire of the second half of the twentieth century, exhausted and depleted after World War II. The U.S. has assets that Britain did not have. It bestrides a continent with four times the population of Britain, whose preeminence depended heavily on its colonial conquests and the geographical reach provided by its possessions. While there are new economic and political realities, the notion is highly overstated of a depleted United States as a beached whale and of a consequently endangered Israel.

Even after the Great Recession, the U.S., with less than 5 percent of the world's population, produces over 20 percent of the manufactured goods in the world and dominates the service and technology economy, the next great wave of economic growth.[146] The U.S. economy hit bottom in mid-2009, and the recovery remains painfully slow and uneven. But the U.S. will come back. It remains the linchpin of global prosperity. Never bet against the U.S. Even in areas where China has the comparative advantage of cheap factory labor, there are signs of an American comeback. China's wages are rapidly rising as its middle class demands higher salaries. With strong increases in U.S. productivity, an open investment climate, and flexible capital and labor markets, American companies are increasingly competitive. In a 2011 report, the Boston Consulting Group forecast that within four years, production in the U.S. will cost about the same as it does in China.[147]

America's universities have been a key reason for U.S. leadership in the world and for the country's attraction to the best and brightest young people in the world. The English language is advancing as the preferred global means of communication. America remains a beacon of freedom for refugees around the world.

But the challenges are real. The U.S. has dug itself into a deep hole from which it will take years to emerge completely. It may be as late as 2017 before employment recovers to pre–Great Recession levels. American creativity and innovation still lead the world even if that lead is shrinking. But these advantages will quickly erode if the United States cannot promptly and directly meet its underlying financial challenges. There are troubling signs of losing the global competitive edge. Only 40 percent of American college students graduate in four years; the rising cost of college is excluding middle-class Americans; and full-time students in four-year institutions are spending far less time actually studying than in the early 1960s.[148]

A recent study by McKinsey & Company has found that to regain the growth the U.S. enjoyed in the past two decades, America will have to increase its labor productivity by more than one-third to a rate not seen since the 1960s, when there was a political and social consensus and American industry dominated world markets that were recovering from wartime devastation.[149]

The U.S. must increasingly work through countries with different agendas and interests to achieve its goals, whether in places such as North Korea and Iran, where problems seem intractable, and the Middle East, where the Arab Spring has created a dangerous vacuum of power that Islamic parties are likely to fill.

Yet the U.S. in the end always rises to a crisis. Despite the seismic changes in the world, the U.S. will remain *primus inter pares* for at least another generation.

Israel's Role in the New World Order

Israel is very much a part of the new multipolar world and is itself part of the swing in economic, political, and military influence. But for its small size, Israel would stand out as a BRIC-type nation. It is a major regional power. Its per capita GDP exceeds that of several members of the European Union, and its military power is among the top ten in the world. It is the dominant economic, military, and technological force in the Middle East.

For sure, Iran is competing for dominance in the Middle East at every front, up to and including efforts to destroy Israel, both through surrogates such as Hamas and Hezbollah and its nuclear program. Iran's population is ten times larger than Israel's and is well educated. It has a strong scientific and engineering base and vast oil and natural gas reserves, which emerging nations crave to feed their growth.

But Israel has a technological and military edge as well as the advantage of an open, democratic system promoting the kind of innovation stifled by Iran's Islamic dictatorship. For all of Israel's internal political problems with its small, single-issue parties and the rise of religious-based militancy, it has a far more stable, sustainable system than Iran's, with its radical Revolutionary Guard and theocratic leadership that have brutally suppressed the opposition. Israel needs to carry on toward further and faster economic liberalization and advancement of high technology and to invest more in an educational system that is faltering, to prevent any slide in the sectors that have made it so successful. Economic power is concentrated in the hands of favored families and monopolies.

The Israeli middle class lacks full access to education and housing opportunities, one of the reasons behind the 2011 social demonstrations. Israel's significant income inequalities have risen over the last three decades, arising from the plight of the Israeli Arab population; elderly who often come to Israel at the last stages of their lives, with no pensions from their host countries; and the growing Haredi population, which is largely outside the traditional labor force.[150]

Israel will be buffeted by the great global shift of power, and since it accounts for a minuscule 0.3 percent of global GDP, it has little influence on wider economic forces. But one utterly unexpected discovery could simplify Israel's role in the new global order—offshore energy. Israelis have long joked that Moses took the wrong turn out of Egypt en route to the Promised Land, while its Arab neighbors were gushing oil and gas. But a Houston-based company, Noble Energy, exploring for natural gas in deep waters off Israel's Mediterranean coast, made its first major discovery in the year 2000 of one trillion cubic feet of gas, called the Mari-B. Noble began producing gas for sale in Israel in 2004, and five years later it found the Tamar field, which was eight times larger and in fact was the biggest natural gas discovery in the world in 2009. Delivery is scheduled to begin in 2012, but more is on the way. In late 2010, a mammoth field was discovered with up to 16 trillion cubic feet of natural gas, appropriately called Leviathan, the third-largest find anywhere on the globe in the last ten years. This means Israel could begin to narrow its energy imbalance, in which it exports 3.2 million tons equivalent of oil, while importing 19.4 million.[151] All of Israel's electricity needs could be met for thirty years with only half that amount, leaving the balance for export.

And even these fields are only the beginning of an energy boom. The U.S. Geological Survey estimates that between 50 and 100 million cubic feet of natural gas lies under Israel's territorial waters. For years Israel imported almost half its natural gas from Egypt, now convulsed by revolution and unable to guarantee pipeline security across the Sinai desert; the pipeline has been bombed on multiple occasions. Israel could strengthen its ties in Europe as a new source of energy in a region heavily dependent on the capricious supplies of Iranian oil and Russian gas. But Israel needs to put in place a stable energy pricing regime that encourages foreign investors rather than seek short-term gain.

Israel should follow the lead of Norway and create a stabilization fund to protect against unexpected international economic events. Some of the revenues could be used to redress Israel's large income inequality and to invest in scientific research and education for its citizens. To fully realize all these benefits, Israel will need tens of billions of dollars in foreign investment to build undersea pipelines and liquid natural gas facilities, but the gas itself will increase Israel's attraction to foreign investors.

Israel nevertheless cannot go it alone and must maintain its strong relationship with the U.S. as the centerpiece of its foreign policy while broadening its base of economic support to include other emerging countries, the BRICs, the Asian Tiger countries, and hopefully Turkey. Israel is already on the way to doing so, as Turkey is taking keen interest in Israel's high-tech products, despite Turkey's political movement away from Israel.

Its lesson from the shift in world power is clear: The days when Israel could rely on the U.S. alone are fast disappearing. Jerusalem must strengthen and deepen relationships with emerging nations, especially those with vibrant Jewish communities such as Brazil, Russia, and Argentina. The outlook is promising.

Trade between Israel and Brazil increased from $449 million in 2002 to $746 million in 2006, and Jerusalem and Brasilia recently signed a bilateral agreement for industrial research and development in the private sector.

Notwithstanding the vitriol following the incident of the Gaza flotilla, Israel must do everything possible to maintain its military and economic relationship with Turkey. Defense ministers of both countries confirmed that the political disagreements should not impact military cooperation and, in particular, arms purchases. As for Russia, Israel is already its leading trading partner in the Middle East, and given Israel's strong base of Russian-born *olim*, Israel has natural advantages as it seeks to expand economic ties with Moscow.

The world in general, and Israel and world Jewry in particular, has a great stake in whether Russia will become more confrontational or cooperative with the U.S. and the West. The Jewish community inside Russia is in no position to be a voice for a more cooperative policy. It would risk the gains it has made if it gets too far ahead of public opinion and challenges Putin. But the Obama administration's reset of relations with Russia has led to more cooperation in a number of cases—a new strategic arms reduction treaty, supply lines for NATO to Afghanistan, and a modicum of support on Iran.

The challenge for Israel is to balance its relationship with Russia against its strengthening relationships with the new states of Eastern Europe and Central Asia, some of whose interests diverge from Moscow's. The necessity for such a balance was thrown into relief during the summer of 2008 when Georgia and Russia came to blows. Georgia has been a major purchaser of Israeli arms, and in fact, the first warning shot between Georgia and Russia came with Russia downing an Israeli-made drone over the Black Sea.

In contrast to Russia, China has no history of anti-Semitism; indeed, during World War II Shanghai was a refuge for tens of thousands of Jews fleeing Nazi oppression. China admires Israel's technological prowess and has sent delegations to the Jewish state. But these ties are strained if not overwhelmed by China's dependence on Iran—its third-largest source of oil, supplying 12 percent of its consumption, and a location for large amounts of Chinese energy investment in the future.

Today, China has a Jewish community of some five thousand, consisting mostly of Western expatriates and Israelis seeking business opportunities. Judaism is not one of the five recognized religions in China, although there are Chabad houses in Beijing and Shanghai and several synagogues in Hong Kong. The State of Israel should encourage Judaism's official recognition, although even without such an imprimatur, Jewish life exists in China and the government places no active restrictions on Jewish religious practice.

Trade with China represents perhaps the biggest prize, but with its rapid acceleration comes a firewall of which Israel should be wary. China is now Israel's second-largest trading partner after the EU, and a survey by the *Jerusalem Post* discovered close to a thousand Israeli companies doing business across China. In 2005, the Israeli Tourism Ministry had only four licensed guides qualified to accompany Chinese tourists, and there were no Chinese-language pamphlets or maps. Since then, Chinese tourism to Israel has boomed, and the Ministry of Tourism has increased its Chinese capabilities.

Israel's greatest asset to China is its high-tech capacity. For example, the Beijiang Power and Desalination Plant is building a major ultra-high-temperature coal-fired generator with the world's most modern pollution controls, by teaming with Israeli equipment manufactured by Brack, using its excess heat to distill seawater into fresh water. Thus, Israel is contributing to another way in which China is seeking to be a leader in new technology and to provide badly needed fresh water for China's growing needs. Beijiang's massive desalination complex was almost totally made in Israel, shipped to Tianjin, and bolted together.[152]

While China has generally taken a pro-Palestinian position in international forums and has criticized Israel's nuclear program, it has not taken the belligerent, one-sided position of the Soviet Union during the Cold War. Indeed, Israel had been a key military supplier to China. But Israel must remain sensitive to American concerns, particularly of those in the Pentagon who see China as a potential military opponent. U.S. Defense Department officials strongly oppose technology transfers to China that could aid its military and missile capacity. Israel's cooperation with China via Israel Aircraft Industries and other defense companies has led to serious tensions with Washington.

The cancellation of the Falcon aircraft sale to China under Pentagon pressure was a severe blow. The scars from this episode required a 2005 memorandum of understanding with the United States for Israel to confirm that it would no longer supply sensitive military-related items to China. Israel will have to navigate a tightrope in maintaining its critical partnership with the United States while trying to find ways to broaden its relationship with China. The recently commenced $350 million Sino-Israel technology fund is less problematic from the U.S. security standpoint because it is focused on start-ups in each country.

Yet, Israel must face the hard fact that its greatest tool for even partly offsetting China's growing dependence on Iranian and Arab oil and natural gas is the sophisticated military equipment that China badly needs but that the U.S. will not permit Israel to exploit fully.

Of the major emerging countries, India is Israel's most likely new ally. Both are vibrant democracies that share a British colonial heritage and secured their independence at the same time. Both have Islamic powers on their borders (indeed, India's Muslim population is among the world's largest). Both nations confront radical Islamic terrorism, and India suffers more Islamic-based terrorist attacks than any other country, including Israel, especially over Kashmir. Both have nuclear weapons capabilities but have not signed the Nuclear Non-Proliferation Treaty, and both have strong military forces that are increasingly cooperating with each other. India-Israel trade is increasingly robust, and former Indian president A.P.J. Abdul Kalam recently supported joint space exploration with Israel. Israel is now one of the top three suppliers of military equipment for the Indian military, without raising the kind of security concerns at the Pentagon as with Israel-China military sales.[153] These parallel interests have the potential to unite Israel in common purpose with a rising Asian power that refused to even have diplomatic relations with Jerusalem until a generation ago.

But there are limits to the relationship. Since its foundation as an independent state from British colonial rule, less than a year before Israel's creation, there has never been a high-level visit to Israel by an Indian political leader because of India's concerns about the reaction of its large Muslim minority as well as its growing economic ties to the Muslim Middle East. And for that reason India keeps its deepening military relationship with Israel away from public scrutiny.

It is therefore important to cultivate a personal dimension through Jewish communities in emerging states, where a surprising number can be found— 110, 000 Jews in Brazil alone, with a disproportionate role in business, academia, and politics. While strengthening these relations, supporting them with domestic policies is crucial. The best scenario for Israel is to continue down the path it set in the 1980s—toward further and faster economic liberalization and promotion of high technology. Israel's Silicon Wadi remains the envy of much of the world. IBM, Motorola, Microsoft, and dozens of other multinational high-technology companies have benefited greatly from locating plants and research facilities in Israel. The wider Israeli economy is attractive enough to have coaxed Berkshire Hathaway out of its American shell when Warren Buffett chose Israel as its first international investment, paying $4 billion for 80 percent of Iscar Metalworking in 2006. Cisco has made nine high-tech acquisitions in Israel and is aiming for more. Such investments are only a part of Israeli foreign direct investment, which reached an astonishing $9.5 billion in 2007, more than 5 percent of the country's GDP.

Other economic factors also suggest that Israel has the potential to thrive even if the U.S. gradually slides economically. Israel spends a greater share of its GDP (4.4 percent) on research and development than any OECD state; almost one Israeli in ten works in the high-tech sector; thousands of start-ups are created every year; and, outside of U.S.-based firms, more companies from Israel are listed on the NASDAQ exchange than from any other nation. The exchange even tracks stocks through a special Israeli index. The government's role in this process has been visionary, with the Ministry of Industry, Trade and Labor creating tech incubators as early as 1991—far ahead of the curve—and the Yuma program subsidizing the establishment of ten venture capital funds. Israel has world-class research institutions, such as the Weizmann Institute and the Technion, and has the capacity to convert basic research into commercial products.

Yet, the risks Israel faces are outgrowths of this success. A recent poll of potential global high-tech investors conducted by consultants Deloitte found that 30 percent intended to invest in Chinese companies, while 25 percent said they planned on investing in India. Israel was not even on the list.

Perhaps most alarming is the Israeli brain drain abroad. The number of Israeli academics working at U.S. universities equals one-quarter of the total senior faculty in Israel. While there are no accurate figures, there may be anywhere from 100,000 to 300,000 Israeli engineers working outside Israel, most in the United States, some 80,000 in Silicon Valley alone. To support Israel's overwhelming comparative advantage, investment in education must be a paramount national policy. There are some signs that Israel's role as a font of innovation has slowed; budget cuts have hampered higher education. Israel can help fill part of the public funding gap by emulating the American model of philanthropy led by Buffett and Microsoft's Bill Gates, who have promised to give at least half of their wealth to philanthropic activities, such as education. Israel should encourage its billionaire entrepreneurial class to do likewise.

For all its accomplishments in sixty years of independence, Israel remains significantly dependent on the U.S. for security, for investment, and even as a cultural model. The hard fact is that Israel has a limited ability to develop truly deep strategic relationships with the BRIC countries and other emerging powers. Their strong economic growth has fueled a growing reliance on Middle Eastern energy. The U.S. has placed significant limits on Israel's ability to sell high-tech products such as missile guidance systems craved by China. And China, India, and Russia, with their sizable domestic Muslim populations, are wary of a too-visible relationship with the Jewish state.

When all is said and done, it is to the United States that Israel and the Jewish people worldwide must continue to look for support in creating a world order based on the rule of law, tolerance, democracy, and global prosperity. America's fate and that of the Jewish people are inextricably intertwined. It is impossible to overstate the importance of the United States of America to Israel's security, and to the protection of Jews worldwide. Little is to be gained outside of domestic Israeli politics from the Israeli prime minister lecturing the American President in the Oval Office before the television cameras and then playing to his political opponents in Congress by criticizing and not properly characterizing President Obama's 2011 peace initiative.

Israel provides real benefits to the U.S. but must recognize the importance of trying to satisfy its major ally's foreign policy goals. When Israel announces new housing units in contested territories during the visit of Vice President Joe Biden, one of Israel's staunchest friends, and again just after President Obama successfully went to the mat to block the UN Security Council from supporting a Palestinian state and the Quartet then launched a new peace initiative, it can only needlessly strain relations with the U.S.

No one has more at stake in continued American strength at home and abroad than the Jewish people and the State of Israel. The U.S. remains the bulwark against attacks against Israel, whether diplomatic from the United Nations or military from Hezbollah or Hamas rockets and missiles; against the Iranian nuclear threat; against the war against terrorism; and in protecting pro-Western Arab nations that have already made peace with Israel or that support normal relations. In all of these areas and more, it is the United States that is the key, often sole nation taking positions that dovetail with Israel's.

In the near and medium term there is no imaginable reality other than that Israel and Diaspora Jews, wherever they live, will continue to depend on the leadership of the United States. Only the U.S. has the breadth of political, military, intelligence, and diplomatic support Israel requires to avoid international isolation. Likewise, Jews in the largest Diaspora community in the world, the U.S., have remarkable freedom, influence, and access to the highest levels of the American government, and they live in a benign and accepting environment unlike any in the long history of Diaspora Jews. The stable, prosperous, tolerant, democratic world the U.S. strives to create is one of the best protections for Jews in Europe and around the world. Anything that challenges the dominance of the U.S. in the world can have negative implications for the State of Israel and Jews the world over.

While the relative economic advantage, and consequent political advantage, of the United States has eroded, and the U.S. must share power with new emerging nations, the U.S. remains the world's major power. Jews around the world are firmly embedded in their Diaspora societies, with rights and protections never enjoyed before in Jewish history. Israel is a strong country, with an unprecedented capacity for self-defense. All of this is reason for modest optimism, despite the earthshaking shifts of power from the West to the emerging powers of the East and South.

2

Globalization: A More Integrated World

G LOBALIZATION IS A MAJOR FORCE shaping the twenty-first century. Vast amounts of capital, goods, and people are moving across national boundaries with dramatic speed, creating an interdependence among countries and people never before witnessed in history. The principal elements are the breathtaking technological breakthroughs of the digital age creating instantaneous global communications that tie us together more closely. The degree of mutual interdependence was most recently punctuated by the global Great Recession of 2008–2009. Few nations were unscathed, and only coordinated action by separate governments in the new G20 organization, for the first time in history including major emerging powers along with established developed economies, avoided a worldwide depression. In contrast to a mercantilist past, most countries now have a mutual interest in the prosperity of others in a tranquil world.

A tsunami in Japan sends radioactive particles from a damaged nuclear reactor into the milk of Washington State and disrupts huge sectors of global automobile production that depend on a supply chain of parts reaching across the Pacific.[1] Virtually every major product contains components from around the globe. There is no such thing as a purely American, or Chinese, or European product in any major industry. Products today should be more properly labeled "Made in the World" because of the sources of their components. The notion that one country makes a distinct product and exports it to another is a thing of the past. Parts for the iPhone come from a half dozen countries. A giant Chinese company, Foxconn, may physically manufacture iPads at its Shenzhen plants in China, but in reality less than 10 percent of its value is added in China, with components coming from around Asia and the U.S.

This replaces the broken model of a central production hub with distribution spokes, such as the U.S. or Britain as "a workshop of the world," shipping goods to other countries. Increasingly, trade takes place within regions and between developing nations themselves. So 70 percent of Europe's trade is within Europe, and 50 percent of Asia's is within Asia.[2]

A more integrated world is ultimately a safer world, including for Israel and the Jewish people. For Israel's entrepreneurs, who have always had to look abroad for expansion because of their small home market, this new integrated and digitally accessible world offers great opportunity, which has also been seized by foreign investors taking advantage of Israel's path-breaking research. Israel has become a high-tech hub, making up in brainpower and creativity what it lacks in natural resources and size. Its inflows of venture capital are more than the UK, Germany, and France combined. It once was joked that the way to make a small fortune in Israel was to come with a large one, but no longer. Israeli success is a product of market reforms championed during Benjamin Netanyahu's tenure as finance minister and the careful monetary leadership of a succession of central bank chairmen from Jacob Frenkel to Stanley Fischer. In a generation this has propelled Israel from a sleepy, state-dominated economy to its 2010 acceptance into the group of the world's thirty-four wealthiest democratic nations, the Organisation for Economic Co-operation and Development (OECD).[3]

Globalization is also characterized by the increasing global reach and influence of nonstate actors. Multinational corporations operate seamlessly across national borders. The American icon Coca-Cola receives about 80 percent of its revenues from sales outside the United States. And every major multinational corporation projects itself as a global presence, with manufacturing and research facilities in major markets around the world. It is a fallacy to see Detroit's Big Three—General Motors, Ford, and Chrysler (in which Fiat of Italy holds a major stake)—as manufacturers of purely American automobiles. Like Japan's Toyota and Honda and South Korea's Hyundai, they source parts across the world and have plants and local partners spanning the globe.

Nongovernmental organizations also have a global reach; benign organizations promote standards for human rights, democracy, and the environment. But terrorist groups also use the modern mechanisms of globalization to plan and fund attacks on innocent civilians from Jerusalem and New York to Mumbai and the once isolated paradise of Bali, recruiting jihadists, even from U.S. citizens, from hideouts in Pakistan, Afghanistan, Yemen, and elsewhere.

The financial sector has embraced globalization most completely, as capital crosses borders with the click of a computer mouse, and global financial institutions maintain loans with each other and partner on major deal financing. Union Bank of Switzerland (UBS) and Credit Suisse, storied Swiss banks that once were secret Alpine bastions of private wealth, now are as much American as Swiss and operate according to transparent global norms. The Hongkong and

Shanghai Banking Corporation (HSBC) is similarly a citizen of the world, with its original geographically identified namesake only a small part of its global operations, its management able to funnel Chinese savings and capital among subsidiaries across the globe, and its iconic advertising in airport terminals the world over, claiming to be the world's local bank. The trading platforms themselves manifest this globalization. Stock markets operate on a 24/7 basis, and there is cross-ownership in many of the major markets. The venerable New York Stock Exchange owns Euronext, a Paris-based, Europe-wide exchange; NASDAQ, the U.S. exchange, historically the home of U.S. high-tech companies, owns the Dubai International Financial Exchange and is now known as NASDAQ Dubai.

Technology: The Key Globalization Driver

We are in the midst of a communications revolution every bit as fundamental as Gutenberg's fifteenth-century invention of the printing press, which allowed the diffusion of knowledge around the world in compact book form, and the Industrial Revolution of the eighteenth and nineteenth centuries, which shifted Western economies from an agricultural to a manufacturing base and, with the help of rail and maritime transport, dramatically increased incomes in nations that could master the new technical skills. The Digital Revolution began in the latter half of the twentieth century and produced an information age, with the most profound implications for moving information freely and rapidly around the globe by shifting from traditional analog, mechanical, and electronic systems to digital technology growing out of several overlapping scientific breakthroughs:

- The development of large computers for governments and corporations began in the 1950s, and the profusion of personal computers began in the 1980s, aided by the genius of Steve Jobs of Apple, along with widely distributed software operating systems from Microsoft, created in 1975 by Bill Gates and Paul Allen while still students at Harvard.
- The Internet was begun in the early 1960s at the RAND Corporation; adapted by the Defense Advanced Research Projects Agency (DARPA) in 1969, when it was called the ARPANET; and developed as a communications network designed to survive an enemy attack by operating in regional segments. From this it morphed into the Internet in the early 1990s through the architecture of the World Wide Web. The basic principle is based on dividing digital messages into bundles of data that are sent around a network and reassembled at their intended destination.[4]
- The speed of innovation occurred at historic levels because the number of transistors that can be placed on computer chips—the workhorses of everything from computers to smart phones—doubles every two years.

This is named Moore's law after Gordon Moore, the cofounder of Intel, and was thought to have reached its limit until the company announced a new 3-D transistor design allowing information to be transmitted at ever-faster speeds with less power consumption.[5]

- Handheld mobile phones in the first decade of this century incorporated digital technology to combine functions of telephones, e-mail communications, music, movies, TVs, and entire encyclopedias of information.
- Social networks linking mobile devices and the Internet connect people around the globe in the most personal ways. Technology, which had been the province of large enterprises and elites, has been dramatically expanded to developing countries in every part of the world. Never before in human history has technology developed so rapidly and so profoundly transformed society.

Computer, cell phone, and Internet access has surpassed virtually all projections. In 1990 there were 12.4 million cell phone subscribers (less than 1 percent of the world's population) and only 2.8 million Internet users. In 2008 nearly 25 percent of the world was accessible online, double the proportion in 2002. By 2010, over 4 billion people, two-thirds of the entire population of the planet, were cell phone subscribers, and 1.8 billion people, or over one-quarter of the world's population, were Internet users. Four billion text messages are sent every day. By 2013, 2.2 billion people around the globe will be online, a 30 percent increase from 2010.

Because we live with this revolution on a daily basis, it is easy to forget how much it has changed our lives. In only twenty-five years since personal computers replaced typewriters, the Internet has evolved from a military network to the worldwide phenomenon it is today; e-mail has become the major mode of written communication; search engines such as Google bring the accumulated world of knowledge from the beginning of time to everyone; social networks such as YouTube, Twitter, and Facebook, begun in 2004 by Mark Zuckerberg before his graduation from Harvard, have matured and now have over 800 million users worldwide; and cell phones and then smart phones, combining every medium of communication, all became everyday objects.

These new digital technologies are having a profound impact on societies, allowing the creation of virtual communities across boundaries of geography, religion, and politics and bringing an immediacy to local and global events. As one digital expert noted, this "technology revolution has sparked a values revolution" in which communications is about connectivity to other people, many of them far distant and from different cultures.[6] More and more computing will be done through "the cloud," an open network with huge data centers that permit increasing numbers of people and institutions to connect in this virtual world.

Small and portable, mobile smartphones are replacing personal computers as a primary gateway to the World Wide Web. Their ubiquity permits the tracking of individuals, where they shop and eat, with whom they meet, their likes and dislikes, which can be used for everything from corporate marketing to law enforcement. It is now possible to know where the vast majority of the world is at any point in time, and as one expert put it, "instead of having a [national] census once every decade, it is now possible to have one every 30 minutes." The Internet has also dramatically reduced the cost of innovation, making it among the most personally empowering inventions in history, allowing people to communicate with anyone, anywhere, anytime, without cost, and to express their unfiltered views through their own websites and blogs. New discoveries permit ever-faster access to, and storage of, more and more information.

Globalization has created a more integrated and interdependent world. Music and film, much of it from the U.S., have become universally shared mediums. Brand-name hotels offer uniform service. International newspapers are sold in newsstands around the world. Even restaurants have become a global commodity, with McDonald's golden arches in every nook and cranny of the world. Yum! Brands expects that in 2011 its American icons Pizza Hut, KFC, and Taco Bell will have a larger share of sales in China than in their home country.

Success in the twenty-first-century world will come to those with the educational skills to master the new technologies and develop ever-newer ones; the flexibility to adapt to rapid change; and the creativity to innovate. These are traits that the Jewish people, wherever they live, have used to survive and thrive for three millennia.

Digital technologies are revolutionizing traditional print journalism, so much so that important regional newspapers such as the *Los Angeles Times* and *Washington Post* have eliminated almost all the bureaus they established around the U.S. as the press expanded during the Cold War and the postwar consumer boom. Delivery of news and classified advertising online destroyed their business model and bankrupted many papers that had borrowed heavily to acquire what they mistakenly believed would be cash cows in cities across the country. Even in news-hungry Israel, which has more newspapers per capita than virtually any other country, young Israelis get their news digitally.

In 1972, Charles Dolan and Gerald Levin launched Home Box Office (HBO), the first pay-TV network, which led to the creation of a national satellite distribution system. Initially, the satellite system was used in geographically remote areas that got poor reception using traditional over-the-air signals. But when Ted Turner created CNN in 1980, using satellites to provide an instant twenty-four-hour news service, seven days a week, he profoundly changed the way the world got its news and tied the people of the planet closer together. By 1998, the number of national cable video networks in the U.S. alone had grown to 171.[7] Round-the-clock cable news stations have since become ubiquitous, giving birth to a news cycle that has been spun faster by blogs and videos posted on the Internet. But this comes with a price, because much of what passes for news online does not go through the traditional newspaper editorial and fact-checking filters and often has a strongly partisan political bent. Instantaneous online sources crowd out the in-depth coverage newspapers can provide, and few publications now can afford the patient expenditure of time, money, and effort that go into investigations of public wrongdoing.

The heavily ideological content of twenty-first-century news in the Digital Era has helped polarize American society and may do the same to other countries, including Israel. Increasingly, people get their news, hold online exchanges, and read blogs on websites that echo their own ideological predilections. Instead of getting their news from the more balanced over-the-air networks of NBC, CBS, and ABC, which predominated in the era of Chet Huntley and David Brinkley, Tom Brokaw, Walter Cronkite, and Peter Jennings, Americans increasingly talk to themselves. They listen to cable news from conservative Fox TV or the more liberal MSNBC, or they are bombarded by bombastic political commentators who add their heavily ideological texture to events, with no pretense of objectivity.

India alone has fourteen twenty-four-hour news stations, and while Chinese news organizations are expanding global coverage, they emphasize the state's views of events. Arab cable news networks, such as Qatar-based Al Jazeera, have brought immediacy to events in the Muslim world. Often presenting a sensationalized and anti-Israel view of the news, the Arabic network has developed a wide following with 40 million viewers. The impact of Al Jazeera on Arab citizens was most noteworthy during the Gaza War in 2008–2009. Its constant broadcasts of highly selective images of the violence in Gaza led many viewers in nations outside the region to protest what they were persuaded was their own governments' passivity in the face of what Al Jazeera portrayed as Israeli "aggression," which viewers felt they were seeing with their own eyes. Little was said of the thousands of rockets that were launched from Gaza into civilian locations in southern Israel. Al Jazeera's English-language channel, however, presented more nuanced and fuller reporting.

The Internet and interactive technologies also have an impact in the spiritual world to which religious groups are struggling to adapt. Groups from high Episcopalians to Orthodox Jews have signed up for Twitter and Facebook accounts with what one observer calls "the same gusto that celebrities and politicians have, and for the same reasons—to gain a global platform and to appeal to young people."[8] Pope Benedict XVI opened a Facebook account in 2009. And even dating has been impacted, with online services such as JDate, which has brought thousands of Jewish mates together, providing a novel way of combating intermarriage.

But the strongest impact of the digital telecommunications revolution is its political empowerment of individuals seeking political change. It has been a major factor in helping opposition groups coalesce into democratic movements that challenged and often overthrew the established order in former Soviet-dominated states, through the Orange Revolution in Ukraine and the Rose Revolution in Georgia but also the "red shirt" demonstrations by the rural poor in Bangkok and the upheavals in what had been the politically stagnant Middle East.

The hero of the youth movement that catalyzed the January 25, 2011, revolution in Cairo was a Google executive who rallied supporters through a variety of social networks. Some young organizers demanding democracy called the extraordinary peaceful overthrow of Egyptian president Hosni Mubarak the Facebook Revolution. While these Arab uprisings had many underlying causes, it was global communications that showed Arab youth another model to which they could aspire, and it was digital technology that permitted them to mobilize support, reaching over the heads of their autocratic leaders without the need of a charismatic leader of their own.

The use of cell phone photos in the Iranian protests has been widely reported, but less well known is an incident in Russia exposing an automobile death caused by a well-connected businessman that was caught on video camera, prompting an official investigation.[9] Even cloistered North Korea is not immune to the new Digital Era: The world learned of Kim Jong Il's 2008 stroke when South Korean agents intercepted a government e-mail containing "Dear Leader's brain scans." In China, citizens are using the Internet to call local Communist Party officials to task for corruption and the abuse of power by posting their grievances online.[10] One striking new example of technology's impact in empowering citizens to hold their governments accountable is a new website leveraging the wiki revolution—the relaying of information and knowledge by allowing any reader to edit and add material, much like the eponymous Internet-based Wikipedia. Following a contested election in her home country of Kenya in 2007, lawyer Ory Okolloh developed an Internet mapping tool called Ushahidi (*testimony* in Swahili) that could change the way of verifying election abuses. The website collects user-generated reports of election intimidation and maps them by location to help election monitors intervene in real time. Because Kenya has few computers, Ushahidi works through cell phones, which are personal empowering devices of extraordinary portability.

But Ushahidi has even broader applications. It helped locate trapped victims of the 2010 Haitian earthquake through an emergency texting number advertised by radio. The SOS messages were translated by a group of Haitian Americans in the U.S. and then plotted on an interactive "crisis map." Rather than having aid workers or foreign journalists highlight a humanitarian crisis and provide assistance as best they can on the ground, Ushahidi allowed the victims themselves to supply the data, mobilize distant volunteers, and supply information to people on the ground to better target relief.

One can only dare imagine how the Holocaust might have been prevented if such technology had been available then; or how the victims of the Cambodian Killing Fields might have limited Pol Pot's madness; or how genocide in Darfur might have been avoided if smart phones could have captured images of the slaughter and shown them to the world on Facebook and YouTube; or what might have happened if something like Ushahidi had been available to map the rapes and deaths at the hands of the Sudanese-backed militias. But it is available now, and as Anand Giridharadas has movingly written, "They say that history is written by the victors. But now, before the victors win, there is a chance to scream out with a text message that will not vanish."[11]

The Developing World: Possible Transformation

The digital technologies are having a profound impact on the developing world. Although a digital divide remains between rich and poor nations and peoples within those countries, Internet usage now penetrates rural villages and schools in Africa, Asia, and Latin America. Among the rural poor, mobile phones function as microlending tools, thus becoming market makers and catalysts of entrepreneurship. In Kenya and India, they are used for banking; with 600,000 villages but only 40,000 branch banks, Indians can now access financial services previously out of reach.

More than 500 million Indians own mobile phones, with 15–20 million new subscribers each month, many of whom had no prospect of ever having fixed telephone lines in their villages. This only scratches the surface of what is possible in lifting the incomes and quality of life of the poor. Less than 10 percent of the population of India uses the Internet, limited by the scarcity of personal computers and the illiteracy of one-quarter of the population (compared to only 10 percent illiteracy rates in China). Telemedicine and long-distance learning are bringing healing, education, and business opportunities to remote places, making Internet access a great equalizer for developing countries and for low-income people in developed countries. Smart phones will give rural villagers an even more powerful tool, with instant access to a massive repository of information, from medical advice to data on crop prices, and will provide poor children access to educational resources of unlimited scope, when their own schools cannot afford modern textbooks. The same can occur in poor neighborhoods in the U.S. and Israel and in Israeli Arab villages.

Today, more than two-thirds of the world's mobile phones are being used in the developing world, and emerging countries are the fastest-growing sector for both handset sales and the construction of mobile telephony infrastructure.

With new 3G and 4G mobile phones, Internet access will soar. All this will prove a boon to Israel, which has pioneered in Internet telephone technology.

People in impoverished countries can gain access to otherwise unaffordable computer tools with a new technology called Nivio; this permits access to a fully functional Microsoft Windows desktop environment through a web browser that users can rent at low prices whenever they need it.[12]

Globalization can also bind Diaspora Jews and Israel closer together. A new online educational service from Israel provides one-on-one interactive Hebrew language training for American youngsters over the computer in visual form, so student and teacher see each other.

The Dark Side of Globalization

But globalization also has a dark side. It allows nuclear technology to spread more easily to rogue nations such as North Korea and Iran and—in a nightmare scenario—to terrorists operating independent of states, as well as their nations themselves, if technology being developed by General Electric using lasers to refine weapons-grade uranium falls into the wrong hands.[13] The instant exchange of information compromises privacy by tracking personal data; enhances the circulation of dangerous content, from pornography to anti-Semitic material; and expedites the theft of trade secrets by hackers and competitors.

The same world-connecting technology also enables criminal gangs to commit cybercrime by hacking into corporate and personal computers, and it allows terrorist groups to communicate across vast distances to plan and finance attacks and recruit fighters through jihadist websites. Al-Qaeda in the Arabian Peninsula produces an online English-language magazine *Inspire* and uses provocative videos with English subtitles uploaded on YouTube.[14] Terrorists in the U.S. have indicated they were influenced by radical Islamic websites as far away as Yemen.

China and Iran are engaged in cyberwars against their own people by blocking social networks and information sources. China has substituted its own sources and penetrated Google's system to trace and target human rights activists. Just as print media are strictly controlled in autocratic nations, including much of the Arab world, some experts believe that at least forty countries filter specific Internet sites or services, as China does by prohibiting access to some foreign news sources. The Mubarak government shut down access to the Internet and cell phones during the revolt in an ultimately futile attempt to abort the uprising in Egypt.[15]

Sophisticated government agencies can monitor local activists through electronic trails. Faraz Sanei of Human Rights Watch reports that Iran's Revolutionary Guard Corps has an Iranian "cyber army" that it can unleash against opponents. Syria, to compensate for its digital deficiencies, brought in Iranian Revolutionary Guard experts to use Facebook and Twitter as offensive weapons against antigovernment protestors, ominously putting Iranian forces closer to Israel. In the face of a popular uprising, Syria lifted its social networking ban—not to try to mollify the opposition but to better track them down. Andrew Tabler, an expert on Syria at the Washington Institute for Near East Policy explained: "Lifting the ban on Facebook helped the regime pinpoint where the [activists] were coming from. It was not about being magnanimous; it was a way to allow more surveillance, leading to thousands of arrests."[16]

With Iranian assistance, Syria crippled Internet service, arrested antiregime bloggers, placed pro-Assad messages on the Facebook pages of opponents, switched their people's Facebook security certificates, and tracked their log-in information and online activity. The regime bombarded the protestors' Twitter accounts with messages to inhibit their use against the government. They created online disinformation videos of future demonstrations and made death threats against prodemocracy activists. In Sudan, the government uses what they call "cyber jihadists" to launch "online defense operations" against their opponents.

Secretary of State Hillary Clinton recognized the perversions of Internet freedom, noting that in a number of countries, activists and bloggers "found their e-mails hacked or their computers infected with spyware that reported back on their every key-stroke. Digital activists have been tortured so they would reveal their passwords." The U.S. State Department has funded "cyber defense" training for five thousand people in the past two years to give them the tools to combat their governments' intrusions and is exploring a new digital "secret handshake" so activists can know with whom they are chatting on the Internet.[17]

A new word has appeared in our vocabulary, *malware*, viruses infecting computers. Cyberwar has become a part of the arsenal of twenty-first-century warfare between nation-states, and Israel has one of the most sophisticated capabilities that it probably has already used as a form of self-defense to slow Iran's nuclear program.[18] But this is all by way of saying that in the end, with all the miraculous promise of the Digital Revolution, human nature will be the determining factor of whether it produces more good than harm. Just as the Nazis harnessed the latest technology to perpetrate the Holocaust, so too will twenty-first-century despots and repressive regimes use digital technology to try to thwart the use of the very technology that can undermine their regimes.

Even as technology brings more of the world into the digital age, one aspect of the digital divide may remain: The younger generation is more adept at using the new technologies than their parents, a unique reversal of roles with broad implications for the relations between generations. In the digital age it is the youth who teach the adults Internet skills. It is estimated that in advanced countries children between eight and twelve spend eleven hours a day "wired" to seven to nine pieces of technology at once, while their parents can handle no more than five at a time and their grandparents few, if any. The diffusion of digital technology gets to younger and younger children, with over one third of American children under eight years old regularly using smart phones and other portable Internet products. Many parents have had to learn to text their children, since telephone calls go unanswered. Digital technology has broad, global effects on the ability of older people to find jobs in aging industrialized societies, where they will need to work well past their early sixties to earn livable pensions. But at the same time their lack of computer and social networking skills limits their employability.

The digital age also has important implications for learning. The generation born after 1980 is constantly connected to one form or another of digital technology; they are always "on" and never alone. Experts see their brains adapting to an online environment of multitasking and processing parallel tracks of information. They can "channel surf television, listen to music, do their homework and chat online with a dozen friends all at the same time"—effectively, they insist.[19] Digital technology also allows young entrepreneurs to connect and share ideas while searching for global partners; there are some 10 million Junior Achievement alumni around the world able to connect with one another.

But traditional schooling and learning patterns are bound to be affected. For better or worse, today's students question information from authorities at school by going on the Internet, and the acquisition of knowledge is far different from the linear fashion in which previous generations were taught from printed books and professors' lectures. Homework and in-depth thinking can suffer as teenagers spend countless hours on Facebook or text messaging each other.

A new phenomenon, cyberbullying, is a threat to impressionable young teenagers. Mobile phones are being used to pass vicious rumors about classmates, resulting in anxiety, isolation, and in extreme cases, suicide. Parents find they have few avenues to defend their children from these cyberattacks, whose origins are difficult to pinpoint. Nor can they protect them from a new phenomenon of what law enforcement officials call "teen sexting," the distribution by teenagers of sexually explicit pictures, videos, and text messages from a sense of bravado or other seemingly innocent motives, but also at times to take revenge for a slight or a love affair gone sour. An Internet poll conducted for the Associate Press and MTV in 2009 found that almost one-quarter of fourteen- to seventeen-year-olds have been involved in "some type of naked sexting." Half of American states are trying to craft legislation to deal with sexting and to educate children about its dangers, and many school districts are banning it and authorizing school principals to search cell phones.[20] But the most dangerous aspect may be the extreme difficulty of erasing this material from cyberspace; juvenile mistakes may follow a child through an adult career.

A loss of privacy is one of the most troubling aspects of the digital era that characterizes globalization. Once people choose to place something on any of the new technologies it can be safely assumed to be open to the world and in the public domain, as several U.S. political figures learned to their chagrin, including promising New York congressman Anthony Weiner, who used the Internet to transmit sexually explicit messages.

Google provoked a transatlantic firestorm by collecting data from home wireless networks in Germany and around the world while assembling its Street View archives. Facebook came under attack by privacy advocates for using users' own information for commercial purposes and has now strengthened its privacy protection. Social network companies have a strong incentive to track the travel and consumption habits of tens of millions of users because the information helps advertisers target potential customers; this has become embedded in the networks' business models.

Government secrets are harder to keep. At one level, the digital era promotes government accountability, but at another, it can intrude on secret information. Wikileaks is a self-described whistleblower website that publishes private, secret, and classified government documents on the Internet ranging from details of combat in Iraq and Afghanistan to Sarah Palin's personal e-mail messages. Much of it was information that traditional journalists had been denied under the U.S. Freedom of Information Act.

Even more sensational and with greater negative impact on American diplomacy was Wikileaks' publication of State Department cables from U.S. embassies around the world.[21] The organization's steady drumbeat of releases has done incalculable damage—in part because of its disclosure of candid but embarrassing content about foreign leaders, but also in demonstrating that the greatest global power was unable to protect its secrets. It has embarrassed close allies, who made unflattering statements about other leaders and countries to U.S. diplomats in confidence and expecting them to remain so. This massive leak will almost certainly curtail the willingness of foreign leaders to share information and candid assessments that are of great value to the United States in fashioning its policies. It may also chill the frank and valuable reporting of U.S. diplomats to Washington lest they further strain relations and damage their careers.

The following extraordinary event could only have occurred in the digital era. Bradley Manning, a twenty-four-year-old private first class operating in a military intelligence unit in Iraq, using a computer, a thumb drive, and a CD disc, was able to download a quarter of a million sensitive cables while telling his superiors he was listening to music on the CD. He then shared the downloads with Wikileaks, which posted them on the Internet for all to see. Of note, the Defense Department received this cache of cables from 2006 to 2009 from the State Department because following the recommendations of the 9/11 commission, which had criticized the absence of intelligence sharing by government agencies as one cause of the September 11, 2011, disaster, government departments were required to share sensitive data with each other to help agencies "connect the dots" in a way that had not been done before the attack on New York's Twin Towers. State Department computers, better protected than the Pentagon's, do not operate if a CD or any device is inserted that can download sensitive material. The Defense Department had no such safeguard. This is but another indication that privacy in the digital era is a perishable commodity.

In the U.S., judges can stop or delay publication of a printed article if the government can demonstrate potential harm to national security. But Wikileaks operates in cyberspace where information is instantly available. British officials went to court to shut down the site, but after granting injunctions, the judges reversed themselves because the ruling was ineffectual; the material was already posted online for the world to see. So did a U.S. judge, who had ordered the site shut down after it published confidential documents about a Swiss bank. Demonstrating the problems with unfettered access to information, the judge said, "We live in an age when people can do some good things and people can do terrible things without accountability necessarily in a court of law."[22]

Globalization also is a factor in the increase in income inequality within industrial countries. The information age demands and rewards skills of the brain rather than the hand. The U.S. has one of the highest levels of income inequality among advanced democratic nations. A recent report found that between the years 2000 and 2007 the wealthiest 10 percent of Americans secured all of the nation's income growth for themselves. For most of the postwar era, the top 10 percent of American families got a third of the average income growth, with the bottom 90 percent getting the rest. But in the digital era, the tables have been turned. In 2009, the top 5 percent held 63.5 percent of America's wealth, and the bottom 80 percent just 12.8 percent.[23] This is an unhealthy development for a democracy.

Globalization also punishes high-wage nations, prompting manufacturing companies in the U.S. and Europe to move plants to lower-wage states, just as imports from low-wage countries depress wages in the developed world. This in turn set off an antiglobalization backlash in the mid-1990s. The benefits of globalization were seen to flow largely to the educated elites. A wider gap opened between developed and developing countries. During the past three decades, while most developing nations have reduced poverty, the rate in sub-Saharan Africa has remained stagnant for a quarter century, and half the population lives in poverty. This inequality may not be solely the fault of globalization, and, in fact, the forces behind globalization will add two billion new people to the middle class by 2030.[24] But it has become a convenient target for antiglobalization forces.

Globalization means more intense worldwide competition. That, in turn, rewards nations that invest in education, research, and development and have a dependable structure of governance and a flexible business environment, like Israel. Nations and peoples who conduct business as usual will lose jobs, income, and influence in the world and fall further behind. Even the most developed countries must run faster to avoid being left in the wake of globalization. A recent OECD study found that among its thirty member nations, the educational advantage the U.S. enjoyed since the end of World War II has eroded. Only four industrialized nations had lower high school completion rates, and a higher percentage of students in an increasing number of countries graduated from high school and college. If the U.S. could do what Poland has done by raising the literacy skills of its 15-year-olds by almost one grade level during less than a decade, it could add billions of dollars to the U.S. economy.[25]

Globalization also accelerates rapid population movements. Yale professor Jeffrey Garten forecasts that every twenty-four hours for the next several decades, 180,000 people in developing countries will be moving from the countryside to cities, in search of work in Shanghai or São Paulo or Johannesburg; this is the equivalent of creating one New York City every two months.[26] As industrial employment moves to low-wage countries, the labor of less-skilled workers who are not part of the technology revolution is devalued.

Globalization has led to vast numbers of people crossing national boundaries in search of jobs and a better economic future, including millions of Hispanics coming into the U.S. and changing the face of America, as they overtook African Americans as the largest minority group in the country. According to the International Labor Organization, between 1989 and 2009, 20 million people immigrated to the fifteen nations of Western Europe, some from Eastern Europe but most from Turkey and the Maghreb states of North Africa, likewise profoundly changing the social structure of their adopted nations.

An anti-immigrant wave has risen throughout Europe in response to the economic hardships. Far-right parties in Germany, the UK, Italy, France, the Netherlands, Norway, and Switzerland are on the rise. Islamophobic campaigns targeting Romas and Muslims have been documented by the forty-seven-nation Council of Europe.

At a superficial level, European Jews can feel relieved that it is Muslims not Jews who are the subject of this public discontent. But at a more profound level, the growth of far-right, populist xenophobic fervor can only make Jews a potential target. It is important for Jewish leaders and organizations not to stand on the sidelines and rest content that Jews are not targeted; they should speak out against attacks on any other minority after so many centuries in which Jews were the targets of opprobrium for being "different." The newfound strength of the Jewish people lies in their mainstream acceptance, but our history gives us a special responsibility lest ignoring it push them back to the future.

The anti-globalization movement has taken many forms. It has caused a sharp increase in protectionist sentiment, retarding progress in negotiating free trade agreements. Labor unions have often led the charge, arguing that free trade allows cheap products from developing states to put downward pressure on the wages of their members, and indeed it does. In November 1998, I attended the WTO ministerial meeting in Seattle as the undersecretary of state. Antiglobalization groups engaged in violent demonstrations, confronting the Seattle police, breaking store windows, defacing buildings, and blocking us from leaving our hotel. This led Secretary of State Albright to fume to me that "we are prisoners in our own hotel." The antiglobalization forces will be with us for years to come—until there is a sense that the prosperity globalization provides has been more widely spread through all levels of society.

The rise of the Tea Party conservative movement, reflected in the 2010 U.S. congressional elections, and the liberal Occupy Wall Street demonstrations have starkly different agendas and operating models, but each represents a backlash against what proponents see as the financial elites, who used taxpayer money to be bailed out of their grievous mistakes in helping bring on the Great Recession of 2008–2009, while average people were left holding the bag and lost their homes and jobs.

Globalization and the Great Recession of 2008–2009

One of the clearest negative impacts of globalization can be seen in the financial crisis that began in the U.S. in 2008 and spread across the world, sucking in many different states and victims. In the Clinton administration, I witnessed firsthand how the fall of a globally insignificant currency, the Thai baht, could ripple throughout Asia, to Russia and Brazil. I headed the U.S. delegation at a regional meeting in Malaysia, when Thai prime minister Mahathir blamed the crisis on international speculators, such as George Soros. This was widely taken to be a thinly veiled anti-Semitic comment, and I issued a strong rebuttal with Washington's approval. With prompt action by the IMF, the U.S. Treasury, and the Federal Reserve, the crisis abated, and the Asian economies recovered within a few years. But the tough IMF medicine, imposed by a Western-based institution, made them determined to never depend on the IMF again. So the Asian nations piled up huge reserves and invested in U.S. Treasury bonds and other government-backed securities, pushing the world economy into a troubling imbalance.

But this paled in comparison to the global impact of the next crisis, which is called the "Great Recession" for good reason. Job losses have been truly global, with some 50 million people laid off, according to the International Labor Organization.[27] Mortgages on homes by the millions, in local neighborhoods around the U.S., were bundled together into poorly regulated, exotic instruments and sold to financial institutions and investors around the world with AAA ratings from American rating services. Such is the integration of today's global economy that when the value of the homes behind these securities collapsed, it impeded growth in Latin America, Africa, and East Asia. Exports from central European countries to Western Europe cratered; their traditional source of credit, major Western European banks, were so harmed by their own investments that they were unable to extend financing. For the first time in the postwar era, the U.S., Europe, and Japan fell into simultaneous recessions, and global growth in 2009 contracted for the first time since the Great Depression.

The globalization of the financial world affected China in a number of ways. Seeking a slightly higher return on their dollar reserves, Beijing had become one of the largest holders of mortgage bonds issued by the U.S.-government-sponsored—now controlled—Fannie Mae and Freddie Mac, exposing a country 10,000 miles away to the deterioration in the housing markets in local U.S. communities. Meanwhile, Chinese and other East Asian exports of cheap manufactured goods to the U.S. and Europe fell markedly. The conceit that China, or any country in East Asia, had totally decoupled its growth from the U.S. was proven patently false. No one was immune in an integrated global economy, stock markets were battered, and supply chains were disrupted for lack of credit to lubricate the world trading and financial system.[28]

The ferocity of the global downturn resulted in angry protests at factories in China and Indonesia, and often-violent labor unrest erupted from Chile to Europe. No area felt more political pressure than the nations of the European Union, whose banks gorged themselves on sovereign debt from relatively small nations in the EU, Ireland and Greece, and set off a crisis that threatens the future of the euro itself.

International anger was directed at the U.S., which was incorrectly seen as the sole culprit in causing the Great Recession. Nevertheless governments around the world—most notably America's creditors in China—questioned the U.S. economic model and its financial and political leadership as never before in the postwar era.

Washington deserves its fair share of the blame for reckless lending, lax regulation, and gross fiscal imprudence, with three large Bush-era tax cuts, two unfunded wars, and higher social spending, after the Clinton administration left three successive annual budget surpluses for the Bush administration, with forecasts of trillion-dollar surpluses for the first decade of the twenty-first century. But there were other culprits as well, including China, which rather than invest its massive trade surpluses at home, loaned the money back to the U.S. so American consumers could buy more Chinese and other imported goods. That kept China's export industries humming but did not fill the pockets of their workers.

There was another unintended consequence to the world order. The former U.S. director of national intelligence, Admiral Dennis C. Blair, warned Congress that the economic crisis was the most immediate threat to American security because of "allies and friends not being able to fully meet their defense and humanitarian obligations," refugee flows, and lack of financial help for Latin America, Eastern Europe, and sub-Saharan Africa. He warned further: "Instability can loosen the fragile hold that many developing countries have on law and order."[29]

The world buckled but did not break, thanks to wise emergency action by the Bush and Obama administrations. But the impact of the great global recession will be with us for years to come. No country has more riding on keeping the arteries of trade and commerce open and avoiding a reversion to protectionism than the State of Israel, whose exports sustain its prosperity. But despite their pledge at the height of the crisis in 2008 to keep trade open, the G20 countries have been among the most enthusiastic at adopting discriminatory trading policies. The EU reintroduced export subsidies and import tariffs on American biofuels. Russia imposed tariffs on cars while injecting hundreds of millions of dollars into its own derelict auto industry. India raised tariffs on steel products. Brazil and Argentina sought higher tariffs on products imported from other South American countries into the Mercosur trade bloc. China blocked food imports and rejected several investments by foreign companies. French president Sarkozy, announcing a government rescue package for French automakers such as Peugeot, called on them to close their plants in EU member states and return to France.

The U.S. Congress inserted "Buy America" provisions in initial drafts of the 2009 stimulus package that were qualified, but not removed, after complaints by the Obama administration. There is even a provision in the Troubled Asset Relief Program (TARP) to discourage firms receiving funds from employing foreign workers at a time when the U.S. should be encouraging the best and brightest from all over the world to come to the U.S.

Israelis are among the most mobile workers in the world and participate in great numbers, for short and long periods, in the American workforce, particularly in high technology. Anything that restricts foreign workers will fall disproportionately hard on Israelis. Professor Garten of Yale notes, "Silicon Valley would be a pale shadow of itself without Indian, Chinese and Israeli brain power in its midst."[30] More broadly international trade has become an unfortunate, unfair villain for allegedly taking jobs from American workers. The WTO's Doha trade round has foundered after ten fruitless years of negotiation, and it took some three years to finally get three free trade agreements with South Korea, Panama, and Colombia, so clearly in America's economic interest, negotiated in the Bush administration, to be tweaked by the Obama administration and passed by Congress.[31]

Reforming Global Governance

Yet, protectionism did not get out of hand, as it did in the 1930s, when it deepened the Great Depression with beggar-thy-neighbor policies. Fitfully but inexorably, the world is stumbling toward developing the institutions necessary to steer globalization in a constructive direction. This does not portend the advent of a utopian one-world government. Though multinational corporations and nongovernmental organizations have entered transnational space, the nation-state will remain the world's basic organizational model. But these states are increasingly recognizing that the health of their societies depends on multinational cooperation, diminishing any one state's ability to act on its own without regard to the impact on others. All the forces that make this a globalized world mean that neither challenges nor solutions are solely national.

The U.S. *Global Trends 2025* report points out that the world faces new challenges from conflicts over scarce food, energy, and water supplies; rogue states outside the integrated world economy that play by their own rules; terrorist groups with a worldwide reach; a widening gap between rich and poor within nations and between nations; and global warming. Each of these challenges demonstrates the lack of an international system to help manage the new globalized world, with many competing power centers but no globally effective institutions to mediate the changes. Writing in the *Financial Times*, Philip Stephens called this "multipolarity without multilateralism," a world of "fragmentation and instability."[32] In the short term, there is a real possibility that the new global order will produce more chaos and disharmony than order and stability unless institutions can be created to generate consensus that once was supplied—even imposed—by the leading nations of the once unchallenged West.

Long before globalization was a reality, a burst of international creativity arose from the ashes of World War II, focusing on world peace, financial stability, growth, and trade in recognition of the fact that a cause of the Second World War was the Great Depression and protectionism: from the United Nations; the International Monetary Fund; the World Bank and later its regional progeny, the Inter-American, Asian, and African Development Banks; to the General Agreement on Tariffs and Trade (GATT).

All of these institutions have been reformed in some way to take into account global integration. The World Trade Organization (WTO) was created in the mid-1990s, and unlike GATT, it is able to adjudicate trade disputes by issuing binding judgments, which every member nation respects.

The OECD, which declined into a think tank from its role as the coordinator of America's postwar Marshall Plan aid, is reviving under the leadership of former Mexican foreign and finance minister Angel Gurria, a champion of Israel's entry, into an organization with international responsibilities. It helps set global standards of best practices for industrial democracies and serves as a forum for binding agreements such as the OECD Anti-Bribery Convention I helped negotiate in the Clinton administration; this make it illegal to bribe foreign officials in exchange for contracts.

Inside Europe, the OECD has been active in exchanging information to stop cross-border tax evasion. It is also the headquarters for the Financial Action Task Force (FATF), created to monitor and control exploding cross-border financial flows that have made it much easier to pilfer official funds and then launder and hide the stolen money in foreign banks. While I was deputy secretary of the Treasury, we published a "name-and-shame" list of major countries that had failed to achieve the highest international standards against money laundering, including Panama, Russia, Liechtenstein, and, yes, Israel. I worked with Israel on improving its program, and within a year it had passed the necessary legislation to require banks to "know their customers" and refuse to accept dirty money, and to put in place a financial intelligence unit to receive reports of suspicious transactions from Israeli banks and trace the money back to its origin.

Meanwhile, regional organizations developed to link nations on all the inhabited continents, although most have little real decision-making authority: African Union (1963); Organization of American States (OAS, modernized in 1970); Association of Southeast Asian Nations (ASEAN, 1967); Arab League (1945, originally five states led by Egypt, now twenty-two); Asia-Pacific Economic Cooperation forum (APEC, 1989). Still other international organizations arose with specific missions, such as the Organization of the Petroleum Exporting Countries (OPEC, 1960) to set production quotas on oil production to ensure high prices for oil producers; OPEC organized the first international embargo of a major commodity with the 1973 oil embargo, aimed at the U.S. for facilitating the Israeli victory in the 1973 Yom Kippur War. This led the major consuming nations to create the International Energy Agency (IEA) to try to reduce their dependence on uncertain and expensive oil supplies.

The most important and effective military institution is the North Atlantic Treaty Organization (NATO), initially created in 1949 to provide collective defense against the Soviet Union, but since the end of the Cold War operating from the Balkan Wars of the 1990s to far afield in Asia (Afghanistan) and Africa (Libya) against general threats to peace and stability.

But the most unique and important civilian regional organization is the European Union, to which I was the U.S. ambassador. Originally created out of the ashes of World War II to preserve peace between France and Germany, the EU is now a twenty-seven-nation institution with a total population of over 500 million people. European countries that had gone to war with each other for centuries created a series of institutions in which they ceded their national sovereignty in a number of areas, such as trade and product standards, and in others pooled their decision-making authority into supranational institutions—an executive arm, the European Commission; a legislative body, the European Parliament, with increased authority; and a judicial branch, the European Court of Justice. The European Union has a common market, in which it is as easy to ship goods from France to Germany as it is from New York to California, now backed up by a common currency, the euro, in which seventeen of the twenty-seven countries participate. While the euro and the entire common enterprise of the EU are challenged by the sovereign debt crisis of 2010–2011, both will survive because of the political will of the member states.

All these organizations can be only as effective as their nation-state members wish them to be. But this web of international organizations has helped to reduce conflict and provide at least some mechanisms to resolve disputes and coordinate action. The United Nations has fifteen current peacekeeping missions, from the Democratic Republic of the Congo and Haiti to Darfur, and since 1974, the Golan Heights in Syria, involving over 98,000 troops, police and military observers, and over 18,000 civilian personnel, or almost 120,000 total men and women. From July 1, 2011, to June 30, 2012, over $7 billion in resources have been approved for these peacekeeping missions, and since 1948, almost $70 billion.[33]

The decision of the Arab League in 2011 to call on the world to stop the slaughter of Libyan civilians by the Qaddafi regime led to UN sanctions and NATO military action, which ultimately led to the end of the regime. its surprisingly aggressive attitude toward the slaughter of opponents who have taken to the streets against Syrian president Bashar al-Assad, and its call for democratic political transition, is another sign of the growing maturity of the organization and the degree to which the Arab Spring has profoundly changed the calculus in the region.

A host of international security agencies, groups, and agreements—some longstanding and some newly formed—have emerged or become more robust to deal with new threats. A number are specialized agencies of the United Nations coordinating health, antihunger campaigns, child protection, and other areas that are rarely controversial. The stakes rise with the Organisation for the Prohibition of Chemical Weapons, under which the 1997 UN Chemical Weapons Convention provided a vehicle to destroy tons of deadly nerve agents and chemical and biological weapons around the world, especially in Russia from Soviet days.

No country has a greater stake than Israel in controlling chemical weapons. Syria, now in turmoil, has the largest stockpile of dangerous chemical weapons in the Middle East, including tens of tons of deadly chemicals they have placed into widely dispersed artillery shells, Scud missiles, small bombs, and movable warheads. Israel has once destroyed Syria's budding nuclear program, but dealing with the widely available nerve gas agent sarin, which is lethal even if inhaled in small amounts, is another story. Using Soviet technology, then president Hafez al-Assad saw chemical weapons as a strategic deterrent against Israel, and now his son President Bashar al-Assad, under siege, has enlarged the size and sophistication of the huge stockpile. While the U.S. and Russia have been eliminating their arsenal of chemical weapons, Syria has refused to sign the Chemical Weapons Convention. Other Middle East countries, including Libya, have lesser quantities of these deadly agents, and with the region in turmoil, their control is up for grabs.[34] One of NATO's first priorities after Qaddafi's fall was to locate and secure these chemical weapons.

In the eye of the storm is the Nuclear Non-Proliferation Treaty (NPT) implemented by the UN's International Atomic Energy Agency (IAEA). The disastrous refusal of the Bush Administration to trust its inspectors was the trigger that started the U.S. invasion of Iraq. The Obama administration has worked more closely with the IAEA in trying to prevent Iran from obtaining nuclear weapons, a development that would touch off a nuclear arms race in the unstable Middle East and threaten far more than the security of Israel, an unacknowledged nuclear power.

The overarching writ of the Bretton Woods organizations provided the stability for the postwar economic revival—chiefly the IMF and the World Bank, which were underwritten by U.S. economic dominance and the dollar's link to gold. This link was severed with President Nixon's decision to go off the gold standard and into the world we have today of floating currencies, whose relative values are to be determined by global markets, based on national and international economic factors. To cope with the new phenomenon of floating exchange rates and the dilemma of "stagflation"—simultaneous high inflation and economic stagnation in the 1970s—the major industrial nations met outside Paris in 1975 and created the Group of Six finance ministers, joined the next year by Canada to form the G7 Group, and later becoming the G8, meeting as heads of state, with the addition of Russia, following the demise of the Soviet Union.

But this narrow world economic steering committee lost its legitimacy with the rise of the new economic powers in the developing world and with the global financial turmoil unleashed in 2008 by the very countries meant to be the stewards of the global economy.

Institutions of global governance do not yet exist to help manage disputes and create consensus in the new multipolar world. But the global financial crisis forced the world's hand, providing an early test of whether global governance could rise to the occasion and create new and more inclusive institutions able to reach consensus on meeting economic challenges. The crisis was an opportunity to shape a new world economic order that can bind the world's major economies into even greater mutual dependence and provide even more countries with a larger stake in peace and stability, certainly benefiting Israel.

Led by President George W. Bush and Secretary of Treasury Henry Paulson, the Group of 20 held its first summit meeting in London in 2008, including for the first time the emerging powers around the world. The 2009 G20 Summit in Pittsburgh, headed by the Obama administration, reached a global consensus on the need for simultaneous, coordinated stimulus to prevent the Great Recession from becoming the second Great Depression. And it worked, as China joined the U.S., Europe, Brazil, and other key countries to prevent a global meltdown. At the same time, the IMF provided more voting power to the emerging giants such as China, at the expense of European nations.

While many regional and multilateral institutions are slowly beginning to reform themselves and take on more responsibility, we are in a transitional phase where the newly emerging giants are demanding and winning more representation in the institutions guiding the global economy but are not yet willing to assume the full responsibilities that come with greater influence.[35]

The difficulty is that while the U.S. must continue to lead, its leadership is increasingly challenged at every turn, and Washington operates in a more complex environment than ever before. One can only hope that over time the very effort of sharing power in international institutions can help rising powers become more responsible stakeholders in addressing the great issues of the twenty-first century—creating growth and jobs, combating terrorism and climate change, limiting the proliferation of nuclear weapons and other weapons of mass destruction, and ensuring energy security.[36] The capacity of the new players to become "responsible stakeholders," in the words of World Bank president Robert Zoellick, will be the test of whether there will be a global consensus on not just economic issues but also global political and environmental challenges, or simply more chaos as additional players in the room complicate the achievement of a consensus.

The Rise of Multinational Corporations and Nongovernmental Organizations as Global Actors

One of the least appreciated but most important aspects of global governance is the transformation of multinational corporations, particularly those based in the United States and Europe, from an unfair image as rapacious entities in the countries where they operate. For sure, there are still large companies that pollute and care little for their local employees, but they are increasingly aberrant. Private companies have been increasingly targeted by shareholders demanding better behavior, and corporations have seen it in their interest to change. Corporations transfer technology to developing countries, provide pharmaceuticals at low or no cost to deal with diseases such as AIDS, and more broadly, behave in accordance with a new set of corporate values.

The UN, long the sole province of states, now recognizes that private industry plays a critical role in many of the areas in which the organization is concerned, such as the environment and worker protection. The UN Global Compact, launched under the leadership of then secretary general Kofi Annan, enlisted many of the world's largest corporations in assisting the UN in alleviating poverty and taking initiatives on climate change. Companies also abide by the OECD's global standards for multinational corporations and partner with environmental groups on important projects, including groups such as U.S. Climate Action Partnership.

The idea of "corporate social responsibility" was pioneered and catalyzed by professor Klaus Schwab, the world's premier social entrepreneur, who created the World Economic Forum (WEF) dedicated "To Improve the State of the World." In 1971, Professor Schwab began holding annual forums, initially for large, multilateral corporations, in the tiny sky village of Davos, Switzerland, in the middle of the winter. More recently the WEF has been extended to regional conferences around the globe. I have participated since 1995 and have seen the changes in corporate accountability brought about under the aegis of the WEF. The forums bring together thousands of chief executives from multinational corporations as well as academics and NGO and government leaders. It is also one of the few places where Israeli business and government leaders have been able to meet with their Arab counterparts. The WEF lives by its often-repeated mantra: "Economic progress without social development is not sustainable, while social development without economic progress is not feasible."

The WEF is itself an NGO and is one of numerous such organizations that, along with the private sector, are growing in importance on the international stage. As I discuss in chapter 1, major corporations have gone beyond good works as an appendage to the essential goal of creating shareholder value to embracing a wider concept of partnering with stakeholders such as local governments and NGOs to improve the international aspects of their business plans. Most NGOs perform admirable work, and the fact that they are not bound by state borders means they often can succeed where states are literally beyond their boundaries. Dozens of environmental groups, who once did battle with multinational corporations, now reach beyond borders to partner with them on climate change, water conservation, and waste disposal.

The Clinton Global Initiative, founded by former President Bill Clinton, meets annually in New York City, at the time of the UN General Assembly, and gets global leaders in every field together. Uniquely, the Clinton Global Initiative requires participating companies and firms to make explicit commitments to help with progress on envirnomental, social, and economic challenges, which are monitored for compliance.

Human rights organizations do important work in bringing their issues to the attention of the press and the public. Some, such as Amnesty International, give a highly biased view on the Palestinian-Israel conflict and outrageously suggested in 2009 that the UN add Israel to the list of arms-embargoed countries such as Sudan and the Democratic Republic of the Congo. Much of the unwarranted scorn heaped on Israel and Jews at the Durban Conference on Racism in 2001 came from NGOs. And indeed, one of the reasons the outcome of the second Durban Conference in 2009 was more moderate than the first was because organizations such as the Ford Foundation, which had funded some troublesome Palestinian NGOs, in the first Durban Conference, tightened their rules to preclude unfair attacks on Israel, and because the U.S. and EU took a leadership role in insisting on shifting the focus from Israel to genuine human rights deprivations around the world.

But in general, most human rights organizations have also called worldwide attention to gross violations of human rights, including genocide, in ways that did not exist a few decades ago. Doctors Without Borders has done a courageous job of publicizing human rights abuses and providing medical service to civilians trapped in genocides and civil conflicts in Africa. Human Rights First undertook an important study of anti-Semitism in Europe, calling attention to the rise of anti-Semitic actions on the continent. Freedom House issues an annual democracy report, which has a sting to it when it downgrades nations, as it did in 2007 with Russia, dropping it into the "not free" category. But its 2009 downgrade of Israel's press to the "partially free" category was a mistake, which I protested as Freedom House's vice chairman at the time, and in 2010 Israel was restored to its highest designation.

Transparency International issues annual reports ranking countries according to their levels of corruption. This has an impact on how investors view prospects of doing business in nations with a high corruption index. To its credit, Israel has never had a low rating, but there is a troubling increase in charges of fraudulent conduct against senior ministers, including former prime minister Ehud Olmert.

When he served as prime minister of Britain, Tony Blair strengthened the anticorruption effort of the OECD with a new voluntary code of conduct, called the Extractive Industries Transparency Initiative (EITI). Companies engaged in mining and oil and gas exploration—long in the vanguard of corruption because they deal most often with officialdom—were encouraged to "publish what you pay" by revealing the royalties disbursed to foreign governments for their mineral wealth. Such codes of conduct, whether orchestrated by official treaty or voluntary participation, are far from perfect but can be extremely useful and in the long run may reduce bribery of foreign officials through public naming and shaming. This can provide a greater share of a nation's bounty to its citizens instead of its corrupt leaders. I saw this operation when I served on a panel, appointed by Lord John Browne, then BP chairman, to provide advice on how the company and commercial partners could make their pipeline from the Caspian Sea to the Turkish port of Ceyhan a model of social and environmental sensitivity. BP was the first oil company to follow the initiative, and Azerbaijan became the first nation to sign on.

Another promising and uniquely modern type of global institution, designed for a diverse globalized world with multiple power centers, can be useful to Israel. These are organizations with no headquarters or secretariat, no charter or rules; they have participants, not members. Professor Amitai Etzioni of George Washington University cites the Proliferation Security Initiative (PSI) and argues that more streamlined and simple groups can form the building blocks of effective global governance in the twenty-first century. It is an organization in only the barest sense of the word but requiring a high degree of informal multinational cooperation among states—a multinational effort led by the United States that involves the interdiction of ships thought to be carrying nuclear materials. More than ninety member countries voluntarily participate, including Russia, France, and the UK, but not China. The participants share intelligence and coordinate their armed forces to interdict suspect ships and aircraft, and they can act swiftly without having to deal with a laborious and often fruitless complaint process through the UN Security Council.

PSI's most prominent accomplishment was blocking a 2003 delivery to Libya of equipment for enriching uranium produced in Malaysia, based on a design provided by the network led by Pakistani scientist Abdul Qadeer Khan. Following a U.S. request, the owner of the ship diverted it to a port in Italy, also a PSI participant, where agents of the Italian government searched the vessel and seized parts for gas centrifuges.[37]

The very fact that the PSI is not a permanent, fixed body but is purely operational in nature makes it an effective player and a less visible target. The Internet can help other informal but potentially effective international bodies by promoting instant sharing of information to meet a variety of shared global challenges. One pressing example is the cooperation of key countries, including China, against Somali pirates boarding commercial ships to hold the crew hostage and extort ransom.

Missing Out on Globalization: The Arab Development Deficit

Israel's adversaries in the Arab world have fallen far behind in virtually all measures of growth valued in a globalized economy. But Israel and world Jewry should take cold comfort. A prosperous, vibrant Arab world means as much to its own citizens as it does to the interests of the United States and Israel. Unemployment, poor governance, and lack of adequate public services drive dissatisfied citizens to fundamentalism and terrorism that would have much less allure in a stable, prosperous Arab society.

The statistics are astonishing. According to the most recent UN-produced Arab Human Development Report, written by Arab experts, the total number of books translated into Arabic in the last *millennium* was fewer than those translated into Spanish in *one* year. Greece, with a population of 11 million, translates five times more annually than all twenty-two Arab countries combined.

Literature is only one aspect of the Arab world's problems. The first Arab Human Development Report, published in 2002, noted that the GDP of all Arab countries combined was less than that of Spain and that over the last quarter century, real GDP per capita has actually fallen. Throughout the 1990s exports from the region (70 percent of which are oil or oil related) grew at only 1.5 percent, far below the average global rate of 6 percent; the total non-oil exports of the Arab world are less than that of tiny Finland.

It is no coincidence that of the world's six major regions, the Middle East and Arab North Africa received the lowest democracy rating from Freedom House. The Arab countries also have the highest illiteracy rates and one of the lowest numbers of active research scientists with frequently cited articles. The 2009 Arab Human Development Report sharpened the critique examining the area through "the lens of human security."[38] It notes the "fragility of the region's political, social, economic and environment structures, in the lack of people-centered development policies and in its vulnerability to outside intervention."

While the Israeli-Palestinian conflict is mentioned, unlike too many Arab political leaders and commentators, the report does not advance it as an excuse for the lack of progress. Instead, the report focuses on repression of political activity, martial law and protracted emergency rule, and the social phenomenon of "ingrained male dominance."

It is precisely these failings that led to the Arab Spring. Hopefully, the energy released by the upheavals against repressive regimes, and the greater political, social, and economic freedom they portend, will unleash the full potential of the Arab people to take their place in the new globalized world. But the early promise of the Arab Spring has already turned into the 2011 summer of discontent and an Islamic winter, as Islamic political parties are assuming power for the first time in the modern era, following elections, with slow progress toward democracy. The Arab Spring will not produce immediate and positive results. It will take far more than demonstrations in the streets, as courageous as they have been, and one election, to build a thoroughly modern society with democratic institutions and economic models that produce growth and jobs at a time when other emerging nations are rushing ahead. Years of hard work and commitment are needed for the Arab world to meet global norms, and time is not on their side.

Indeed, there is a likelihood that rather than opening up the economies of the Arab world, the populist resentment at decades of repression may express itself in state-dominated, protectionist economic policies that will set back the Arab world still further. In an age of globalization, Arab growth and development will remain stagnant until structural barriers can be overcome.

Whether these conditions will be alleviated by the political upheaval across the Arab world is impossible to foresee. But whatever the outcome, the Arab world is sitting on a demographic time bomb. Population is expected to grow by about 40 percent during the next two decades—almost 150 million additional people, the equivalent of two new Egypts. But these countries already have the world's lowest employment rates and some of the highest rates of youth unemployment.[39]

Israel and the Diaspora in a Globalized World

Historically, change has been threatening to world Jewry. Events that have harmed the world at large, from the Black Death of the Middle Ages to the Great

Depression of the 1930s, have had a uniquely severe impact on Jews, who were often also blamed for the calamities. But I do not believe the disruptive changes wrought by globalization and the technology revolution will have a similar impact on Jews in this century. Despite the enormous pain wrought on millions in the Great Recession, anger at Wall Street has rarely been aimed at Jews.

For sure, the blogosphere has been fertile ground for traditional attacks on Jewish bankers and businesses as economic crises deepened, but there is little evidence of such old-fashioned Jewish scapegoating. The Bernard Madoff scandal has not helped, but a majority of his victims were Jewish individuals or Jewish charitable and educational institutions, and this has done long-term damage to Jewish philanthropy.[40] Even though financial institutions from as far away as Spain suffered large losses as well, the Madoff scandal did not set off a wave of anti-Semitism, even in the midst of the financial crisis. For most people, Madoff was seen for what he was: a crook and con man extraordinaire. The lessons of the Holocaust and the rise of the rule of law are increasingly embedded in Diaspora societies, and these help protect Jews from threats that might have otherwise arisen.

The age of globalization and the digital revolution are net positives for Israel and world Jewry. An interconnected and interdependent world can make the Jewish state and the Jewish people safer. The mutual interdependence of a globalized world makes conventional wars between nations less likely and undercuts support for terrorist groups and countries that seek to upset the new globalized world order. The more Israel can embed itself and its citizens in the global economy and global economic governance, the more secure they will be.

The recent financial turmoil presents a mixed picture. Individual Israeli investors were buffeted by the crisis, and Israeli investment in East European real estate has been largely funded by Eastern European banks that fell victim in turn to the credit crunch. Israeli entrepreneurs, who relied on a quick turnaround during the boom period, are stuck, and many are fearful of not being able to meet their debts.

But Israel was largely shielded from the worst effects through excellent monetary management and prudent supervision by Israel's central bank under Stanley Fischer; Israel's banks purchased few U.S. toxic assets and were not fully integrated into the global financial structure. Growth declined and unemployment rose, but Israel emerged faster than the United States and Europe from the Great Recession and enjoyed solid growth in 2011, while the U.S. and Europe struggle to regain their balance.

Clearly, the past few years have seen Israel play a larger role in many key multilateral institutions than ever in history: Israel was a founding member of the World Trade Organization and has worked hard in trade talks. In 2000, after years of exclusion, Israel was finally accepted into a regional grouping at the UN, which is where most of the UN's serious diplomacy takes place. In 2006, Israel's Magen David Adom was accepted as a full member of the

International Committee of the Red Cross, after decades of campaigning. And in 2008, in an unprecedented move, King Abdullah of Saudi Arabia invited Israelis to participate in an international gathering on interfaith dialogue. In 2010 Israel was admitted to the Organisation for Economic Co-operation and Development (OECD), the club of advanced industrial nations.

However, Israel remains on the periphery of many key institutions and the focus of disproportionate attack and attention by many international organizations. While the United Nations has moved beyond its infamous 1975 resolution condemning Zionism as "a form of racism and racial discrimination," its Commission on Human Rights was for years a prime launching forum for attacks on the Jewish state. The body was led by flagrant abusers of human rights—Zimbabwe, Cuba, and Sudan are members—and Israel was its perpetual whipping boy. Boycotted by the Bush administration, the commission metamorphosed into a Human Rights Council in 2006, because of concerns that serial human rights violators were members of the commission and that it had become overly politicized. As a result, the Obama administration agreed to take a seat on the body, designed to be more robust and less politicized. Little has changed, and Israel is still the focus of disproportionate attacks. In 2006–2007, for example, a majority of the country-specific resolutions passed by the UN General Assembly involved Israel. This pattern also can be observed in less egregious form in other UN institutions such as the Security Council, where Israel's interests are protected by an American veto.

In the 1960s the UN Commission on Human Rights shifted its focus to colonial abuses and especially apartheid in South Africa. Once Israel captured Palestinian territory in the Six Day War, occupied it, and then began settling it as a matter of official policy, Israel became a human rights target. Anne Bayefsky, an international law professor at York University in Toronto, found that for over thirty years, Israel had been the subject of one-third of the resolutions condemning human rights violations. In 2002, the UN Commission on Human Rights approved a resolution affirming the right of Palestinians to fight Israel "by all available means, including armed struggle." This led Alfred Moses, a former U.S. ambassador to the commission, and later chairman of UN Watch, to declare that "a vote in favor of this resolution is a vote for Palestinian terrorism."[41]

The Goldstone Commission's 2009 report on the Gaza War has done more political damage to Israel's reputation than any single document since Israel's founding, notwithstanding Judge Richard Goldstone's later recanting of its major finding that Israel had committed war crimes. The Gaza investigation was authorized by the Human Rights Council.

The international judicial arena could pose challenges for Israel. International criminal justice has been publicly legitimized with the creation of the Hague-based International Criminal Court (ICC), established in 1998 when 120 states, not including Israel and the United States, adopted the Rome Statute. It is the first permanent treaty-based international criminal court designed to end the immunity of political figures for serious human rights violations. Before the ICC, there was a series of ad hoc courts created, such as the International Criminal Tribunal for the former Yugoslavia to persecute the perpetrators of "ethnic cleansing" and for the genocide in Rwanda. This should be heartening for a nation born after the Holocaust and in the shadow of the Nuremberg trials, which prosecuted Nazis for crimes against humanity, then a new concept.

But for Israel, the misuse by the international community of human rights against Israel led it not to participate in the ICC. Most recently, the ICC has threatened to investigate Israel's conduct in the Gaza War. The U.S. military strongly opposed the ICC because of fears of politically motivated trials against U.S. soldiers, so that while President Clinton signed the Rome Treaty it was never ratified by the U.S. Senate. If the ICC can focus on genuine genocides and war crimes, it has the potential to do much good, but it must prove itself capable of impartial judicial decisions.

Some states have attempted to extend their judicial reach beyond their borders in the name of human rights, and with notable success. Spain boxed in the retired Chilean dictator Augusto Pinochet while he was visiting Britain with a warrant for his arrest on human rights charges, driving him home to Chile until he died there. But this process can be heavily politicized. Belgium attempted to prosecute Ariel Sharon for alleged crimes during the 1981 Lebanon War, while refusing to investigate militant extremists on Israel's borders. The UK has an investigation against then Foreign Minister Tzipi Livni and Defense Minister Ehud Barak, which prevents both from going to England, for fear of arrest.

The rise of multilateral organizations to cope with globalization suggests that Israel needs a stronger focus on this aspect of its international engagement. Active diplomacy is equally important in bilateral relations and within formal institutions. A good opportunity exists for Israel to reintroduce itself to the world. Throughout the 1960s, when Israel itself was facing existential threats and still building its own economy, Jerusalem dispatched hundreds of experts across Africa and other parts of the developing world. Israel was celebrated as a leading donor to Africa by focusing expertise and resources on the newly independent states of the continent, and for a time Israel was also rewarded with their diplomatic support at the UN. The Six Day War left Israel isolated from them, but since the end of the Cold War, Israeli diplomats have returned to Africa. They should be followed by Israeli businessmen and the return of Israeli government development aid.

Globalization is far from an unvarnished positive. Israel faces a challenge similar to that of other industrial democracies in a globalized world economy, leading the former president of Ben-Gurion University, Avishai Braverman, now a member of the Knesset, to warn: "Globalization is a greater threat to Israel than even Iran." His concerns rest primarily on globalization's unequal distribution of benefits in Israeli society, which were foreseen well before the wave of demonstrations in 2011 protesting a perceived lack of social justice.[42] As far back as 2007 one in five Israelis (15 percent of Jews and half of Israeli Arabs) reported cutting back on food because of straitened finances, compared with only 10 percent in Europe. Israel has a significant income disparity compared to the twenty-seven nations in the European Union.[43]

Close to one in four Israelis live close to poverty despite the nation's high-tech boom—or perhaps because of the high-tech sector's propensity to reward the educated and their already rich investors.[44] In 2011 thousands of Israelis took to the streets in one of the first social protests in Israeli history. The broad, peaceful demonstrations urged more comprehensive benefits for average Israelis flowing from Israel's stunning economic success in the global world, from housing to better social services, educational investments, and job opportunities. As a result, Prime Minister Netanyahu appointed a distinguished panel of experts and has endorsed many of their findings for action to benefit the middle class and poor. The Knesset is considering action on some of the panel's recommendations.

But the gap within Israel is made more severe by the condition of its Arab citizens and the ultra-Orthodox Jews, most of them wards of the state because they lack education essential to work in a modern society. There is a troubling parallel between the economic status of Israeli Arabs and Israeli ultra-Orthodox, but for far different reasons. For Israeli Arabs it is lack of education and job opportunities excluding them from the Israeli Jewish mainstream, intensified by discrimination. For the Haredim, large families keep young mothers at home, often tending to up to a dozen children while the fathers spend the day studying Talmud and Torah at subsidized yeshivas.

There is an even greater gap between Israel and its Palestinian neighbors. The lack of integration between the Palestinian and Israeli economies and the Palestinians' absence of access to modern technology and quality education have placed them in an economic straitjacket. In a very real way they are being shut out of the globalized modern world. Although Israel legitimately feels constrained by security from integrating the Palestinians more fully, the economic and political price has been high.

Before the Second Intifada, there was hope for a nascent, mutually beneficial economic relationship. During the Clinton administration, I was responsible for the economic dimension of the peace process. With U.S. encouragement and the cooperation of then prime minister Netanyahu and later prime minister Ehud Barak, Israel allowed more than 100,000 Palestinian workers into Israel daily. Half came legally and the rest with government acquiescence, offering Israel reliable, inexpensive labor and accounting for 40 percent of the Palestinian Authority's GDP. Some 20,000 VIP passes were granted to Palestinian businessmen to travel by car into Israel proper. The Gaza Industrial Estate, which I visited in July 2000 as deputy Treasury secretary, was made a qualifying industrial zone by American legislation to offer tariff-free imports for products containing a minimum of Israeli content that stimulated the economy. From 1997 to 2000 GDP grew by an annual average of 5 percent in the Palestinian territories, and unemployment fell to 8 percent in the West Bank and 14 percent in Gaza.

But politics trumped economics, as it so often has in the Middle East. Yasser Arafat declared the Second Intifada, following the failure of the Camp David Summit in 2000 and Ariel Sharon's provocative visit to Jerusalem's Muslim shrine on the Temple Mount. But this sort of economic stimulus through trade and investment concessions remains the model to seek now. While an economic dimension does not guarantee political progress, it nevertheless helps create the space for a political solution. And though the heady days of 2000 have not returned, there are some signs of an economic rebirth, at least in the West Bank. Under the tutelage of Prime Minister Salam Fayyad, a former IMF economist who preaches and practices incorruptibility and institution building from the bottom up, the West Bank is slowly rebuilding economically and beginning to again reach out to the world. GDP growth in 2009 in the West Bank was about 7 percent and near double-digit levels in 2010 and 2011. But with Fayyad a potential casualty of the 2011 pact between Fatah and Hamas, if it is ever implemented, economic progress is uncertain even though it is essential for maintaining a relative peace in the West Bank.

Despite its dislocations, globalization offers special advantages for world Jewry and Israel. The new globalized digital world allows Jews to connect to people of other religions and has the potential to break down barriers of mutual distrust. The globalized economy puts a special premium on education, flexibility, and mobility, historic Jewish strengths gained from centuries of adapting to oppression. Mobility has been a requirement of survival, and young Jews work for global institutions, from Hong Kong and Shanghai to São Paulo and Mumbai.

As "People of the Book," Jews have historically prized education, now the key ingredient for competing in a globalized world. In the U.S., more than 80 percent of American Jewish college-age students pursue higher education, a proportion twice that of the total population. Israel's advantage over the Arab world in science and technology is demonstrated by the dramatic fact that between 1980 and 2000, 7,652 patents were registered by Israelis in the United States. The Arab world registered only 367 during the same time period.

The absence of Jewish communal life in the places around the globe where the best and brightest young Jewish men and women increasingly will be working, living, and finding mates (in Asia, for example), threatens even more assimilation and intermarriage with the local population. This will greatly complicate the maintenance of Jewish identity and the creation of a critical mass necessary to maintain a Jewish community. To accomplish this, new Jewish communal institutions must be built, including "virtual" communities on the Internet.

Cohesive Jewish communities exist in major Latin American cities, such as Buenos Aires and Rio de Janeiro, and in Hong Kong. The Chabad Lubavitch movement, which originated in the eighteenth century in Eastern Europe, is the most global Jewish institution. With four thousand rabbis and 150-plus Chabad houses around the world, they are often the only Jewish presence in some of the fastest-growing Asian cities, from South Korea, Thailand, and Cambodia to two in Vietnam, in Ho Chi Minh City, and Hanoi. They all offer hospitality; religious, social, and recreational activities; a welcoming Jewish presence; and kosher meals. Non-Orthodox groups such as the American Jewish Committee are also beginning their outreach to far-flung Jewish communities.

An excellent book by Dan Senor and Paul Singer, *Start-Up Nation: The Story of Israel's Economic Miracle,* describes how the leadership skills learned in compulsory military service, along with immigrants, who must build a new life from scratch, have led Israel to have more companies listed on the American NASDAQ index than any other foreign country.[45] With a third of its population born outside the country—a product of waves of immigration from Eastern Europe, the Arab countries, and Ethiopia as well as aliyah from throughout the Diaspora since 1948—and more than half of the population traveling abroad at least once a year, Israel is more globally aware than nearly any other nation-state. It boasts the highest number of engineers per capita (135 per 10,000 people, compared with 85 per 10,000 in the U.S.) and the highest number of cell phones per capita. Three-quarters of Israelis use the Internet, with 1.25 million households online—95 percent of which have broadband connections.[46]

From a business perspective, this represents a significant advantage. Connections to the wider world by personal and, increasingly, digital experience can help Israeli entrepreneurs break out of their classic constraint of a small home market and seek foreign markets to nourish their companies. Some of the most successful borderless technologies—such as those finding a home on the web—have Israeli roots, including the world's first Windows-based instant messaging software systems (ICQ) and one of the first Internet firewall and billing companies (Checkpoint, Amdocs). Even Israel's kibbutzim, which lost some 50,000 members since the mid-1980s, have moved from their socialist roots to seek world markets for their products.

Kibbutz Gan Shmuel, where some of my relatives live, is an example as it exports juice concentrate and tropical fish to Europe and around the world. Kibbutz Kissufim, established after independence as a frontline fighting commune on the Gaza border, progressed over the years from field labor to manufacturing eyeglasses to growing high-value organic fruits and vegetables for export to Europe.

For the Jewish people, the growing interconnectivity of the planet is a profoundly positive development helping to overwhelm the inevitable anti-Semitic blogs that also travel globally. It can break down barriers of distrust, diminish negative stereotypes, and integrate the Jewish people and the State of Israel. Even the Hebrew language need not be a barrier for Israelis in communicating with the rest of the world, as Google, Yahoo!, and Microsoft now have software that provides instant translations.

Globalization necessitates global interdependence and cooperation, one of the greatest protections of Israel and the Jewish people, and must be reflected in a style of governance that can no longer go it alone. The benefits of such interdependence are far greater than economic survival and financial success. Countries that are dependent on each other for their economic health rarely go to war. This was the main impetus for creating the postwar structures that coalesced to become the European Union. The more Israel can leverage its global connectivity to promote investment and interdependence, the more it can be embedded in the global economy, the greater advantage the nation takes of globalization, the more secure it will be.

Israel can learn from the United States. Despite its size and wealth, the U.S. is as dependent on other countries as other states are on it. More than 5 percent of the U.S. workforce is employed by U.S. operations of foreign companies, jobs that generate an equal number of secondary jobs. One in ten Americans directly relies on foreign investment for employment and is consequently *personally* invested in the health of not just America but also the home countries from which their employers are based. The more Israel can encourage other states to become similarly bound up in its own success and stability, the better the outcome for Israel. Israel must make itself more central to the economies of as many countries as possible.

But there is also an unsettling scenario that can be imagined in which the Israeli bureaucracy, alternatively described by some Israeli entrepreneurs and manufacturers as sclerotic or simply backward, impedes development, and an antiquated tax code has intensified the inequality of Israeli incomes. The red tape and high tax rates are relics of the determinedly egalitarian past, with its socialist ideological tenets that have failed to adjust to rising wealth. A 2006 study suggested that the Israeli middle class pays the world's highest taxes; Shraga Brosh, the president of the Manufacturers Association of Israel, argues that "Israel has opened itself up to globalization and free trade [and can compete; but Israel] lags behind the world it is competing with in the areas of taxation and governance."[47]

In measuring the ease with which Israelis can commence and operate businesses, the state is ranked in the middle of the pack—right behind Moldova and ahead of Turkey but far below Saudi Arabia, Tunisia, and Mongolia, let alone the Western states to which Israel rightfully compares itself. Amnon Rubinstein, a liberal lawyer and former cabinet member, writes that this "red tape mania" has sent developers fleeing abroad with their capital and energies, "causing damage greater than any Arab boycott."[48] There is also growing international competition for the technical and engineering talent in Israel so prized by foreign investors in the nation's firms. Israel may have the highest number of engineers per capita, but that still adds up to fewer than 100,000—or about one-sixth of the number of engineers graduated *every year* by China and one-third by India. Israel must work to retain its homegrown talent to keep its competitive edge, but as mentioned in chapter 1, has experienced a significant exodus of scientists and engineers living outside of Israel, most in the United States. Israel needs to differentiate its engineering talent by quality and ingenuity to avoid being buried under the growing weight of Asian expertise. Israel will maintain its comparative advantage and Israeli talent will be sought out only as long as Israel continues to focus on ensuring that its engineers are among the highest quality, best paid, and most innovative.

Still, Israel has the third-highest rate of entrepreneurship in the world—and the highest rate among women and people over fifty-five—which is even more impressive in light of the high taxes necessary to support a large military as well as the hurdles of licensing that must be overcome to start a business, let alone to make it a going concern.

But there are troubling indications that Israel's educational system is not receiving the funds necessary to maintain the quality of its workforce. Technical education must get as much priority as yeshiva learning. Nothing is more important to Israel's long-term standing in the new globalized world order than an educated population, and not just among elites.

Finally, to reap the full benefits of globalization, peace with the Palestinians, and eventually with the wider Arab world, is an important precondition. Evidence comes from the economic advantages of the 1993 Oslo Accords, which directly promoted a global embrace and attracted more multinational corporations to Israel in the hope of long-lasting peace and security that businesses need to flourish anywhere.

Israel must help ensure that the Palestinians are allowed to prosper and take advantage of globalization as well, because the alternative scenarios are unpleasant. The Israeli government's policy of encouraging the expansion of settlements has serious consequences for Israel's relations with the U.S., and for its global reputation, while angering the Palestinians and complicating their economic plight. This is not a viable policy for dealing with what is already a poverty-ridden, violence-prone territory on Israel's doorstep.

Instead, Israel must seek an economic interdependence with the West Bank and eventually Gaza, as it did before the Second Intifada of late 2000. There are obviously security imperatives before Israel completely relaxes restrictions, but isolating the territories from the Israeli and wider global economy raises even more compelling security considerations. The seemingly inexorable expansion of settlements and the restraint of movement by checkpoints, even though significantly reduced by Prime Minister Netanyahu, undercut the West Bank moderates and strengthen the argument of Hamas and the radicals that only violence will succeed. When Palestinians must spend several hours to reach jobs, schools, and hospitals, it can only build up anger and frustration and impede economic development. Obviously, restrictions on movement must be balanced against the threat of terrorism—but that is the purpose of the security fence, and it has worked remarkably well to reduce the incidence of Palestinian violence within Israel.

If peace comes to the territories and the region, Israel will be far better positioned to address its challenges and choose its own best course. Israel would do well to follow the late Yitzhak Rabin's wise counsel of fighting terror as if there were no negotiations, but simultaneously negotiating as if there were no terror.

At the end of the day, globalization and internal innovation will lead Israel to fare as well as any developed economy coming out of the Great Recession. This process makes the early decades of the new century one of the most challenging and exciting periods in history. Dealing with globalization, and adapting to its best and worst aspects, is not a choice but a necessity. The closer integration of the world economy, the growing interdependence, and the technological advances can no more be stopped than the legendary King Canute could order the waves to halt. What can and should be done is to both prepare for this irreversible tide so that more people can benefit from it and adopt programs, such as lifetime learning, job retraining, and adjustment assistance, to mitigate its negative impacts on the less educated and less skilled members of society. If architects of the new global economic structure are able to fashion a more stable foundation, world Jewry and Israel will be more secure. Modern society cannot flourish without it. I believe global problems are so palpable, and affect so many nations, that a consensus will form to strengthen global institutions to deal with them, to the benefit of the United States, Israel, the Jewish people, and the world.

3

Uncharted Waters: The Struggle for the Direction of Islam

<hr>

T HE CHOICES MADE DURING the early decades of this century by more than one and a half billion Muslims around the globe about the way their religion affects their personal and political lives, and whether or not they choose to be fully integrated into the globalized world and its institutions and to adopt its emerging international norms, will have a profound impact on the West in general and the Jewish world in particular.

Hundreds of millions of Muslims, particularly in Asian nations such as Indonesia and Malaysia, have enjoyed the fruits of global integration. The Gulf States and Saudi Arabia are modernizing but at a glacial speed in a world moving at digital speed. And a small but lethal minority of Islamic terrorists, many supported by Iran, have perverted their religion into a jihad to destroy the modern world, the West and Muslim states allied with the U.S., and Israel; to violently destroy the modern order; and to impose an Islamic caliphate in the region, based on fundamentalist sharia law.

The battle for the direction of Islam has been joined with breathtaking speed in the broadest upheaval within Arab Middle Eastern autocratic states since most gained their independence after World War II. Too often oversimplified as a "war of civilizations" against the West, it is as much an internal battle for the mind of the Muslim world, and it will also engage the energies of the Arab peoples and the Western world for decades. The tectonic plates of the Arab world have violently shifted with the political earthquake called the Arab Spring, first in Tunisia, then Egypt, Bahrain, Yemen, Libya, and even Syria. If the hope of the 2011 Arab revolution is realized, which is much in doubt, it will free up the suppressed energies and talents of the Arab world to the betterment of its people and the world. But it has already profoundly and irreversibly changed established pro-American alliances, leading to less U.S. influence in the region and to increased hostility toward Israel, which will continue at least until the Palestinian issue is resolved with a Palestinian state, alongside Israel.

The Intersection of the Muslim and Jewish Worlds

There was a long period of time when Jewish history and the development and spread of the Islamic faith overlapped in profound ways. The founding of the Muslim religion by the Prophet Mohammed in the late sixth century had an immediate impact on the Jews; defeat of a Jewish tribe and its allies by the Muslims of Medina in 628 ended in the Jews being granted protection, with conditions. The Koran's attitude toward infidels whether Christians or Jews is read in different ways by the Muslims themselves, but relations between Jews and Muslims were shaped throughout the Middle Ages by the Koran's mandate to tolerate "the People of the Book" in exchange for tribute payments (*jizya*) and the Jews' acceptance of an inferior social status.[1]

With the dramatic expansion of Islam into the Arabian Peninsula, Persia (now Iran), the Middle East, North Africa, and southern Europe, as many as 90 percent of medieval Jews lived in countries that had fallen to the great wave of Muslim conquest. Jewish language and culture were profoundly affected by Islam. Jews lived in a golden age in Spain as high officials and advisers to Muslim not Christian rulers, and Maimonides flourished in Egypt, where his most famous works were produced and almost magically found in Cairo only a few decades ago.

While the Jewish minorities were never fully integrated into Muslim majority countries, the Jews were treated far better, up to the time of the birth of the modern State of Israel, than at the hands of Christian-majority nations, where for much of Jewish history, the brutality was extraordinary.

For much of what we think of as modern history, from the Middle Ages to the twentieth century, the relationship with the expanding Christian world affected Jews most directly. From the violence of the first Crusade in 1096, along their path to the Holy Land, and in their capture of Jerusalem, fate of the Jews was in jeopardy. Jews were blamed for the Black Death in the mid-fourteenth century. The Christian reconquest of Spain led to the expulsion of Jews in 1492 from Spain, and the inquisition of those who converted and remained, and then a few years later from Portugal. But even before that, Jews had been expelled from England in 1290 and from large parts of France in 1501. By then Jews were almost nonexistent in Western Europe. They resettled in the Ottoman Empire, where they were protected and flourished under Muslim sultans. This again is in sharp contrast with Central and Eastern Europe and Russia, where pogroms and discrimination, special dress requirements, severe limitations on occupational opportunities, the Czarist requirement to live in the Pale of Settlement culminated in the Holocaust, the destruction of two-thirds of European Jewry.

The Islamic world went into centuries of retreat. But today, a confluence of factors again makes the Muslim religion and culture a central force in Jewish as well as world history. With the founding of the modern State of Israel the status of Jews in Arab lands dramatically changed. The Arab nations united in their determination to expel the Jews from what they considered an Islamic land. They went to war against Israel in 1948, 1967, and 1973, in an attempt to "throw the Jews into the sea." And with the founding of the Jewish state, Jews who had lived in relative peace and tranquility in Arab countries for centuries were forced to flee to Israel, leaving behind their personal possessions and their businesses.

Other factors have brought the Muslim world back to the center of the global arena. Lacking job opportunities in their home countries and invited to Europe as guest workers, Muslims from North Africa and Turkey immigrated en masse and stayed; more than 15 million Muslims, their number likely doubling in thirty years, are profoundly changing the face of Europe and its politics. In France, the Muslim community represents 10 percent of the population and close to that in Belgium. In Austria, around half the first graders in Vienna's public schools are Muslims or children of immigrants. In many European countries they have been poorly integrated. In Germany it was only during the government of Chancellor Gerhard Schroeder in the 1990s that Turkish immigrants could become citizens regardless of how long they had been in the country, and in 2011 Chancellor Angela Merkel proclaimed that "multiculturalism" had failed in Germany and could not work.

The demographics are compelling. Muslims in Europe have three times the birthrate of Christians and Jews. If one million Islamic immigrants continue arriving on the continent each year, by 2050 one in five Europeans will likely be Muslim. The chairman of the Green Party in Germany is from a Turkish Muslim family, and the mayor of Rotterdam is also a Muslim. Even if these population and immigration trends moderate and are constrained by political backlash, they presage a change in European politics that is likely to push European policies in directions unfavorable to Europe's Jews and Israel. Now only 0.4 percent of the European population, European Jewry, with its falling birthrate, will be even more marginalized.

There is a broader demographic reality that ensures the Muslim world a major place on the twenty-first-century agenda. Islam is the world's fastest-growing religion, and in 2008 it surpassed Catholicism as the world's largest.[2] In the Arab countries alone, the population has nearly tripled since 1970, to over 350 million in 2010, and by 2050, with rapid population increases, the Arab world will increase by two-thirds, to almost 600 million people. The populations of only four countries or areas, Somalia, Yemen, and Iraq, all of which are in the midst of violent conflicts, and the Palestinians in the West Bank and Gaza, on Israel's backdoor, are expected to double between today and 2050.

Children under fifteen years of age make up an astounding one-third of the entire Arab population, and 54 percent is now under the age of twenty-five. The Palestinian Authority has the youngest median age in the Middle East and one of the youngest in the world at only 17.6 years of age. This is a force to be reckoned with, which the U.S. and Israel ignore at their peril. Time is not on Israel's side for peace with a restless, heavily unemployed young population next door.[3]

The dependence of the U.S. and Europe on Middle Eastern oil also makes the Muslim world critical to the West and has a special impact on Israel. By the early 1970s, domestic production in the U.S. declined, and the U.S. began importing oil in large quantities from the Middle East and the Gulf States. The implications were first seen dramatically in the 1973 Arab oil embargo imposed during the Yom Kippur War, and then a second oil shock in 1979 followed the Iranian Revolution. Much of America's foreign policy in the Middle East, including enormous arms sales to Saudi Arabia, the largest producer of crude oil, and the Gulf states has been driven by the need to secure oil supplies for the West. Although the U.S. dependence on Arab oil is actually declining, and the U.S. imports more oil from Canada than Saudi Arabia, it remains a major geopolitical factor. Certainly, the first Gulf War, in which President George H.W. Bush properly injected U.S. forces when Saddam Hussein's Iraqi forces invaded Kuwait, was recognition of the importance of the region as a crucial source of energy.

It would be a tragic mistake to view the Muslim world as a whole through the prism of Islamic terrorism, which is as much a threat to the vast majority of peaceful Muslims as it is to the populations of western countries and Israel. But at the same time, the most dramatic force behind the revival of the Muslim world's importance on the global agenda is the rise of an unconventional form of warfare—terrorism, supported by Iran and Syria but performed by Islamic non-state terrorist organizations and actors. Terrorism takes many forms and is as old as recorded warfare. The official U.S. government definition is a violent act dangerous to human life intended "(i) to intimidate or coerce a civilian population; (ii) to influence the policy of a government by intimidation or coercion; or (iii) to affect the conduct of a government by assassination or kidnapping."[4] Islamic radicals have no monopoly. For example, the Irish Republican Army through much of the twentieth century sporadically terrorized its own people, the British army, and civilians in England to end British rule in Northern Ireland.

But a number of elements have made twenty-first-century Islamic terrorism distinctive. Its global reach and its wide geographic operational capabilities increasingly extend far beyond the Middle East to major Western and Asian cities that have no direct connection to the Islamic world's dispute with Israeli in locations as diverse as Buenos Aires, Mumbai, London, Bali, Madrid, Dar es Salaam, Islamabad, Baghdad, Kabul, and parts of northern Nigeria. Three BRIC countries—Russia, India, and China—face high levels of attack from radical Islamic movements, and even Brazil is exposed, as Hezbollah profits from human and narcotics trafficking in the traditionally lawless tri-border region between Brazil, Paraguay, and Argentina. China faces a surge of attacks in its far western provinces, where the Uyghurs, a Muslim Turkic group in Xinjiang, demand political freedom and economic benefits equal to the Han Chinese. Russia has fought its own brutal battles with radical Muslims in Chechnya, who seek secession from Russia.

Many of the Middle East and Asian Islamic terrorist groups, such as the Afghan and Pakistan Taliban, al-Shabab in Somalia, and affiliates of al-Qaeda in Yemen, have a similar agenda of imposing sharia law, forcefully taking over the territories in which they are based and expelling all Western military presence. The destruction of Israel is not high on their agenda. The Islamic terrorists do not hesitate to attack other Muslim nations allied with the West or who practice a different (and usually more tolerant) brand of Islam. Meanwhile, they work to create safe havens by embedding themselves in failed, failing, or weak Muslim states such as Yemen, Somalia, Pakistan, and Afghanistan that cannot fully control their borders, most graphically Afghanistan, weakened by generations of rebellion, invasion, and civil war.

Other terrorist groups, particularly Hezbollah and Hamas, closer to Israel, have as a prime goal the forceful elimination of the Jewish state, and they strengthen their hand with social service and welfare capacities that exceed and replace governments, along with creating political wings in the fashion of the Irish Republican Army's ties to Sinn Fein. Hezbollah in Lebanon has become a virtual state within a state. Crime also plays a role in sophisticated recruitment and funding, through the informal hawala banking system employed in parts of the Muslim world.

Modern technology is an essential element of planning and operations—using all digital platforms, including satellite TV stations, websites, and cyberspace communications. In dirt poor Somalia, militants use Twitter to communicate with each other, as easily as young people from Tel Aviv to Manhattan. But for major organizations such as Hezbollah and Hamas, state support by Iran and Syria provides vast financial, moral, religious, and military underpinning, most notably Hezbollah's tens of thousands of missiles and rockets, exceeding those of many nation-states. Significantly, while all support the elimination of Israel, only Hezbollah in Lebanon and Hamas in Gaza have made this their primary goal.

Some groups such as Hezbollah have declared that they distinguish between Zionism and Judaism. But this is consistent neither with their charters and statements, which vilify Jews in terms classically used by anti-Semites through the ages, nor with their targets, which have included a Chabad house in Mumbai and the Jewish community center in Buenos Aires, as well as the Israeli Embassy there.

Terrorism in the Middle East was largely a regional threat to Israel, but at its inception it took a secular and political form. In 1955 Egyptian president Nasser began to import Soviet arms to prepare for another war with Israel. Before attacking he formed and trained the *fedayeen* (one who sacrifices himself) to infiltrate Israel and commit acts of terrorism, sabotage, and murder.[5] Nasser's creation became part of Webster's dictionary, and now in a different name has become a staple of twenty-first-century life.

The first major nonstate terrorist group was the Palestine Liberation Organization (PLO), created in 1964 by the Palestinian National Congress in Arab Jerusalem. Muslim in character, it was essentially secular in orientation, with the goal of destroying Israel as a Jewish state and replacing it with a secular Palestinian state. Shortly thereafter, Yasser Arafat became its leader and, with funding from major Arab governments, made the "liberation of Palestine" its goal. Black September 1970 became the first example of what we live with today, with Islamic terrorism directed not only against Israel and the West but against moderate Muslim states as well. The PLO launched an attack against Jordan to take over the state and was defeated only with covert Israeli help, at the request of the U.S., to save Jordan's King Hussein. The PLO was expelled from Jordan to Lebanon, where it established a "state within a state," much as Hezbollah has done in Lebanon today. After the 1982 Israeli invasion the PLO fled to Tunis. It was not until 1974, after the Yom Kippur War, that the PLO was formally recognized by the Arab world as the sole representative of the Palestinians.

Terrorism burst most spectacularly into world consciousness on September 5, 1972, when the Palestinian terrorist group Black September, an arm of the PLO, took a large number of the Israeli Olympic team hostage in the Munich Olympic Village and murdered eleven Israeli athletes and coaches. Most of the terrorists were later killed by the Israeli secret service.[6] Then Palestinian terrorists moved to hijacking airliners. The PLO was not alone. Carlos the Jackal (Ilich Ramirez Sanchez, a Venezuelan militant) worked variously with Communists and Islamic groups such as the Popular Front for the Liberation of Palestine to carry out a series of notorious airplane hijackings and attacks against other Western targets and even OPEC headquarters.

By the late 1980s, the first Intifada had broken out in the Palestinian territories to protest the Israeli occupation. It was not until the 1993 Oslo Accords signed by Israeli prime minister Yitzhak Rabin and PLO chairman Yasser Arafat on the White House lawn in the presence of President Bill Clinton that Arafat and the PLO were permitted by Israel to return to the West Bank and Gaza.

Prime Minister Yitzhak Rabin himself was assassinated by an Israeli nationalist fanatic, and with one bullet the prospects of a peace agreement with the Palestinians died with him. By then terrorism had become an established fact of life, largely directed against Israel.

The major change in its nature and scope came with the Iranian Revolution in 1979, following the overthrow of Iran's Shah Mohammad Reza Pahlavi, one of America's and Israel's closest friends in the Middle East. A popular revolution inspired by Ayatollah Ruhollah Khomeini changed the dynamics of the Middle East: He not only created the first Islamic Republic but also made its radical Shiite views one of its chief exports through support of Hezbollah and Hamas.

The face of terrorism moved beyond Israel in the 1980s to attempt to uproot the U.S. military presence in the Middle East and to attack Muslim allies of the U.S. In this decade, three major terrorist groups took root: Hezbollah in Lebanon, Hamas in Gaza (both supported by Iran), and al-Qaeda in the Afghanistan-Pakistan border region.

Since its formation in the 1980s, Hezbollah (the Party of God) has grown from the small Islamic jihad militia into a disciplined and heavily armed organization. It first mounted more than thirty suicide attacks in Lebanon against U.S., French, and Israeli forces. The most devastating was the attack on the Marine barracks in Beirut that killed 241 American servicemen, forced the Marines' withdrawal, and made it politically impossible for American troops to remain on station in the Middle East. Achieving this goal was not enough. Islamic jihadists attacked the U.S. Embassy compound with a powerful truck bomb explosion that killed twenty people and almost took the life of my personal friend, U.S. Ambassador Reginald Bartholomew. He described to me how the force of the bomb tipped a large bookcase over him; he survived only because a visiting British diplomat rescued him from the rubble.[7] Hezbollah staged airline hijackings, was behind kidnappings of American hostages, and became a major player in Lebanon's civil war through political assassinations and support of its militia.

Hezbollah receives anywhere between $60 million and $200 million annually from Iran for an estimated 1,000 full-time members and another 6,000 to 10,000 volunteers; they have amassed as many as 40,000 rockets and Iranian-made missiles that can reach Haifa and Tel Aviv. By 2010 Hezbollah had become Lebanon's kingmaker, helping squeeze the moderate prime minister, Saad Hariri, from office and replacing him with someone more to its liking, Najib Mikati. Hezbollah reaches far beyond the Middle East: With the direct help of Iran, it carried out the suicide attack on the Israeli Embassy in Buenos Aires in 1992, killing twenty-nine people, and two years later on the Jewish community center there, killing ninety-five. After years of fitful investigation, the Argentine government expelled seven Iranian diplomats.

Hezbollah employs sophisticated methods to fund its operations. The Lebanese Canadian Bank, in Beirut, for example, was found by the U.S. to be involved in a global money laundering exercise, facilitating Hezbollah officials engaged in the South American cocaine trade by moving enormous sums of drug money into their hands through the legitimate banking system. One U.S. law enforcement official ruefully said that Hezbollah operates "like the Gambinos on steroids," referring to the infamous Mafia family. The funds they receive from both Iran and Syria enables them not only to acquire weapons to use against Israel, but to fund their social service network to compete with the Lebanese state, and to acquire large plots of land in Lebanon in militarily strategic locations, mainly in Christian areas.[8]

Hamas, the acronym for the Islamic Resistance Movement, was formed during the turbulent 1980s, with a focus on eliminating the State of Israel and replacing it with an Islamic state.[9] It began in 1987 at the outset of the first Intifada as a product of Egypt's Muslim Brotherhood, the new power broker following the fall of Egyptian president Hosni Mubarak in 2011. Hamas follows Hezbollah's structure with a political leadership and a military wing, the Qassam Brigades, formed in 1991. A corps of several hundred fighters receives military training in Iran and Syria, and some 10,000 supporters are committed to violent action against Israel. Its political wing engages in Palestinian politics and has a well-developed social welfare wing, which gives it legitimacy and popularity among the people by providing social services in its main base in Gaza. Its most senior leadership is based in Damascus, but it is funded principally by Iran and Islamic charities in Saudi Arabia and in the Gulf and by Palestinian expatriates.

Hamas's history illustrates the risk of state support for terrorist groups—what intelligence experts call blowback. In Hamas's early years, Israel supported it as a counterweight to the secular nationalists in the PLO, allowing it to build mosques, schools, and social clubs in Gaza. But the violent side of Hamas soon became clear, with suicide bombings starting in 1993, the year of the Oslo Peace Accords. Hamas has sent mixed signals for years on whether it would stand by its demand for Palestinians to return to Israel in exchange for an end to Israeli occupation. In 2004 Sheikh Ahmed Yassin said Hamas would cease its armed resistance against Israel in return for a Palestinian state in the West Bank, Gaza, and East Jerusalem, leaving to "future generations" the "historical rights" of Palestinians to return to Israel. In 2006, Hamas proposed a ten-year truce in return for complete Israeli withdrawal from the territories and East Jerusalem and recognition of the Palestinian "right of return." But Hamas leader Khaled Meshal added that Hamas was not calling for an end to armed attacks against Israel.

The year before, in 2005, then Israeli prime minister Ariel Sharon withdrew troops and the civilian settlers they protected from Gaza, evicting 7,000 Israelis from twenty-one settlements in northern Gaza, along with all Israeli security forces. Nothing transformed and hardened Israeli public opinion more than what followed. Rather than accepting the withdrawal as a major step toward peace, Hamas responded by sending thousands of rockets into southern Israel, killing almost 400 Israelis and wounding more than 2,000.

Human Rights Watch independently confirmed that Hamas has launched thousands of rockets into Israel since 2001, for the direct purpose of striking Israeli civilians and threatening nearly 800,000 Israeli men, women, and children. Israel finally responded in 2008 by sending an invasion force to attack Hamas command posts and its militia, both cynically deployed among civilians to maximize the danger to its own citizens when Israel attacked, and thereby rally world opinion against Israel. It worked. While the world focused on accusations that Israel had committed war crimes, the UN's Goldstone Report found that both Hamas and Israel had committed "war crimes," the world's focus was on the accusations, later recanted by Judge Goldstone, against Israel.

But no terrorist is a more widely known product of espionage blowback than the most infamous and successful terrorist of our age, Osama bin Laden. Born in 1957 to a prominent family in Saudi Arabia, he was raised in the Wahhabi Muslim tradition, as severe and aggressive in its own way as the Shiites with whom he later allied himself against the U.S. and Israel. Like Hezbollah and Hamas, bin Laden believed that innocent civilians—men, women, and children—are legitimate targets of Islamic jihad. What radicalized him was his service funneling arms, money, and fighters from around the Arab world and the United States to the Afghan War against the Soviet invasion.[10] I was in the Carter White House when we began the military and financial support of the Afghan mujahideen in a CIA program called Operation Cyclone, to fight the Soviets, later expanded during the Reagan administration. Some of the same weapons, including the decisive handheld Stinger missiles fired against Soviet helicopters, were used against American troops by the Taliban decades later.

Bin Laden's al-Qaeda ("the database") was formed in 1988 out of the merger of thousands of militants who fought the Soviet Union in Afghanistan with the Egyptian Islamic Jihad. Al-Qaeda's goal was nothing less than the creation of an Islamic caliphate. But the pivotal turning point for bin Laden was Saudi support for the 1993 Oslo peace accords with Israel. He and his organization raised terrorism to a global level by fusing a radical jihadist interpretation of Islam with an informal network of unregulated Islamic banks and money changers known as the hawala banking system, which underwrote a seemingly endless supply of suicide bombers inspired by bin Laden and trained in camps based mainly in Afghanistan.

Bin Laden had an obsession with attacking the U.S. directly by targeting the skyscraper symbols of its financial power in Wall Street. In November 1990, the FBI razed the New Jersey home of El Sayyid Nosair, an associate of an al-Qaeda operative, finding evidence of terrorist plots to do just that. And in 1993, almost a decade before 9/11, the World Trade Center was bombed through an internal device set by Nosair, who also was convicted of murdering Rabbi Meir Kahane in 1990. Trying to duplicate Hezbollah's success in forcing the U.S. military out of Lebanon, bin Laden had the same goal in forcing the U.S. out of Saudi Arabia, where they were protecting the kingdom after Saddam Hussein's troops had been driven from Kuwait in 1991.

Al-Qaeda struck anywhere bin Laden could destroy U.S. facilities, first in 1996 at the Khobar Towers in Dhahran, Saudi Arabia, killing nineteen U.S. Air Force personnel, and then on August 7, 1998, in twin attacks against American embassies in Dar es Salaam, Tanzania, and Nairobi, Kenya. I felt the personal impact of the deaths when, as undersecretary of state I accompanied Secretary of State Albright to Dover Air Force Base in Delaware to honor the return of the flag-draped coffins, in a heart-wrenching ceremony with the families of the victims.

In 2000, al-Qaeda struck again, attacking the U.S. Navy destroyer USS *Cole* in the Yemeni port of Aden, killing seventeen American sailors. The climactic September 11 attacks on the World Trade Center and the Pentagon followed. On April 29, 2003, the normally triumphalist Defense Secretary Donald Rumsfeld announced that U.S. troops would be withdrawn from Saudi Arabia.

When the 9/11 attacks occurred, I was in my law office on Pennsylvania Avenue in Washington. My colleagues at Covington & Burling, who had just heard the news, flocked into my office to tell me of the attacks on the Twin Towers and the Pentagon. I looked out of my window and saw smoke rising from the Pentagon. The first words out of my mouth were "Osama bin Laden." As deputy secretary of the Treasury in the Clinton administration, I had been involved in the decision to place bin Laden and al-Qaeda on the terrorist financing list and freeze their assets. I felt only he could have masterminded such a complex and evil plot.

From that day to this, terrorism has been a central organizing factor in American foreign policy and a major preoccupation of the American people, changing American lifestyles and habits of thought. Bin Laden escaped his American and Afghan pursuers to a lawless mountain border area between Afghanistan and Pakistan and planned the 2004 Madrid train bombings and the July 2005 London subway and bus bombings.

His assassination on May 1, 2011, by daring and courageous Navy Seals and CIA personnel boldly ordered by President Obama, has removed the most recognizable face of global terrorism. Relentless U.S. drone attacks in the lawless Pakistan-Afghanistan border region have killed many of bin Laden's senior aides, including Atiya Abdul Rahman.[11] But while the weakened al-Qaeda central command holds out under attacks by remote-controlled aerial drones, which also killed al-Qaeda's second most important figure, it has inspired affiliates in weak or failed states as well as stronger nations in North Africa. While they still represent the greatest threat to the U.S. homeland, their looser ties with the home base and less central direction may make their thrust less predictable, their plans harder to track, and the results more scattered but still dangerous.

Al-Qaeda's most dangerous affiliate now is Al-Qaeda in the Arabian Peninsula (AQAP), based in Yemen. AQAP was behind several attempts to attack the U.S. (e.g., placing parcel bombs in a UPS cargo plane headed for the U.S. via stops in Germany and the UK). I am on the UPS board, and our board meeting came just after the discovery of the bomb through a last-minute tip from Saudi intelligence. Until then, the sophisticated plastic chemical, PETN, placed in an HP printer cartridge in a package addressed to a Chicago synagogue, had eluded detection from chemical-sniffing dogs and X-rays. Even after the cartridge was dismantled, just before the UPS plane was ready to leave for the United States, the explosive material was not initially detected. The entire operation cost AQAP less than $5,000. The intention was to disrupt the global air cargo system, adding millions to the system's security costs.[12] Even though the plot failed, there are few more striking examples of what the military calls asymmetrical combat.

Undeterred, AQAP has been trying to produce a highly lethal poison, ricin, that can kill people from just inhaling, which they are attempting to pack around explosives to target American airports and shopping malls.[13]

Fortunately, a 2011 U.S. drone attack in Yemen killed the American-born jihadist leader of AQAP, Anwar al-Awlaki, who was the mastermind behind these plots aimed at his native country. But AQAP remains the greatest threat to the U.S. homeland.

Weak States and Terrorism

AQAP's base in Yemen underscores the degree to which Islamic terrorist groups rely on bases in weak Middle Eastern states. State failure is emblematic of a further consequence of globalization that could empower the forces of militant Islam. Global economic integration has only stimulated the strengthening of tribalism; separatist groups within countries seek independence, autonomy, or secession—in Kashmir, Kurdistan, the former Yugoslavia, Sudan, Congo, and elsewhere in Africa. The resort to particularism has been accentuated as many people reject the universalism of globalization and the integration of societies by technology, which poses a challenge to their desire to retain their distinctive differences. This is particularly so for radical elements rejecting modernity in the Muslim world. They nest in Muslim states with weak governments that do not control all their own territory, such as Yemen and Somalia, and in the lawless provinces at the Afghan-Pakistan border, confident that the governments are unable or unwilling to uproot them. They attack mosques, markets, and other public places while planning what they hope will be spectacular new acts of terrorism in the U.S. and Europe.

The breakdown of Somalia is a direct cause of modern-day maritime buccaneers raiding the sea-lanes. But the consequences of failed or weak Middle Eastern states go far beyond the nuisance of Somali pirates.

Yemen is the perfect example of a failed state providing a vacuum that militant Islamic groups such as AQAP and local militants rely on. Yemen's pro-Western president Ali Abdullah Saleh was finally forced to step down after three decades in power. But his successor faces secessionist forces in the south of the country; and AQAP and Shiite rebels who have taken over significant parts of Abyan Province, including its capital city of Zinjibar.[14] Likewise, one of the factors behind the Taliban's success in Afghanistan is the inability of Pakistan to control its lawless northwest provinces, where the Taliban and al-Qaeda have their bases.

If the Israeli-Palestinian dispute were resolved tomorrow, it would certainly strengthen the hand of the moderate pro-Western regimes, but the fierce battle would nevertheless continue within the Islamic countries. In 2004 I cochaired the Center for Global Development's Commission on Weak States and U.S. National Security,[15] which included future Obama administration leaders, such as Susan Rice, now U.S. ambassador to the United Nations. The commission's mandate was to investigate how the weakness of even minor and distant states could have a devastating impact on American national security and America's close allies. We identified a set of conditions, the combination of which could lead to state failure: a "security gap," in which governments were unable to exercise full control over their territory; a "capacity gap," in which they were unable to meet the basic needs of their citizens; and a "legitimacy gap," which described a lack of identity and respect held by peoples for their leaders. These act as centrifugal forces if not addressed, stretching and perhaps breaking links that hold states together to control their borders, deliver basic services, and provide honest governance.

Failed, or weak and failing, states become security threats as havens for terrorists or drug lords, sometimes working in tandem to combine murder and money, destabilizing their neighbors and becoming focal points for radicalism and instability. Weak states are a refuge for terrorists training in Afghanistan and Somalia; transnational crime networks based in Burma and Central Asia; drug lords in Latin America who overwhelm law enforcement officials. Poverty, disease, and humanitarian emergencies overwhelm governments in Haiti and Central America. Our commission concluded that weak and failing states "form the fundamental foreign policy and security challenges of our time."

The challenge for Israel is twofold. First, neighboring Lebanon and Syria now are firmly installed on the list of states at risk, particularly with the revolution in Syria. If President Assad is forced to leave office and Syria descends into chaos, Israel will feel the brunt more than any other nation in the region. And second, failed states provide a haven for various malefactors who could harm the West and Israel. Israel is as reliant on safe sea-lanes as any export state and oil importer; Somali pirates could be devastating. Israel's continued engagement in the Horn of Africa, especially Eritrea, will also be made much more difficult. State failure in neighboring Sudan has already affected Israel through an influx of more than a thousand Darfuri refugees fleeing unspeakable abuses. Israel, born out of the ashes of the Holocaust, is obviously sympathetic but cannot manage massive inflows from African civil conflicts.

The Battle for the Soul of Islam: Extremism or Modernity

Too often, Israel and the West see Islam and its people only through the eyes of the small percentage of radicals who use their religion to justify launching their terrorist wars against the West. In fact, the Muslim world is far from monolithic, and the Islamic polity can be measured through an almost kaleidoscopic number of conflicts: Sunni and Shiite governments; states with sharp tribal lines and those with more unitary populations; jihadist states and independent terrorist groups; modernizers and fundamentalists; democratic and autocratic states; secularists and religious fundamentalists; global integrationists and rejectionists; and those who align broadly with the West and those who reject Western values and culture and seek to expunge from Islamic lands all traces of the rule of law, open expression, and representative government.

No matter what the measure, complexity renders all these simple dichotomies illusory. Muslim states in Asia, North Africa, and the Gulf are taking significant strides toward modernity that, together with the 2011 Middle Eastern revolutions propelled by the unfulfilled expectations of the educated young, have shaken the stagnant Arab world.

Indonesia, the world's most populous Muslim country, has become the world's fourth-largest democratic state since the end of the Suharto regime in 1998,[16] an adamant foe of Islamic militancy, and hence the target of jihadist terror.[17] The same is not true for Syria, which although a secular power has an odd twist: Political power is centralized in the Alawite Muslim minority and passed down among the Assad clan, which is aligned with Islamic fundamentalist Iran to support Hezbollah in Lebanon. Yet even before the popular revolt against the ruling Assad clan, Syria acted to reduce the influence of conservative Muslims, including banning the niqab, the traditional Islamic veil for women, in universities and elsewhere, much like the French.[18]

The deep and often violent schism between Sunni and Shiite Islam dates back to an eighth-century dispute over Mohammed's legacy. Shiite theology holds that divine authority was passed to holy men, or imams, beginning with Ali, son-in-law of the prophet Mohammed, who was killed in battle; suffering and martyrdom infuse their creed. Sunnis stress community and prayer, leaning toward temporal authority and stability. It is easy to see how these religious and political differences dovetail. Sunni Muslim governments are generally more favorably disposed to the West and more willing to entertain a peace accord with Israel. Iran and its radical surrogates—which include both Shiite (Hezbollah) and Sunni (Hamas) groups—are virulently anti-Western and anti-Jewish, and they refuse to accept Israel's right to exist. How these internal divisions are managed during the next decade will be crucial.

Israel can indirectly help strengthen the moderate Islamic forces by demonstrating it is doing all it can to improve the lives of the Palestinians and to reach a peace agreement, even if the divided Palestinians are unresponsive. In fact, the bitter divisions between the Palestinians in the West Bank and Gaza, even with their attempt at a unity pact, reflect the divisions within the Arab world. The Palestinian Authority, under President Mahmoud Abbas and Prime Minister Salam Fayyad, and the dominant political party in the West Bank, Fatah, are generally more moderate. The Palestinian state they wish to create would be secular and only on territory Israel did not control before the 1967 war. Hamas, on the other hand, is a radical offshoot of Egypt's Muslim Brotherhood, receives support from Iran, and refuses to recognize Israel within any borders. They fought a civil war following the 2006 Palestinian elections. The Palestinian Authority's U.S.-trained police force cooperates with the Israeli intelligence and army to track down Hamas terrorists in the West Bank.

The need for Israel to support the Palestinian Authority's leadership and strengthen it in its struggle should be obvious. Yet, for all the benefits of the 2011 agreement with Hamas that freed Gilad Shalit from his long imprisonment by Hamas, reuniting him with his family (with whom I have met) and reinforcing Israel's pledge never to abandon one of its soldiers, by exchanging more than a thousand Palestinian terrorists with Hamas, rather than to President Abbas, this action strengthened Hamas and weakened Abbas, in the eyes of the Palestinians.

At its most apocalyptic, the interaction between the Muslim world and the West including Israel, can be seen as a "clash of civilizations," in the words of the late Harvard political scientist Samuel P. Huntington, a former fellow staff member of the Carter administration who served on the National Security Council. In a 1993 *Foreign Affairs* article and then in his 1996 best seller, *The Clash of Civilizations and the Remaking of World Order*, he warned that conflicts in the post–Cold War world focus on religion and culture rather than dueling ideologies. One of those civilizations in Huntington's thesis was the Muslim world of the Middle East, which as a result of a massive population explosion and resurgence of Islamic fundamentalism he forecast would have a "bloody" confrontation with Western civilization and Israel. The 1979 Iranian Revolution was an opening chapter in this saga.[19] Elements of this conflict are certainly now evident, but even for this small, violent fringe of the Muslim world, the clash of civilizations underway inside the Muslim world is as intense if not more so than its aggressive stance toward the West and the modern world. There is more a civil war for the future of Islam than a battle between Western and Islamic civilizations.

To the extent there is a war of civilizations, it has been declared by a small but deadly group of Islamic radicals. That war of course is real, as evidenced by the number of radical Islamic terrorist attacks on targets around the world. But the war is as much a civil war within the Muslim world as it is a war against the West. But more Muslim civilians have been killed or maimed at the hands of fellow Muslim terrorists than the total of their American, European, and Israeli victims. A subplot of the Iraq War was the murderous attacks by elements of the Sunni minority to regain its control over the Shiite majority that it lost when the U.S. deposed Saddam Hussein. The wars in Afghanistan and Pakistan, the conflicts in Yemen and Somalia, all have aspects of internal religious, jihadist, or clan aspects. And the largely nonviolent uprisings of the Arab Spring stemmed from internal struggles between secular democratic forces, Islamic forces, and autocratic secular regimes.

The battlefield within the Muslim world extends from Casablanca to Jakarta, from Kabul to Khartoum, from Tunis to Islamabad. In geopolitical terms, the struggle is also one for regional hegemony. It pits the largely Sunni and pro-Western regimes of Saudi Arabia, most of the Gulf states, Jordan, and the moderate states of North Africa against an Iranian-led rejectionist coalition that includes Syria, Qatar, and their nonstate terrorist clients, Hezbollah and Hamas. Before the Arab Spring, Egypt was firmly part of the moderate, anti-Iran coalition, but it is likely to strike a more neutral posture in the future.

The internal divide between pro-Western and anti-Western Muslim states is even more complex, because the populace in the so-called Arab street is generally more religious and suspicious of the West, as well as more virulently anti-Israel than its leaders.

President Obama has reversed the Bush administration and declared in his National Security Strategy there was no "global war against Islam" but a war "against a specific network, al-Qaeda, and its terrorism affiliates." If Huntington's view of a war of civilizations was too sweeping, President Obama's is too narrow. He has defined the war on terrorism as one against al-Qaeda and its affiliates. But radical Islam extends well beyond al-Qaeda, from Hamas and Hezbollah to al-Shahab and the Taliban. An essential aspect of the hot wars in Afghanistan, Pakistan, and Iraq and the civil wars in Somalia and Yemen is the titanic struggle *within* the Muslim world between moderate, pro-Western forces and fundamentalist, rejectionist elements.

Clearly there are multiple and varied flash points between the Muslim and non-Muslim worlds, from terrorist attacks against New York City, London, and Madrid and against U.S. troops in Iraq and Afghanistan, to differences on how cultural and religious expression is dealt with in Western society. They range from the permissibility of satirizing the Prophet Mohammed to the suitability of wearing head scarves by schoolgirls to the location of new mosques and even, in Switzerland, to whether to ban minarets in a public referendum. There are multiple signs of tension between Western and Islamic cultures. A *Financial Times* poll in March 2010 showed majorities supporting a ban on the public wearing of the burqa in the UK, France, Italy, Spain, and Germany; only a third of Americans supported it.[20] Responding to anti-Muslim immigrant feelings in her country, German Chancellor Angela Merkel starkly declared that Germany's efforts at creating a multicultural society had "utterly failed" and that the idea of people from different cultural backgrounds living happily "side by side" had not worked.[21]

This would be a strange concept for a mainstream political leader to voice in the U.S., where people with a rich diversity of ethnic and religious backgrounds live in relative harmony as Americans. But still, in the U.S. the intense controversy over locating a mosque and Islamic community center headed by a moderate imam two blocks from the Twin Towers in Manhattan underscores the intense anti-Muslim emotions stirred up by the 9/11 attacks. At the fringes of society, the 2011 Koran burning by a little-known Florida pastor, Terry Jones, evoked wide condemnation in the U.S.[22]

Af-Pak

But the heart of the battle over the direction of Islam remains within Muslim countries. This is no better demonstrated than in Pakistan and Afghanistan. It is here that there is a unique and dangerous intersection between Huntington's clash of Western and Islamic civilizations on the one hand, and the internal civil war within Islam on the other.

As a result of the almost ten year American military involvement in Afghanistan following the 9/11 attacks, and the enormous U.S. and NATO military intervention in Afghanistan, and military assistance program to the Afghan and Pakistan armies, along with U.S. drone attacks against al Qaeda and Taliban militants on both sides of the border, the West has become interwoven with the internal struggle between moderate Muslims in both countries and fierce, radical Islamists seeking to turn both nations into fundamentalist theocratic states.

Pakistan's president Asif Ali Zardari knows firsthand about what he called the "cancer" of Muslim terrorism, because it struck down his wife, Benazir Bhutto, as she was bidding to return to power.[23] After her assassination he declared: "There is an internal tension within Muslim society. The failure to resolve that tension peacefully and rationally threatens to degenerate into a collision course of values spilling into a clash between Islam and the West. It is finding a solution to this internal debate within Islam—about democracy, about human rights, about the role of women in society, about respect for other religions and cultures, about technology and modernity—that shall shape the future relations between Islam and the West."[24]

He stands at the crosshairs where the two battles converge in Afghanistan and Pakistan, dubbed "Af-Pak" by the Obama administration because it is an interlocked battle. They share many of the attributes of failed or failing states. Afghans have at least as much loyalty to their clan as they do to their nation; they count on their clan to protect them and advance their prospects, and they have little expectation of security or advancement from the central government, such as it is. If it is possible to win the war in Afghanistan, the U.S. must succeed at what it has not done well before—nation building while fighting a hot war, empowering the tribal leaders to combat the Taliban while trying to coax the corrupt central government to deliver services through these leaders.

But it is even more crucial to any winning strategy to end the safe haven Pakistan has granted for the Afghan Taliban and other radical groups such as the Haqqani network, largely through Pakistan's own intelligence services, the Inter-Services Intelligence agency (ISI). The ISI and the powerful Pakistan military see the Afghan Taliban, which is daily engaged in trying to kill American and Afghan government troops, as their instrument to serve as a buffer against their archenemy India and to exert influence over Afghanistan. They are the principal actors in creating these and other terrorist groups as instruments of state policy and sustaining them even as the United States pours billions of dollars of military and economic support into the strategic goal of eradicating the roots of terrorism.

Pakistan is the most dangerous nation on earth, with 190 million people, a nuclear arsenal growing faster than any other country's, a strong radical Islamic antigovernment insurgency, little control over their border with Afghanistan, and a weak civilian government. The country has become the target of increasingly frequent, deadly, and bold attacks against its key cities, including its capital, Islamabad, and its cultural center, Lahore.[25] The gaps in the state's governance are so evident that President Obama himself has publicly expressed his concerns about the viability of a government that does not "seem to have the capacity to deliver basic services: schools, health care, rule of law, [or] a judicial system that works for the majority of the people."[26]

This incapacity has provided gaps that Islamist radicals have been glad to fill. Pakistan's future is crucial in the conflict between a modern, moderate Islam and a jihadist Islam, and it is inextricably linked with Afghanistan to form what Secretary of State Clinton described as the "nerve center of world terrorism." But Afghanistan cannot be stabilized without Pakistan winning its own battle against terrorists, and that would mean Pakistan's ISI cutting their ties with the Afghan Taliban they have nurtured since the 1990s to help control the destiny of their weaker neighbor and to keep Afghanistan unstable.[27] Pakistan's rulers see Afghanistan as a country giving them strategic depth against India, whom they regard as their enemy.

It is impossible to exaggerate the complexity of the multibillion-dollar U.S. effort to support Pakistan's government against terrorism. Its chief weapons have been CIA agents on the ground to identify militant targets and drones that swoop in and attack al-Qaeda and Pakistani Taliban sites in the tribal areas of Pakistan's mountainous northwest. Both have long been at risk because of Pakistan's ambivalence about the campaign; Pakistan has threatened to hobble the drone attacks and has harassed the CIA agents.

Once President Obama announced that the U.S. would begin leaving Afghanistan, the Pakistani military felt it could only look to its terrorist clients to harass India and control a post-American Afghanistan. Prominent Republican opinion makers such as George Will have joined liberal Democrats in arguing that Afghanistan is a lost cause and America should pull out. In my view this would be a serious mistake. The U.S. must make a long-term commitment despite the certain loss of American lives. Because Afghanistan and Pakistan have many elements of failed states, success will require a combination of military, economic, diplomatic, and nation-building programs that will be a test case in the war against terrorism. Success would mark a historic turning point, while failure would encourage jihadists all over the world, and not only Hamas in Palestine and Hezbollah in Lebanon but also their state sponsor, Iran.

A series of incidents in 2011 have strained relations between America and Pakistan almost to the breaking point, dramatized the different worldviews of the two countries, creating the opportunity for further leverage by the Taliban. While Americans celebrated the assassination of Osama bin Laden in a massive compound in Abbottabad, near a large Pakistan military base and academy,[28] Pakistanis were incensed they had not been consulted and that their airspace had been violated. Instead of celebrating the end of the world's most infamous terrorist and redoubling efforts against al-Qaeda or the Taliban, the embarrassed Pakistani military and intelligence were blamed for not detecting the U.S. force as it flew in literally under the radar.[29] Americans disbelieved that bin Laden could have lived in the compound without any knowledge of the ISI, the military, or the government. Other incidents have inflamed popular passions in Pakistan against the U.S. and NATO. For example, a CIA operative was involved in an accident that took the lives of Pakistani civilians. And NATO forces bombing what they believed were Taliban bases inadvertently killed two dozen Pakistani soldiers.

In Afghanistan, the innocent destruction of what turned out to be a Koran by American soldiers, has led toa furious reaction in the Afghan public, threatening the ability of the U.S. to safely transfer power in 2014 to the Afghan Army. Men dressed as Afghan security guards and soldiers have infiltrated into secure locations and killed several French soldiers,leading President Sarkozy to announce an early withdrawal of French troops, and a number of American soldiers as well. Levels of distrust between the erstwhile allies, the U.S. and Afghanistan, is as high as that between the U.S. and Pakistan.

But in the end, each country needs the other. The U.S. needs a stable Pakistan and a self-sustaining Afghanistan. Pakistan is essential for NATO forces that must rely on it for supply routes to its troops in Afghanistan. The U.S. can ill afford to allow Pakistan's nuclear arms to fall into the hands of the Taliban or al-Qaeda. The Pakistani military cannot turn its back on billions of dollars of U.S. aid. If the partnership is permanently weakened, it will complicate the task of the U.S. and NATO in Afghanistan.

Pakistan tried to reach out to China to create a counterweight to the Americans after the bin Laden assassination. While China has provided substantial military assistance to Pakistan; has helped Pakistan's nuclear program with two new reactors in retaliation for the U.S.-India nuclear agreement; shares Pakistan's concerns about India; and cooperates on intelligence sharing, Pakistan has recognized the limits of China as a substitute for the U.S.

China is concerned about Pakistan's inability to curb terrorism, particularly the Uyghur Muslim separatists who use Pakistan as their base, and has publicly rebuked Pakistan for harboring the Uighurs. Two-way trade between China and Pakistan is small. And China gave a cold shoulder to Pakistan's request to build a naval base on the Arabian Sea.[30]

Although Pakistan's weak democratic tradition is flawed by frequent military interventions, the country has an aggressive, independent press and a vibrant civil society led by the legal profession. But there is a deadly internal struggle that, if lost, would move a nuclear-armed country from an imperfect democracy to an Islamic theocracy, joining Iran in the heart of the Islamic world. To bring Pakistan to the brink, the Pakistan Taliban and their allies are using a combination of anger of the poor and landless against wealthy landlords in a country that has never redistributed their huge landholdings, along with a murderous campaign of intimidation. Despite a robust military offensive in the summer of 2009 the army appears unwilling or incapable of successfully challenging the militants. To the disaffected, unprotected by the state, radical Islam seems an attractive solution.

Pakistan is a deeply divided nation, in which Islamic strains are strong and widespread. Beginning with the military dictator General Mohammad Zia ul Haq in the 1980s, Islam was promoted in the schools as a uniting force for the country. Islamic jihadists were supported to fight the Soviet Union in neighboring Afghanistan. Now nuclear-armed Pakistan is reaping what it sowed, as Pakistani society is suffused at every level with Islamic conservatives, even in the military and professional ranks.

The 2011 assassination of Salmaan Taseer, the governor of Punjab and an outspoken opponent of the country's tough antiblasphemy laws against any perceived slight of Islam, by his own bodyguard, while the rest of his protective force stood by, brought the internal divisions to a head. Within a few hours, some 25,000 messages of support for the assassin were posted on Facebook, and the very lawyers who courageously took to the streets against Pakistan's military dictatorship in 2007–2008 showered rose petals on the confessed killer when he appeared in court and have taken up his defense for standing up for Islam.[31]

Pakistan's internal struggle is mirrored throughout the Arab world, as pro-Western governments are unable to provide opportunities for their young people to offset the pull of fundamentalist Islam, while militant forces are better organized and more infused with a sense of mission than are moderates.

The stakes in Af-Pak are high. If the Taliban is successful in undermining both governments, it would be a blow to the U.S., the West, and Israel in combating their own terrorist threats. Defeating or co-opting them could have great ramifications for Israel in combating local terrorist forces and have an important psychological impact on extremists in Europe. But in the end, only the governments themselves can come to the realization that time is running out on their need to produce internal economic and political reforms and strong military action to combat surging Islamic fundamentalism.

The Obama strategy therefore departs from the Bush strategy in several ways. There is a bold but risky effort to bring elements of the Taliban into reconciliation. U.S. intelligence estimates that less than 10 percent are hardcore terrorists.[32] This may bear fruit, with the increasingly aggressive military actions against the Taliban. In early 2012, the Taliban suddenly announced they were creating an office in Qatar to begin negotiations with the U.S. to end the war, following the Obama administration's decision to release several Taliban fighters in Guantanamo Bay, Cuba, to house arrest in Qatar.[33] Although with reluctance, Afghan president Karzai has supported the U.S.-Taliban talks, with the understanding his government would take the lead in the negotiations.[34]

Just how difficult these negotiations would be was underscored by an almost simultaneous announcement by four major Pakistani radical groups to unite with the ruthless Afghan Haqqani to end their infighting, stop targeting Pakistani civilians, and focus their firepower on American and NATO forces in Afghanistan.[35]

The tribal chiefs along the Pakistan frontier want U.S. aid channeled through them instead of corrupt Pakistani officials and to have the U.S. train tribal militias rather than relying on the Pakistani army. They want to improve schools to reduce the influence of militant Islamic *madrassas*—small local schools almost entirely devoted to rote memorization of the Koran.

In Pakistan, at the urging of the U.S., President Zardari has taken steps to satisfy some tribal concerns by allowing political parties to campaign in the tribal belt area, called the Federally Administered Tribal Areas, where militants are prevalent, and by relaxing an antiquated law that held whole tribes could be imprisoned or their businesses blocked if even one member of the tribe was suspected of a crime.[36]

In both Pakistan and Afghanistan, there is a greater emphasis on economic development, with particular emphasis on Afghan agriculture.[37]

Delivering basic services and jobs is crucial to fighting a terrorist insurgency, and this cannot be done without legitimate and credible government.[38] This faces huge hurdles in Afghanistan, where three-quarters of the population is illiterate, and there is virtually no modern infrastructure to deliver assistance—few paved roads, no rail lines, and few airports. The U.S. has learned a lesson from the Soviet failure in Afghanistan. Rather than relying solely on a corrupt central government, U.S. and NATO aid is directed toward local and village authorities.

An Afghan Public Protection Program is being developed to supplant the ineffectual national police force. This policy of bypassing Kabul may account in part for the attacks on Washington emanating from Afghan president Hamid Karzai.

But as unpopular as the Afghan war has become, the U.S. cannot permit itself to be seen as defeated by the Taliban, as the Soviets were by their predecessors, the mujahideen. As former secretary of state Henry Kissinger has noted, this would fuel jihadists in the region, including those in Russia and China, and Hamas and Hezbollah on Israel's doorstep, and potentially destabilize Afghanistan's neighbors. Kissinger properly sees the need for a regional security agreement for Afghanistan, involving all of its neighbors, with a reliable multilateral enforcement mechanism.[39] With the new offer by the Taliban to commence talks in Qatar, Washington should bring in Russia, China, Pakistan, India, and even Iran, if it is willing to play a constructive role in creating a stable Afghanistan, rather than try to dissuade the Taliban from reaching an agreement with Washington.

Iran: The Rise of State-Backed Fundamentalism

The 1979 Iranian Revolution was a watershed event in the modern history of the Muslim world. A radical theocratic state was born, with a patina of democracy, bent on eliminating every vestige of Western influence in the Middle East and supporting terrorist groups seeking to destroy Israel, fused with a determination to become a regional hegemon to restore the glory of the ancient Persian Empire, backed by nuclear weapons. What was revolutionary in the Islamic world was the fusion of politics and Islam in which the religious authority was supreme and the civilian government subordinate, a radically different model from the secular governments of Egypt, Syria, Tunisia, and Algeria and the monarchies of Saudi Arabia, the Gulf states, Jordan, and Morocco.

Iran is the only Shiite republic in the world and sees itself charged with the messianic mission of restoring the Mahdi, the incarnation of the twelfth imam or holy prophet, for the final war between the believers and the infidels. What makes Iran such a challenge is its lethal combination of radical Shiite theology with a significant military, economic, and political capability, one of the largest oil and gas reserves in the world, OPEC's second-largest oil exporter, and a budding nuclear ability.

The regime formed the Islamic Revolutionary Guard Corps shortly after the 1979 revolution to eliminate opposition. The Revolutionary Guard has morphed into more than a feared security service, with tentacles reaching throughout Iran's society, controlling Iran's missiles, overseeing its nuclear program, and having a multibillion-dollar commercial empire which reaches into virtually every sector of the Iranian economy.[40] I worked in the White House through the Iranian Revolution of 1979 and the ordeal of the American hostages that helped destroy Jimmy Carter's presidency, a crisis inadvertently touched off by President Carter's decision to shelter the deposed Shah of Iran as he was mortally ill with cancer. The Shah owed his throne to a CIA coup in 1953 that overthrew a popularly elected prime minister opposed to American and British interests. Over the years he became a loyal ally of the U.S., developed a close military relationship with Israel, and guaranteed its supply of oil. It was the Shah who began Iran's nuclear program, not the radical Shiite regime that toppled him.

Iran's relationship with Jews and with terrorism is complicated. For several thousand years, a sizable Jewish community had lived in relative tranquility and prosperity in what used to be called Persia. I first came in contact with that community in 1979, shortly after the Iranian Revolution confirmed Ayatollah Khomeini as its leader. A delegation of Iranian Jews visiting the U.S. came to see me in the White House and in feverish and emotional terms described their fears for their families, their friends, and their fellow Jews under Khomeini. They reported that thousands had converged on U.S. embassies in Europe seeking visas to flee to safety in the United States but were being turned away and told to return to Iran. Their moving story evoked harsh memories of American consulates in Europe turning back Jews and others targeted by the Nazis in the 1930s and the early days of World War II. I was determined not to see a repeat of the disastrous immigration policies that helped doom European Jewry.

Still, we had a dilemma. Designating Iranians as refugees would have infuriated the new Khomeini government, with which Washington had hoped to salvage something positive before the hostage crisis erupted in November of 1979. Along with White House counsel Robert Lipshutz, we proposed a new visa category and obtained the strong support of President Carter. Upon our recommendation, he ordered the creation of an unusual travel visa that allowed some 50,000 Iranian Jews, Baha'i, and Christians to travel to the U.S. and stay. Indefinitely until the *status quo ante* was returned—that is, the return of the Shah! I still receive New Years greetings from the Los Angeles–based Iranian Jewish community. Today, there are only a few thousand Iranian Jews left in Iran, and they keep a low profile. There is one Jewish representative in the Iranian parliament, Maurice Motamed.

From their perverse perspective, the mullahs in Tehran have reason to celebrate three decades of radical, theocratic government in a country of 70 million with a long and culturally rich history; a highly educated populace; a modern and sophisticated military financed by revenues from huge oil and gas reserves; and advanced scientific, technological, and growing nuclear capacity. After the debilitating war in the 1980s against Iraq's Saddam Hussein, in which over a million soldiers were killed, the U.S. removed their archenemy in the Iraq War. Without firing a shot, Iran was the major strategic victor in the Iraq War: The parliamentary majority of the Shiite prime minister Nouri al-Maliki depends on the support of the political party of the virulently anti-American cleric Muqtada al-Sadr, who in turn draws support from Iran's clerical autocracy. Iran is also the premier state sponsor of terrorism; when missiles fly from Gaza to Israel they are largely homemade, but Iran is supplying longer-range rockets to Hezbollah and components of roadside bombs that have done so much damage to motorized troops in Afghanistan and Iraq. Its program to develop a nuclear bomb is the overriding security threat to Israel and a destabilizing factor in the Arab world.

In 1997 and again in 2001, a relative moderate, Sayyid Mohammad Khatami, was elected president on a platform of reform and liberalization. With an outpouring of young voters, his was the most open presidential election since the revolution.

Efforts were made to reach out to him during the Clinton administration, end Tehran's rupture with Washington, and establish a "dialogue of civilizations" that both Khatami and the Clinton administration sought. To back this up, we took unilateral steps such as lifting the ban on some Iranian products, like pistachios, and cultural exchanges were launched. But there was little reciprocal response from Iran, and during the Bush administration these halting measures stopped.

In the 2009 presidential election, dozens of potential candidates were whittled down to only four by the Guardian Council, but the openness of the campaign was unprecedented. A series of televised debates captivated the usually apathetic public, and former prime minister Mir Hossein Mousavi criticized President Mahmoud Ahmadinejad's public denial of the Holocaust and his foreign policy of "adventurism, illusionism, exhibitionism, extremism, and superficiality."[41] Despite a huge turnout and only hand-counted paper ballots, within two hours of the closing of the polls, Ahmadinejad was declared a landslide winner in a farcical outcome, as Supreme Leader Ayatollah Ali Khamenei declared Ahmadinejad's "victory" a "divine assessment."

Then followed the most convulsive period since the Islamic revolution, which presaged the Arab Spring two years later. Using the same social media employed in the Arab revolutions in the Middle East, more than one million Iranians gathered to protest fraud. The demonstration was put down by the Revolutionary Guard in ruthless patrols. A show trial was launched in August 2009 against one hundred leading opponents, including a nineteen-year-old member of the Jewish community, Yahotil Sha'oolian.

The opposition is weakened but unbowed. In November 2009, anti-U.S. demonstrations planned by the regime to mark the anniversary of the 1979 takeover of the American Embassy were met with tens of thousands of Iranians staging anti-regime demonstrations.[42] Again, in the winter of 2011, inspired by the democratic forces in Tunisia and Egypt, the opposition reemerged and was again brutally suppressed.[43]

Ahmadinejad is a shrewd populist politician who has used extreme language denying the Holocaust, threatening to destroy Israel as a way of consolidating his support at home and in an attempt to become a leader of the Arab Middle East. He appointed Ahmad Vahidi as defense minister, the subject of an Interpol "red alert" after the Argentine government sought his extradition for his role in the 1994 bombing of the Buenos Aires Jewish community center, AMIA. At the same time, he has pulled back the patrols that harass Iranian women about their dress deviating from strict Islamic codes and has nominated the first women to cabinet positions.

But Ahmadinejad's most serious opposition is not from the moderate clerics and secular middle class but from the person who anointed him president, Ayatollah Khamenei, with whom he is engaged in a power struggle Khamenei is winning. Ahmadinejad supported the 2009 agreement with the U.S. and the West to defuse the nuclear standoff, but he was overturned by Ayatollah Khomeini and the Revolutionary Guard, which controls Iran's nuclear program. His appointments have been blocked by the Ayatollah. But whoever prevails, the balance of power for now remains with the most radical, anti-Western elements in Iran.[44]

Iran's self-styled Cyber Army, linked to the Revolutionary Guard, is not prepared to cede cyberspace to prodemocracy forces, is engaged in highly sophisticated efforts to interfere with Internet access, and is using modern spying technology to identify opponents. But I believe that over time, Iran's highly trained and talented people, their yearning for a genuine democracy and for contact with the outside world, together with biting Western economic sanctions, may lead Iran to a more moderate posture, even as it races forward with its nuclear program.

As history demonstrated with the fall of Communism, governments that lose their legitimacy ultimately lose their power. The current leadership of the theocratic state has lost popular confidence on a broad scale. In this circumstance, even the unthinkable—a fundamental move from radical, political Islam—becomes possible to contemplate. As Iran modernizes, globalization is affecting it as much as any country, even China. There the regime has attempted an à la carte version of globalization, providing citizens with technology and connections abroad but limiting the political and social effects. This has proven difficult.

As in China, the main reason for optimism about a more moderate Iranian government is its educated citizenry and growing middle class that are increasingly exposed to the outside world through the same technology that promoted the Arab Spring. So it is a race against time, as the hard-liners try to push their nuclear agenda and consolidate their eroding power until a new generation, which wants to be part of the modern world, takes over, one way or the other.

U.S., European, and, more indirectly, Israeli policy should be aimed at empowering this growing reform movement among the young and better educated, and avoiding actions that allow the hard-liners to consolidate their power and to continue to aim their terrorist proxies toward Israel.

Iran's very radicalism has served to isolate it. Iran is so out of step with the stirrings in the Middle East from the Arab Spring that the government will be more isolated in the region. Ahmadinejad's statements denying the Holocaust and his grossly perverted Holocaust denial conference in 2006 provoked leaders throughout the world and flew in the face of the UN's own commemoration of the sixtieth anniversary of the liberation of the Nazi concentration camps. His calculated attacks on Israel at the UN conference on racism in Geneva occurred on Holocaust Memorial Day and led to a walkout by over forty diplomats from more than twenty countries (including one Arab state, Morocco). He characterized Israel as a "cruel and repressive racist regime" that "occupied Palestine on the pretext of suffering under the Nazis" and then raised his sights beyond Israel to Jews in general, raising the old canard of world Jewish power.

This led to a rare public rebuke by UN Secretary General Ban Ki-moon urging members to "turn away from such a message in both form and substance." One of the few countries to defend Ahmadinejad was America's erstwhile ally Pakistan, whose ambassador to the UN in Geneva said, "There were things in there that a lot of people in the Muslim world would be in agreement with, for example the situation in Palestine, in Iraq and in Afghanistan, even if they don't agree with the way he said it."[45]

Anti-Iranian sentiment in the largely Sunni, moderate, pro-Western Arab world is palpable. The official Saudi government daily, *Al-Watan*, said that Arab countries were being subjected to "Persian colonialism." After the Lebanon War, the Egyptian foreign minister at the time, Ahmad Abu Al-Gheit, accused Iran of "trying to use Arab cards to realize interests and goals that are not Arab" and opposed Iran's nuclear ambitions. This was also reflected in the Egyptian press. The secretary general of the Palestinian Authority, General al-Tayeb Abdel Rahim, accused Iran of encouraging Hamas to resume the resistance against Israel and blocking it from a dialogue with the Authority.

This backlash may not last. One outcome of the Egyptian revolution is likely to be a rapprochement, although not an alliance, between Cairo and Tehran through a normalization of diplomatic relations. Two Iranian warships were permitted to pass through the Suez Canal on their way to Syria, for the first time since the 1979 Iranian Revolution. Iran's direct leverage in the Palestinian territories through Hamas puts Israel in a diplomatic pincer, with a changing Egypt on the other side.

There is at best a glimmer of hope in certain overlapping areas of security interest between Iran and the United States, particularly in Afghanistan, where Iran seeks to reduce the opium traffic and wants a stable government on its border. It offered help to the United States when it attacked al-Qaeda in Afghanistan after 9/11, has never been a supporter of the Taliban, and tried to develop close relations with Afghan president Hamid Karzai, at times by cash payments. During the height of the Cold War, the U.S. was able to find areas such as arms control to negotiate with the Soviet Union, even as it was challenging Soviet power around the world. Afghanistan offers a similar area for tentative efforts at dialogue, if for no other reason than to ensure that Iran does not exert disproportionate influence on the country after U.S. and NATO forces depart in 2014.

But hopes for Iranian cooperation to facilitate an eventual American exit from Afghanistan are likely to be dashed. Iran is mounting an aggressive campaign to deepen its strained ties with the Taliban, expanding its contact with Afghan political leaders and trying to dissuade Afghanistan from negotiating a long-term security agreement with the U.S. after the U.S. and NATO troops leave in 2014. Concerned about the long-term presence of U.S. troops on their flanks, and the intelligence-gathering capacity from U.S. bases into Iran, they have negotiated their own defense agreement with Afghanistan. Iran has used its oil wealth to provide millions of dollars to Afghan leaders convened by President Karzai to provide advice on the nature of the long-term relationship Afghanistan should have with Washington.[46]

This is a virtual repeat of the strategy they successfully used in Iraq, to convince the Iraqi government, after so much blood and money had been expended by the U.S., that it should not allow any long-term American troop presence if it meant granting immunity to U.S. troops. As a result, all U.S. troops withdrew from Iraq at the end of 2011.

Iran is at loggerheads with the U.S. in other areas. Tensions were heightened when a U.S. drone crashed in Iran. In the nuclear field, as I will discuss in more detail in chapter 4, Iran's program has led to the imposition of four sets of UN Security Council sanctions, backed up by strong U.S. and European sanctions. In sanctions legislation passed by Congress in the closing hours of its 2011 session, the Central Bank of Iran was directly targeted, prohibiting any bank or corporation that does business with the Iranian central bank, and many use the bank for their oil transactions, from doing business in the U.S. At the same time, the EU has agreed in principle not to import any oil from Iran, the lifeblood of its economy. For the first time, Iran is cracking from the cumulative weight of the sanctions. The value of its currency, the rial, has plunged; consumers are having difficulty purchasing basic goods; the Iranian central bank is being forced to require money changers to post artificially low exchange rates and block websites that list real-time rates; inflation has soared and along with it commodity prices have gone through the roof; and whole sectors have stopped production.[47]

Iran has retaliated by warning the USS *John C. Stennis*, a nuclear-powered aircraft carrier, not to return to the Persian Gulf; by threatening to close the Strait of Hormuz; and by preparing a bill to close the Persian Gulf to ships unless they received permission from the Iranian navy.[48] These are all empty threats, since these are international waters, but they signal how much pain the nuclear-related sanctions are exacting, and they rattled nervous oil markets, sending the price of crude oil well over $100 per barrel—which also helps fill the coffers of Iran with badly needed cash.

Iranian president Mahmoud Ahmadinejad is trying to expand his country's influence in the backyard of the U.S. through a January 2012 swing to Venezuela, Ecuador, Nicaragua, and Bolivia. In addition, Iran has opened six new diplomatic missions in Latin America and expanded its embassies in five other countries. Particularly troubling is that Iran is embedding its feared Quds Force, a part of the Revolutionary Guard, and military personnel in these Latin diplomatic posts. Given Iran's clear linkage to the two bombings in 1992 and 1994 of the Jewish community center (AMIA) and Israeli Embassy in Buenos Aires, this is a highly troubling development not only for the U.S. but also for Israel and the Jewish communities throughout Central and South America.

Iran has become the biggest importer of Brazilian beef, has dramatically increased trade with Argentina, and has opened bank branches and transportation companies in Hugo Chavez's pro-Iranian Venezuela to help it circumvent sanctions.[49]

At the same time, Iran has now indicated it wishes to resume negotiations over its nuclear program, a clear sign that sanctions are working.

The Sunni-Shiite Division

Iran punctuates one of the great historic divides in the Muslim world, between the Shiite and Sunni branches of Islam. This gulf goes back to the very founding period of the religion but has important manifestations today. In Bahrain, an important American ally and the location of the U.S. Fifth Fleet, a minority Sunni monarchy is facing a revolt from its majority Shiite population, which has been systematically discriminated against for generations. The government has even arrested emergency room doctors who treated Shiite demonstrators, for somehow aiding the revolution. Sunni Saudi Arabia sent in troops to help quell the Shiite unrest.

In Iraq, a subplot of the bloody and divisive aftermath of the war was the upending of the long-standing Sunni-Shiite power struggle under Saddam Hussein. Saddam was a Sunni, and his Sunni-dominated Ba'ath Party had long suppressed the majority Shiite population, often brutally. The U.S. invasion and the elections that followed put in place a Shiite-led coalition government, headed by Prime Minister al-Maliki. In response, parts of the Sunni population attacked both U.S. troops and the new Shiite power structure. It took a "Sunni Awakening" initiative by American general David Petraeus to gain the confidence of the Sunni minority.

But ominously, the key Shiite opponent of the U.S. was Muqtada al-Sadr, who spent years in Iran during the Saddam regime. Al-Sadr has been a key part of the Maliki coalition, and it was his pressure on Maliki, at Iran's insistence, that prevented agreement on the long-term presence of even a small contingent of U.S. troops in Iraq. Because al-Sadr, undoubtedly at Iran's instance, refused to agree to American assistance that any remaining U.S. troops be shielded from legal liability for any inadvertent injuries they might cause in the line of duty, all American troops have been withdrawn by the end of 2011, Iraq has reaped a whirlwind since the departure of the American troops, with a spasm of bombings against Shiites, leaving Iraq unstable, threatening to revive the Sunni-Shiite civil war, and leaving Iran as the dominant external force.

To further strengthen fellow Shiite Iran's influence in Iraq, Prime Minister Maliki has invited an equally militant Shiite group, Asaib Ahl al-Haq, into his coalition, led by Qais al-Khazali, who has been trained and financed by Iran's dangerous Quds Force.[50] More broadly, the key Arab allies of the U.S. in the region (Egypt, Jordan, Saudi Arabia, and the Gulf states) are all Sunni majority countries. Until this historic Sunni-Shiite divide can be resolved through mutual tolerance, it will remain a divisive factor in the region and will greatly complicate American foreign policy.

Dealing with Islamic Militancy: Positive Signs in the Muslim World

Even before the Arab Spring, the prospects in part of the Muslim world were not as bleak as the headlines of the day suggest. Many Muslim countries are attempting to incorporate parts of Western culture and its political principles. One reason for cautious optimism is that radical forces are characteristically overreaching and upsetting the lives of average citizens. While their political stature grew for a time, extremists may be going the way of the radicals who were thrown out of the tranquil and isolated Swat Valley in Pakistan. Citizens demanded an end to the zealotry—the imposition of sharia law by the Taliban and their extreme punishments imposed on so-called apostates: with girls' schools torched and criminals' hands chopped off.

Muslim countries outside the Middle East, such as Indonesia and Malaysia, have become thriving, modern, moderate, democratic nations. The Gulf States and even Saudi Arabia have made major educational reforms, creating universities with Western curricula, the major presence of American institutions of higher learning, and equal education for women. Abu Dhabi is creating a modern Arab cultural identity with a striking new art museum and a degree-granting campus of New York University with Jewish faculty members, even offering Hebrew as a noncredit course. Doha in Qatar has a new Museum of Islamic Art designed by I.M. Pei, and Dubai is the Gulf's major financial center. Another example of an effort at integration into global norms is Education City in Doha, Qatar, the creation of Emir Al-Thani, a reformer. Education City offers full degree programs from a number of U.S. universities, such as Virginia

Commonwealth, Carnegie Mellon, Northwestern, and Texas A&M. Dubai's Knowledge Village is doing the same. Qatar is actively seeking partnerships with American and European science and technology firms. Roger Mandle, the former president of the Rhode Island School of Design told me how positive he is about his new position as head of the new Qatar Museum Authority in Doha. Before September 11, 2001, there were only three American universities operating in the Muslim world; today there are over thirty.

The Gulf Cooperation Council (GCC) countries have spent as much as $50 billion on education since 2004.[51] On the cultural front, the UAE will be home to the world's largest Guggenheim Museum. A new literary prize for Arab fiction was launched by the Booker Prize Foundation together with the Emirates Foundation and the Weidenfeld Institute for Strategic Dialogue, an English-based charity named for Lord Weidenfeld, who has extensive ties to Israel. The Gulf states are trying to diversify their oil-based economies by promoting tourism, drawing on hotel expertise from India's Oberon chain and, in Dubai, the South African Jewish hotelier Sol Kerzner.

The Internet is opening up politics wherever it is allowed to operate unfettered. In Malaysia, Internet blogs were the major vehicle for mobilizing the opposition in the 2008 elections that denied the long-ruling National Front Party its typically overwhelming majority. Then prime minister Mahathir was an architect of his own downfall: Seeking to create a cyberhub near Kuala Lumpur, he was told by Western high-tech companies that they would invest only if there were an uncensored Internet.[52]

Business associations and chambers of commerce are increasingly involved in public policy in Morocco, Tunisia, Egypt, Jordan, and Kuwait. And an unprecedented number of businessmen now sit in Arab parliaments.

But whether these liberalizing trends become permanent rests largely with the course charted by the religious and cultural anchors of the region—Saudi Arabia and Egypt. The aging but reformist Saudi king Abdullah recognized the rise of militant Islam as a threat to his regime and suppressed radicals within his borders. But he has gone further, hosting an international interfaith gathering that included Israel in 2008, declaring that "nothing can purify Islam's reputation except for the extension of Muslims' hands to their brothers in other religions."[53] How serious that purification becomes in practice will be gauged by the ruling family's relationship with the strict Wahhabi clerical establishment, which was given domain over all religious and social morals in return for loyalty to the ruling House of Saud. The most serious of several shocks to this relationship was the disclosure that almost all the September 11 terrorists as well as their leader Osama bin Laden were Saudi nationals inspired by radical Wahhabi.

It was not a coincidence that Saudi peace proposals for the region followed the attacks on New York's Twin Towers by only a year; the ruling family recognized that it could not buy security at home from the enforcement of a strict religious code. King Abdullah checked the power of the more radical Wahhabi clerics and their ubiquitous religious police and also created a University of Science and Technology on the American model. It is the first coeducational institution in the kingdom's history. Female lawyers will be permitted to appear in court on behalf of female clients in family cases. Other signs that the modern world is infiltrating the kingdom are the creation of special economic zones encouraging investment by foreign companies to help create local start-ups, a new financial center in Riyadh, and a less aggressive tone in the official Saudi press treatment of Israel and Jews. King Abdullah announced in 2011 that women can participate in local elections in 2015.

There is a real risk that once eighty-two-year-old King Abdullah passes from the scene, his handpicked successor, Prince Nayef bin Abdul Aziz al-Saud, the conservative former interior minister, may repudiate even the small steps the king has taken toward modernization. He has flatly opposed the king's initiatives for women, and following the September 11 attacks, involving more than a dozen Saudi-born terrorists, Prince Nayef proposed the preposterous notion that "Zionists benefitted from the 9/11 attacks" because they rallied world opinion against the Muslim world.[54]

Uncharted Waters: The Arab Spring and the Next Generation

I have spent considerable time in the Middle East and North Africa in my official responsibilities during the Clinton administration and later in my private activities. I helped create the U.S.-North African Economic Partnership as under secretary of state. I have been from Dubai and Doha to Algeria, Morocco, and Tunisia, from Egypt and Jordan to Gaza and the West Bank. I saw firsthand the grinding poverty in Egypt and Gaza, the lack of free expression there and throughout much of the Arab world. But in frequent meetings with government officials and business leaders, I developed a respect for their seriousness of purpose in trying to resolve their many endemic problems.

It also became clear that they were not moving rapidly enough to keep up with the changes of the new twenty-first century and the desires of the bulk of the young people, stoked by their digital contacts with the wider world. Yet, I never anticipated such rapid changes in the firmly entrenched pro-American order throughout the region.

Mohamed Bouazizi is an unlikely historical figure. But when this humble twenty-six-year-old street vendor burned himself on January 4, 2011, on the streets of the small Tunisian town of Sidi Bouzid, distraught at the confiscation of his wares, the harassment by local officials, and the lack of economic opportunity, he was the spark that set off a massive fire in the Arab world. A starting series of revolutions toppled decades-long autocratic, pro-Western rulers in Tunisia, where one-quarter of the population is under the age of fourteen,[55] and in Egypt, one of two Arab nations with a peace treaty with Israel, which President Hosni Mubarak carefully maintained, even after Israel's bombing of the Syrian nuclear site and the Gaza War; led to the grave wounding of the president of Yemen, who was forced to flee to Saudi Arabia, briefly return home before seeking medical care in the U.S., and stepping down in favor of his vice president, who was elected in 2012 with overwhelming public support; ousted the longest-standing ruler in the world, Libya's Muammar Qaddafi; shook the foundations of the ruling family in Bahrain, which had governed the nation for over two hundred years; threatened the brutal family rule of Syria's Bashar al-Assad, one of Iran's closest allies, who assumed the presidency from his father, Hafez al-Assad; and spread to the seemingly popular monarchies of Jordan, where the motorcade of King Abdullah II was pelted with stones and demonstrations demanded democracy,[56] and Morocco.

Each country has different historical circumstances, but there were common factors. The combination of the youth bulge, lack of jobs and education, failure to deliver basic public services, and disgust at repression and corruption led to the most profound upheaval in the Arab world since it gained its independence from Britain and France following World War II. Without any charismatic leader around whom they could rally, but using social media and other digital tools, they have shaken up ossified political structures in Arab societies, with uncertain results. Only one result is clear: The Arab Spring has thrust the Muslim world back into a dominant position on the global agenda, complicating the problems of creating a stable region for growth and moderation.

This has given voice to the Arab masses so long suppressed and offers potential that the creativity of the Arab people, and the skills of the new generation, will make their societies more profitable and dynamic over time. But in the short term it has unleashed public anger by the "Arab street" at Israel, which the security forces of the pro-Western regimes had carefully controlled, content to do the bidding of the U.S. to support peace with Israel, or at least a state of nonhostility.

The pro-American autocratic leaders played a double game. To create a safety valve, the pro-Western governments at the same time directed the anger and frustration of their citizens against Israel, particularly the occupation of Palestinian territories, as the source of their impoverishment.

When I was under secretary of state, I received permission to speak with then foreign minister Amr Moussa (likely Egypt's next president), during a meeting in Cairo on economic issues, about the U.S. government's concerns over the viciously anti-Israel and anti-Semitic nature of the cartoons in Egypt's state-run paper, *Al-Ahram*, depicting jackbooted Israeli soldiers, with Nazi swastikas on their helmets, brutalizing innocent Palestinians. I told the foreign minister that the U.S. felt these were incendiary and contrary to the maintenance of public support for the Egypt-Israel peace treaty. The foreign minister, whom I have come to respect, told me cavalierly that Egypt had a free press, and the government could not interfere!

The other part of this double game by the moderate, secular autocrats was to convince successive U.S. administrations that if they failed to fully support them and pushed for a democratic opening, the result would be the election of Islamic regimes. But at the same time they prevented moderate, democratic, non-Islamic parties from gaining any footing in their countries, making it more likely that the warning may become a self-fulfilling prophecy. The opportunity to encourage internal reforms leading to carefully planned transitions was lost.

The convulsions of the Arab Spring created a vacuum of power, since the autocratic rulers allowed the creation of no alternative political parties, forced Islamists underground, and prohibited the formation of the foundations of civil society: nongovernment organizations, an independent judiciary, and the rule of law. It is not a conceit that the Arab world is unable to create a viable democracy; rather their rulers destroyed any effort to create democratic institutions. The vacuum is fast being filled by the Islamic forces that are the best disciplined, have grassroots organizations that have long provided social services the governments failed to deliver, and are viewed by the Arab publics as incorruptible because of their religious scruples.

Whatever long-term benefit a more free and open society may have for the Arab nations in the decades ahead, the geopolitical impact on their foreign policy is profound, like shaking up a deck of cards and casting them to the wind. Before the Arab Spring, there were two groups of Muslim nations in neat stacks: the moderate, largely Sunni-dominated pro-Western autocracies (Egypt, Yemen, Somalia, Tunisia, Algeria), monarchies (Jordan, Saudi Arabia, the Gulf states, Morocco), and democracies (Turkey) lined up against the radical anti-Western Muslim nations (Iran, Syria), with their nongovernmental terrorist groups (Hamas, Hezbollah, Islamic Jihad). A number of countries are in play and could tip either way—Iraq, Libya, Afghanistan, Pakistan, and Lebanon. Israel was either legally accepted by treaty in two countries, Egypt and Jordan, or more or less tolerated by the other pro-Western nations. Now the lineup is more tenuous, with troubling implications for Israel, at least until a two-state solution can be reached with the Palestinians and with new challenges for the U.S., which has lost clout and influence in the region.

Yet, the forces unleashed by the Arab Spring are so profound, that alliances in the post-revolutionary period are very much up for grabs. If Bashar al-Assad falls in Syria, Iran will have lost its only real ally in the Arab Middle East. Already, in early 2012, Hamas, an ally of Iran, has turned on Assad and called for his ouster, a remarkable development.

As the pro-Western leaders fell like dominos, it is revealing that every free election held since the Arab Spring has been dominated by Islamic parties, which will be charged with writing new constitutions for their states. Indeed, this began well before the current uprisings, with the 2006 Palestinian parliamentary elections, in which Hamas shocked the world by overwhelming the more moderate Fatah Party, winning more than half of the 132 seats. In Tunisia, the Islamic Ennahda Party was the clear winner. After the final round of Egyptian parliamentary voting, the Muslim Brotherhood had 40 percent of the vote; the more fundamentalist, hard-line al-Nour Party of Islamic Salafists finished second with 20 percent, giving the two parties dominance in the new legislature.[57] The poorly organized secular parties barely scratched the surface, leaving the young people who sparked the January 25th revolution against President Mubarak effectively sidelined.

In moderate Morocco, the Islamic Justice and Development Party won 27 percent of the parliamentary seats, earning the right, under the commitment made by King Mohammed V in the face of street demonstrations, to have its leader, Abdelilah Benkirane, appointed as the new prime minister, along with the foreign and justice ministries.

These stunning election results for the Islamic parties were not a vote on foreign policy. Israel was not an issue for the vast majority of voters; jobs, freedom, and accountability were the major issues. But the elections have major geopolitical implications for the U.S. and for Israel, bringing to power parties historically antithetical to both Israel and the West and who will play on an underlying Arab public need to end perceived subjugation to the West. Like the Hamas victory in 2006, these elections will emphasize that democracy is not one free election; it is a state of mind to encourage tolerance of differences, compromise, transparency, and the creation of institutions guaranteeing the rule of law.

Alternative Scenarios from the Arab Spring

There is a spectrum of alternative scenarios arising from the Arab Spring. The ones at either end of the spectrum are unlikely.

The worst-case outcome would be the development of Iranian-style radical Islamic republics, which export revolution and seek the expulsion of Western influence and the destruction of Israel. This is not a road down which Tunisia and Egypt, Morocco, and even Libya will travel, because of their more moderate version of Sunni Islam, their significant middle-class and business interests, their desire for Western investment to create jobs, and their strong military and political relationships with the U.S. and Europe.

Neither is there a likelihood of a Western-style democracy, after so many decades of autocratic rule and the role that the Islamic religion will play in the governance of the state given the recent elections. But there is the realistic prospect that entering into government, and being responsible for the delivery of services and the creation of jobs, will have a sobering impact on the newly empowered

Islamic parties. The Arab publics may have little patience with imposition of strict sharia law or foreign policy dalliances, like the Iranian government engages in, when jobs, economic opportunity, free expression, and personal empowerment are priorities.

There are several Arab countries that offer reason for optimism. Morocco, for example—because the Alaouite dynasty has a great deal of public legitimacy, with a history of tolerance toward minorities, including Jews; because King Mohammed VI publicly embraced reform only days after demonstrations began; and because the Islamic party seems genuinely moderate—could be a beacon for other countries in the region, particularly Jordan, with a fellow modern-thinking monarch.

The king put a new constitution to the voters in July 2011, before parliamentary elections, that pledges to appoint as prime minister the leader of the party with the largest number of seats but reserves for him the national security decisions. The Islamic Justice and Development Party asked that the constitution make Morocco a religious Islamic state. The king refused. Importantly, in a preamble, the new constitution specifically notes the long history of minorities, such as the Berbers and Jews, and guarantees them equal rights. The new Islamic prime minister Abdelilah Benkirane has made his first public priority the encouragement of foreign direct investment and his second the establishment of the rule of law.[58] He made a point of leading the funeral procession during the funeral of Jewish leader Simon Levy.

Tunisia's winning Islamic party, Ennahda (Renaissance), is also moderate and has pledged to respect minority and women's rights. Rachid al-Ghannouchi, the founder of the party and a major figure in the Arab and Muslim world, has long argued that Islam is compatible with pluralism and democracy. While secular forces in Tunisia doubt the sincerity of Ennahda not to impose strict sharia law, time will tell. There is a realistic prospect that to avoid civil strife with Tunisia's large secular population, and to encourage Western investment, Ennahda will not overreach.[59]

There are other positive straws in the Arab wind. In Kuwait, free elections saw four women being seated in the parliament for the first time, over the objection of conservative Islamists; women only won the right to vote in 2006. Bahrain named Houda Ezra Ebrahim Nonoo as the first Jewish Ambassador to the United States from an Arab nation in 2011, one of Bahrain's 36 Jewish citizens.

Turkey

Turkey is held up as a model for the new Middle East, with its Islamic-party controlling government, free elections, a booming free-market economy, and the rule of law, along with a Western orientation through its NATO membership. But while the country has many enviable features under its Islamic prime minister, if Turkey is the high-water mark of what the West and Israel can expect from the new post–Arab Spring governments, such as Egypt, there is trouble ahead given Turkey's strained relationship with Israel, its independent foreign policy on issues like Iran's nuclear program, and its recent crackdown on an independent press and dissenting political voices.

Turkey has a centuries-long relationship with the Middle East and is crucial to the Muslim world's direction. The Ottoman Empire captured Jerusalem in the fifteenth century and controlled Palestine until 1917; the British took over following World War I. Turkey has been a Middle Eastern power in a historical relationship with the West, with the Jews, and, in modern times, with Israel. The modern Turkish state, founded by Mustafa Kemal Ataturk after the Ottoman collapse at the end of World War I, was based on a fierce secularism, defended by its military, and modernism. Turkey, which welcomed Jews expelled from Spain in 1492, and protected its Jewish citizens from the Nazis in World War II, was the first Muslim state to recognize Israel. Its military maintained a close relationship with the Israeli Defense Forces for decades.

But with the landslide election of Recep Tayyip Erdogan's Justice and Development Party in 2002, Turkey got its first Islamic-oriented government. Gradually Turkey has distanced itself from Israel, not coincidentally when Erdogan pushed the generals out of politics. The troubling move away from secularism is partly a result of disappointment at the European Union's decades-long refusal to accept Turkey. This spells bad news for Israel. Prime Minister Erdogan has seen his popularity within Turkey and the broader Arab Middle East rise in direct proportion to the vehemence of his opposition to Israeli policies.

He was deeply angered and embarrassed when Israel responded to incessant rocket attacks by launching the incursion into Gaza within days of hosting then Prime Minister Ehud Olmert for serious negotiations with Syria over the Golan Heights.

He has escalated his attacks. In 2009, my wife Fran and I witnessed his walkout from a panel on which he was speaking with Israeli president Shimon Peres over the Gaza War, from the main plenary session at the World Economic Forum. In 2010 he was furious over the killing of Turkish citizens in the flotilla challenging the Israeli blockade of Gaza. And in 2011, he withdrew his ambassador to Israel and expelled Israel's ambassador in Ankara when he was dissatisfied with the conclusion of the UN panel examining the attack, which concluded that while Israel had used "excessive force," it had not violated international law by the blockade, aimed at keeping weapons from Hamas. This was aggravated when Israel refused to apologize over the incident.

Not to be outdone, he has threatened to use Turkish military vessels to accompany future flotillas to Gaza to prevent Israeli commandos from boarding the ships and, equally troubling, to block Israel's efforts to exploit its newly found natural gas reserves in the Mediterranean, pursuant to an agreement Israel reached with Cyprus, which Turkey partly occupies, to divide the gas between Cyprus and Israel.[60] In the run-up to the UN vote on Palestinian statehood, Erdogan called Israel "a spoiled child of the West."

This impacts on U.S. interests as well. To temper Washington's concerns, he has pledged to accept a Turkish location for a radar station that will be a key part of an antimissile shield aimed at Iran, over Iranian objection, even as he tried in 2010 to reach his own agreement with Iran over its nuclear program, undercutting U.S. efforts for a strong UN Security Council resolution.[61]

But if Turkey is held up as a model for Egypt and other new democratically elected Muslim governments, it is departing from what should be expected of them. The Erdogan government has been actively suppressing opposition dissent and cracking down on journalists with the temerity to criticize the government, on the fallacious grounds they are helping terrorist organizations. Human rights groups in Turkey see a clear pattern of suppressing freedom of the press. The European Court of Human Rights received almost nine thousand complaints against Turkey for breaches of free expression and press liberties. Distinguished writers, such as Nobel laureate Orhan Pamuk, have been fined, and Nedim Sener, winner of the 2010 International Press Institute's World Press Freedom Hero award, has been arrested for reporting on the murder of a prominent Turkish-Armenian journalist.[62]

Egypt: Linchpin for the New Arab Middle East

Although Saudi Arabia has the wealth and the religious legitimacy as the guardian of the Muslim holy places in Mecca, Egypt remains the heart of the Arab Middle East with more than 80 million people, a major military, and a significant economy as well as millennia of unbroken history. It is the site of the Arab League. So goes Egypt, so goes the new Arab Middle East. What happens in Egypt has enormous implications for the direction of the Arab world, for the U.S., and for Israel, which has complained of the "cold peace" with Egypt from the time of the 1979 treaty. Israelis are likely to look back on the Mubarak era as warm and secure compared to the future. President Mubarak never severed diplomatic relations with Israel, even after Israel's strikes against Iraqi and Syrian nuclear sites, which he quietly supported. He protected Israel's flanks in Gaza and the Sinai, which soon became permeable after the collapse of Mubarak's rule. The natural gas pipelines from Egypt were repeatedly blown up, Gaza began receiving supplies from Egypt, and Israelis en route to Eilat were killed when a tourist bus was fired on at the Sinai border.

For the United States, Egypt remains a centerpiece of American foreign policy in the region. The military establishments of the two countries have a close working relationship, and hundreds of Egyptian officers receive specialized training in the U.S. every year. President Obama was certainly correct in calling for an orderly and prompt transition of power once it appeared that Mubarak's days were numbered, but Mubarak's departure is a setback for the U.S. and for the pro-Western moderate coalition of Arab nations opposed to Iran.

It underscores the limits of American influence in the region; American-backed governments have lost their popular legitimacy, and aid now is limited by budget deficits; the U.S. aid package for post-Mubarak Egypt amounts to only $2 billion. Meanwhile Egypt faces major challenges in moving toward a democratic state. Under Mubarak, Egypt had gradually begun to liberalize its economy with U.S. support, but growth was uneven and corrupted by crony capitalism. Highly educated young Egyptians are unable to find jobs; with almost half of its population under thirty, and a third under the age of fourteen, Egypt faces the same challenge of a youth bulge as the rest of the Arab world.

Egypt is not Iran with its dominant Islamic fundamentalist forces, nor Lebanon with its warring religious militias. It is a more moderate nation with an educated elite, and while the Muslim Brotherhood has been in Egypt since the 1920s, the movement lacks the jihadist impulse of al-Qaeda, and if it did, it would quickly lose influence. But at the same time, the Muslim Brotherhood is vehemently anti-Western and anti-Israel and is the mother organization for the Muslim Brotherhood organizations in Jordan, Tunisia, and Libya, as well as jihadist Hamas in Gaza.

Moreover, the Egyptian military is a force for stability. But its performance as the interim government until the new parliament takes office and a new president is elected in 2012 demonstrates its limits in the revolutionary fervor that has swept Egypt. It has succeeded in alienating both the secular forces that spearheaded the ouster of Mubarak and the Islamic forces that have decisively won the parliamentary vote, by insisting on keeping its own military budget and large commercial holdings out of parliamentary scrutiny, by having a role in drafting the new constitution through its own council, and by suppressing demonstrators who have come back to Tahrir Square in Cairo, the site of the initial demonstrations against Mubarak.

With the parliament that will write Egypt's new constitution firmly in the hands of the two major Islamic political parties, the stage is set for a titanic confrontation with the military and a dramatically new Egypt that may follow sharia law. An even greater threat than the Muslim Brotherhood is the opening Egypt's nascent democracy provides for militant groups that have no interest in democratic forms except to exploit them. The Salafi Islamic group follows the fundamentalist Wahhabi movement; it was an Egyptian fundamentalist and former military officer, Aboud al-Zumar, who supplied the bullets that killed President Anwar Sadat after he signed the peace treaty with Israel. Other Egyptian fundamentalists have emerged in public; the sons of Omar Abdel Rahman, the blind sheikh serving a life sentence in the U.S. for the 1993 conspiracy to bomb the World Trade Center, spoke at a conference in a leading Cairo hotel to demand the release of their father.[63]

Ali Gomaa, the grand mufti of Egypt, took to the op-ed pages of the *New York Times* to try to provide reassurance that while it is "inevitable that Islam will have a place in our democratic political order," "this should not be cause for alarm for Egyptians or for the West," and that "equal citizenship will be guaranteed regardless of religion, race or creed."[64] Only time will tell if these words will be translated into deed.

While a new regime may be more democratic, it will not be as close an ally of the U.S., as determined to fight terrorism and confront Iran, or as committed to working for peace with Israel. Even before the parliamentary elections demonstrated the political power of the Islamic forces, the interim government allowed Iranian warships through the Suez Canal for the first time. The Egyptian Sinai has become a lawless area, where the pipeline providing Egyptian natural gas to Israel has been repeatedly bombed, and terrorists transit from Gaza into Israel, killing a number of Israelis in the summer of 2011. Following the Eilat attacks by militant Palestinians through the Egyptian Sinai, Israel chased the terrorists across the border, inadvertently killing several Egyptian soldiers. This produced a furious response, with crowds tearing down the Israeli flag and replacing it with an Egyptian flag, to great public support. More seriously, a mob of secular soccer fans stormed the Israeli Embassy, with the Egyptian military and police standing idly by, forcing the evacuation of the Israeli ambassador and staff, and requiring Prime Minister Netanyahu to enlist the emergency assistance of President Obama to prevent a deadly attack against the remaining Israeli security guards.[65]

So goes Egypt, so goes Jordan, the other Arab nation with a peace agreement with Israel. Shortly after the attack against the Israeli Embassy in Cairo, the Israeli government removed all of its personnel from its embassy in Amman, Jordan, because of intelligence indicating an attack was imminent following Friday prayers.

Just as Egypt's Islamic forces will play a disproportionate role in the new democratic institutions, so too in Libya, a generally moderate Arab state, where Muammar el-Qaddafi's autocratic government has been ousted by NATO and U.S.-backed rebels, the opening created may be filled by the well-organized Islamists. The nation's most powerful post-Qaddafi military leader is Abdel Hakim Belhaj, who led a militant group aligned with al-Qaeda and is seeking to oust the interim prime minister, American-trained Mahmoud Jibril, after he criticized the Islamists. Ali Sallabi, a key leader of the uprising against Qaddafi's forty-two years of oppression, while pledging to respect democracy and equal rights, is aligned with the Libyan branch of the Muslim Brotherhood, which, as in Egypt, has come "out of the cold" and will use its superior organizational capabilities to potentially dominate a new democratic Libya.[66]

In the end it is the evolution of the Muslim Brotherhood that will determine the direction of the Arab Middle East in Egypt and other key countries. Will the exercise of power in a democratic system temper its fundamentalist views, as the group struggles to bring tranquility, government services, jobs, and economic opportunity to the countries in which it has been newly empowered? Will the Arab Spring bring about the birth of a new moderate Islam, or will it simply enable Islamic parties long on the outside of political power to implement their strict sharia law and anti-Western and anti-Israel policies?

In Egypt, the Arab bellwether state, there will be an uneasy balance of power between the pro-Western democracy and the anti-Western Islamists for years to come, with the young secularists who initiated the revolution gradually regaining their voice. I believe the imperative of Western investment to create jobs and the need for U.S. military and economic assistance will temper Egypt's domestic and foreign policy agenda and will keep its peace treaty with Israel intact, even as it more openly champions the Palestinian cause and restores diplomatic relations with Iran. There is already indication that the newly empowered Islamic forces in the parliament recognize that the secular leaders, such as Wael Ghonim, the young executive from Google who was the face to Egypt and the world at Tahrir Square, must be accommodated, even if they are now in disarray. The Muslim Brotherhood is keeping a distance from the Salafists and prefers to align with more moderate Islamic and secular elements. They will find if they push sharia law too far, that long-empowered Egyptian women will provide a potent opposition force and will be unwilling to go back to medieval days.

The uneasy and unpredictable balance of power in Egypt was graphically demonstrated by two conflicting events. One was the tense standoff with the U.S. over the charges leveled against U.S. supported pro-democracy groups like the National Democratic Institute, the International Republican Institute (including the son of the U.S. Secretary of Transportation Ray LaHood), and Freedom House (which I had served as vice chairman) for failing to properly register as foreign-supported NGOs. At the same time, the interim government of Egypt swallowed its pride and sought an IMF loan to heal the hemorrhage in its budget from the economic downturn occasioned by the Egyptian revolution. Charges have been dropped against the American NGOs and they have been allowed to leave Egypt, but the incident pointed up the anti-American sentiment in the country.

But it is critical to be clear-eyed in looking at the new Islamic forces. In Tunisia and Morocco, they are genuinely moderate. But in Egypt, the Salafists, who have won close to one-fifth of the parliamentary vote, are a different story. They are more fundamentalist, following the Saudi Arabian Wahhabi model. Salafi leader Kamal Habib was jailed in the 1980s in connection with the assassination of President Anwar Sadat, following Sadat's historic visit to Jerusalem and the peace treaty with Israel. The Salafists burned Coptic Christian churches in Cairo. Leaders such as Habib say they have reformed and will focus on jobs and fighting corruption.[67]

Since its founding in 1928 in Egypt, the Muslim Brotherhood has been the central Islamic force in Egypt and much of the Arab Middle East. It is not monolithic.

Its offshoot in Gaza, Hamas, is radical and unrepentant in its goal to eliminate Israel. Its branch in Jordan, the Islamic Action Front, is the principal opposition force and has not called for the end to the rule of the Hashemite king. In Egypt, the Muslim Brotherhood has long rejected violent jihad and has focused on providing social services, such as free medical clinics and schools, to poor Egyptians.

Still, the Muslim Brotherhood, let alone the Salafists, remains committed to a religious state following strict Koran law. It is sobering to remember that this newly elected power center has long had the rock-bottom belief that "Allah is our objective. The Prophet is our leader. Quran is our law. Jihad is our way. Dying in the way of Allah is our highest hope."[68]

The American Role in Addressing Islamic Extremism

How the U.S. can best address Islamic extremism is a challenging question with few clear answers. On the one-year anniversary of the self-immolation of Mohamed Bouazizi in Tunisia, the *Washington Post* recognized the differences between the Arab Spring and other prodemocratic revolutions in the former Soviet bloc countries of Central Europe, East Asia, and Latin America. While those revolutions were largely peaceful, the violence in Syria, Libya, Yemen, and even Egypt has been in sharp contrast. While the other revolutions adopted clear democratic and free-market economic policies, the new Islamic-dominated governments are likely to adopt more populist, state-dominated policies that will discourage needed Western investment. And finally, while the new democracies in Latin America, Central Europe, and Asia have become firm allies of the U.S. and the EU, the new Islamic parties are likely to take a more arm's-length relationship with the West and, by extension, with Israel.[69]

The administration of George W. Bush originally championed democratic elections across the region, one of the strategic justifications advanced by the neoconservatives for the Iraq invasion. The theory was that democratic regimes would be more amenable to the West and to a wider peaceful orientation and would give voice to a discontented Arab public. But when the Bush administration pushed for Palestinian elections in 2006 over the objections of Israel and moderate Palestinian leaders who feared a Hamas victory, Hamas won in Gaza and then violently ousted Fatah and the Palestinian Authority.

Even before the 2011 Arab uprisings, opinion polls suggested if elections were held, Islamists might win power in Jordan, Egypt, and across the Maghreb and the comparatively moderate Gulf states. This could result in more capable, more legitimate, but also more anti-Western, anti-American, and anti-Israeli governments surrounding the Jewish state. Here, Professor Huntington was prescient when he warned in his *Clash of Civilizations* fifteen years ago that in the short term, "[i]n the Arab world . . . Western democracy strengthens anti-Western political forces."[70]

The U.S. now has no other alternative to maintain its influence in the region than to embrace the new democratic forces, to fully engage with the new Islamic parties and governments, but to do so in ways that urge compliance with the genuine principles of democracy, free speech, the rule of law, respect for differences of opinion and for the rights of women, and an open economic system. In a major May 2011 speech, President Obama, building on his 2009 Cairo speech, did just that in setting out the policy of the U.S. in the new revolutionary environment. He stressed that "it will be the policy of the United States to promote reform across the region, and to support transitions to democracy"; supporting a "set of universal rights," including freedom of speech, assembly, religion, and the "right to choose your own leaders," was a "top priority that must be translated into concrete actions."

In the process, he took on pro-American leaders not following these principles, such as the royal family of Bahrain for its "mass arrests and brute force" in putting down peaceful Shiite demonstrators, and Yemen's President Saleh for failing to "follow through on his commitment to transfer power," which he has done at last. Obama offered debt relief, economic assistance, and new trade initiatives for Egypt and Tunisia.[71] So, too, Secretary of State Clinton has strongly embraced the right of Arab women to make their own choice, without compulsion, in whether to wear a hijab or a head covering, and on their right to fully engage in the political process.[72] A Gallup poll taken before Obama's election showed more than two-thirds of Muslims admired American democracy, education, and technology. So there is a base on which to build.

To the extent that economic reforms in the Arab world can produce a middle class, it will be easier to promote reform since extremists will hold less attraction. The Bush administration's mistake in pressing elections on the Palestinian territories was to do so before the foundations for democracy were in place. But with the Arab upheaval, the U.S. role must be to help channel the energy that toppled the autocrats into constructive democratic directions and prevent radical groups from hijacking the promise the revolutions have brought to the Arab world.

The United States remains a force in the region and can still play a major, even if less dominant, role in strengthening the moderate, pro-Western camp of Egypt, Jordan, Saudi Arabia, and the Gulf states against the rejectionist camp of Iran and Syria, and in so doing help buttress Israeli support abroad. In just the past few years, the U.S. has reached agreements with a number of Gulf states (UAE, Qatar, Kuwait, and Bahrain) to deploy two Patriot missile batteries to each country.[73] This provides assurance of American support against Iran's growing military power. In the fall of 2010, the Gulf states and Saudi Arabia concluded a huge arms deal with the U.S. to protect against a resurgent Iran.

The U.S. must remain directly engaged on every front but must do so with discernment. In contrast to the strategically essential first Gulf War, the geopolitical sum of the Bush administration's Iraq War equals the rise of Iran as the dominant foreign force in that country now that American troops have left, enforced by the close ties between Iraq's majority Shiite population and the Iranian Shiite government.

The U.S., in the years ahead, must fully engage with the new democratic governments, even if controlled by Islamic forces; support the Egyptian military while trying to steer it away from self-defeating policies; condition future U.S. aid on compliance with existing international agreements with Israel; provide substantial economic assistance and technical help in building new democratic institutions; and continue to work toward an Israeli-Palestinian two-state solution, which will help temper opposition to Israel from the newly empowered Islamic forces in the Middle East.

At the same time, the U.S. should continue to directly confront Iran's budding nuclear program through harsh sanctions, show stronger support for Iran's opposition as it insists on the same democratic opening the Arab Spring has brought in the Middle East,[74] and reassure Arab countries in the region of U.S. protection against Iran. This is a tall order, but one that is achievable.

Israel's Role

No country is more directly affected than Israel by the unprecedented turmoil of the neighbors that surround it. The twin pillars of its relationship in the Muslim world, Egypt and Turkey, are distancing themselves in every way from Israel. The situation in Lebanon to Israel's north, which looked so promising following the expulsion of Syrian troops and the 2009 election of a pro-Western prime minister, Saad Hariri, the son of the murdered former prime minister Rafik Hariri, has drastically changed for the worse. Hariri has been ousted by the same Hezbollah that killed his father (as a UN judicial panel found in 2011), and its candidate was installed as the new prime minister, Najib Mikati, a Sunni Muslim and one of the richest men in the country.[75]

And Israel's Palestinian negotiating partner, Mahmoud Abbas (Abu Mazen), has signed a pact with Israel's archenemy Hamas and is ignoring pleas from the U.S. by seeking a unilateral vote on statehood in the United Nations. The conventional wisdom is that these convulsions in the Arab world will lead Israel to pull back even further from negotiations with the Palestinians, concerned that trading land for peace could put radical forces in power. Prime Minister Netanyahu seemed to confirm this by arguing that the basis for peace and stability "lies in bolstering the might of the state of Israel" and casting doubt on whether the gaps between the Israeli and Palestinian positions could be bridged.[76]

At such a period of enormous uncertainty, Israel's military prowess is important to emphasize, along with heightened security guarantees for any peace agreement. To show its military resolve to the world, Israel took the rare step of opening Palmachim Air Force Base to foreign reporters, highlighting Israel's Iron Dome antirocket missile defense system and its Arrow antiballistic missile system. But this also served to underscore a major shift in Israel's military doctrine by providing multilayered defenses beyond the traditional deterrence and attack capabilities. Its new Iron Dome antimissile system was first used successfully in April 2011, to intercept incoming Katyusha rockets from militants in Gaza. The newly modified Arrow 2 system, with an Arrow 3 generation being developed, intercepts missiles high up in the atmosphere. And a new Ballistic Picture Control Center that detects incoming threats and alerts the public became operational in 2010.

But as critical as military strength is in a hostile Middle East, it would be a tragic mistake if Israel only adopted a defensive posture and hunkered down, circling the wagons. Just the opposite should occur. For sure, the Fatah-Hamas pact enormously complicates the process. Both the Obama administration and the Israeli government have properly refused to negotiate with a government that includes Hamas, so long as it remains dedicated to Israel's destruction and refuses to accept the Quartet's conditions for negotiation. Still, Israel must be more forthcoming in its vision of a two-state solution so that, at the least it is seen to offer the Palestinians a peaceful path toward their own state, even if the Palestinians turn their back on realistic solutions. This is the best way for Israel to remove itself from the turmoil in the Arab world.

Now is the time for Israel to act strategically. Israel's choices can serve either to increase support for or undermine pro-Western forces in the Muslim world. There is little indication that Israel is thinking in such a strategic fashion. Yet, nothing is more important to Israel's long-term national security than doing its part, even at the margins of the great internal struggle within the Muslim world, to strengthen those Arab nations that have already made peace with Israel, as well as Palestinian moderates, and to work toward silencing jihadists and radicals who so expertly use the Israeli-Palestinian conflict to incite support. The Obama administration and Secretary of State Hillary Clinton understand this dynamic and are doing all they can to encourage the peace process. President Obama's May 19, 2011, speech and a follow-up speech a few days later to AIPAC not only embraced the new democratic movements in the Arab world but also recommitted the U.S. to the Israeli-Palestinian peace process, laying out explicitly for the first time that negotiations should be based on Israel's 1967 borders, but with agreed land swaps to take into account the major settlement blocs in the West Bank and West Jerusalem. Yet, it is unclear if the Israeli government is prepared to raise its strategic horizons to exploit the divisions within the Arab world.

In the American outreach to Muslim moderates, Israel has its role to play. The U.S. strategy calls for Israel to cooperate in the peace process with the Palestinians and help America and its allies show the region's constituencies there can be a better future based on economic growth, tolerance, and integration and not violent Islamization. The U.S. and the West would assist in the creation of an institutional framework in the Palestinian territories, and elsewhere in the region, which over time could lead to stable democracies in the Middle East with strong, civil societies, independent courts, and respect for human rights and the rule of law.

The Saudis advanced a plan, first in 2002 and again in 2008, offering full acceptance of Israel as a sovereign state and normalization of relations. While the offer came with several unrealistic conditions, such as a complete pullback to pre-1967 borders, it is nevertheless an important step forward and did not insist on the "right of return" for over one million Palestinians but calls for a "just solution" to the refugee problem, probably involving compensation, which could involve an international monetary payment. The broader message of the Saudi plan demonstrates a new willingness to end sixty years of conflict and is a far cry from the three "nos" the Arabs sent to Israel at the Arab League's Khartoum Summit after their defeat in the 1967 War—no peace, no recognition, and no negotiations. Over fifty Muslim nations in the Organization of the Islamic Conference have endorsed the Saudi two-state peace process, with the exception of Iran.

It would have been useful for successive Israeli governments to have publicly recognized the importance of the Saudi plan without formally accepting it and then offering negotiations. No such recognition ever was announced. Now Israel must act quickly and not allow itself to be paralyzed by the uncertain political outlook in the Middle East. The current cycle of violence against Israel makes compromise by any Israeli government more difficult. On the Palestinian side, despair is increasing popular support for violence and for Hamas even in the West Bank.

While combating terrorism with military force is important, it must be only part of a broader strategy of engagement including economic development and empowering moderates in the territories by making it clear that a peaceful path pays greater dividends than violence. This would mean continuing to relax restrictions on the movement of Palestinians within the West Bank; beginning to allow Palestinians with no personal record of terrorism to seek work in Israel; and reinforcing the institutions of the Palestinian Authority.

The role of Israeli nongovernmental organizations is too often ignored—and given the entrenchment of official views, quick progress requires resorting to extragovernmental actors. Bottom-up efforts to promote more contact, cooperation, and dialogue between Israelis and Palestinians are essential for building a viable peace. Many organizations doing important grassroots work should be leveraged further—the New Israel Fund concentrates on improving relations between Israeli Jews and Arabs and helping Israeli Arabs; the PeaceWorks Foundation, Seeds for Peace, One Voice, and the Leo Kramer Foundation for Applied Research focus on bringing together Palestinians and Israeli professionals, businessmen, and young people. There is a natural Israeli-Palestinian marketplace: Small Israeli high-tech companies and American giants in Israel are outsourcing engineering and computer programming to Palestinians because of their low costs, proven skills, and work ethic. They often communicate with each other by the Internet, circumventing the security barriers that prevent direct meetings.[77] These efforts deserve support from the U.S., EU, and Israeli government. But legislation in the Israeli Knesset, sponsored by Foreign Minister Avigdor Lieberman, would sharply limit foreign donations to NGOs considered "political," a contravention of Israel's long-standing support for free expression.

Still, there is only so much that nongovernmental organizations and corporations can do. Governments remain the primary players, and Israel must demonstrate to the Palestinian public that the path to peace produces a better way of life and more opportunity than the Hamas path of violence, even if they are conjoined with Fatah in a pact of cooperation.

Many of the Palestinian Authority's goals, from delivering public services in a noncorrupt manner to rooting out Hamas militants in the West Bank, were put in jeopardy by the Hamas pact. The Palestinian Authority had been making progress in developing a functioning police force with U.S. assistance and training. In fact, for all of its political downsides, Israel's intervention in Gaza belied the notion that pressure could force a similar unilateral withdrawal from the West Bank, and weaken Hamas as a military force, limiting its ability to cause havoc in the West Bank.

The U.S. role in training Palestinian policy to combat Hamas terrorists in the West Bank threatening Israel and the Palestinian Authority is too little appreciated. Starting in 2005 in the Bush administration, and enhanced in the Obama administration, a special unit called the office of the United States Security Coordinator (USSC) was established on the ground in the West Bank to train the national security forces and police force, first under Lieutenant General Kip Ward, for five years under Lieutenant General Keith Dayton, and now under Lieutenant General Michael Moeller. From 2007 to 2010 $392 million was appropriated through the State Department with $150 million more for 2011.[78]

American training of the Palestinian police has proven far more effective than even Israel could have imagined, and the Israel Defense Forces are increasingly willing to pull back in their favor in Jenin, once a center of violence.[79] An important lesson from the Jenin project is that Hamas is not strong in many parts of the West Bank, and the situation was eased by the evacuation in 2005 of several outposts illegal under Israeli law. Israeli authorities have removed many checkpoints, granted VIP passes to some 1,500 Palestinian officials and businessmen, issued work visas to others, and encouraged sewing workshops in the Jenin refugee camp to sell clothes to shops in Tel Aviv. Jenin is located in the Gilboa region, where there is a history of Arab-Jewish cooperation; it persists in the regional council headed by Daniel Atar, who is Jewish, and his deputy Arab.

Aside from the economic benefits, the Jenin program inculcated pride and determination among Palestinians to build a peaceful state that combats terrorism. Brigadier General Munir al-Zoubi, who commands the Palestinian Presidential Guard, said: "We are here to enforce law and order and to use all means to fight terrorism."[80] He noted that only a few years ago he would have been branded a collaborator for using the term *terrorism*, but now "We have discovered that many people commit terrorist acts under the resistance to occupation. And we are fighting that."[81]

Yet progress in the Middle East never follows a linear path. In April 2011, an Israeli Arab, Juliano Mer Khamis, who headed a children's theater in Jenin, the Freedom Theatre, was assassinated by Palestinian militants in Jenin.[82]

The Arab world must also be prepared for symbolic acts that will encourage Israel to take bolder action. The Obama administration's efforts to get countries such as Saudi Arabia to make even minimal gestures toward Israel, like allowing Israeli planes to fly over Saudi air space, have been summarily rebuffed. Peace with Egypt became possible when Anwar Sadat came to Jerusalem; Israelis need to see neighbors and potential partners willing to extend the same hand. Palestinian negotiators have never been willing to recognize Israel as a Jewish state because it would undercut their effort, futile though they know it is, to have their refugees return to Israel; in turn this undercuts support among the Israeli public for the peace process.[83]

Another initiative on the Israeli side would be to dramatically improve public services to its Israeli Arab citizens who make up 20 percent of Israel's population. They have the right to vote, equal treatment in the Israeli medical system, to schooling in state-supported institutions, to property, and to redress in courts for grievances. While discrimination exists, the only official barrier is exemption from military service, where few Israeli Arabs would choose to serve but from whose ranks Israel's leadership is drawn.

But their incomes are far below those of Israel's Jewish citizens, their public services are more meager than those extended to Israeli Jews,[84] and gross insults fly in public from time to time: In December 2010, the chief rabbis in a dozen cities declared that Jewish landlords should not rent to non-Jews.[85] Most Israeli-Arabs nevertheless prefer to remain in Israel than live in the more economically depressed West Bank, let alone the authoritarian Arab states outside Israel.

Yet at the same time, Israeli Arabs commemorate what they call "Nakba Day" (day of catastrophe) on the same day each May that Israeli Jews celebrate victory in the war of independence, perhaps the only minority group in any country that considers the creation of the state in which they live a disaster.[86]

Nevertheless, there should be a supreme effort to improve Israeli Arabs' economic circumstances and to treat them as equal citizens, not, as Israeli foreign minister Avigdor Lieberman has proposed, forcing them to swear loyalty and advocating land swaps in any peace agreement that would annex Arab districts to a Palestinian state.[87] Prime Minister Netanyahu cannot silence him without bringing down his governing coalition.

Prime Minister Netanyahu, with whom I worked during the Clinton administration, is genuinely committed to the economic betterment of the Palestinians.[88] With his unique background as both a graduate of MIT's business school and a student of political science, he is well aware that nothing threatens Israel more than having a seething, poverty-ridden population on its borders. Within Israel, he was the most forceful champion for Israel's economic liberalization, which sparked Israel's phenomenal economic boom. But the economic dimension can carry the process only so far. At the end of the day, he will have to confront the need for a bold political effort, even at the expense of his conservative governing coalition.

There is a great need for a convergence of policies on key issues between the U.S. and Israel—on how to resuscitate the peace process, on the future of Israeli settlements, and on how to deal with the new Hamas-Fatah reconciliation. Israel is increasingly isolated on these issues around the world, and only the U.S. stands in the way of even further isolation.

Early in the Obama administration, a critical mistake was made calling for a complete settlement freeze, without prior consultation with the Israeli government, thereby creating a condition the Palestinians used as a bar to resume peace negotiations with Israel, terminated at the end of the Olmert government. Even so, Prime Minister Netanyahu agreed to an unprecedented ten-month settlement freeze, but it failed to unlock Palestinian participation until the ninth month. When President Obama asked for a three-month extension of the settlement freeze, it was denied by the prime minister.

The critical need for cooperation in the post–Arab Spring world has not gotten off to a promising start. There was a contretemps over President Obama's speech of May 19, 2011, largely devoted to the U.S. reaction to the Arab Spring, but in which he called for the starting point for renewing stalled Palestinian-Israeli negotiations on the basis of Israel's pre-1967 borders with agreed land swaps. There was no prior consultation with the Israeli government. While this had been the implicit position of American presidents going back to President Clinton, it was stated with more clarity than before and elicited a furious and historically unprecedented reaction by Netanyahu in an Oval Office meeting, during which he ignored the president's condition for "agreed land swaps" and lectured his host before the television cameras. Obama had to clarify his position in a speech to the American Israel Public Affairs Committee (AIPAC), the powerful pro-Israel lobby, on May 22, that the 1967 borders would not be final and would take into account major settlement blocs Israel would keep in any two-state outcome. This was essentially a reiteration of the policy of President George W. Bush.

To reconcile differences on settlements, Israel should limit them to genuinely natural growth and keep them within their current boundaries, building up rather than out. This would provide some room for maneuver by the Palestinians. A coordinated mapping exercise with the U.S. to establish boundaries could help prevent misunderstandings. While it is commonly understood that the largest settlement blocks would remain under Israeli control in any final peace agreement, many others would have to be dismantled. Prime Minister Netanyahu's speech to a joint session of Congress implied as much. But, if settlements continue at their current pace, a two-state solution with a viable Palestinian state with contiguous borders will become impossible.

Another dimension to the deadlock over control of the West Bank is the dispute over its natural resources. Israeli companies quarry rocks to produce gravel and sand to build settlements, as well as transporting it out of the West Bank to build roads and other projects inside the original 1948 armistice boundary, known as the Green Line. Israel's Supreme Court has never found the Israeli settlements or the Israeli use of West Bank natural resources to be illegal, ruling that since the status of the West Bank before the 1967 Six Day War was unclear, the area has not necessarily been "occupied" by Israel in the sense of wider international law—a view widely disputed in other countries.

While I believe Israel is correct as a legal matter, this does not change the fact that Israel is depleting the natural resources of a future Palestinian state over the objections of its present leaders. Nor does it defuse the anger and frustration of many Palestinians in the West Bank, who are growing disillusioned with the potential for peace and of the viability of whatever state may emerge. When radical Jewish settlers poison Palestinian olive trees and burn mosques, passions are only inflamed.

There is a convergence of thinking between the president's views and the prime minister's on refusing to negotiate with Hamas while it remains committed to Israel's destruction, although Israel dealt with Hamas, through Egypt, to gain the release of Gilad Shalit. But this is only part of the answer. With the unity agreement between the Palestinian factions, there must be some way to continue a dialogue. Perhaps the best of a bad situation would be to continue to engage with Palestinian president Abbas, and whatever technocratic government emerges, and rely on him to obtain agreements from Hamas. During the most intense battles with the IRA in Northern Ireland, Britain maintained a dialogue with the IRA's political arm,

Sinn Fein. By simultaneously fighting IRA terrorism and reaching out to Northern Ireland's political leaders, peace was ultimately achieved.

The lesson for Israel is clear. If a unity government of some sort eventually emerges in the Palestinian territories, and this remains uncertain, Hamas may agree to abide by any agreement and avoid climbing down from its professed desire to obliterate Israel. This will pose a difficult challenge for Israel. The European Union will almost certainly recognize such a government, and the U.S. may be hard pressed not to do likewise, at least to keep economic aid and training funds for the Palestinian security forces in the West Bank. Here again, an agreed approach must be worked out in intensive discussions between Israel and the U.S.

Israelis must not be lulled into a false sense that the status quo will provide the long-term security they need. If the peace process collapses, it will be hard for the Palestinian Authority to sustain support for the internal reforms on which it is embarking. Cooperation will erode between the Palestinian police and the Israel Defense Forces and Israeli intelligence. Hamas will be able to capitalize on the vacuum and to assert that only violence produces results. And Israel's increasing isolation in the world community will be amplified. For Israel, peace is a national security imperative. Permanently controlling too much territory and too many hostile Palestinians is futile and self-defeating. It will inevitably lead to increasingly repressive measures to maintain control, made all the more so because of demographic realities.

At the onset of the first Intifada in the mid-1980s, Itamar Rabinovich, later Israeli ambassador to the U.S., and his wife Efrat organized a small dinner for my wife Fran and me with Leah and Yitzhak Rabin. I asked Rabin why the Palestinians were in revolt. In his characteristically taciturn manner, between puffs of a cigarette, he said simply, "They do not like to be occupied by us." The longer the occupation lasts, the more expanding settlements collide with a rapidly expanding population of Palestinians; and the more anger and resentment that swells up among the Palestinians, the more the moderates committed to a peaceful two-state solution will have the ground cut from beneath them.

The Israeli-Palestinian impasse entered a new, even more dangerous phase as Palestinian president Abbas has spurned Washington's entreaties, from whom his Palestinian Authority receives over $200 million annually in economic assistance, and sought a declaration of statehood in the U.N. Only the Security Council can accept a new member state, and the Obama administration is pledged to veto their application. The administration worked hard and effectively to prevent the necessary nine votes to bring the issue before the Security Council. There remains the possibility that the UN General Assembly may vote to change the status of the Palestinians from an "observer entity" to an "observer state," like the Holy See (the Vatican).

This seemingly minor change in status has earthshaking consequences. It would permit the Palestinian "state" to join the International Criminal Court and bring suits against Israeli occupation of what they will claim is their state. UN sanctions may be sought against Israel for "occupying" what they will claim is their sovereign territory. Scores of countries may place embassies in the new "state," some in East Jerusalem, and may insist that the IDF provide unimpeded access. Palestinian demonstrators may march on settlements, demanding their removal, setting up potentially violent confrontations with the settler movement. A third intifada is not an impossible scenario.

Israel will not stand idly by. It may impound the tax revenues it collects and normally forwards to the Palestinian Authority on products sold in the territories. Israel could try to annex some territory, as it did in East Jerusalem and on the Golan Heights, making a peacefully negotiated two-state solution even more complicated to achieve. Caught in between will be the U.S.

This will have broad ramifications in the Muslim world, already on a knife's edge between moderates and radicals in an intense battle for the heart and soul—and direction—of the Muslim world that will be fought in the Middle East during the years ahead, and it will determine its future.

On a hopeful note, at the beginning of 2012, at the initiative of Jordan's King Abdullah, for the first time in sixteen months, the Palestinians and Israelis have commenced a new round of negotiations under the terms set by the Quartet.[89] With a new round of settlements announced around Jerusalem, and with both sides locked into fixed positions, progress is far from certain. But for the first time the two sides are exchanging specific proposals on borders and security arrangements. Progress here can help bolster American efforts to steer the volatile Middle East in a more positive direction, help block implementation of the Hamas-Fatah pact for a "unity" government, and prevent efforts by Congress to cut off funds for the Palestinian Authority. But so far nothing tangible has resulted from the talks.

One unadulerated positive is that amidst all the turmoil in the Arab Middle East, the Obama administration has reached new heights in the military relationship with Israel, strengthening the IDF with the most modern weaponry, and helping to finance an effective anti-missile defense system, the Iron Dome.

4

Nontraditional Global Security Risks

G LOBAL SECURITY IS challenged by a number of forces that when viewed together are new in the scope of history and pose unprecedented destructive
dangers. These nontraditional security challenges include the potential spread
of nuclear weapons and chemical weapons to radical states such as Iran and to
terrorist groups; cyberwarfare as a new form of arms race; worldwide environmental threats to water and climate; and demographic challenges with profound
political implications for the world, including Jewish continuity.

Although they appear disparate and disconnected, they have much in common. Many seem intractable and require states to work together through imperfect international institutions over decades. If unresolved, their effects cannot
be reversed, and the entire planet will suffer. As in so many other issues, U.S.
leadership is critical, but the State of Israel also has a role to play despite its small
size, which paradoxically makes some issues more pressing. Demography has a
special impact on world Jewry and Israel: While much of the world must cope
with a rapidly expanding population, Jews must struggle to maintain their influence with too few—a stagnant population of about 13 million in a world that
officially reached 7 billion people in 2011.

Nuclear Proliferation

By far the most immediate and dangerous challenge is the spread of nuclear
weapons technology. Since the end of the Cold War, a number of states have
acquired nuclear weapons or the technology to produce them.

At the height of the Cold War, the U.S. and the Soviet Union possessed a total of 70,000 nuclear warheads, but each superpower kept its stock under tight control. There was a balance that effectively kept a check on their use. Soviet leader Nikita Khrushchev's rash action of placing nuclear weapons in Cuba, 90 miles from U.S. shores, and President John Kennedy's successful confrontation is likely one of the reasons the Politburo dismissed him. China, with a far smaller arsenal, has also followed a responsible policy.

At the time the Soviet Union was formally dissolved on December 25, 1991, both sides together had deployed more than 19,000 strategic warheads. So the world is safer in terms of the two great nuclear powers but more dangerous with the number of countries with nuclear weapons. As President Obama noted, "in a strange turn of history, the threat of global war has gone down, but the risk of a nuclear attack has gone up."[1] Since the end of the Cold War more countries have acquired nuclear weapons or the technology to produce them. China has some 240 total warheads, India and Pakistan between 80 and 100 each, and North Korea only a few. Israel is thought to have an estimated 80 to 200 warheads in its arsenal.[2]

Thirty-one countries operate a total of 441 civilian nuclear power reactors, but nine, led by the U.S., and including France, Japan, Russia, South Korea, the UK, Canada, Ukraine, and Germany, produce the vast majority of civilian nuclear power. By 2050, it is estimated there will be 1,800 nuclear reactors, many in countries that have none today. But with proper controls, these civilian reactors need not become factories for nuclear weapons.

The greatest threat to the world in general, and to Israel in particular, would be for nuclear arms to get into the hands of Iran, al-Qaeda, the Taliban, and other radical nonstate actors.

The history of Iran's acquisition of nuclear technology through the network of A.Q. Khan is a stark reminder of how difficult it is to prevent nuclear proliferation. The builder of Pakistan's "Islamic bomb," operating almost certainly with the knowledge of Pakistan's security establishment, has admitted running the world's largest nuclear proliferation network, reaching out to North Korea and Libya as well as Iran.[3] In the last years of the twentieth century, Washington convinced a host of countries—Argentina, Brazil, Ukraine, Kazakhstan, Belarus, South Africa, and Taiwan among them—to abandon their nuclear weapons programs. Libya, even under Qaddafi, followed in 2003. It now appears these diplomatic successes were merely a pause before the storm.

Mohamed ElBaradei, then director general of the UN's International Atomic Energy Agency (IAEA), has indicated that as many as thirty nations have the technology to build nuclear weapons quickly if they choose to do so. His successor, Yukiya Amano, is deeply concerned that terrorist groups could acquire the means to disable a city by using conventional explosives to spread a suitcase full of nuclear material in a so-called dirty bomb. He told a World Economic Forum in 2011 in which I participated that his agency receives information about illicit trafficking in nuclear materials every two days.

The fear is not fanciful that in the near future terrorist groups, along with Iran, will be more easily able to enrich uranium, a key ingredient in nuclear weapons. General Electric has developed a new laser beam technology that makes it much cheaper and faster to enrich uranium than using today's large centrifuge. GE is seeking U.S. government permission to build a $1 billion plant using laser enrichment to make nuclear reactor fuel on a mass basis—enough to fuel up to sixty reactors and power more than a third of all the housing units in the nation. Iran has successfully tested laser enrichment in its laboratory, kept the results secret, and when the IAEA discovered the cover-up in 2003, insisted it had dismantled the facility. But in typical Iranian fashion, in 2010 Iranian president Mahmoud Ahmadinejad praised the "relentless efforts" of their scientists in building lasers for enrichment. Iran has rebuffed efforts by the IAEA to obtain more information. Given Iran's closeness to Hezbollah and Hamas, the fear of misuse and the threat to Israel are chilling.[4]

Henry Kissinger put it bluntly: "The proliferation of nuclear weapons in the face of the stated opposition of . . . major powers severely damages the prospects for a homogenous international order promoting non-proliferation; . . . it would be unreasonable to expect that those weapons will never be used."[5]

Even for stable nations such as India, careful management is essential. India, like Israel, has not signed the Nuclear Non-Proliferation Treaty, but the U.S. Senate approved a nuclear treaty with India granting it the right to reprocess American-supplied nuclear fuel under strict conditions. India and its rival Pakistan have fought several wars, and both have exploded nuclear weapons; this puts 1.4 billion people under the threat of mutual nuclear attack. Pakistan, with a shaky civilian government, a strong terrorist insurgency, an intelligence service focused more on India than the Taliban, and a military at odds with the U.S. over its counterinsurgency strategy, has the fastest growing nuclear arsenal in the world. As Bruce Riedel, an expert in the area put it, Pakistan "has more terrorists per square mile than any place else on earth, and it has a nuclear weapons program that is growing faster than any place else on earth."[6]

Equally problematic, but of less imminent threat, is North Korea, which has been intransigent despite more than a decade of negotiations, threats, sanctions, and more negotiations. Even though it cannot adequately feed its own people, at some point in the next several years North Korea will almost certainly master both the construction of a weapon and its missile delivery mechanism unless its program can be aborted. While the direct threat from a nuclear-armed North Korea cannot be discounted, the danger is largely confined to the Korean Peninsula. Still, Israel and the West remain at risk—*not* from the direct threat of nuclear attack, but from efforts by the cash-strapped North Korean regime to sell its technology to belligerent and unstable states, who might in turn share it with terrorist groups. The nascent nuclear facility in Syria, bombed by Israel in 2007, was made of North Korean components.

Surprisingly, a break came in February 2012, shortly after a new leader, Kim Jong-un, took over for his deceased father, when North Korea unexpectedly announced a suspension of its nuclear weapons testing and uranium enrichment, a moratorium on tests of its long-range missiles, and agreed to allow international inspectors to inspect its main nuclear facility. In return, the Obama administration pledged to ship food aid to the starving population in the country.[7]

The Unique Iranian Threat

Iran's drive for nuclear weapons is the paramount threat to the security of Israel but poses an equal danger to the U.S. and Europe, as well as the West's moderate Arab allies. Armed with nuclear weapons, Iran would try to become the regional hegemon, tipping the balance of power away from the moderate, pro-Western Muslim states and emboldening radical states and Tehran's terrorist clients, Hezbollah and Hamas. A nuclear-emboldened Iran might step up subversive activities against the Gulf sheikdoms and could demand that all U.S. troops get out of the Middle East.[8] This in turn would likely spur some pro-Western Arab states to pursue their own nuclear programs. By November 2006, six pro-Western Muslim countries—Egypt, Saudi Arabia, United Arab Emirates, Algeria, Morocco, and Tunisia—responded to Iran's growing threat by announcing their intentions to pursue "more robust" nuclear programs.[9] Saudi Arabia is in the process of establishing a civilian nuclear and renewable energy center, and Egypt announced plans for several nuclear reactors even before Mubarak's overthrow.

This validated the prediction by General Brent Scowcroft, national security adviser to Presidents Ford and George H.W. Bush, that a nuclear-armed Iran would "start an eruption of proliferation among the Gulf states, and would reach as far as Turkey and Egypt, with states doubting the U.S. deterrent umbrella that had heretofore provided states some comfort against a growing Iran," and might even cause reverberations in East Asia, igniting proliferation in Japan and South Korea.[10]

A nuclear-armed Iran would also undermine what is left of the nonproliferation efforts led for decades by the U.S., and might be the death kneel for the Non-Proliferation Treaty. Even without a nuclear weapon Iran is the world's most dangerous rogue nation, having already blown up the Israeli Embassy (1992) and the Jewish community center (1994) in Buenos Aires; murdered its own former prime minister, Shapour Bakhtiar in Paris (1991); played a role in the bombing of the housing complex for U.S. soldiers in Khobar, Saudi Arabia (1996); funded and armed Hezbollah in Lebanon and Hamas in

Gaza; supported Syria's assassination of the pro-Western prime minister of Lebanon, Rafiq al Hariri (2005);[11] and tried to murder the Saudi ambassador to Washington, working through a Mexican drug cartel (2011). In addition, Iran's president pledged to wipe Israel off the face of the earth. One can only imagine how much more emboldened Iran would be with a nuclear weapon in its pocket. The speaker of Iran's parliament, Ali Larijani, has put their case baldly: "If Iran becomes atomic Iran, no longer will anyone dare to challenge it because they would have to pay too high a price."[12]

By the end of 2011 Iran already had 4.9 tons of low-grade enriched uranium, enough to make four to six atomic bombs, if enriched to a weapons grade, and is producing more daily.

Iran's rapidly developing nuclear program represents more than a pure military threat at a time of unprecedented upheavals in the Arab world, when Iran and Syria continue supporting terrorist groups. Iran has built several nuclear facilities and dispersed them throughout the country. Iran admits to enriching low-grade uranium at Natanz, near Tehran, suitable for only civilian uses, although Iran is now enriching it to a higher level. IAEA inspectors visit regularly.

At Bushehr in the south, the Russians have gone forward with construction of a nuclear plant and the provision of critical technology to Iran over strong U.S. objections. It is a civilian reactor and since Russia controls the nuclear fuel, there is little direct weapons threat. But the reactor provides Iranian scientists experience in nuclear technology for Iranian scientists.[13]

At Isfahan, the Iranian government inaugurated its first plant to manufacture nuclear fuel on April 10, 2009, its self-declared National Nuclear Day, marking the date three years before when the regime publicly declared it had succeeded in enriching uranium, although the actual date is murky because of failure to notify the IAEA. The Isfahan plant produces low-grade fuel for a forty-megawatt research reactor in Arak, in central Iran.

Though Iran has claimed that its nuclear goals are solely peaceful, the notion that Tehran would limit itself to civilian nuclear power is not credible for a number of reasons: the reactionary nature of the theocratic regime (including the issuance of a fatwa in January 2009 by a cleric close to the leadership, sanctioning the use of nuclear weapons against Iran's enemies);[14] Ahmadinejad's pledge to destroy Israel; Iran's support for radical groups on Israel's borders; Iran's limited cooperation with the IAEA; its development of missiles with increasingly long ranges; and Iran's historic ambition to restore regional Persian hegemony. Had Persia defeated Greece in battle, there might have been no Western civilization as we know it.

Iran's failure to cooperate with the IAEA has been an especially telling marker and is the basis for four rounds of UN Security Council sanctions; the country is sharing less information as its nuclear program advances. The IAEA declared its most recent inspection trip in early 2012 a "failure," given Iran's failure to permit inspections at some of its nuclear sites and to satisfactorily respond to IAEA inquiries about suspicious parts of its nuclear program.

For eighteen years, Iran concealed its nuclear work outright. To this day, Tehran refuses to disclose if it is working on a heavy water nuclear reactor at Arak to produce plutonium, an explosive material that has only highly limited civilian use. Many experts believe that many of Iran's nuclear facilities remain undisclosed.[15]

There is wide disagreement, especially between Israel and the United States (and even within the United States), over how long it might take Iran to build an operational nuclear weapon, although not over the direction of the Iranian nuclear program. The production schedule of a bomb that could be placed on a delivery vehicle and targeted on Israel or parts of Europe was thought to be anywhere from two to ten years. But even with the widely acknowledged success of the Stuxnet computer worm that slowed Iran's centrifuges, generally thought to have emanated from Israel, by mid-2011 Iran had regained pre-Stuxnet levels of uranium enrichment.

Despite four rounds of UN sanctions and stiff U.S. and EU sanctions, along with the Stuxnet computer attack, widely believed to have emanated from Israel, Iran has never stopped running its centrifuges, which spin out more and more enriched uranium. The IAEA data indicate that Iran is enriching more uranium and at a faster rate than ever before, an average of over 100 kilograms (220 pounds) of low-enriched uranium per month, or twice the rate before the Stuxnet attack. It is now estimated to have produced 3,000 kilograms (6,600 pounds), and the amount grows each month.

To have weapons-grade material, Iran would need to enrich the uranium to 90 percent from the 3.5 percent low-grade uranium it is now producing. Particularly troubling, Iran is enriching uranium to a medium-grade level of 20 percent, which can be quickly upgraded to weapons level, and now has 80 kilograms of the 225 kilograms it would need to build a bomb.[16] Iran would have no civilian need to boost its low-grade uranium if it were interested only in a civilian program.[17] No matter how one looks at the data, the rapidity of Iran's progress is disturbing—all the more so, to paraphrase Prime Minister Netanyahu, when viewed from the banks of the Jordan rather than the banks of the Potomac. At the inauguration of the Isfahan plant, the head of the Atomic Energy Organization of Iran, Gholam Aghazadeh, boasted that his country had increased the number of the critical spinning centrifuges needed to enrich uranium to 7,000, above the estimate of some 5,500 made by the IAEA two months earlier. This would be enough to produce one ton of low-enriched uranium hexafluoride, which if further enriched could produce enough fissile material for one atomic bomb.[18] And each succeeding IAEA report has been more pessimistic.

By the time President George W. Bush left office in January 2009, American intelligence estimated that Iran had installed eight thousand centrifuges, of which half were operational, enough to produce one "bomb's worth of uranium" every eight months.[19] In its first report under Mr. Amato's leadership, the

IAEA provided a chilling conclusion: "the information raises concerns about the possible existence in Iran of past or current undisclosed activities related to the development of a nuclear payload for a missile."[20] Then director of U.S. National Intelligence Admiral Dennis Blair noted in 2009 that "Iran is clearly developing all the components of a deliverable nuclear weapons program: fissionable material, nuclear weaponizing capability, and the means to deliver it."[21]

In a dramatic disclosure at the end of the 2009 G20 Summit in Pittsburgh, President Obama, together with French president Sarkozy and then British prime minister Gordon Brown, presented evidence of another Iranian nuclear enrichment plant at Fordow, near the holy city of Qom. Iran's response was belligerent, pledging to open ten new enrichment facilities and announcing it would enrich uranium to a level closer to weapons grade.[22] Two years later, in 2011, they openly announced they were moving centrifuges to Qom, in a facility deep underground, to avoid a military strike from Israel or the U.S.

By the Spring of 2012, this operation will be substantially completed, and any military intervention more complicated and less likely to be successful. Fereydoun Abbasi, the head of Iran's Atomic Energy Organization, has openly stated that the underground Fordow plant near Qom will shortly start production of enriched uranium, making it the second uranium enrichment plant after the one at Natanz, which is more exposed to a military strike.[23]

Time is not on the side of the U.S., the West, or Israel. Western intelligence agencies and Israel now believe that Iran will reach nuclear weapons capability within no more than a year, a time frame explicitly cited by Defense Secretary Leon Panetta. Indeed, Israel will reach by the middle of 2012 what Israeli Defense Minister Barak calls the "immunity zone," when any Israeli military action would be unable to stop Iran's nuclear program, in part because they will have moved much of their nuclear program, including their centrifuges, to the deep underground facility at Qom.[24] It is critical to prevent a nuclear arms race from becoming a common motif of the new century, which an Iranian nuclear weapon would catalyze.

The principal question remaining is whether Iranian scientists and engineers have the technical sophistication to design and build a bomb. The answer is yes. The most recent IAEA report in 2011 is the most explicit of any in the past about the military dimension of the Iranian program, expressing great concern that Iran's "past or current undisclosed nuclear related activities" have "possible military dimensions" and that a "credible" case has been discovered that "Iran has carried out activities relevant to the development of a nuclear device." While the report did not conclude that Iran had a nuclear bomb or was making one, it contains one thousand pages of documents and data and interviews from ten countries; foreigners who had helped Iran describe actions that have no other purpose than a military one: computer models of nuclear explosions, experiments on nuclear triggers, and construction of large containment vessels at its Parchin military base to test the feasibility of explosive compression.

While the IAEA agreed with the U.S. National Intelligence Estimates in 2007 that Iran had dismantled its focused efforts to build a bomb in 2003, the new conclusions make it clear that work has now resumed in earnest; indeed, the enrichment of fuel was never suspended.[25]

There can be no doubt now that Iran's nuclear goals are military. I cochair with former senator Chuck Hagel an Iran study at the Atlantic Council in Washington, in which we have brought the foremost experts around the country together. In a paper for our group by Barbara Slavin and a 2011 seminar, which included Olli Heinonen, a senior official with IAEA until 2010, and David Albright, president of the Institute for Science and International Security, they connected the dots. These include the combination of Iran's unwillingness to respond to questions from the IAEA and permit full on-site inspections; their decision to conceal their intentions about nuclear facilities such as the new one near Qom; the dramatic increase of nuclear fuel enriched from 3.5 percent purity to 20 percent, closer to the 90 percent needed for weapons-grade fuel; and their efforts to acquire carbon fiber, maraging steel, vacuum pumps, and other components unnecessary for a civilian program.[26]

The IAEA report supports the conclusions heard at the Atlantic Council that Iran has mastered a number of crucial steps needed to build a nuclear weapon, with help from experts in North Korea and Pakistan.[27] Especially compelling is the IAEA disclosure that a former Soviet nuclear scientist, Vyacheslav Danilenko, has assisted the Iranians for at least five years in building a R265 generator, an aluminum shell loaded with high explosives that detonate with split-second precision and can compress the enriched uranium Iran is developing to trigger a nuclear chain reaction.[28]

I believe Iran wants to master all the steps to build a nuclear weapon, including the ability to pack a nuclear device on the top of a missile that can reach Israel and parts of Europe and the Gulf states, announce they are "nuclear capable," meaning they could put all the pieces of the nuclear puzzle together in short order, but stop just short of testing a nuclear device. Thus, Iran's likely goal is to enrich enough uranium to break out of the Nuclear Non-Proliferation Treaty at any chosen moment and produce nuclear weapons-grade fuel and nuclear weapons they can place on top of missiles. As the U.S. director of National Intelligence told the Senate Armed Services Committee in March 2011: "We continue to assess that Iran is keeping open the option to develop nuclear weapons in part by developing various nuclear capabilities that better position it to produce such weapons, should it choose to do so. We do not know, however, if Iran will eventually decide to build nuclear weapons."[29]

More colorfully, but with a similar conclusion, General Michael Hayden, former director of the CIA in the Bush administration, told me personally that Iran wants "to have all the components for a nuclear weapon in the garage, so they can assemble it whenever they want."[30]

It is now frighteningly clear that there has been a pact between the world's two most dangerously rogue nuclear states, Iran and North Korea, to work toward this goal. North Korea's advanced missile, the BM-25, could carry a nuclear warhead and would extend the 1,200-mile range of Iran's current maximum-range ballistic missile, the Sajjil, which already can reach Israel. These new missiles could send nuclear or conventional warheads from Iran to targets as far away as parts of Eastern Europe, all of the Middle East, and Turkey. A UN panel of experts confirmed the routine sharing of ballistic missile technology between North Korea and Iran, in violation of UN sanctions against North Korea, on flights transshipped through China. Tellingly, China refused to sign off on the report.[31]

Iran's missile program alone underscores its determination to become a regional hegemon. In a show of its military prowess, in mid-2011 Iran unveiled underground silos carrying missiles for the Shahab-3, with a range of 1,240 miles, putting Israel, U.S. military bases in the Persian Gulf, and even parts of Eastern Europe within range. Again, North Korea provided assistance in building the underground silos, which are difficult to successfully attack.[32]

And North Korea is not the only source. Working without fanfare, China, Russia, India, Italy, and North Korea have all helped Iran obtain technology.[33] Tehran operates a sophisticated network of front companies posing as schools and private laboratories, which when unmasked simply close shop and reopen under different names and locations to acquire electronics and other items supposedly blocked by UN sanctions.[34]

Iran thus presents a dire threat to Israel and a grave danger to the West—all the more reason for the wide support among Iranian politicians for their nuclear program as a way of achieving regional preeminence. The desire for a nuclear capacity goes back to the pro-American shah, and the modern program began under two relatively "moderate" presidents, Ali Akbar Hashemi Rafsanjani and Mohammad Khatami. Even the leaders of the Green opposition movement publicly support Iran's nuclear program.[35]

Options for Dealing with the Iranian Threat

Building on the work of the Bush administration, the Obama administration has developed a preemptive strategy through a series of bilateral nuclear agreements with moderate Arab states, inducing them to use fuel from reliable suppliers, such as the U.S. and France, that is more difficult to convert to weapons-grade material. The goal is to duplicate the "gold standard" agreement between the U.S. and the United Arab Emirates under which the Emirates forswear enrichment and processing in return for access to the global market for nuclear technologies. Similar agreements are being negotiated with Jordan, Bahrain, and soon Saudi Arabia.[36]

Iran already has enrichment technology, but there is still time and several options to stop the weaponization of that technology, and some of them overlap: engage Tehran in the hope of a grand bargain; impose sanctions severe enough to carry a high price tag for Iran; and attack with arms, cyberwarfare, and sabotage.

In its first year in office, the Obama administration vigorously pursued the engagement option, sharply changing the policy of the Bush administration and following the example of previous administrations in dealing with North Korean nuclear weapons (to little effect) and with Libyan weapons (with greater success). Negotiations would be paired: robust economic incentives with an end to sanctions *or* tougher sanctions in the face of noncompliance. The Obama administration was prepared to negotiate even before Iran suspended its nuclear enrichment program—a precondition set by President Bush—and this included a bargain combining economic incentives with political and diplomatic steps. The U.S. would recognize Iran if it would abandon its enrichment program under strict IAEA supervision and end its support of terrorist groups. The Obama administration viewed engagement as a way to test Iran's intentions and to marshal support for stronger sanctions if Iran rejected the offer.

There was a fleeting moment when it appeared a first step toward resolution of the nuclear standoff might work. Iranian negotiators tentatively agreed in Vienna in October 2009 to a joint American, European, and Russian proposal to ship most of their enriched uranium from their Natanz plant to Russia and France for reprocessing into fuel for a medical reactor, making it difficult to convert into weapons-grade fuel. President Ahmadinejad accepted the deal, but it was rejected by senior political leaders in Tehran. Iran's supreme leader, Ayatollah Ali Khamenei, responded by accusing the U.S. of deceptively plotting to bring down his regime.[37]

The second option, sanctions variously described by Washington as "biting" or "severe," is the natural consequence of the failure of the engagement policy. Having taken a leading role on sanctions in the Clinton administration, I am painfully aware of how difficult it is to fashion an effective sanctions regime against Iran. The country has the world's seventeenth-largest economy, and its huge oil and gas reserves are second only to Saudi Arabia's.[38] The EU is Iran's largest trading partner in goods, with Germany the single biggest exporter. Russia provides almost all of Iran's arms, and China, which imports 12 percent of its oil from Iran, has invested billions in Iran's energy sector and in 2010 supplanted the European Union as Iran's top trading partner, significantly because of its importation of Iranian oil. Turkey imports 17 percent of its natural gas from Iran and desperately wants to reduce its dependence on Russia.

Can any combination of sanctions prevent Iran from developing a nuclear bomb if it is determined to do so? The most effective way to slow down Iran's nuclear program is to deny them the ability to obtain items such as carbon fiber and maraging steel they cannot make themselves and which are essential to a nuclear weapon. What sanctions can also do is substantially increase the cost to Iran and buy time for negotiations on an effective oversight program and a change in leadership to one that would make a more balanced cost-benefit analysis against a bomb. Iran's oil production is down to about four million barrels per day from six million in the shah's time, and its economy is suffering from sanctions imposed by the UN, plus those imposed on top of them by the U.S. and EU, effectively three rings of sanctions. The combination of sanctions on Iran make them in my experience, having helped lead the sanctions effort during the Clinton administration, among the most severe and broad-based against any nation in modern times. Sanctions block any U.S. person or corporation from dealing with more than three dozen Iranian banks, universities, and insurance companies; the economic arm of the elite Revolutionary Guard Corps; and individuals linked to the nuclear and biological weapons programs.[39] Among the most effective sanctions are those that block dollar-denominated transactions that can be monitored as they pass through the U.S. clearing system. Credit Suisse, the large Swiss bank with substantial U.S. operations, was fined $536 million for its transactions with Iran.[40] The administration has compelled major U.S. and European companies to withdraw from Iran. A 2010 bill passed by the U.S. Congress effectively bars financial institutions around the world from conducting any business in the U.S. if they assist Iranian state-owned companies involved in key sectors of the Iranian economy; these institutions must choose between doing business with Iran or the United States.

In December 2011, the U.S. Congress enacted an amendment that for the first time targets the Iranian central bank for sanctions, meaning that any bank, financial institution, or corporation that does business with the Iranian central bank (e.g., financing oil transactions) would itself be subject to sanctions.

Moreover, the EU has agreed to forswear purchases of Iranian oil, its major source of foreign currency beginning July 1, 2012. Together these will severely stress the Iranian economy. Their currency, the rial, has dropped precipitously in value, and basic commodities are expensive and difficult to find. The key now will be to induce at least some of the major Asian purchasers of Iranian crude oil—China, India, Japan, and South Korea—to end or curtail their purchases. The U.S. has the most leverage with Japan and Korea. The most effective move would be to block the export of refined petroleum products to Iran by boycott or embargo; Iran's domestic refinery capacity is so limited that it must import some 40 percent of their needs. The difficulty of buying insurance for ships calling at Iranian ports has already increased the cost of refined oil products. Sanctions, together with cyberwarfare against Iran's nuclear infrastructure, have at least delayed Iran's nuclear weapons program. Meir Dagan, the outgoing director of Israel's Mossad, stated that he believes Iran will be unable to build a nuclear weapon before 2015 at the earliest, several years later than previously thought.[41]

It seems clear that the U.S. and the EU will have to bear the brunt of expanded sanctions. Efforts at tougher multilateral sanctions through the UN are likely to be blocked by China and Russia. Moscow has proposed a step-by-step process to lift sanctions in return for gradual Iranian agreement on addressing outstanding IAEA questions, but this will only give Iran more time to enrich increased amounts of uranium and develop other aspects of its nuclear program, which feeds into Iran's hands and takes pressure off them.[42]

And sanctions have downsides, as well. The risk of conflict with Iran has been a principle reason that the price of crude oil has sharply increased to over $100 per barrel, even at a time of modest economic recovery from the Great Recession, crimping growth globally, and casting a dark cloud over America's rebounding economy in a presidential election year.

Broader internal opposition to Ahmadinejad's economic policies may play an important role in the long run, and as sanctions hit harder, foreign and domestic policy consequences may merge. One of the disturbing difficulties of broadening support for sanctions has been the refusal of the very Arab countries that fear a nuclear Iran to apply these economic countermeasures with force. Oman, less than 50 kilometers (30 miles) from Iran across the Strait of Hormuz, is intent on supporting U.S. interests, but not at the expense of maintaining good relations with Tehran, lest it be overrun by its more populous neighbor. Qatar is in a similar situation.

And the Egyptian Revolution will remove an Arab ally against Iran. The foreign minister in the interim civilian government, Nabil Elaraby, declared that "Egypt has turned a page with every country in the world. If you want me to say it—Iran is not an enemy. We have no enemies. Anywhere."

The sad reality is that if the radical leaders in Tehran are hell-bent on acquiring a nuclear weapon regardless of the cost to their country, it is difficult to stop them, short of taking more dramatic action. Many experts in the U.S. are already turning to a deterrent strategy against what they see as the inevitability of an Iranian atomic bomb, rather than an interdiction strategy to stop Iran from acquiring it. This is a dangerous policy, sending a green light to Iran to proceed. Unlike the mutually assured destruction policy the U.S. employed against a rational Soviet opponent during the Cold War, the Iranian leadership is distinguished by radical theology and an erratic decision-making process. Preventing mutual annihilation involves prudent game theory; even though the Persians invented chess, it is not the Iranian way today.

There were indications that the Obama administration has shifted its policy toward Iran from declaring, as President Obama did in 2009, that a nuclear Iran was "unacceptable" and that the U.S. would "use all elements of American power to prevent Iran from developing a nuclear weapon" to a policy of seeking to "isolate" Iran through increasingly tougher sanctions. This is a subtle move away from prevention to containment.[43]

On the eve of Israeli Prime Minister Netanyahu's early March 2012 visit to Washington and speeches by the Prime Minister and President Obama to the AIPAC conference, the President toughened his rhetoric to return to his original 2009 formulation at a nuclear weapon in Iran's hands was "unacceptable." President Obama more clearly put the military option on the table, declaring "When the United States says it is unacceptable for Iran to have a nuclear weapon, we mean what we say."[44]

The Obama administration recognizes the futility of forcing Iran to forswear its low-grade nuclear enrichment program and is instead focusing on demanding that Iran cooperate with the IAEA and disclose its nuclear sites. But divisions within the Obama administration came into the open in a leaked memorandum from then defense secretary Gates shortly before his retirement, warning the president that Iran might produce all the major parts for a nuclear weapon but "stop just short of assembling a fully operational weapon."

The embarrassing disclosure prompted the administration to draw a more precise line to block Iran from developing the capability to break out suddenly and build a nuclear weapon. But only through the clearest reassurances from Washington to Israel and its anxious Arab allies that the U.S. is willing to act with force against Iran can the administration avoid a dangerous shift in the regional power balance that could in turn invite Israeli military action.

In fact, the U.S. "red line" for the Iranian nuclear program keeps moving, as Iran constantly crosses one red line after another. Initially then secretary of state Condoleezza Rice set the red line for U.S. action at forcing Iran to stop its centrifuges from enriching uranium.[45] Now the red line is denying Iran a nuclear capability they will shortly have. Then it will be stopping Iran from actually building a nuclear bomb. Israel has a critical role to play in strengthening these pro-Western Arab governments that share a deep antipathy to Iranian ambitions.

As President Obama has indicated, if all else fails, the third option of military action remains. But despite ritualistically stating that "all options are on the table," both then secretary of defense Robert Gates and the current secretary of defense Leon Panetta have thrown cold water on the military option. Panetta stressed the "unintended consequences."[46]

It should be the last alternative. It is strongly opposed by the overstretched American military, which would have to participate either with troops and pilots or, at a minimum, logistical support for an air attack by Israel in a well-established pattern set in Iraq in 1981 and Syria in 2007. It is evident that Israeli forces are training for such an operation, but despite confidence expressed by their commanders, many experts doubt its chances for success.[47]

Former Mossad chief Meir Dagan has publicly cast doubt on the success of any military effort and has stressed the collateral damage to Israel of such an attack. The distances to Iranian nuclear plants, the number of key facilities that would need to be targeted, and their dispersion and even burial in underground bunkers, like near Qom, would make the operation far more difficult than the successful mission in Iraq twenty-seven years ago. The consequences of a unilateral attack could prove horrific. Admiral Mike Mullen, chairman of the U.S. Joint Chiefs of Staff, warned that an Israeli strike would be "profoundly destabilizing" to the region.[48] It would lead to a dramatic rise in oil prices, solidify public support for the Iranian regime, give them a justification for moving beyond having a nuclear capability to actually developing a nuclear weapon, and perhaps ignite open warfare with Iran's proxies in the Palestinian territories, Lebanon and Syria, and even with Iran itself—to say nothing of the political conflagration in the Muslim world.

Even if Israeli jets made it to Iran, there is no guarantee that a successful strike would dissuade Iran once and for all. At best, it would only buy time. Lieutenant General Gabi Ashkenazi, the head of the Israel Defense Forces (IDF), has estimated it would set back Iran's program by two to three years, as assessment shared by Defense Minister Barak. Amos Yadlin, former head of the Military Intelligence Directorate of the IDF, has expressed similar doubts.[49] The Americans felt it would delay the program only by a matter of months.[50] Moreover, a successful strike would probably only lead Iran to redouble its development, hide and secure facilities even more comprehensively, or, in a truly nightmarish scenario, decide that mastering the nuclear fuel cycle was uneconomical when it could follow the path of others and use its petrodollars to buy a ready-made, albeit crude, weapon from a cash-poor nuclear state such as North Korea or Pakistan.

These risks were succinctly linked by Mohamed ElBaradei when he was IAEA secretary general and, in my view, too lenient in his interpretation of Iranian intentions. He said: "I don't believe the Iranians have made a decision to go for a nuclear weapon, but they are absolutely determined to have the technology because they believe it will bring them power, prestige and an insurance policy." But if Israel bombed Iran, he warned, that would "put Iran on a crash course for nuclear weapons with the support of the whole Muslim world."[51]

Toward the end of the Bush administration, the then Israeli prime minister Ehud Olmert tested the waters to see if Washington would supply bunker-busting bombs, but the Bush administration made clear it would not.[52] The Israeli government has about 100 GBU-28 bunker-busting bombs, but a report by the Bipartisan Policy Center's National Security Project indicates that Israel needs an additional 200 precision-guided GBU-31 bombs, with a Boeing global positioning system, along with several KC-135 aerial refueling tankers for the long trip from Israel to Iran.[53] The Obama administration, even before Netanyahu's inaugural visit, warned the Israeli government that it would be "ill-advised" to try to bomb the Natanz facility.[54]

The Obama administration, however, has worked tirelessly to pursue nonmilitary means and ease Israel's fears. It enlisted Russian assistance by delaying, probably permanently, the installation of a central European antimissile system and obtaining Russian agreement to cancel a sale to Tehran of the S-300 surface-to-air missile system that could have served as an additional deterrent to an Israeli air strike.[55]

The U.S. and Israel are already emphasizing missile defense systems to interdict any Iranian attack, and both nations have long been working on what they hope will be an effective antimissile shield. Israel Aerospace Industries and Boeing have developed and deployed two batteries of the Arrow II system in Israel. Its sophisticated technology relies on a fragmenting warhead designed to explode near its target, rather than hitting an incoming missile, but the technology is far less perfect than the standard facilities for launching a missile attack. Sea-based missile interceptors are also being deployed by the end of 2011.

But a containment policy is not a way to avoid a military confrontation. To be effective, it must be clear that the U.S. or Israel is prepared to use preemptive force if necessary. Any threat of retaliation *after* Iran obtains a nuclear device would be too late: Why would Iran believe the threat if the United States, having said it would never allow Iran to get a nuclear capability, then allowed it?[56]

If Iran's current intentions are to master all the steps for a nuclear weapon, but not to cross the red line of actually building one, would the U.S. and Israel have any warning if Iran suddenly tried to "break out" and actually build a bomb? The answer is likely yes. One overt sign would be the expulsion of the IAEA inspectors, who still have access to the plants at Natanz and Fordow. This would be a sure signal that Iran is intent on enriching uranium to a weapons grade. It would then take several months for the country to do so. Another sign would be further disclosures by the IAEA determining that Iran had actually developed weapons-grade materials.[57] And the active intelligence efforts by Israel and the U.S. might detect weapons activities. Moreover, to actually have an operational nuclear weapon would require far more time. Iran would need to be able to place a weapon atop a missile, which they have yet to master.

Israel is maintaining its traditional prudence, hoping for the best and preparing for the worst, perfecting a robust second-strike capability while trying to deny Iran a first-strike capability.

But Israel is not defenseless. It has a superb intelligence capacity that allowed it to destroy most of Hezbollah's long-range rockets stored in underground warehouses in Lebanon on July 12, 2006;[58] strike the production line of a facility at Al-Safir jointly operated by Syria and Iran in July 2007; destroy the Syrian nuclear facility in September 2007; and assassinate key Hezbollah and Hamas leaders.

By sabotaging Iran's centrifuges with the Stuxnet computer virus, Israel delayed the nuclear program, and Israeli prowess in cyberwarfare may reap more results.

Richard Clarke, a top antiterrorism official in the Clinton and George W. Bush administrations, indicates that Israel may have also used cyberwarfare against Syria's air defenses, clearing the way for its jets to attack the Syrian nuclear facility. A series of assassination attempts, some successful, have been made against leading Iranian nuclear scientists; including Majid Shahriari, who had managed a major nuclear program for Iran's Atomic Energy Organization and was killed in broad daylight in Tehran.

Defensively, Israel's strength comes from its capacity for massive retaliation, of which Iran must be aware; its second-strike capability now includes Dolphin-class submarines bought from Germany.

Israel should also gain confidence from the fact that it is not alone in its deep concern about an Iranian bomb. Even if Washington shies away from a first strike on Iran, it has projected an American military presence in the Persian Gulf, where the Navy's Fifth Fleet makes its home in Bahrain.

Britain, France, and Germany have stood with the United States in making it clear that it would be unacceptable for Iran to acquire nuclear weapons, with French president Nicolas Sarkozy being especially emphatic. Disquiet extends to general concerns about Iranian expansionism. Arab officials have made clear to the U.S. government that Iran's influence is as threatening to them as its nuclear program,"[59] and Morocco cut diplomatic ties with Tehran after Iranian diplomats in Rabat were discovered seeking to convert Sunni Moroccan citizens to Shiism. Saudi Arabia dangled the carrot of a large purchase of Russian military hardware in exchange for Moscow's cancellation of a sale of S-300 antiaircraft missiles to Tehran.[60] Riyadh also promised China that it would trade a guaranteed oil supply in return for Chinese pressure on Iran to drop its nuclear weapons plans.[61]

The remarkable set of diplomatic cables posted by Wikileaks show the grave concerns of moderate Muslim governments. Lebanon's former prime minister Saad Hariri told American officials that the U.S. "must be willing to go all the way" to stop Iran's nuclear program if diplomatic efforts fail. The Saudi ambassador to Washington reported that King Abdullah "told you to cut off the head of the snake." Fears of Iranian political ambitions were expressed by leaders of Yemen and the Gulf states, and the crown prince of Abu Dhabi said: "Ahmadinejad is Hitler."[62] Such strong sentiments in the Sunni Arab world are a key reason why the outcome of the 2011 Arab upheavals is so critical to the U.S. and Israel. It is difficult to imagine the new governments taking as strong a line against Iran as their deposed predecessors.

Although Israel rejects any linkage between the peace process and the fight against terrorism, progress would strengthen the anti-Iranian, pro-American countries. Jerusalem therefore should do all it can to demonstrate progress toward peace with the Palestinians in order to give these governments more running room to align their policies toward Iran with those of the United States.

The Netanyahu government initially indicated it would not move forward with the Palestinians until the U.S. shows progress against Iran. But the U.S. emphasizes that progress on the Palestinian front helps the Obama administration build a moderate Arab coalition to curb Iranian influence. There is a genuine opportunity for a regional alliance against Iran, but every nation must pull its weight, including Israel.[63] Senior Obama administration officials have stressed this linkage; in the words of Secretary of State Clinton: "For Israel to get the kind of strong support it's looking for vis-à-vis Iran, it cannot stay on the sideline with respect to the Palestinian . . . peace efforts."[64]

Prime Minister Netanyahu has accepted the idea of a two-state solution as long as the Palestinians accept Israel as the state of the Jewish people. But from his earliest meetings with the Obama administration, Netanyahu insisted on clear U.S. progress in its diplomatic efforts to stop Iran's nuclear weapons program. There is room for compromise between Washington and Jerusalem, although there are many barriers on the Palestinian side. But Jerusalem would be well served if its deeds as well as its words placed the onus for action on Palestinian shoulders rather than on what many nations regard as Israel's refusal to bargain in good faith.

Unless the latest round of sanctions against the Iranian central bank and an oil import ban by the EU bring Tehran to its senses to negotiate an agreement to forswear nuclear weapons with a credible inspection regime, or leads to a regime change, at some point within the next two or three years, Israel and the U.S. will likely be faced with a monumental decision of choosing between two unpalatable options: accepting an Iranian nuclear weapon and seeking to contain it or pulling the trigger on military action with all its negative consequences. These include setting a torch to the volatile Middle East; likely attacks against U.S. assets; rocket attacks against Israel from Hezbollah and Hamas, soaring crude oil and gasoline prices, as well as potentially strengthening the Iranian regime,

It is important to be frank about the stark choices and not to split hairs. The U.S. intelligence community, burned by their horrific misjudgment of Sadaam Hussein's non-existent weapons of mass destruction, and recognizing the cataclysmic consequences of going to war with Iran, continues to cling to the notion that while Iran is manufacturing all the components of a nuclear weapon, Tehran has not decided to assemble them into a bomb.[65]

I likewise believe their goal is "nuclear capability," not a nuclear bomb, at this point. But to take satisfaction with this state of affairs is distressing, since it leaves Iran with the ability to abruptly break-out into a nuclear weapons state when they choose. Secretary of Defense Leon Panetta, one of the finest public servants of this or any another generation, put the administration's position this way: "The intelligence doesn't show that they've made the decision to proceed with developing a nuclear weapon. That is the red line that would concern us."[66]

Because accepting an Iranian nuclear capability, or even worse a nuclear weapon or going to war with Iran over their nuclear program, is such a Hobson's choice, more direct support for Iranian opposition movements, and even more severe economic sanctions should be emphasized. If North Korea buck-led under the pressure of international sanctions and genuinely implements its pledge to suspend its nuclear program and allow international inspectors, perhaps this may serve as a precedent for an Iranian agreement, under even more severe sanctions.

The prognosis for Iran may depend on its internal political debate and the impact of economic sanctions. But Iran is a police state, and its nuclear weapons program is controlled by the most radical institution in the country, the Revolutionary Guards (Army of the Guardians of the Islamic Revolution). Unless and until the mullahs and radicals are dislodged, or the economic vise of sanctions takes a greater toll, it is unlikely that Iran will give up its nuclear option. Sanctions have drawn Iran back to the bargaining table, and combined with a credible threat of military force and cyberattacks, it may be stopped short of developing a nuclear weapon.

But Iran's goal of nuclear capability will be more difficult to stop as it moves closer to mastering the nuclear fuel cycle and developing more powerful missiles that can reach Israel, all of the Middle East, and major parts of Europe. An end-game agreement might be for Iran to keep its uranium enrichment capability, but stop short of "nuclear capability," in return for a carefully phased-out sanctions regime, calibrated to clear and verifiable implementation on Iran's part keeping its commitments to avoid weaponizing its existing nuclear capability. This agreement would have to be backed up by Iran signing the additional protocol to the Non-Proliferation Treaty, which gives the IAEA unlimited inspection rights. This "nuclear latency" agreement, forestalling further steps by Iran toward a nuclear weapon may be the best than can be achieved at this stage, short of war.

This bleak picture for the U.S., Europe, and especially Israel will be tempered by what are likely to be further breakthroughs in anti-missile technology by Israel and the U.S., plus the promise of a U.S. nuclear umbrella for moderate, pro-Western Muslim states to provide comfort against Iran, especially in the unsettled landscape following the 2011 Arab Spring.

One thing is certain: Iran will be a major preoccupation for Israel and the U.S. well into the twenty-first century.

Other Nuclear Risks and the Potential of Nuclear Disarmament

Effectively dealing with nuclear proliferation involves more than solely focusing on Iran. Among nuclear powers the security of existing nuclear stockpiles must be upgraded to be certain that countries like Pakistan, Russia, and China do not become unwitting proliferators. Theft, let alone purchase, of nuclear-related goods also remains a high concern. If there is a more dangerous place on earth for nuclear weapons than Iran, it is Pakistan. It has the fastest-growing nuclear inventory on the planet. While its nuclear weapons program is focused solely on India, the potential for "loose nukes" from Pakistan reaching terrorist groups such as the Taliban is greater than anywhere else because of its weak government and resilient radical opposition. Al-Qaeda's remaining leaders are based in Pakistan. Leaked U.S. Embassy cables from Islamabad underscore the unwillingness of the Pakistan government to allow the U.S. to remove nuclear fuel from a research reactor.

The U.S. has made significant strides toward securing nuclear materials in Russia and elsewhere in the former Soviet Union, and there is expanding cooperation in nuclear security between the U.S. and China. Belarus, the former Soviet republic with a very hard-line regime, announced with Secretary of State Clinton in the fall of 2010 that it would eliminate its stockpile of highly enriched uranium by 2012, which could have been used for nuclear weapons.[67]

As noted, nuclear security, along with opportunities for trade in civilian nuclear materials, was also part of the historic 2008 treaty between the U.S. and India reached by the Bush administration, even though India had not signed the Nuclear Non-Proliferation Treaty.

In 2010, President Obama hosted a meeting of over forty countries in Washington, with the goal of preventing nuclear material from falling into the hands of terrorists. There were some concrete accomplishments. The former Soviet state of Ukraine has about 100 kilograms (220 pounds) of highly enriched uranium at its civilian reactors, enough to make several bombs; it agreed to convert the reactors to low-enriched uranium, which is more difficult to transform into a nuclear weapon. Canada announced it would return its spent nuclear fuel to the U.S., and Chile said it had given up the last forty pounds of its highly enriched uranium. Prime Minister Najib Razak of Malaysia agreed to adopt stricter import and export controls to prevent the country from being used as a point of transshipment for nuclear materials and technology.[68]

President Obama's commitment is long-standing, and his signature legislation during his time in the Senate was his work on securing nuclear arms. President Obama has another far-reaching goal that may impact Israel directly, much more than nonproliferation—nuclear disarmament. In a 2009 speech in Prague, he rejected the fatalist idea of a destiny in which more nations and more individuals would possess the ultimate tools of destruction, stating that "if we believe that the spread of nuclear weapons is inevitable . . . then . . . we are admitting to ourselves that the use of nuclear weapons is inevitable."

His plan is based on an ambitious effort to have a world free of all nuclear weapons, first enunciated as a goal by President Ronald Reagan and President Mikhail Gorbachev of the then Soviet Union at the Reykjavik Summit in 1987, led by a bipartisan group of luminaries, including former secretaries of state George Schultz and Henry Kissinger; former secretary of defense William Perry; former senator Sam Nunn, who was chairman of the Senate Armed Services Committee; and Ambassador Max Kampelman, a longtime leader in American government and in the world Jewish community. They have developed concrete steps to support

President Reagan's bold statement at Reykjavik, calling for the abolishment of "all nuclear weapons," which he considered to be "totally irrational, totally inhumane, good for nothing but killing, possibly destructive of civilization."[69]

While there have been significant reductions in the stock of nuclear weapons in the hands of the U.S. and Russia, other states such as North Korea, Pakistan, India, China, and now Iran seem intent on building a new stockpile of twenty-first-century nuclear weapons.

Today, after several arms control agreements with the Soviet Union and with post-Soviet Russia, the global nuclear arsenal is still formidable but has been reduced to about 20,000 nuclear weapons worldwide, with several thousand ready for launch at an instant.[70] A modest first step toward the president's goal is START, the new strategic arms reduction treaty between the United States and Russia to cut the number of deployed strategic warheads to 1,550 on each side, down from 2,100 for the U.S. and 2,600 for the Russians. Both sides have thousands more in reserve.

President Obama's seriousness of purpose was underscored by a new doctrine he announced in the 2010 Nuclear Posture Review, which renounces the development of any new nuclear weapons and commits the U.S. to not using nuclear weapons against nonnuclear states in compliance with the Nuclear Non-Proliferation Treaty, even if they attack the U.S. with biological or chemical weapons or launch a cyberattack. Iran and North Korea are not provided such assurance, and they are warned that the U.S. reserves the right to use nuclear weapons against them if they sell or transfer nuclear technology to terrorists or other states.

In the 2010 Quadrennial Defense Review, the president supported development of a new class of super nonnuclear weapons, one of which is particularly important to Israel, since it could fly straight up the middle of the Persian Gulf and then make a sharp turn toward Iran. These new nonnuclear weapons do far less collateral damage than nuclear weapons and could be more readily used against Iran's deeply buried nuclear facilities. The Pentagon hopes to have an early version by 2015.[71]

There is one element of the president's vision of a world without nuclear weapons that is of concern to Israel. The administration has publicly called on Israel, along with other nonsignatories to the Non-Proliferation Treaty, to ratify the treaty. At the same time, the Arab nations regularly call for a nuclear-free zone in the Middle East. Since none possesses a nuclear weapon, this would amount to unilateral nuclear disarmament by Israel. It is difficult to imagine a circumstance in which Israel would wish to bind itself to the intrusive inspections of the IAEA, a UN body, on a nuclear program it has never officially admitted having, let alone give it up as the Arab states have demanded, at the very time Iran is going full speed ahead to develop a nuclear capability. Israel's nuclear deterrent is its ultimate defense against efforts to end the Third Jewish Commonwealth.

In the end, it is difficult to be optimistic about the course of nuclear proliferation. While the U.S. and Russia probably will agree to a further reduction in their stocks of nuclear weapons, even those reductions indicate a pragmatic rather than principled response on behalf of Moscow. Russia is not interested in disarmament per se. It is eager for a deal because its nuclear arsenal is rapidly deteriorating, and it lacks the money to upgrade its own weapons.[72] Meanwhile, North Korea, even with its newly professed interest in suspending its nuclear program, may continue to try to arrange covert sales of its nuclear technology to the highest bidder, continue to cooperate with Iran, and continue to work on refining its delivery mechanisms and miniaturizing its nuclear warheads.

If there is any hope of preventing the inexorable spread of nuclear capability, it lies in a proposal first made by President Dwight Eisenhower some sixty years ago but now gaining renewed currency. In his Atoms for Peace program he recommended an international nuclear fuel bank to provide its member nations the material for civilian nuclear power while controlling the processing of by-product isotopes so they could not be weaponized. There is growing support for reviving this initiative, even from oil-rich Saudi Arabia. Russia has set up its own bank as a commercial venture, and the thirty-five members of the IAEA board voted to create a global nuclear fuel bank. Spearheaded by former Senator Sam Nunn and his bipartisan group of former senior U.S. government officials, more than $150 million—enough to buy eighty tons of fuel—has been pledged by the U.S., EU, Norway, and the UAE, topped off by an unlikely source: $50 million from a remarkable private donation by the billionaire investor Warren Buffett (Israel's largest foreign investor). This may persuade states seeking civilian nuclear power to draw from the international bank to enrich their fuel and thus strike a critical blow against weapons proliferation.[73]

Cybersecurity

Two of the great strengths of the Internet are its open architecture and its accessibility; but these characteristics have also made the Internet vulnerable to misuse by individuals, governments, and terrorist groups.

Cyberspace and the Internet undergird much of the new global economy but are also widely used by terrorists and criminal groups to plan, finance, and recruit.[74] Advanced societies such as the U.S. and Israel have invested far too little in preventing cyberattacks against nonmilitary targets that could compromise hospitals, computer systems in corporations, and government agencies.[75] The authorities need to stay one step ahead of the criminals by planting false trails and exercising constant oversight. Unfortunately, computer hackers for hire are hijacking data and entire computer systems by using increasingly sophisticated methods.

Attackers often use malicious software—malware—that nests inside corporate computer networks for industrial espionage, transmitting digital copies of trade secrets, customer lists, and contracts. Over two million computer viruses, worms, back doors, and other infiltrating programs have emerged in just the past two years and permit the invasion of personal computers and the theft of personal data, including social security numbers, bank accounts, and credit card information.[76] Most of the basic infrastructure of modern countries, from transport to electric power and financial systems, depend on these vulnerable computers.

The groups that hack into computers has changed, from random high school or college kids showing off their high-tech skills, to organized criminal gangs who make huge sums from hacking into individual and corporate computer networks, and to nation states, particularly developing countries like China, who use hacking as a way of stealing technology and competitive secrets from corporations, state secrets from other governments, and, within the last few years, use malicious software called "malware" to attack their enemies. Defenses that work for less sophisticated attacks do not stop highly sophisticated ones. Attacks are customized against specific targets.[77]

Thus, cyberattacks are increasingly skilled, progressing from individual hackers to organized criminal groups using identity theft and other methods to steal financial data on a vast scale, and despite billions of dollars spent to combat them, the gangs seem to be gaining the upper hand. A Cybersecurity expert estimated the annual loss of intellectual property and investment opportunities from China's cyberattacks against industries around the world at $6 to 20 billion, a large percentage from the oil industry, which has sensitive data on the oil fields on which the industry spends vast sums before bidding on them.[78]

Cyberattacks are part of corporate and government espionage from France to China, but most emanate from or target the U.S. and are directed against American individuals and firms from sources that are presumed to be trusted partners. The attackers frequently target vulnerable employees within organizations, not simply technology. This presents a special challenge in a world in which the modern workforce has mobile devices which access company information, or they simply work from home, or they travel abroad where they can be targeted. There is recent trend to extend data to less secure, employee-owned devices like iPads and iPhones. And Social Media can be misused to gain information on employees electronically.

Law enforcement is minimal. When a group called Anonymous went after Visa, MasterCard, and PayPal because they had stopped processing donations to Wikileaks, the hackers disabled the payment companies for a day.[79] In 2011, hackers stole credit card information from over 350,000 customers of Citigroup, and in 2010 the Nasdaq stock exchange was attacked, with malware detected on the Nasdaq board of directors communication system.[80] The level of sophistication of the attackers was dramatized in March of 2011 when the core security of EMC, a world leader in computer security, was compromised by a highly advanced attack, affecting millions of corporate and government users. That same month, millions of email addresses were exposed as a result of the breach at Epsilon, an email marketing provider. Hackers known as Lulz Security and Anonymous have attacked the websites of the CIA, Public Broadcasting System (PBS), International Monetary Fund, Lockheed Martin, and U.S. Senate. It is estimated that in 2011, 22 million Americans had their personal online data compromised, and some 90 percent of U.S. corporations had an online attack in 2010. These attacks can undermine confidence in the Internet economy, an increasingly large percentage of the global GDP.[81]

But serious as it is, cybercrime is dwarfed by computer attacks launched by nations on military or industrial targets to steal secrets or disable basic infrastructure, almost all of which are run by computers. Imperceptibly a new version of the Cold War arms race has begun—a cyber-race, with both offensive and defensive weapons that can be disguised to appear as if they are based in other countries. Even if the world can avoid military confrontation with Iran, the country has already been the site of one of the hardest-fought digital battles of this new century. While all countries are vulnerable to such attacks, Israel is likely to continue its edge over its adversaries. Indeed, it has likely already deployed such weapons against Iran.

Unlike most military attacks, cyberattacks are difficult to trace, and experts believe at least ten countries have the ability to launch them. A series of attacks has been linked to China through a system that Canadian researchers call "Ghost Net," controlled by computers based almost exclusively in China. They say it has infiltrated nearly 1,300 computers in 103 countries, including embassies, foreign and defense ministries, and even Dalai Lama centers. Attacks have also been made on the U.S. military air traffic control system, the civilian electrical grid, and multinational corporations, revealing major gaps in U.S. computer defense systems.[82] On July 4, 2009, while America celebrated Independence Day, a coordinated attack linked to China was launched against a dozen U.S. government agencies. The Pentagon's computers are scanned every day.

The fiercest recorded attack by one nation against another was Russia's on Estonia, in 2007, in what some have called Cyber War I, in retaliation for Estonia's decision to remove a Soviet-era war memorial in the former Soviet Baltic state. The attack disabled or disrupted business and communications at banks, government offices, and the media as well as bank web servers. The following year, Russia's cyberattacks against Georgian communications were coordinated with the Russian military advances in the Russia-Georgia War.[83] Even isolated North Korea, which cannot adequately feed its own people with basic staples, used an Internet virus to attack American government and business websites in the U.S., including those in the White House and the New York Stock Exchange.[84]

In a remarkably blunt 2011 report entitled "Foreign Spies Stealing U.S. Economic Secrets in Cyberspace," fourteen American intelligence agencies pointed to China and Russia as two foreign governments most active in cyberespionage—stealing U.S. technology over the Internet as a matter of their national policy. The report said that "Chinese actors are the world's most active and persistent perpetrators of economic espionage," while "Russia's intelligence services are conducting a range of activities to collect economic information and technology from U.S. targets." The Office of the National Counterintelligence Executive estimated that tens of billions of dollars of corporate trade secrets, technology, and intellectual property were being stolen by online piracy each year.[85]

Here Israel and the U.S. have a high-tech edge over their adversaries. The Bush administration developed plans to undermine the electrical and computer systems and other networks that serve Iran's nuclear program, and they have been accelerated by President Obama.[86] The opening salvo in Cyberwarfare in the Middle East was launched in 2010 against Iran's nuclear program, most likely by Israel. The Iranian government's nuclear agency confirmed that a sophisticated computer worm, or malware, Stuxnet, infected the centrifuge machinery that produces enriched uranium, that 30,000 computers used in the enrichment operation had been infected, and called it "part of the electronic warfare against Iran."[87]

The head of the U.S. Department of Homeland Security's cyberspace center told a U.S. Senate committee in the fall of 2010 that this attack was a "game changer" because of the skillful targeting of specific Iranian nuclear equipment.

But even the downside of this technology can be an advantage for Israel, which has the ability to defend its vital infrastructure against possible enemy attack, as well as developing offensive and preemptive cyberweapons. And it is not far-fetched to think that one of the most effective defenses against any Iranian nuclear threat would be not a traditional preemptive military strike, which would disrupt the entire region, but a covert cyberattack to disrupt Iranian nuclear and missile programs and other vital infrastructure. Indeed, Israel has heavily invested in computer, signal, and electronic facilities within its military intelligence in an organization known as Unit 8200. With its technological prowess, Israel should be in the best position of any nation in the region to protect its own vital computer-driven infrastructure and to attack others if necessary.

The U.S. has begun to act aggressively. The Obama administration developed a new White House office headed by a "Cyber Czar" after Mike McConnell, the former U.S. director of National Intelligence, warned that computer attacks on financial structures were the equivalent of nuclear weapons and that "America's failure to protect cyberspace is one of the most urgent national security problems."[88] The degree to which cyberwarfare has moved up the agenda of the U.S. government is demonstrated by the inauguration in 2010 of a new U.S. Cyber Command to provide an integrated cyberdefense system, covering all defense networks, with "layered protections" supporting "military and counterterrorism missions with operations in cyber space." It is also working with private industry to share intelligence on cyberthreats to them. The new command has a direct reporting chain to the president, because in the words of Deputy Secretary of Defense William J. Lynn, "milliseconds can make a difference."

In addition, in May 2011, the Obama administration proposed legislation that requires companies involved in critical infrastructure services, such as the power grid, to have adequate systems to reduce the risk of an online attack that could imperil millions of people; that stiffens penalties for computer crimes; and that gives the Department of Homeland Security new power over federal computer systems.[89] U.S. Attorney General Eric Holder called the initiative a "historic strategy" to deal with "the 21st century threats that we now face to both our national and international security," which "really have no borders."[90]

A key to the new cyberdefense strategy is using the tools of the super-secret National Security Agency (NSA), called Tutelage, to defend against attacks against the U.S. military networks, and then bringing similar tools to the private sector. *Washington Post* columnist David Ignatius reported that in May 2011, the Pentagon and Department of Homeland Security launched a pilot project dubbed the DIB Cyber Pilot to protect the nation's critical defense industrial base of around two dozen defense companies from cyberattack, as well as four major Internet service providers. This has already blocked many attempted intrusions.[91]

We may be entering another era of mutually assured destruction through cyberweapons rather than nuclear weapon. The West's openness and technological advances make it more vulnerable because the Internet has democratized this weapon. The risk of cyberattack comes from both state and nonstate actors. Attacks administered today by high-end, classified government computers will undoubtedly be tomorrow's run-of-the-mill attack.[92] Al-Qaeda already uses the Internet, a portal for Google Maps to locate targets and plan attacks in Pakistan—and with greater sophistication than the Pakistani national police.[93]

Nations have begun to deploy digital technology to open new fronts in "spycraft." The computer infrastructure of the U.S. Naval War College in 2006 shut down its website and e-mail system for two weeks. In 2011, U.S. deputy secretary of defense Lynn made public a 2008 cyberattack in which he said the Defense Department "suffered a significant compromise of its classified military computer networks," which began when an unnamed foreign intelligence agency had an infected flash drive inserted into a U.S. military laptop at a base in the Middle East. Lynn indicated this was only the tip of the iceberg and that during the previous decade there had been an exponential increase in the frequency and sophistication of intrusions into the U.S. military network, so that now "Every day, the U.S. military and civilian networks are probed thousands of times and scanned millions of times."[94]

Further indicating the depths of the challenge, Pentagon officials revealed that computer spies had broken into the U.S. Air Force's air traffic control system and into the design system for the new F-35 Joint Strike Fighter Program, potentially making it easier for adversaries to defend against the new aircraft.[95] This directly impacts Israel, as the Israeli Air Force has publicly set its sights on the F-35 as its next-generation air superiority fighter.

The dimensions of the threat are staggering, with 15,000 U.S. military networks worldwide, seven million computing devices, and more than 90,000 people in the defense establishment working to maintain the networks.[96]

The ease with which one low-level private in an intelligence unit stationed abroad could intercept over 250,000 classified cables and transfer them to Wikileaks is only one indication of how readily sensitive information can be compromised if it is not properly protected.[97] America could take a page from Estonia's new cyberdefense playbook. Estonia is one of the world's most wired nations. Its Cyber Defense League is integrated into its total defense mobilization to protect its hard-earned freedom from Russia. In an emergency, the new force can mobilize the Estonian private and public sectors under a single paramilitary command to protect the country's thoroughly computerized nervous system. It has established digital ID numbers for online transactions; a similar system is opposed in the U.S. by privacy groups.

Estonia's unique public-private collaboration does not exist in the United States, where the private sector incorrectly believes it can protect itself without government collaboration. Free-enterprise, small-government advocates should take a lesson from NATO, which created the Cooperative Cyber Defense Center of Excellence and based it in Estonia.[98]

While NATO can command large standing armies, navies that patrol the seas, and traditional air power, asymmetrical warfare pitting nations against terrorist groups is not accounted for in time-honored measures of power. One of the most potent U.S. weapons deployed against the Taliban and al-Qaeda is the unmanned aerial vehicle (UAV), better known as the drone, which beams videos of suspected terrorist outposts to a soldier with a remote digital terminal at a base thousands of miles away. The airmen firing on targets from video screens at their Nevada airbase go to work in uniform to remind them that they are at war. A highly improved new drone dubbed the Gorgon can send videos scanning much larger areas using several cameras as well as a storage drive.[99]

Israel was a pioneer in drone technology as far back as 1982, when drones were used against Syria and Lebanon, and now drones are regularly used for surveillance across and beyond Israel's frontiers. It is a world leader: Russia apparently offered Israel $1 billion for its technology in return for canceling the sale of its antimissile system to Iran (Israel turned down the deal lest the technology end up in Chinese hands).

Such tactical tales only scratch the surface of how modern technology can transform the battlefield. Published Defense Department documents point to plans for space weapons (China for the first time in 2010 launched as many space vehicles as the U.S.); gamma rays, lasers, and microwaves to disrupt enemy weapons; and high-powered electromagnetic radiation to bombard enemy computers. These weapons can potentially cripple the most expensive traditional ships and airplanes.[100] The lesson for the U.S. and for Israel is clear: to be the first to develop these technologies and to collaborate on developing these capabilities with Western allies. Israel's technological prowess will be a great asset in an age of cyberwarfare.

Cyberattacks also have an internal political dimension. China has shut down more than seven hundred websites and placed restrictions on their citizens setting up their own sites.[101] Individuals are prohibited from registering new websites ending in China's country code domain name (.cn), making it more difficult for Chinese citizens to communicate on the Internet worldwide. Unwittingly, some U.S. high-tech companies, such as Cisco Systems, have supplied the Chinese government standard Internet equipment, which the Chinese government has used to maintain its Golden Shield system to track and target dissidents online, such as the Falun Gong group. At the Chinese government's demand, Yahoo! handed over data several years ago about a Chinese journalist, who was later sentenced to ten years in prison. This led firms such as Microsoft and Google, as well as Yahoo!, to join a Global Network Initiative to establish principles protecting "the freedom of expression rights of their users when confronted with government demands, laws and regulations to suppress freedom of expression."[102]

Going a step further, it would be useful for Western high-tech firms to warn users in countries such as China that they are at risk of being discovered by the government. Laws should also be strengthened to bar firms from selling technology that will allow China to eavesdrop on Internet conversations or from tailoring their products to enable governments to repress their citizens.[103]

Google had about 30 percent of China's search market and threatened to withdraw unless China stopped forcing it to censor results of their users' searches. The government dug in, and an uneasy compromise was reached, but without really threatening Chinese Internet censorship. Cyberattacks were launched on human rights advocates, Chinese think tanks, and U.S. companies in strategic sectors where China has been lagging. The attacks were traced to a Chinese university and vocational school with links to the military. The restrictions and attacks raised tensions between China and the U.S. extending beyond the widely publicized Google dispute. A paper by a Chinese graduate student at China's Institute of Systems Engineering of Dalian University of Technology described how an attack on a small U.S. power grid subnetwork could lead to a nationwide shutdown of America's power grid.

Prompted by hacking in China and digital shutdowns in Iran to hobble postelection protests in 2009, the Obama administration made Internet freedom a central tenet of American foreign policy, equivalent to free speech. In 2010, for example, a small Chinese Internet service provider, IDC China, briefly rerouted some 15 percent of the world's web traffic, which was then retransmitted to China's state-owned China Telecommunications, forcing data from the U.S. and other countries, including American government and military data, to pass through China's computer servers. China has an encryption master key that could have been used to break into sensitive data.[104]

All of this led Secretary of State Hillary Clinton to forcefully articulate a new strategy demanding that cyberattackers face international condemnation: "In an Internet connected world, an attack on one nation's networks can be an attack on all." Following up, the Treasury announced that it would permit exports of free personal Internet services and software to Iran, Cuba, and Sudan despite a general U.S. trade embargo.

The U.S. is integrating Cybersecurity into another facet of its foreign and defense policy, as the Obama administration is leading a worldwide effort to deploy what are called "shadow" Internet and mobile phone systems to enable dissident movements in autocratic states to undercut their repressive governments' efforts to censor them or shut down their own networks. Secretary of State Clinton equated today's "viral videos and blog posts" for dissidents to the movements by dissidents in the pre-Internet era, including Soviet Jewry.[105] This involves highly secret efforts to create cell phone networks inside these countries independent of the national telecommunications systems. These systems can fit into a suitcase and be placed across borders quickly to allow wireless communications with a link to the global Internet. By this State Department–funded project, revealed publicly in 2011, democratic-oriented dissidents can use hidden wireless networks to communicate inside their countries with fellow dissidents in countries such as Iran, Syria, and Libya and with the outside world.[106] This is a way of providing Internet service in countries that restrict use of the Internet by political opponents, human rights organizations, and religious groups.[107]

Israel must not only develop a strategy of deterrence and preemption but also coordinate it closely with the U.S. The Obama administration's developing cyberstrategy is aimed at many of the same nations and terrorist groups that threaten Israel, and this overlap should provide an extra measure of confidence to Israel. Cooperation is essential because one challenge of the new technologies is the uncertain collateral effects on innocent users; the new cyberwarfare race therefore must be dealt with on a multilateral basis.

This Cyberwar capacity raises many questions. At what point would a cyberattack be considered an act of war? What would be proper retaliation in response to a cyberattack? What deterrence can be put in place? With 4.5 billion computer users around the globe, there is no international framework to address, let alone investigate, these issues.[108]

Responding to cyberattacks will involve an entirely new set of rules about when and how the U.S. military should react, particularly since the identity of the attackers is so difficult to determine. It is reasonable to assume that returning fire in cyberspace is lawful under current laws of war. It is clear that this will demand new U.S. procedures and international agreements since there is no international consensus on what constitutes the use of force in cyberspace and at what point it rises to the level of a national security attack. A cyberattacker's intentions and physical location may be unclear—whether for spying alone or disrupting vital infrastructure—so retaliation, like a nuclear response, could adversely affect computer systems in countries far from the counterattack.[109]

The Pentagon has declared that a computer attack from a foreign nation can be considered an act of war that may lead to a conventional military response from the U.S. But we are at an early stage in developing these policies. Thus, the new policy is silent on the threshold level of cyberattack that could lead to a military response, and it says nothing about the response to a cyberattack from a terrorist group.[110] Unlike a conventional attack, the source of a cyberattack is often difficult to locate, making any response problematic.

There are no international rules for what is permissible, what constitutes an attack, and how to trace its origins and respond appropriately. A new approach is needed to deal with the new international cyber arms race. That is why the Obama administration in 2011 called for international cooperation to halt computer attacks and to neutralize potential cyberattacks.[111]

Cyberwarfare has its limits. Individuals still have to execute digital battle plans, so for all the sophistication of the Stuxnet virus, its delivery system was as simple and as challenging as that of the Trojan horse. A human being still had to insert an infected thumb drive into a computer.[112] And despite the attack, Iran regained its production levels of enriched uranium and eventually returned to pre-Stuxnet levels of uranium enrichment.

Global Warming, Energy Security, and a Looming Water Crisis

Global Warming

Global warming is the greatest environmental threat to the planet. Rising temperatures, surging seas, and melting glaciers will affect the economic interests and physical security of countries everywhere, possibly driving a billion people back into poverty. I have been directly involved in global warming challenges since I served as the chief U.S. negotiator for the Kyoto Protocol in 1997.

Global warming is an extremely difficult issue to successfully attack because people around the world are being asked to take unpopular measures to deal with a problem they cannot easily see and feel in their daily lives; because of severe disagreements between developing and developed countries on their respective responsibilities in dealing with the challenge; and because of strong political opposition in the U.S., whose leadership is essential for any global action.

Though some climate scientists have presented exaggerated findings, there is wide consensus among the world's climatologists that a man-made buildup of greenhouse gases is causing temperature increases that will reach dangerous levels during the next twenty-five years if carbon dioxide levels in the atmosphere are not stabilized. Human-generated greenhouse gases have helped reverse a 2,000-year cooling trend, leading to higher average temperatures during the past decade than at any point in two millennia.[113] The 12 warmest years of the last 125 have all occurred since 1990, and 20 of the 21 warmest since 1800 since 1980. The last 50 years appear to have been the warmest half century in 600 years.

Carbon dioxide in the atmosphere measured about 280 parts per million (ppm) before the Industrial Revolution; it is now at 380 ppm. The last time concentrations were greater than 300 ppm was 25 million years ago. The gas has a long life in the atmosphere, so what has built up will not go away for perhaps a hundred years. As temperatures rise, low-lying areas such as south Florida are at risk, where a large number of Jewish senior citizens live, and the entire nation of the Maldives in the Indian Ocean may vanish under water. With the current greenhouse gas buildup in the atmosphere, the world was already consigned to a 2 degree Celsius (3.6 degree Fahrenheit) increase in temperatures above preindustrial levels. The goal of the United Nations-led climate change negotiations is to avoid even larger temperature increases.

This makes "natural" security a part of *national* security. The U.S. Navy recently established its own task force on climate change to map out a future with limited Arctic ice, realizing that the "warfare enterprise" will likely change.[114] The Russian Navy's nuclear subs will have to adopt new tactics; their commanders like to use the thick Arctic ice to hide from American detection, and as the ice thins, so does a strategic asset.

As the effects of climate change and growing demand for resources collide, the U.S. National Intelligence Council's *Global Trends 2025* predicts that resulting scarcity will create "conflict on a geostrategic level." Especially hard hit will be the world's poorest. By 2020 between 75 and 250 million people will be under severe environmental stress, with Africa disproportionately impacted.[115] Global warming is already significantly impacting crop yields in many countries, leading to food price increases and causing stress to consumers in both developed and developing nations. Wheat yields in Russia, for example, have declined more than 10 percent in recent years, and also in India, France, and China, compared to what they would have been without rising temperatures.[116]

Climate-induced price spikes since 2007, with some grain prices doubling, have created a demand for the four basic staples that supply the bulk of calories we consume—wheat, rice, corn, and soybeans—that has far outpaced production and drawn down stockpiles to troubling levels. After decades in which the number of undernourished people fell, there has been a sharp rise in recent years, in part because of soaring food prices. Four decades ago, one-third of the population in developing countries was undernourished. By the mid-1990s, with the Green Revolution, that percentage dropped to less than 20 percent, and the total number dropped below 800 million people for the first time in modern history. Now the UN Food and Agriculture Organization (FAO) estimates that in 2010 the number soared to 925 million and is rising.[117]

There has been modest improvement over the years in global governance concerning climate change, but the mechanisms remain imperfect. At Rio de Janeiro in 1992, action by all countries was purely voluntary, and the U.S. Senate unanimously approved the Rio Treaty. But once the UN process moved toward legally binding reductions, fissures developed between the industrialized nations and the developing world. I found in serving as the chief U.S. negotiator for the 1997 Kyoto Protocol that the gulf between developed and developing nations is too large, and the inability of the U.S. to take bold action too distant, for a traditional treaty limiting emissions to be realistic. Led by China and India, the developing world refused to make any binding commitments to reduce the level of increase in their emissions, even as the U.S., the European Union, Japan, and the developed nations were making binding commitments to reduce their greenhouse gas emissions by 2012 to levels of 1990. The developing nations blamed the industrial nations for causing the climate change crisis and asserted that only those nations should fix it. This north-south divide remains today.

The Copenhagen Climate Change Conference in 2009, which I attended in a private capacity, was another test of the capacity of the international community to reach an agreement in which all key countries, including the newly emerging giants, would make binding, although not identical, commitments to forestall what is truly a global problem. The world failed the test badly.

China can no longer stay on the sidelines. In 2008, it became the world's largest carbon emitter; four of the five top greenhouse gas emitters are emerging economies—China, India, Brazil, and Indonesia. There will be no solution to climate change unless they and other emerging nations take on some obligations, whether by reducing the growth of emissions, imposing energy standards tied to economic growth, or making agreements in areas such as autos. But it is difficult to be optimistic about an agreement that key developing countries refuse to join, and the U.S. fails to follow the EU in adopting binding targets.

Still, there are some promising global efforts to attack climate change. For example, Chinese fuel-efficiency standards are higher than those in the U.S. Moreover, for the first time, China in 2011 built in reductions in the growth of their greenhouse gas emissions into their new five year plan. There is also a growing recognition of the impact on global warming from the cut-and-burn destruction of tropical forests in countries like Brazil and Indonesia. Huge tracts of tropical forest, home to about two-thirds of the world's species, are being cut at the astounding rate of one hectare per second to make room for soybeans, roads, and other development. This boosts annual carbon emissions by almost 20 percent, more than all the world's modes of transportation.

A group of developing countries with fast-depleting tropical forests have created a "rain forest coalition" to reduce or cease the deforestation that has boosted their short-term development while devastating the absorption of carbon from the atmosphere. They seek direct compensation or broader foreign assistance and credits from developed countries. Brazil has pledged that if it receives the right incentives, it will reduce the rate of Amazon deforestation by half over the next decade.

A year later in 2010 at Cancun, Mexico, a new type of international agreement was conceived, a "bottom-up" nonbinding approach, under which the major nations, developed and developing, make specific "best-effort" commitments to reduce their greenhouse gas emissions and submit to international monitoring. The advantage of this approach is that it is more inclusive. China pledged to substantially reduce the level of its "energy intensity"—the amount of energy and thus emissions generated per unit of GDP—and has built this into its new five-year economic plan. Penalties or sanctions for failure will not work, so peer pressure is the best that can be hoped for at this point, even as temperatures and sea levels continue to rise. This slow environmental crisis remains invisible to most of the world, and so too does the political will to combat it.

An even more significant step was taken at the Durban Climate Change Conference in South Africa at the end of 2011.

The most exposed developing nations broke from the developing country ranks and demanded that both developed and emerging developing nations bind themselves to act. As a result, a major step forward was taken to end the developed–developing country impasse that has bedeviled global climate change negotiations. The Durban Platform for Enhanced Action was adopted requiring all 194 participating nations to develop over the next four years "a protocol, another legal instrument or an agreed outcome with legal force," in which "all parties" will reduce greenhouse gas emissions. Language used in the past to shield developing nations from acting was deleted, including economic development as the key priority for developing countries. This represents a sea change in global climate change negotiations.[118]

But the United States remains the pivotal nation for leading the effort to deal with climate change. When I was negotiating the Kyoto Protocol, I was faced with a 95 to zero vote for the Bryd-Hagel Resolution making it clear the U.S. Senate would not ratify any climate change treaty in which key emerging powers like China were not required to take actions, fearing a competitive disadvantage for American companies.

The U.S. has to execute a huge turn in policy. Almost half of the country's electric power comes from cheap and plentiful coal, the energy source that produces the most greenhouse gases. President Obama included in his first major bill, the 2009 Economic Stimulus Package, some $70 billion to accelerate work on energy efficiency through home insulation and weatherization, electric meters that monitor usage to save power, and incentives for alternate energy projects, including biofuels, wind, solar and geothermal energy, as well as coal sequestration technology. The Obama administration also issued the first major, tough auto and truck fuel efficiency standards, since those I helped create in the Carter administration in 1977, to reduce greenhouse gas pollution.

The administration also supported a major climate change bill, called Waxman-Markey, after its key sponsors, that passed the U.S. House of Representatives in 2009, that would have sought to meet the Kyoto Protocol targets through binding caps on overall emissions, with a trading system between companies to reduce costs, it stalled in the Senate. In today's political environment, a combination of regional interests, concerns about cost burdens on corporations, and a vocal conservative group that disbelieves the basic scientific findings on global warming, will block any binding legislation for the foreseeable future.

Attitudes have changed in the U.S. toward climate change, but not enough to generate the political will to pass nationwide legislation that would both curb America's appetite for fossil fuels and begin to limit the amount of greenhouse gases emitted into the atmosphere.

But major corporations and states have filled the void of direct federal government action. Major U.S.-based multinational companies have taken the challenge of climate change seriously, developing their own greenhouse gas footprint and taking steps the reduce their emissions, joining groups like the Pew Center to cap their emissions. Wal-Mart has used its enormous market leverage to require its suppliers to reduce their emissions. Major utilities and manufacturers have supported a "cap and trade" policy using a market system as an incentive to install carbon filters.[119] More than half of American states now require their utilities to rely increasingly on fuels other than oil and coal over the next ten years. California, the most populous state, enacted mandatory reductions in greenhouse gas emissions for its businesses, and its voters refused to repeal the law.

President Obama added to the momentum by including in his first major piece of legislation, the Economic Stimulus Package of 2009, some $70 billion to accelerate work on energy efficiency through home insulation and weatherization, electric meters that monitor usage to save power, and alternative energy projects, including biofuels and wind, solar, and geothermal energy as well as coal sequestration technology. In the fall of 2009, the U.S. administration issued tough new fuel-efficiency standards for cars and trucks designed to reduce greenhouse gas pollution.[120]

But the U.S. has to execute a huge turn in policy. Almost half of the country's electric power comes from domestic sources, primarily from cheap and plentiful American coal, the energy source that produces the most greenhouse gasses. Regional interests have stalled congressional legislation, which is opposed by the Republican majority in the U.S. House of Representatives.

Although not a major player at this point, Israel can be a leader in meeting the challenge of global warming. Long before climate change was recognized as a global environmental challenge, the fledgling State of Israel, through the Jewish National Fund, recognized the importance of forests, which absorb greenhouse gasses. Its historically unprecedented program of planting a staggering 240 million trees, going back to 1901, long before Israel became a state, has been of enormous importance in improving Israel's environment.

If there is a solution to climate change, given the international political impasse, it will come from technology. Israel has long recognized the problems of climate change and to its credit has signed international agreements to do its part. A state that has so famously made the desert bloom has the potential to show the world how to avert a global catastrophe. In doing so Israel can build on its comparative technical advantages. The possibilities increase when one realizes the strides Israel has already made in alternative energy—270 firms are engaged in research and development, and a similar number of individual scientists are engaged in such endeavors. Israel has the highest per capita number of solar collectors in the world, and Israeli companies have been partnering with European and American companies for more than twenty years to develop its solar energy and other alternative energy initiatives. The German government has funded joint German-Israeli alternative energy projects. And in 2007, President Bush signed a joint American-Israeli energy research bill to focus on a range of alternative energy technologies.

Israel also demonstrates the economic potential of green industries. In 2007, Israeli exports generated from renewable energy sources totaled $110 million. The ten-year target is an increase to $1 billion a year. R&D investment is expected to increase to $350 million, and Israel is following up on its goals with concrete actions. A national research and development center on global warming and renewable resources has been established in the Negev, and the government is partnering with academic institutions.

In the Diaspora, there is a Jewish Climate Change Campaign, part of a worldwide effort to mobilize religious groups, organized by Prince Philip's UK-based Alliance of Religions and Conservation. Its founder, Rabbi Yedidya Sinclair, believes that "Judaism has profound things to say [about environmentalism] and people will realize that."[121] Diaspora Jews have been drawn to the professions and finance. But a greater contribution would come if more went into engineering and technology focused on clean energy alternatives and conservation.

The Water Crisis in Israel and the Middle East

Two-thirds of the world's population face severe water stress in the coming years. By the middle of the next decade, almost two billion people will live in regions of severe water scarcity. Two-thirds of the world's water is used to grow food, and nearly 70 percent of the fresh water is locked in ice; most of the rest is stored in underground aquifers that are being drained much more quickly than the natural recharge rate from rain and other runoff. In the U.S., the water level of the Colorado River, which half a century ago raged through pristine areas such as the Grand Canyon, has dropped precipitously, at least in part because of mass irrigation of crops on a primitive industrial scale. With about 80 million more people on earth each year, demand for water will keep rising unless nations change the way they use it.[122] In the Middle East, Arab groundwater reserves in renewable aquifers are also being withdrawn faster than they can be replenished. Desertification is swallowing up more than two-thirds of total land area, with almost 90 percent of the Arabian Peninsula already desert and 78 percent of North Africa.[123] The world needs to invest more than $1 trillion in water infrastructure during the next fifteen years in order to meet the growing demand. The number of people living in water-stressed countries is expected to triple to more than three billion by 2025, one-third of the global population.[124]

As a coastal state dominated by desert and one that rightly treasures water as much as any strategic asset, Israel knows the global warming threat is all too real. Over the past century the Middle East has seen a 30 percent reduction in precipitation, and as a direct result of global warming, Israel is predicted to have 40 percent less water at the end of the twenty-first century than at the beginning. The long-term drought was a major cause of the devastating December 2010 forest fires, which destroyed 5,000 hectares of the Carmel Forest near Haifa, one of Israel's national treasures, and is all the more alarming because Israel had only 1,500 firefighters in the entire nation and was inadequately equipped to deal with the most significant natural disaster in its history. Global warming promises to impact world Jewry disproportionately because a large proportion of the world's Jews who live in coastal regions are likely to be the first affected by rising sea levels.

But shortage rather than deluge is the more immediate challenge for the coastal state of Israel. Its way of life, prospects for peace, ability to gain friends in the international community, and economic and demographic growth rely in large measure on its ability to continue to provide the state and its inhabitants with sufficient water. Despite a recent drought, average rainfall has been fairly constant. But due in part to global warming, showers have become shorter and more intense, increasing runoff to the sea instead of soaking into aquifers. The Jordan River has been reduced to a trickle, and the level of the Dead Sea is falling by around one meter a year.[125]

Yeshayahu Bar-Or, chief scientist of Israel's Environment Ministry, predicts that global warming will contaminate the coastal aquifer with salt water, reduce rainfall by 35 percent by 2100, and lead to pollution of the Kinneret (Sea of Galilee).[126]

However, there is an opportunity as well as a challenge for Israel. Compelled to deal with scarce water and other resources from the time when Jewish settlement in prestate Palestine began, Israelis have followed the biblical injunction to make the desert bloom by pioneering sophisticated agricultural techniques. The most celebrated is drip irrigation, developed in the late 1950s by the doyen of Israeli water engineers, Simcha Blass, at Kibbutz Hatzerim. It was so successful that within a decade drip systems were employed by major agricultural producers throughout the Americas and Australia. The technology, simple in conception if not in execution, uses a hose punctured with holes that is hooked to a computer regulating the flow of water for minimum evaporation and maximum absorption by crops. It has been critical in increasing Israel's agricultural output twelvefold since 1948 while using the same amount of water.

Israel has also been aiding African farmers to set up drip systems and sells the technology worldwide. This comparative advantage creates "green collar" jobs, promotes a sector in environmental technology, and places itself in the vanguard of the fight against climate change—another way for Israeli scientific and technological expertise to serve as a cultural and diplomatic bridge.

If Israelis can develop drip agricultural technology, they should be able to devise a method to harvest water from the ground, from rainfall, or from the Mediterranean Sea. Israeli expertise has contributed to the fortunes of Kadima-based IDE Technologies, which in 2005 opened the world's largest desalination plant at Ashkelon—and three years later won a $100 million contract to build China's biggest desalination plant. The problem with desalination is that it uses large amounts of energy and reduces incentives to conserve water. This has made Israeli agriculture more water intensive, focusing on such export fruits as bananas and citrus that are not native to the Middle East. Agriculture is estimated to use more than half of Israel's drinking water, even though it accounts for less than 3 percent of GDP and employs less than 4 percent of the workforce.

Although the importance of water might appear to generate conflict in the Middle East, in fact, water is one of the few issues on which Israelis and Arabs have sustained cooperative effort, especially with Jordan.[127]

Very early after its establishment, the State of Israel and the Hashemite Kingdom, though legally at war, realized the importance of jointly managing their shared water resources in the Jordan Valley. The two sides met, often in secret, two or three times a year in a decidedly informal setting: at a picnic table near the confluence of the Jordan and Yarmouk rivers. Regardless of the wider political tensions, these "Picnic Table Talks" were held for decades and in large measure accounted for fairly convivial relations between Amman and Jerusalem on this issue.

Such binational or even regional management agreements with respect to water resources could be equally helpful throughout the Levant, where the main aquifers extend under the territory of Israel, Jordan, and the Palestinian territories into Syria. But continued population pressures threaten to break down the fund of goodwill, and Israel is more vulnerable than some of its neighbors because Lebanon and Turkey do not suffer from grave water shortages. The West Bank's annual shortfall of 70 million cubic meters of water is a source of considerable anger among Palestinians. As the demographic pressures on both sides of the Green Line exacerbate the effects of the shortfall, water has incendiary potential and will have to be part of any peace agreement.

Energy Security

Few things would provide more security for the U.S., Israel, and the Jewish people than for the industrial nations to free themselves from energy supplied by one of the world's most unstable regions and to reduce their dependence on Middle East oil and gas, which is the source of the power and influence of much of the Arab world and Iran.

There are major economic and national security imperatives. Post–World War II recessions have generally been preceded by a run-up in oil prices. The twin oil shocks of the 1970s, the first from the 1973 Arab oil embargo and the second from the 1979–1980 Iranian revolution, ushered in a period of "stagflation," a totally unprecedented phenomenon of simultaneous high inflation and high unemployment. I know from personal experience in the White House that it was a major factor in the 1980 defeat of President Jimmy Carter by Ronald Reagan.

The United States had been significantly self-sufficient in energy until the 1970s, producing a peak of 10 million barrels of oil per day. Today, the U.S. produces only 8 million barrels of oil daily but consumes 19 million barrels per day, having to import the difference. About 72 percent of the oil used by the U.S. is for our transportation sector—cars, buses, trains, airplanes.

The Organization of the Petroleum Exporting Countries (OPEC) was created in 1961 but did not exercise its muscle until the 1973 Yom Kippur War, when the Arab members imposed an embargo in retaliation for U.S. support of Israel at its time of maximum danger. But U.S. and Western dependence on Middle East oil was already a significant part of American foreign policy, and has been since. President Dwight Eisenhower's demand that Israel, the UK, and France withdraw from the Suez Canal in 1956; the dramatic 120 percent spike in oil prices within a year of the 1979 Iranian Revolution; the 1991 Gulf War to push Iraq out of Kuwait and to protect the oil fields of Saudi Arabia; the massive arms deals with the Saudis and Gulf states, which have been a bipartisan staple of American foreign policy for decades, all demonstrate how the Middle East and its oil wealth has been inextricably tied to U.S. national security interests.

But the major change in energy demand in the twenty-first century is that the emerging nations, such as China and India, as they develop large middle classes, have become major users of energy, catching up with the West in consuming more fossil fuels and further enhancing the influence of the energy-rich states on the foreign policies of the importing nations. In 2010, all of the increase in energy demand came from the developing world, not the industrial world, in barrels of oil equivalent.

World energy demand is likely to increase by at least 2.5 million barrels per day each year, and the lion's share will be from the emerging nations. The U.S. Energy Information Administration estimates that world energy consumption will grow by 53 percent by 2031, most driven by strong economic growth in developing countries—85 percent of the growth there compared to only 18 percent for the OECD industrial democratic countries, of which Israel is a member.

This will place great pressure on oil prices, threaten economic growth, and enhance the power of producing nations, to the disadvantage of the U.S. and Israel. While American political leaders often focus on China's contribution to America's massive trade deficit, in fact 60 percent of that deficit comes from importing oil. Growth in developing nations is placing upward pressure on the price. One example underscores this. In 2010, there were 11.5 million vehicles sold in the U.S., but in China, which only a decade ago had few automobiles, over 18 million vehicles were purchased by increasingly affluent Chinese citizens; in the first half of 2011, 11.5 million vehicles were sold in China, the total year's level for the U.S. in 2010. All obviously consume fossil fuels.

But this has national security implications as well. As China takes a more assertive foreign policy profile, its voracious appetite for imported oil has soared. In 2009, China supplanted the U.S. as the largest customer for Saudi Arabian crude oil. And in the midst of international sanctions against Iran, backed up by even stronger ones from the U.S. and the EU, China is a large buyer of Iranian oil, and has plans for huge investments in Iranian energy. With the EU ban on the importation of Iranian oil, the largest consumers of Iranian oil, in addition to China, are in Asia- India, Japan, and South Korea.

There can be little question where China will tilt on Middle East peace issues involving Israel and stiffer sanctions against Iran. India is in a similar situation; Saudi Arabia supplies 25 percent of the Indian oil market and aims to double that amount in the next few years.[128]

Nor will this improve. The International Energy Agency forecasts OPEC's share of world oil production, particularly from the Middle East, will grow from 44 percent now to 51 percent by 2030.[129]

Nations too dependent on oil and gas revenues often catch what is called "the Dutch disease" and fail to develop other sectors of their economy. This is one of the reasons parts of the oil-rich Arab Middle East have stagnated economically. Norway is a good example of a nation that has avoided the worst impact of large energy discoveries and has put its revenues to good use in promoting social equality and capitalist innovation.

When substantial amounts of profits from the unexpected discovery by Noble Energy of large offshore natural gas deposits in Israel flow into government coffers in the next ten years, the nation can best use the money to help reduce its already serious income inequalities—including that of its Arab minority—and invest heavily in education and job training for all citizens.

Expanded oil revenues give greater flexibility to oil-exporting countries such as Iran, Venezuela, and Russia to adopt aggressive policies contrary to U.S. and Israeli interests. When crude oil prices declined dramatically after July 2008, the impact was immediate in reducing the belligerence of Venezuela's Hugo Chavez. Oil below $50 a barrel would do more than anything else to curb his power and to temper his diplomacy.[130]

This calculus is true throughout the oil-producing world. At the onset of the Great Recession in 2008, the Gulf oil producers had foreign assets valued at more than $1 trillion. They seemed well positioned to deal with the financial crisis and to complete many ambitious projects that had been planned on a baseline price of $50 oil or lower. But as oil plunged below $40 per barrel in early 2009, Dubai, which the year before employed more than 15 percent of the world's active construction cranes, became a ghost city. Construction stagnated, and 1,500 foreign workers' visas were canceled each day. The president of the UAE Federation, Sheikh Khalifa bin Zayed al-Nahyan of Abu Dhabi, took extraordinary steps to support Dubai's banking system and its infrastructure programs by tapping its sovereign wealth funds.[131]

This all seems a world apart from 2011, when the upheavals in the Middle East have spooked global markets and led to a dramatic increase in oil prices. With gasoline prices climbing near $4.00 per barrel, jumping in part because of jitters over a possible Israeli attack on Iran, the real impact may finally be hitting home. Two bipartisan groups ran an Oil Shockwave war game in 2007 postulating oil at $150 per barrel. I participated in a 2011 version sponsored by a nonprofit energy think tank, Securing America's Future Energy. The projections included a greater threat from Iran, a more difficult Russia, and severe strains on the global economy. With oil cresting over $147 per barrel in July 2008, and in 2012 exceeding $100 per barrel, such nightmare scenarios are not fanciful.

Energy conservation and efficiency are one important way to reduce Western dependence on imported fossil fuels, with environmental benefits as well. For all of the technological breakthroughs, we have been living in an era based on fossil fuels. But energy efficiency is one way to curb greenhouse gases and reduce dependence on foreign oil. It need not require great technological advances.

A 2008 McKinsey & Company study concluded that most of the carbon abatement needed to combat global warming could be achieved by 2030 by using *existing* technologies to insulate homes and improve fuel efficiency. Relatively simple consumer behavior changes can also help, such as switching to concentrated laundry detergents to reduce packaging and transportation costs.[132] An especially promising technology is LEDs—light-emitting diodes, already being utilized from Buckingham Palace to the Herzliya marina. A complete conversion to LEDs could decrease carbon dioxide emissions from electric power usage for lighting by as much as 50 percent in about 20 years.[133] Conversion from incandescent light bulbs to fluorescents would also generate substantial savings. This is already underway in the European Union but is unlikely to be required in the U.S.

There are other surprisingly simple tools and strategies. For the past decade all new Walmart stores have had roofs made of a shiny plasticized white coating that absorbs less of the sun's heat. The National Laboratory in Oak Ridge, Tennessee, found that houses with reflective roofs use 35 percent less electricity. Buildings lose almost a third of their energy because of poor construction standards and lack of insulation; strict building codes can reduce the waste of energy and create retrofitting jobs. Smart electrical grids allow better data collection from home and industrial meters, permit utilities to maintain a better balance between supply and demand for energy, and integrate solar and wind energy. The twenty-first century will see an information-based infrastructure as the foundation for sound energy and environmental policies, which also provides an opening for Israeli software.

Alternative energy is another source of energy that can be produced in the U.S., Europe, Israel, and the West.[134] Car manufacturers are ramping up electric cars with long-life batteries. Apart from going electric, a related way to keep pressure on Middle East oil producers is to develop fuel for cars and homes with substitutes for oil-based products. The U.S. Congress has mandated that 10 percent of the gasoline produced by refineries must come from ethanol, largely corn based. The real breakthrough will occur when alternative fuels are developed with such nonfood biofuels as wood-based products and algae. This is hardly a pipe dream: A majority of cars in Brazil run on fuel from domestically grown sugarcane.[135]

Methanol, a natural gas–based product, represents 8 percent of the fuel mix. Electric cars are now just coming onto the American market, with the General Motors Volt and Nissan Leaf offering a seventy-five-cent equivalent per-gallon cost. But there is a need for a nationwide plug-in system, probably in traditional gasoline stations, and for a huge increase in the number of batteries, far beyond today's capacity.

A concerted effort by the Western democracies as well as China and India to move toward alternative energy sources will help reduce the threat of global warming and increase their own energy security. But this is a long-term process. In the U.S., experts estimate that by 2020, only around 10 percent of the country's energy needs could be satisfied by alternative energy sources.

Israel can transform a challenge into an avenue of international leadership. Already, an Israeli entrepreneur, Shai Agassi, has teamed with Renault/Nissan to create the first national network of battery-exchange stations for electric cars in Israel that could rival and eventually overtake gasoline stations.

A new generation of young, largely Western-educated leaders in the Middle East is intent on hedging its bets on hydrocarbons. The Crown Prince of Abu Dhabi announced in 2008 that his country would invest $15 billion in renewable energy, as much as President Obama proposed to the U.S. Congress for the entire United States. King Abdullah University of Science and Technology in Saudi Arabia gave a Stanford scientist $25 million to start a research center devoted to making solar power economically competitive with coal. In November 2008 Qatar signed an agreement with then British prime minister Gordon Brown to invest more than $220 million in a British low-carbon technology fund.[136] The U.S. and the West could, over time, become as dependent on Middle East alternative energy as on Middle East oil. But to the extent the Gulf states are linked to the West in developing new technologies, it will enhance their stake in stability and in American leadership, an essential ingredient in Israel's security.

High energy prices are sparking private sector investments in low-carbon, alternate energy, now $710 billion annual around the world, and by 2020, likely to be over $2 trillion, according to one leading energy analyst.[137] (Citing Nick Robins, energy and climate change analyst at HSBC in London, cited in John M. Broder, "Climate Change: A Battle on Many Fronts," *International Herald Tribune*, January 25, 2012)

But coordinated efforts are needed. The EU has committed $7 billion to build a dozen plants to capture and store carbon from coal-burning power plants. The Obama administration included $2.4 billion in its economic stimulus package for similar carbon storage projects, but these must still conquer high cost hurdles. The money would obviously go further as part of a joint effort that could also include China, already one of the world's foremost users of hydro, solar, and wind power.

For the first time in a generation U.S. utilities are pursuing nuclear plants, although they have been slowed by the disaster at Japan's Fukushima nuclear reactor. If the U.S. is serious about dealing with the challenge of climate change and reduced dependence on foreign oil, nuclear energy must play a bigger role. There have been no new American nuclear power plants since 1974, although around 20 percent of the nation's electricity is generated from nuclear power. U.S. utilities have been planning some thirty new nuclear units during the next decade, and China, India, and Russia all plan to build more. France is the world leader, with more than 70 percent of its electricity from nuclear power—and a half-century record of no major accidents.

But Germany is risk averse, in part for political reasons as the rising strength of the Green Party threatens the ruling coalition. After the Fukushima disaster, Chancellor Angela Merkel announced that Germany would close down all its nuclear power plants by 2020. This can only mean more dependence on foreign imported natural gas from Russia and elsewhere—to say nothing of power that will be imported from France's nuclear-powered grid.

Moving the West away from its oil addiction is a political as well as technological challenge Israel is well positioned for because it has long conducted world-class alternative energy research at institutions such as the Weizmann Institute and the Technion. The alternative energy sector can be as important a driver of economic growth as the Internet and digital technologies, but caution is necessary.

There is likely to be a long lead time for commercial development of alternative energy from its theoretical base. Wind energy is an exception. Texas already gets 10 percent of its electricity from wind, Spain more than 10 percent, and Denmark more than 21 percent. But in the United States there are inevitable problems where energy-conscious but influential citizens fight to be sure that wind farms are located somewhere else. Several projects in the northeastern U.S. face fierce legal challenges backed by the tourist industry and prominent summer residents complaining that the tall turbines will spoil the view.[138] While wind generators are now connected to the general power grid, there is a problem with the intermittent nature of wind power.

The U.S. consumes one-quarter of the world's energy, and changing course to alternative sources is like maneuvering a giant ship: It can only be done slowly; the scope of the challenges is immense. So while we dither, China has become the world's top producer of wind turbines, as it is the number one producer of solar panels. Despite the slower pace of U.S. solar energy, the U.S. became a net exporter of solar products in 2010.[139]

A New Western Hemisphere Fossil Fuel Reality

With all the emphasis on alternative energy, it is important to recognize these energy sources have long lead times and will make up only a small share of global energy use in the near future. Nuclear energy, which should become a greater part of global electricity usage, suffered a setback because of the Japanese tsunami. Crude oil and natural gas will remain central to U.S. energy usage, but with an important twist. More of it will come from the Western Hemisphere, and the U.S. itself, rather than from the Middle East. Indeed, even today, only about 10 percent of U.S. oil imports come from the Persian Gulf, and they represent 5 percent of consumption. The Middle East will remain a crucial geostrategic region, but increasingly the oil and natural gas resources of the Arab nations are going to Asia, not the U.S.

In an exciting new energy development with great strategic importance to the U.S. and to Israel, Pulitzer Prize–winning energy authority Daniel Yergin has noted that a new world oil map is emerging in the early part of the twenty-first century, centered on the Western Hemisphere, not the Middle East, running from Alberta, Canada, to North Dakota and south Texas, off the coast of French Guiana to enormous offshore oil deposits near Brazil. It is the result of technological breakthroughs.[140] Since 2007, the U.S. has cut its imports from OPEC by a million barrels per day, as imports from Brazil, Colombia, and Canada increase.

This new, more energy secure oil map is not based on the Venezuela of Hugo Chavez, the anti-Western, anti-Israel president, where oil output has fallen by one-quarter since 2000, nor Mexico, where oil production is also declining. Rather its centerpiece is Canada, with its vast oil or tar sands; presalt deposits in Brazil; and "tight oil" in the U.S.

Production from the oil sands of the great U.S. neighbor to our north, Canada, has risen to 1.5 million barrels daily, more than Libya even before the civil war that ousted Qaddafi, and that output will double by the beginning of the next decade to over 3 million barrels per day on top of its conventional oil production. Along with its other oil production, this will make Canada, in a few short years, a larger oil producer than Iran, and the fifth largest in the world, next to Russia, Saudi Arabia, the U.S., and China. Canada will soon become the top source of U.S. imported oil, supplying the same amount as Saudi Arabia and Kuwait combined.[141]

By 2030 Daniel Yergin predicts more than one-third of all U.S. oil imports will come from Canadian oil sands and other Canadian conventional crude oil production. To get the full value of this great oil sands resource, a new pipeline must be built to bring it to refineries in Texas. Unfortunately, the U.S. State Department has refused to grant a permit to build the 1,700-mile Keystone XL pipeline because of environmental objections. But I have no doubt the pipeline, when partially rerouted, will be built—or Canada will be sending China, not the U.S., this newfound oil.

A second component of this new energy map is Brazil, where new technology discovered enormous oil reserves off its southeast coast, which had been hidden below a salt belt a mile thick. By 2020, less than ten years from now, Brazil will be one of the world's largest oil exporters, producing 5 million barrels of oil per day, twice Venezuela's current output and half of Saudi Arabia's production. This would make democratic Brazil, not autocratic Chavez, the key Latin American energy power.

The third new crude oil source comes in the U.S. itself, from "tight oil" trapped in dense rock; with new "fracking" technology, the crude oil can be released in significant amounts. The U.S. Geological Survey estimated in 2009 that the Bakken formation in North Dakota and Montana may hold 3.65 million barrels of oil. In only eight years, North Dakota has become the fourth-largest oil-producing state in the country. By 2020, Yergin estimates that tight oil production in the U.S. could reach 3 million barrels per day, one-third of U.S. oil production.[142]

Another potential game changer for the U.S. is the Marcellus shale rock formation from sediment deposited over 350 million years ago, extending from upper New York State throughout much of the Appalachian basin, including parts of Pennsylvania, Ohio, Maryland, West Virginia, and Virginia, which holds enormous quantities of clean-burning natural gas—enough to significantly reduce America's dependence on foreign energy. New horizontal drilling techniques make access to this gas a reality.

There are environmental concerns of potential contamination to underground drinking water supplies, but a study conducted by former deputy secretary of energy and MIT professor John Deutch, with whom I worked when he was deputy secretary of energy in the Carter administration, found that these concerns are remote and can be managed with proper regulation.[143]

U.S. companies in Texas, Louisiana, Oklahoma, and Pennsylvania have developed this technology, and leading European companies are trying the same techniques to reduce Europe's growing dependence on Russian natural gas. If the environmental dangers can be removed—and I believe they can—the additional natural gas production would further reduce the need for imported crude oil to heat homes and generate electricity. It will also save billions of dollars in U.S. balance of payments for imported crude oil.[144] For Israel, this will mean that the U.S. and Europe will be less dependent upon Middle East oil, a positive development.

The dimensions of the shale gas revolution are demonstrated by the fact that in 2000 it was less than 2 percent of U.S. natural gas supplies, today it is 30 percent, and by 2035 it is expected to be 45 percent.[145] There is substantial disagreement over how much shale gas is available in the U.S., with the Energy Information Agency in early 2012 cutting by 40 percent their estimates, from 827 trillion cubic feet, enough to meet America's demands for 17 years, to 482 trillion cubic feet, a six-year supply. But still the Agency believes the share of natural gas produced by drilling in shale formations will more than double, to 49 percent by 2035, and that the U.S. will become a net exporter of liquefied natural gas by 2016.[146]

The benefits of unlocking shale gas are not limited to the U.S. The U.S. Energy Information Administration recently estimated that shale gas basins are located in thirty-two countries, with recoverable amounts in Europe of 624 trillion cubic feet of natural gas, compared to 862 trillion in the U.S. The European Centre for Energy and Resource Security estimates that the potential shale gas in Europe could cover European natural gas demand for at least another sixty years. This would significantly reduce European dependence on Russian and Iranian gas.[147]

If shale gas is a potential game changer for the U.S. in the future, Israel is fortunate to have one available right now. A Houston-based energy company, Noble Energy (which I have represented), began searching for natural gas off the Israeli coast when no other company was willing to do so and made discoveries that can change Israel's energy profile, now under serious threat by both actual sabotage and political attacks on the gas pipelines from Egypt following the toppling of the Mubarak regime. Noble first discovered a field it called Mari-B, with 1 trillion cubic feet of natural gas that it began piping to Israel in 2004. In 2008, the much larger Tamar field was discovered, with 8.4 trillion cubic feet, and in 2010, Noble discovered the appropriately named Leviathan field. While the company is still evaluating its gas reserves, independent experts believe there could be more than 20 trillion cubic feet—with possibly more below the Mediterranean, in what is clearly Israeli territory. This could make Israel an exporter of natural gas.

In the Middle East, nothing comes without political controversy. Lebanon is claiming parts of the natural gas reserves are in its territory, which is demonstrably inaccurate. And Turkey, as part of its increasingly tense relationship with Israel, has sharply criticized and threatened to disrupt an Israel-Cyprus agreement to divide the offshore eastern Mediterranean resources, because Turkey occupies part of Cyprus and wants to be included in any agreement.

The irony of Israel's becoming a Middle East energy supplier in competition with the Arabs is not without future diplomatic potential. If resource-hungry China is interested in investing in Israel's gas fields and building terminals to liquefy and ship it to China, this could provide closer links in the decades ahead, based on more than the currently thriving but limited trade in high technology. To take full advantage of its newfound natural gas, it is critical that Israel put in place a tariff system that encourages its further development.

With crude remaining the primary source of energy in the West in the near future, and with emerging markets using increasing amounts of crude oil and natural gas, oil prices will remain high. Saudi Arabia, the world's largest OPEC producer, with the excess capacity to directly affect world prices, has preferred prices at around $80 per barrel—high enough to generate massive resources but not high enough to speed the development of alternative energy sources.[148] But Saudi Arabia has raised its target price to $100 per barrel to help pay for the massive social investments it is using to try to avert the Arab Spring revolutions coming to the Kingdom.

In 1980, Congress passed a bill I helped draft in the Carter White House to support pilot projects for developing oil-shale and coal-based resources through a new government-created corporation, the Synthetic Fuels Corporation. But it was killed by the Reagan administration, and decades of progress were lost. There is no time for similar mistakes now. All alternatives to Middle East oil, from fossil fuels in the U.S., Canada, and the Western Hemisphere, to biofuels, wind, solar, and geothermal power should be vigorously pursued.[149] America's future security, and Israel's, depends upon it.

Demographic Realities and Challenges

Demography is the study of human population, but it is not just about dry numbers. Population significantly influences the relative power of nations, and changes have major impacts that can be foreseen but are often not appreciated until they actually happen. While the size of a country often has a significant relationship to its global impact, size alone was not as crucial as industrial and scientific discoveries and the maturing of political institutions in raising the small country of Britain to a great empire. Countries can have rapidly growing populations and become more wealthy, such as South Korea and Taiwan over the past fifty years, or can be overwhelmed by their populations and sink under their weight, as several countries in sub-Saharan Africa, Pakistan, or the Middle East have done.[150] Other characteristics can be dispositive, such as governance structures, educational levels, and security.

Technological achievements, educational levels, productivity, and creativity can partially make up for size. So Israel, with only 7 million people, has the forty-second-largest economy in the world and the twenty-seventh-highest GDP per capita. With a relatively small number of troops, it deploys one of the world's most effective militaries, eleventh in global firepower by one rating.[151] Likewise, tiny Singapore, with many of the same attributes as Israel, ranks thirty-ninth in the size of its economy and fifteenth in GDP per capita.

But size is an increasingly important factor in a nation's global reach. It is not coincidental that the top three economies in the world (the U.S., China, and Japan) all have large populations; that the major emerging powers all have large and growing populations; and that even regional powers such as Iran and Turkey, each with 70-plus million people, have large numbers, with the tax base to supply the revenues for extensive defense, intelligence, and, in the case of Iran, nuclear programs.

The economic growth of emerging powers has spawned new global institutional arrangements to ensure they have a voice commensurate with their size and growing might. The Group of Seven of the 1970s has become the Group of Twenty, diluting the influence of the industrial democracies, with their more stagnant populations and economic growth. There are now 7 billion people in the world. During the twentieth century, global population leaped from 1.6 billion, and as recently as 1950 there were only 2.5 billion people. By 2050, new World Bank projections indicate there is likely to be over 10 billion. The overall population growth, combined with a huge surge in the growth of a worldwide middle class with increased demands for consumption that will power global growth, will put pressure on scarce natural resources, especially water.

It is not only the total population of a country that matters, but also the movement of that population within and among countries. Millions of Muslims arriving in Europe from North Africa and Turkey have created a backlash and generated support for anti-immigrant, right-wing parties in generally tolerant countries such as France and the Netherlands. This influx will also influence the foreign policies of European nations as Muslims become voting citizens of their adopted countries. One of the reasons the U.S., alone among the industrial democracies, continues to experience large population increases is Hispanic immigration, both legal and illegal, spawning political division and angry political battles. But immigration is also a volatile issue in America, with the status of the some 12 million Hispanics illegally in the country unresolved, with the Bush and Obama administrations seeking ways to legalize them, while some conservatives seek their expulsion; tough laws in states like Arizona and Alabama allowing law enforcement authorities to demand immigration papers from Hispanics they suspect are illegal; major debates in the 2012 presidential election over whether children born in the U.S. to illegal parents should be permitted to stay and go to college; and with the status of U.S. citizens.

Outmigration can also deplete nations of some of their most energetic people and supply a new energy to the countries receiving them. This was one of the results of the historic migration to the United States in the nineteenth century. Now Israel, the country for whom immigration was its very foundation, is experiencing a second phase. Significant numbers of engineers and software professionals have migrated to the U.S. and elsewhere. While the total numbers are subject to dispute, the worrisome trend is not. By 1980, the Israel Central Bureau of Statistics estimated that around 270,000 Israelis were living abroad for more than a year, or 7 percent of the population. More recently, the Israeli Ministry of Immigrant Absorption estimates 750,000 Israeli emigrants, 10 percent of the population, while the Netanyahu government estimates from 800,000 to a million, or 13 percent of the population, relatively high for an OECD country.[152] At the same time, the million Russian Jews who emigrated to Israel have made an immeasurably positive contribution to Israel's economic growth, creativity, and culture.

The Consequences of Aging Societies

Another demographic dimension is the age of the population within countries. Western European countries are aging rapidly, with low birthrates to support a growing number of retirees. Japan's population is shrinking and aging at staggering rates. With almost no immigration permitted, Japan has just ceded to China its status as the world's second-largest economy next to the U.S., and its influence in Asia has declined proportionately. Even in the U.S., which has a growing population, unfunded pension liabilities for states and local government retirees amounting to over $2 trillion.

Aging populations in Western societies will also have to adjust their life cycles, as older people work beyond what they had thought would be retirement age. In France, President Sarkozy's decision to raise the retirement age from 60 to 62 led to mass demonstrations on the streets of Paris. Russia's population is declining rapidly, with males living an average of only 59 years, limiting the nation's ability to sustain a massive army. One reason Russia was anxious to reach an arms control agreement with the U.S. in 2010 was the limit on its financial ability to sustain its nuclear arsenal.

China also has an unusual demographic problem. As the result of its one-child policy, the birthrate of 1.5 children per couple has fallen below replacement level, and the nation can expect an explosion of senior citizens during the next twenty years. This also leads to an increase in the number of young men who will never marry because of the shortage of women; couples tend to abort female fetuses in favor of sons. Nicholas Eberstadt of the American Enterprise Institute warns that these "serious demographic challenges could slow economic growth more than is currently expected."[153] As China has a fall-off in younger workers entering its workforce, its economic growth will be reduced, and it will have fewer workers to support a sharply aging society.

In the G20 countries, 450 million people will turn sixty-five over the next decade. Low fertility rates combined with longer life spans will lead to what some experts see as fiscally unsustainable older populations in the first half of the twenty-first century.[154]

In the Middle East and the Muslim world the youth bulges of rapidly growing working-age populations threaten economic and political stability.[155] An underlying factor in the dramatic upheavals in the Arab Middle East is the lack of economic opportunity for its youth bulge; about half the population is under thirty years of age, and one-third of Egypt's population is under fourteen. Demographic realities will put great pressure on postrevolution governments to deliver more jobs.

The U.S. Dimension: Growth and Diversity

The United States has a healthy demographic profile. The country is growing, faster than China and aging less than most industrialized democracies. But the face of America is rapidly changing. The year 2010 was a demographic landmark; for the first time in American history, more Hispanic, African, and Asian Americans were born than non-Hispanic Caucasians, and by 2050 groups traditionally considered minorities will cumulatively be in the majority.

In California, the nation's largest state (in population), more than half the children are Hispanic, and the Hispanic migration has spread to population centers in the Midwest as well as New York. As the number of Hispanic and Asian American children has grown, today only about 25 percent of Californians under the age of eighteen are non-Hispanic whites. As recently as the 1990s, Hispanics made up only 26 percent of the state's population and are now at 38 percent, almost equal to the white population.[156] And the Hispanic population is likely to increase between now and 2050 by 200 percent.

Hispanics have passed African Americans as the largest minority group in the U.S., and they are also the youngest. This is already having significant political implications. Between 1998 and 2008, the number of eligible Hispanic voters rose from 16.1 million to 19.5 million, more than 20 percent.[157] The number of congressional districts in which minorities make up at least 30 percent of the population nearly doubled from 109 to 205, almost half of the 435 seats in the House of Representatives.[158]

For American Jews this puts a premium on developing relationships with the rapidly growing Hispanic, Indian, and East Asian communities, who traditionally have had little contact with Jews and even less with Israel, while continuing to make common cause with the African American community based on their historic support for the civil rights movement. Groups such as Project Interchange of the American Jewish Committee have for years identified rising young Hispanic leaders for trips to Israel, and this program should be broadened.

There is a broader impact. Immigrant populations, including Africans from countries such as Ghana and Ethiopia, as well as Hispanics, are one of the reasons the U.S. Census Bureau predicts that the American population will grow from 300 million now to around 400 million by 2050. Compared to other mature countries, and even some developing countries, the U.S. will be relatively young. In the next twenty years, there will be 85 million more Americans, while on a much larger base of 1.3 billion, China will add only 60 million more people due largely to its one-child policy.[159] This will make the U.S. the third-largest country in the world, after China and India.[160] In 2050, only about 25 percent of Americans will be over sixty years of age, compared to 31 percent in China and 41 percent in Japan.[161]

The Implications of Growth of the Muslim Diaspora in Europe and the U.S.

As the Muslim population is driven higher by birthrates and immigration, second and third generations of the original immigrants will become citizens and begin, properly so, to become active and more influential in politics. The Lord Mayor of Rotterdam is Muslim. In Germany, after decades of exclusion, Turks are now citizens, and in the 2005 national elections more than half a million voted. In 2008, for the first time, a major political party, the Green Party (which holds more than 10 percent of the seats in parliament), selected a German Muslim, Cem Özdemir, the son of Turkish immigrants, as its leader.[162] This trend can be seen in the next generation as well. In Austria, half of those entering kindergarten in Vienna are Muslim or other immigrants.[163]

At one level, this is to be admired as Europe becomes more multicultural and European Muslims exercise their democratic rights. There are around 500,000 Jews in France and 4 million Muslims, many from former French colonies in North Africa. But as dramatized by the upheavals in suburban Paris, integration of these immigrants has not been easy. "Islamophobia" has replaced Europe's historic anti-Semitism as the principal concern of parts of the continent, and one clear sign is the movement to ban not only the burqa concealing women's bodies and faces but the more widely worn hijab head scarf, seen in France, Belgium, the Netherlands, and Italy. In Switzerland a nationwide referendum in 2009 banned the construction of minarets on mosques. All of this signals a growing European public apprehension with the increasing presence of a Muslim minority.

A more direct threat to European Jewry is the anger of young men in the French Muslim community, predominantly those of Algerian origin, at their continued alienation from mainstream society. Their struggles, exacerbated by the Great Recession and enflamed by the Gaza War, led to street demonstrations with anti-Israeli slogans and anti-Semitic expletives. This tumult can be explained in part by the speed of change in Europe that has taken place in the postwar period. In the middle of the twentieth century there were virtually no Muslims in Western Europe, and today there are 15 million.

While immigrants of the past were forced by distance to cut ties with their homelands and assimilate, in a globalized world with air travel, the Internet, cell phones, global social networks, satellite television, and finally the local mosque and imam, the countries of origin are never far away. Tensions have been aggravated by attacks and bombings by native as well as foreign-born Muslims; the murder of a young Israeli-born Jew by a Muslim gang in suburban Paris; the Danish cartoon controversy over the depiction of the Prophet Mohammed; and the assassination of Dutch film maker Theo Van Gogh by a Muslim incensed with his film *Submission,* which criticizes Islam's treatment of women.[164] Recent studies show that xenophobia is gaining ground in Germany and across Europe—with Muslims a common target, highlighted by the 2009 killing of a young Egyptian mother in a Dresden courtroom.[165] German chancellor Merkel proclaimed that efforts at multiculturalism in Germany had "utterly failed."

Over time, European policy toward Israel will begin to reflect the impact of the emerging political force of European Muslims. European policy toward Israel has already cooled. In 2009 the UK publicly refused to supply replacement parts and other equipment to the Israeli Navy because of its participation in the Gaza War.[166] Many of the rising generation of European Muslims have become animated by the Palestinian issue, emerging into the streets to protest conflicts in Lebanon and Gaza. While it is always possible that Europe's animosity toward its Muslims can turn to sympathy toward its fellow Jewish citizens, it is unlikely to lead to more pro-Israel sentiment; in any event, Jews have never thrived in an environment of anger toward minorities. While it will not be easy, European Jewish institutions should speak out for religious tolerance toward Muslims, just as they would want it for themselves.

In America, statistics are less precise, but there are between 1.8 million[167] and 2.35 million[168] American Muslims, less than 1 percent of the U.S. population. But the Muslim population increased substantially in the last part of the twentieth century, and with rising immigration and relatively high birthrates, it will continue to increase. Sixty five percent of American Muslims are foreign born. One in five native-born American Muslims is African American, many of whom are converts to Islam.[169] Fortunately, there is less tension in the U.S. with its American Muslim population, but there are isolated and highly publicized incidents of violence and prejudice—a murderous attack by an American Muslim officer at Fort Hood, Texas; the American leader of the al-Qaeda branch in Yemen (recently killed by an American drone airplane); and the controversy over the location of a new mosque and American Muslim community center near the World Trade Center.

But American Muslims are nevertheless more integrated into American society than European Muslims and less socially isolated. The Pew Research Center's nationwide sample of American Muslim attitudes in 2007, the first ever conducted, concluded that most were largely assimilated, satisfied with their lives, and moderate with respect to many of the issues dividing the Muslim and Western worlds. Their educational levels and income generally mirror the general public; nearly two-thirds see no conflict between being a devout Muslim and living in a modern society. And they reject Islamic extremism by larger margins than Muslim minorities in Western European countries.[170]

Indeed, a Gallup poll in the summer of 2011 indicates that Muslim Americans are more optimistic about their future than other major faith groups, with almost two-thirds stating that their standard of living is increasing, an 18 percent increase since 2008 despite the recession. American Muslims are less likely to be registered to vote than other religious groups, 65 percent compared to 91 percent of American Jews and Protestants, and one Muslim serves in the U.S. Congress.

However, on foreign policy, their views diverge from mainstream American views in certain areas. They are more likely than people from other religions to see the wars in Iraq and Afghanistan as mistakes and to blame anti-Americanism in Muslim countries on U.S. policy rather than on the rulers of those countries. Relatively few believe the U.S.-led war on terrorism is a sincere effort to reduce terrorism, and only 40 percent believe groups of Arabs carried out the 9/11 attacks. One positive note from the Gallup survey is that Jewish and Muslim Americans share similar perceptions of U.S. Muslim attitudes toward al-Qaeda: 92 percent of American Muslims and 70 percent of American Jews do not believe that Muslim Americans sympathize with the terrorist group.[171]

Rapid Growth in Developing Countries
and the Response of the U.S. and Israel

Most of the 227,000 people added to the world's population each day do not live in the U.S. or Europe but in less developed nations. Better health care in developing nations will reduce the number of deaths, which may mean an even larger population increase.[172] As James Wolfensohn, the former president of the World Bank, noted at the 2009 Israeli Presidential Conference hosted by President Shimon Peres, around 1 billion of the 7 billion people in the world today live in the rich, developed world.[173] But as the world population reaches 10 billion by 2050, the population of the classically defined rich world will remain stagnant at roughly the same 1 billion. This means that nearly 90 percent of the world's population growth will be outside that part of the world where Israel has its historically closest contacts.

These numbers are a wake-up call for the U.S. and for Israel. It is essential for national security reasons that both countries develop closer relations to the fastest-growing nations. One billion people in the world's poorest countries live on less than $1.25 a day. By 2050, these numbers are projected to more than double to over 2 billion people—over 20 percent of the world's population by that time, but their income will not rise commensurately. Incomes are projected to rise to only about $1,700 to $3,000 per year, compared with $40,000 per citizen in China and India, $50,000 in the oil-producing states in the Middle East, and an average of $100,000 in the rich countries. This can create an unstable world. President Obama and Secretary of State Clinton are working to meet this challenge. Her travel schedule reflects this, as does Obama's outreach to the developing world.

Israel does not seem to be making a priority of a similar shift in focus, although in its early years Israel was one of the most active countries in spreading technical and other assistance to African countries. Israel could reap long-term benefits, not only in larger markets for Israeli exports but also in urgently needed political support. But for all of Israel's technological, military, and scientific prowess, there are inherent limits on its influence and power because even with a healthy demographic increase, Israeli Jews will still be an increasingly smaller percentage of the world's population and—more telling—of the Israeli Arab and Palestinian populations. For Israel to maintain its Jewish majority, it must reach a peace agreement.

The Jewish Dimension

If Israel's most challenging external threat is Iran's nuclear ambitions, the most serious internal threat is demographic. There are only a little over 13 million Jews in the world,[174] at least 4 million fewer than before the Holocaust. While the global population is projected to increase from some 7 billion people today to more than 9 billion by midcentury and over 10 billion by 2100,[175] it is difficult to believe the Jewish people will increase much beyond current numbers. Diaspora Jews make up an ever-smaller percentage of the countries in which they live, with the potential for a loss of influence; numbers matter. In the United States, there are around 5 million Jews out of a population of over 300 million, and this tiny percentage, some 2 percent, will certainly decline over the decades ahead.

The Diaspora: A Demograpic Crisis and What to Do About It

In virtually all Diaspora communities, the demographic crisis arises from birth rates below levels to even keep the Jewish population stable, which is an erosion of Jewish identity, a rapidly aging population, and disaffiliation from Jewish communal and institutional life. Much of this is the result of assimilation, low birthrates, and growing intermarriage without non-Jewish spouses converting to Judaism— the most celebrated recent example being the marriage of President Clinton's daughter Chelsea to a Jew who proudly wore a prayer shawl at the ceremony.

In this astonishing age of medical science and good nutrition, the average lifespan in most developed countries is increasing by two and one-half years per decade.[176] A child born today can on average expect to live over ninety years. But it is doubtful that even by 2050 Jews will recover their pre–World War II population levels.[177] We simply have never recovered from the terrible crimes of Hitler and his allies; there were 11 million Jews left after the Holocaust. During the first thirteen years after World War II, a million new Jews were added, but it took more than forty years to add the second million.

With the ironic exception of the Diaspora community in Germany (due to the large influx of Jewish immigrants from Russia), there is a slow, steady decline in the Jewish population. Diaspora Jews have the lowest birthrates of any group in the world, between 1.5 and 1.9 per couple on average compared to the standard replacement rate of 2.1 births per couple, so every single Jewish community outside of Israel will have fewer Jews in 2020 than today. Only in Israel will the number of Jews increase (5.4 million in 2007 to a projected 6.2 million in 2020). The differences are significant. For example, whereas Israeli Jewish women in their forties have an average of 3.4 children, in the United States it is just 1.9, below levels needed for the American Jewish population to stabilize.

There are three great Jewish population centers today: North America (the United States and Canada), Israel, and Europe, with significant numbers also living in Latin American countries (primarily Argentina and Brazil) and in Australia and South Africa. But about 80 percent of the world's Jews live in the United States and Israel. In a major demographic study, the Jewish People Policy Institute (JPPI), whose board I cochair, found that in 2008, Israel became the largest national Jewish community in the world, surpassing the United States. Israel's Jewish population grew since 2004 by 300,000, and the Jewish population in the Diaspora declined by 100,000. This was the first time since the destruction of the Second Temple in 70 C.E. that the largest Jewish community resided in the Land of Israel. The other significant Jewish population centers are found in Europe, a total of 1.1 million, mainly in France (483,500), Britain (292,000), and Germany (119,000); the former Soviet Union (400,000, of which Russia is 205,000); Canada (375,000); Australia (100,000); and South America (700,000, mainly Argentina with 182,300 and Brazil with 95,000).[178] The world's Jews are fairly concentrated in five urban areas: 52 percent live in Tel Aviv, New York, Jerusalem, Los Angeles, and Haifa, and 75 percent live in urban areas with over 100,000 other Jews.

The demographic problem of the Diaspora is particularly pronounced in Europe. In the UK there were 390,000 core Jews in 1970, 297,000 in 2006, and only 238,000 projected in 2020. For Europe as a whole, outside the former Soviet Union, the Jewish population is projected to decline from 1.3 million to barely over a million by 2020. This decline will have a bigger political impact in Europe because of a massive increase in European Muslims, now totaling 15 million.

While American Jews will only slightly increase from current numbers of 5 million, and only then if there is an increase in birthrates and decrease in marriages without conversion of the non-Jewish spouse to Judaism. The demographic crisis in the Diaspora is the direct consequence of the successful integration of the Jewish communities in most countries, affording Jews a sense of security and decreasing the historical sense of alienation. Ironically, at the very hour of our success, many Jews have chosen to abandon their identity. At the very time in history when Diaspora Jews can openly and proudly assert their Jewishness in countries with no social or economic cost, and where the rule of law fully protects Jews and others in their religious and cultural expressions, too few are willing to do so. Many Jews are not only integrating into secular society but also abandoning their Jewish identification. The United States and all Diaspora countries are stronger for the beautiful mosaic of which they are a part and which is at risk of being lost. As a people who thrive on irony, the ultimate irony is that Jews, not external enemies, are threatening Jewish continuity outside Israel.

American college campuses are a microcosm of the challenges. A remarkable 85 percent of American Jews now go on to universities, and of the approximately 250,000 American Jewish students, 47 percent of self-identified Jews have only one Jewish parent.[179] It is there that many Jewish students meet their mates, a large percentage of whom are non-Jews. There has also been a decline by age group in commitment to the Jewish people—the younger the Jew the more tenuous the identification. There is a dramatic drop by age cohort in the number of Jews who report that most of their closest friends are Jewish and in the proportion joining Jewish organizations or donating to Jewish causes.

Addressing the Demographic Challenge

Several options are available. One choice is a turn to Orthodoxy, with a more insular, religious life and strikingly larger families and much smaller rates of intermarriage. The other is Aliyah to Israel, where Jewish continuity is more assured and intermarriage is virtually nonexistent. A third option is a major effort directed at lifelong Jewish education in every dimension and for every age group, with a massive infusion of funds and talent to reach the younger generation with teachings of the beauty of Jewish life, values, and traditions. While a Jewish day-school education is not a certain barrier against drift away from the community, the fact remains that intermarriage rates among Jewish day-school graduates are lower than those in public or secular private schools, and conversion by non-Jewish spouses is more prevalent. The biggest barrier to full-time day-school education is its high cost, and subsidizing that should be a focus of waning Jewish philanthropy.

Orthodox Jewish Diaspora communities have high birthrates, low rates of intermarriage, and a strong focus on Jewish education; they are the only part of the Diaspora Jewish communities that are growing in size. They are energized and devoted to propagating and passing along their religion with all of its time-honored traditions and values. But they remain only a small part of the Jewish population in the Diaspora. While they have a beautiful lifestyle, with strong family and communal bonds, their mass appeal is limited by the necessary restrictions that are part of their lives, including the role of women.

Likewise, immigration from the Diaspora is an option, particularly for communities under pressure in Turkey and parts of Europe, and for those with a strong desire to be part of the exciting process of continuing to build a still-young Jewish sovereign state through Aliyah. But it does not fundamentally address the demographic crisis in the Diaspora. Indeed, it decreases the number of Jews outside Israel.

The best alternative is to strengthen and deepen Jewish life in the Diaspora, to encourage larger families, and to reach out aggressively to mixed marriage couples.

Throughout Jewish history significant elements of the Jewish population have lived outside Israel, and such communities, ever since Babylonia, have not lost their essential Jewish nature or been depleted by assimilation. Babylonian Jews advanced Judaism through the creation of their own Talmud, considered more authoritative by many Jewish sages than the Jerusalem Talmud. If not for the maintenance of Jewish identity throughout the Diaspora, the survival of Judaism would not have been possible, even with small numbers of Jews always living in Israel, even during millennia of exile.

From Germany and across Central and Eastern Europe, I have personally witnessed the inspiring revival of Jewish life after the twin evils of the twentieth century, Nazism and Communism, albeit in the tragically small numbers left after the Holocaust. Likewise, in the U.S. and Western Europe all is not dismal.

American Jewry: Two Communities Moving in Opposite Directions

In America, by far the largest Jewish Diaspora community, there are two distinct Jewish communities of roughly equal size—one committed to Judaism and continuity, whether in its religious *or* secular dimension, the other disaffiliated and at times disaffected from Jewish or Israel-related causes. But there is much to build upon.

For those deeply committed to Jewish continuity, there are encouraging signs across denominational lines. A substantial core of American Jews is intensely engaged in Jewish life. They are creating outreach programs to intermarried couples. As intermarriage with conversion skyrockets, so does the number of American Jewish schoolchildren in full-time Jewish day schools, now 225,000, double the number twenty years ago. Kosher-certified food sales are the fastest-growing segment of the food market, outstripping organic foods and rising from $32 billion in 1993 to over $200 billion in 2010.[180] Somewhere between 500,000 and 1.8 million American Jews keep a kosher home or at least a semblance of one.[181]

There are more Jewish day schools with intensive Jewish education than ever before. Michael Steinhardt has spearheaded a bilingual public charter school in New York City teaching the Hebrew language and focusing on Jewish culture rather than religion to avoid controversy over the American constitutional separation of church and state. Synagogues are developing alternative *chavurot* services, in which smaller numbers of people have more intimate services within larger synagogues. Adult Jewish educational opportunities are flourishing. Jewish primary and secondary education is exploding in the United States, with over seven hundred Jewish day schools teaching over 200,000 children.

Other Diaspora communities are similarly thriving: In Toronto, some 45 percent of Jewish children are enrolled in Jewish day schools, in Australia more than 50 percent, and in Mexico more than 90 percent. Day-school education is no longer the sole domain of the Orthodox community.[182] In my native Atlanta, the Davis Academy is a Reform day school, which would have been unimaginable only a few decades ago. And for all the limitations of part-time, after-school, synagogue-based Jewish education, tens of thousands of Jewish children participate in it.

On college campuses, with the financial assistance of Edgar Bronfman and Lynn Schusterman, Hillel centers are reviving and thriving as the largest Jewish organizations serving universities throughout the United States and Canada. At Atlanta's Emory University, 1,300 of the 2,000 Jewish students participated in some Hillel activity in 2010. Around 70 percent of Jewish college students celebrate some Jewish holidays; 78 percent say that "being Jewish is important to me"; 79 percent have a sense of responsibility for fellow Jews; and 83 percent light Chanukah candles, although less than half (48 percent) believe that raising their children Jewish is very important.[183] Several hundred campuses offer credit courses in Jewish studies, and many offer major or minor degree concentrations; there were literally none when I went to college in the 1960s.

Outside campus and academic life, synagogue membership is slightly increasing, and most American Jews still attend a temple or synagogue at least once a year on the High Holidays; 70 percent participate in some type of Passover Seder;

three-fifths light Chanukah candles; over half fast on Yom Kippur; and up to one-third light candles on the Sabbath.[184]

It is critical to strengthen the healthy base while reaching out to the equally large percentage that is abandoning Judaism. The American Jewish community has always embraced diverse forms of practice—Orthodox, Conservative, Reform, Reconstructionist, and secular Jews. Although up to 70 percent do not identify with Judaism as a religion or are not actively involved with worship, they remain culturally identified with Judaism.

In the U.S., the rate of out-marriage—Jews marrying non-Jewish spouses—has risen from virtually zero in the early 1950s to over 50 percent for new marriages today.[185] In varying degrees, almost all Diaspora communities are struggling with this, from a low of 20 percent in Canada to 25 percent in Australia, and 45 percent in Argentina. Few non-Orthodox families are untouched. The demographic challenge is sharpened by the fact that the percentage of non-Jewish spouses who convert to Judaism ranges from only 7 percent to 20 percent, not much higher than the percentage of Jewish spouses who convert to Christianity. Where there is a conversion to Judaism, as high a percentage of children will retain their Jewish identity as if they had been born to parents who were both Jewish at birth. But where there is no conversion, only around 10 percent of the children of mixed marriages will be raised as Jews.

The great divide between the committed and disaffected elements of Diaspora Jewish life is significantly measured by whether or not there is out-marriage, and if so, whether the non-Jewish spouse converts. Out-marriage without conversion is the single greatest threat to Jewish continuity throughout the Diaspora. The trend puts real pressure on Jews who do *not* out-marry to ensure continuity. In the U.S., since Jews who marry non-Jews without conversion raise their children as Jewish less than 10 percent of the time, the roughly half of American Jews who marry in the faith are raising three-quarters of the next generation of Jews.

Jewish parents are the first line of defense. While it is no guarantee, if parents provide a strong Jewish experience for their children starting with a daily home life emphasizing Jewish practices, and in the form of Jewish schools, camps, and experiences in Israel, it substantially diminishes the frequency of out-marriage. In mixed marriages a formative Jewish experience increases the likelihood of the non-Jewish spouse converting.

Because young Jews between ages eighteen and thirty are the most vulnerable and detached from Jewish life as they pursue higher education, they are a prime target of outreach, as recognized by the revitalized Hillel movement. The most successful Jewish identity builder for this group of young American Jews is Michael Steinhardt's and Charles Bronfman's Taglit-Birthright, which initially sent more than 20,000 young Jews to Israel each year for a ten-day immersion. So far more than 200,000 have learned from the brief but intense Israeli experience. And there is clear evidence that programs such as Birthright contribute to Jewish continuity, so much so that the Jewish Agency is helping to expand it, doubling the number of young people who come annually. (The demand so greatly exceeds the available places that participants are selected by lottery.)

The Cohen Center for Modern Jewish Studies at Brandeis released a 2009 study comparing Birthright Israel trip participants to nonparticipants who had sought to participate. The study found that those who made the trip had a stronger sense of Jewish identity and demonstrated a stronger relationship to Israel.

This Israeli Birthright experience translated directly into Jewish continuity. Of those who are married, 72 percent of participants have Jewish spouses, while 46 percent of nonparticipants are married to a Jew. Of those who come from inter-married households, participants were three times more likely to in-marry; and of those married to spouses who were not born Jewish, there is a higher rate of conversion among spouses of participants. Of unmarried respondents, participants were nearly 50 percent more likely to view marrying a Jew as very important.

Equally significant, the study found that 74 percent of participants felt raising children as Jews was very important, compared to 57 percent of nonparticipants. Intermarried participants are almost twice as likely to hold that view—52 percent view raising children as Jews as very important, compared to 27 percent of nonparticipants. These findings have led one expert to declare, "Birthright Israel may very well be the most successful Jewish continuity program ever."[186] Full-time Jewish education is exceptionally expensive and out of reach for many middle-class Diaspora families who might otherwise send their children to Jewish schools. Federations are putting more resources into Jewish education but not enough. When there is an Israeli crisis, the Jewish Federations of North America (JFNA) engages in emergency campaigns and raises staggering sums of money. But the crisis in Jewish identity has yet to become a prominent cause for donations. It requires nothing less than an emergency education campaign in which all Jewish federations and other Jewish groups should participate, with the goal of a $2 billion endowment nationwide to raise the quality of after-school programs and make the cost of full-time Jewish day schools more affordable. The impact can be swift and significant. In Seattle, a donor willed $100 million to Jewish education, which dramatically reduced the cost of day-school tuition and led to a 50 percent increase in enrollment. But, in Los Angeles, with a far larger and wealthier Jewish population, established Jewish schools are struggling or even being forced to close as more families seek ever more meager financial aid.[187]

The more that successful Jewish business and professional leaders are constructively challenged to reset their charitable priorities toward Jewish causes and particularly Jewish education, the more the Jewish enterprise in the Diaspora will flourish.

There is an Americanization of Jewish philanthropy, underscoring how Jews have been integrated into American life. Of the hundred largest foundations in the U.S., eight were founded by Jews. There are two Jewish foundations with assets of $2 billion or more. And a score of other major foundations have been initiated by Jewish families. But few devote a significant part of their programs to Jewish causes. Of the ten largest foundations established by American Jewish families, only 21 percent of their total dollars went to Jewish institutions, and 79 percent went to general cultural causes—universities, symphonies, and art museums. Of the funds donated to Jewish causes, less than 15 percent go to primary and secondary education, where the money is desperately needed to support the continuity of Jewish life and family.[188]

The same is true of megagifts of $10 million or more.[189] Although they constitute only about 2 percent of the population, Jews made over 29 percent of the megagifts in the U.S. in a recent year, indicating that the Jewish impulse to give *tzedakah* remains strong. But most of these gifts go to higher education, the arts, and medicine. If more major philanthropists followed the example of Michael Steinhardt, Charles and Edgar Bronfman and the Bronfman Foundation, Lynn Schusterman and the Schusterman Foundation, and the Harry and Jeanette Weinberg Foundation and made Jewish causes a central focus, their gifts would make an enormous difference in strengthening Jewish life in the U.S. and around the world.

While all these efforts can strengthen the base, a new approach is needed for those on the margins of the Jewish community: a more open, accessible, welcoming, nonjudgmental Judaism for anyone who wishes to identify as a Jew. Consider the possibilities: In the U.S., among Jewish students of mixed parentage, 91 percent identify themselves as ethnically Jewish, and 50 percent identify as Jews by religion. One of the most exciting efforts is the special outreach program of the Combined Jewish Philanthropies of Greater Boston (CJP), led by the visionary Barry Shrage.[190] It was started in 2000, born of anxiety over soaring out-marriage rates and general disaffiliation. Within five years, one-half of all Jewish children in Boston will be raised in intermarried families. The program focuses not only on mixed couples but also on a general deepening of Judaism as a way of life, including a commitment to social justice. It stresses Jewish education in day schools and synagogue after-school programs as well as an intensive two-year, hundred-hour adult education program taught by university professors. Thus far, over three thousand adults have participated. The program makes a conscious outreach to mixed couples and their children by making Jewish life more open and free of barriers to entry, "not by lowest common denominator experiences," in Shrage's words, but with the proposition that "interfaith households and alienated Jews will only be attracted to experiences of real meaning, passion and depth."[191]

The importance of the CJP efforts can be seen in the population of just one of Boston's Jewish day schools—the Rashi Reform Day School in suburban Newton. Twenty-five percent of Rashi's students are children of intermarried parents with no history of conversion. The school reports that as of 2009, some 60 percent of the children of these mixed families are raising their children as

Jewish—more than triple the national average. These children have a profile similar to Reform Jewish children of two Jewish parents. Another visionary, Barry Rosenberg, who heads the St. Louis Jewish Federation, is doing similar outreach to mixed couples, while strengthening Jewish programming in general. Out-married couples should be welcomed and not turned away by suspicion and prejudice.

It is time for non-Orthodox rabbis to perform mixed marriages if the non-Jewish spouse commits to raising the couple's children as Jews and takes premarriage instruction in Judaism to gain a basic knowledge of what the commitment means. Some Reform rabbis already follow this practice.

The new Internet technology and social networks, such as Facebook, Twitter, and YouTube can create a new set of interactive connections. JDate, an online Jewish dating service, has led to thousands of Jewish marriages that might not otherwise have occurred. And a new service, JDate, unveiled by professors at Brandeis University, will provide the first comprehensive online location for all Jewish institutions and services in the United States. Another new service is JewishGen, a Jewish genealogy network that helps Jews around the world connect with their family histories. Students at New York University are working on a new Diaspora Internet project that will facilitate communications between Jews across the globe.[192]

It is time to go further.[193] Out-marriage is an inevitable outcome of the mainstream integration so long sought by American Jews. If we circle the wagon we will find fewer and fewer Jews inside.

It is time to promote a proactive conversion program among non-Jews, with the principal targets non-Jewish spouses of Jews, the children of mixed marriages, individuals with some Jewish heritage, and many who are simply attracted to a Jewish way of life. In the near future there may be more people claiming some Jewish heritage than those with both parents born as Jews. They should be viewed as an opportunity to increase our Jewish ranks and not to be abandoned as failures.[194] This program need not lower standards for conversion. Ritual entry should still be required, but rabbis should reach out to encourage conversion and not make it more onerous and intimidating. Converts should not be required to be more observant than nonconverts. Patience is required, because conversions might not come immediately, and for many, conversion will never be possible, to avoid offending non-Jewish parents and family. Even in these circumstances, the Jewish community should be warm and welcoming in the hope the children will be raised as Jews.

Moreover, when we consider how to address intermarriage, it is important to focus not only on the non-Jewish spouses but also on the Jewish partners, who should be encouraged to carry their Jewish heritage into the marriage.[195] Most Jews who intermarry probably do not do so out of hostility to Judaism, but simply because, in our open society, they have fallen in love with a non-Jew. Jewish schools, camps, community centers, and synagogues should be open, accessible, and welcoming to mixed couples, since the non-Jewish spouses and their children are potential Jews.[196] The Jewish community should sponsor creative and engaging workshops, education forums, and Seders for mixed marriages.

American culture inculcates the value of individual choice as a birthright. Americans face a bewildering number of choices each day—in clothes, consumer products, news, associations, friends, and even where to worship. Judaism must compete in the marketplace of religion and ideas to continue to be relevant in the twenty-first-century Diaspora life.

Orthodox and traditional Jews are also deeply impacted by American culture and society. Observant Jews can comfortably go to baseball games in Washington, Baltimore, and New York and eat at strictly kosher stands, and in Yankee Stadium, they can join a formal prayer service. The White House, under both Presidents George W. Bush and Barack Obama, has an annual Chanukah celebration for Jewish leaders, with strictly kosher food from the famous White House kitchen. And Hershey Park opens its gates and rides, after closing for the summer, to Orthodox Jews for one day during Sukkoth, with a giant sukkah, kosher meals, and Jewish music piped in throughout the vast facility. Over 10,000 traditional Jews take advantage of this unique American Jewish experience.

And for over thirty years since I helped them obtain a license, over the initial objection of the Interior Department, when I was President Carter's chief domestic adviser, Chabad Lubavitch has a giant menorah lit each Chanukah on the Ellipse behind the White House, next to the National Christmas tree, with the U.S. military bands in full regalia performing Chanukah songs with thousands of people present.

Judaism must be a religion of choice and not just a religion of birth that is reserved for those born Jewish. Looking ahead, Barry Shrage of the Boston Federation says, "All our children and grandchildren will be Jewish by choice."[197] A significant percentage of Americans change their religion at least once during their lifetime. Diaspora Jews are in a competition for religious identification. Being born Jewish is no guarantee of staying Jewish or raising one's children Jewish. It is not just non-Jews who must choose to be Jewish; it is those born Jewish as well. It will take a heroic effort simply keeping the Diaspora population constant; the real challenge is to create more Jews from non-Jews.

Jonathan Sarna said it best: "Today, like so often before, American Jews will find creative ways to maintain and revitalize American Judaism. With the help of visionary leaders, committed followers, and generous philanthropists, it may still be possible for the current 'vanishing' generation of American Jews to be succeeded by another 'vanishing' generation, and then still another."[198] This vision should animate Diaspora Jews around the globe.

Israeli Demographics and the Peace Process

Just as there are fault lines in the Diaspora over the various streams of Judaism, these exist in Israel as well. A significant percent of Israeli Jews are secular and rarely go to synagogue, even if they observe all major holidays in their own ways; but as citizens of a Jewish state, they identify as Jews as well as Israelis. There is a great variety of more observant Jews, from modern to traditional Orthodox and Haredi, and within the Haredi movement a withering variety of different movements, some going back to Eastern European origin. There is a chief Ashkenazi Rabbi, for religious Jews of European origin, and a chief Sephardic Rabbi, to whom many Jews whose ancestors from Spain and many Arab countries look for guidance. There has been a limited penetration by the American Conservative and Reform movements, with central offices, and several dozen synagogues in Israel, but they are no match for the Orthodox rabbinate.

There is a growing movement in Israel to adopt a civil alternative to the rabbinical monopoly on matrimony, founded on the agreement struck by David Ben Gurion to obtain support for the foundation of a Jewish state. Many young Israelis trek to Cyprus to get married in a secular service because the established Israeli rabbinate is Orthodox and refuses to accept conversions by Reform, Conservative, and even Orthodox rabbis outside of Israel. Rabbi Seth Farber, an American-born Orthodox rabbi in Ra'anana, has led a movement for acceptance of Orthodox conversions and conversions undertaken by the IDF. The massive wave of Russian and Ethiopian immigrants further inflamed the controversy, since many of the Russians were children of mixed marriages in Russia, and some doubted the authenticity of the Judaism of the Ethiopian Falashas. Today, the religious status of a quarter million Russian-born citizens of Israel is in limbo, although increasingly as they go into the army, this problem is disappearing.

The Geopolitical Impact of Israeli Demographics

Harsh demographic realities are not limited to the Diaspora and play a central role in Israel, directly affecting the peace process. Demography is an especially powerful lens through which to observe the State of Israel. Israel is the one country other than Germany in which the Jewish population is growing, with in-migration and birthrates that are more than double those in the Diaspora. Israel is an industrial democracy with a young, growing profile. Richard Jackson, a demographic expert at the Washington-based Center for Strategic and International Studies, recently told me that Israel is at the very top in terms of a healthy demographic picture for major industrialized nations.[199]

But the demographic composition of Israel is not like that of other industrial democracies. Israeli Jewish birthrates are at healthy levels (just under three children per family), 50 percent higher than the Jewish Diaspora. But this is well below the rate for Israeli Arab citizens, already nearly 20 percent of Israel's population, and the birthrate is even higher for the Palestinian population under Israeli control.

This means that over time, if Israel insists on maintaining control of the entire West Bank, it will have difficulty remaining a democratic, majority Jewish state.

In recent years, Israel's Jewish population grew by 1.4 percent, while the rest of world Jewry declined by 0.3 percent. The Jewish population of the Diaspora is aging, while in Israel over 25 percent of the population is below the age of fifteen, the largest percentage of young people among the major industrial democracies. From its founding, Israel's Jewish population has exploded from half a million to ten times that number.

Yet the challenge for Israel is that the population of Arab Israelis and Palestinians in the territories is increasing at a greater rate. According to the Israel Central Bureau of Statistics (ICBS), while the Jewish population averages some 2.8 children per family, the Muslim population inside the Green Line marking the boundaries agreed to after the 1948 armistice averages 3.9.[200] Within Israel, Jewish birthrates are far surpassed by every other major group other than Christian Israelis—nineteen per thousand for Jews, thirty-four per thousand for Muslims, and twenty-four per thousand for Druze. These numbers are sobering.

Demographic Trends in Israel, by Ahmad Hleihal, takes a more optimistic view, calculating that by 2020 there will be 6.3 million Israeli Jews (approximately 78 percent of the population) and 2 million Israeli Arabs, only a slight decline in the Jewish majority. However, if Israeli Arab numbers are added to those of the Palestinians in the West Bank and Gaza, the picture changes markedly. By 2020, there will be as many as 6.1 million Palestinian inhabitants of the present territories and nearly 8.5 million non-Jews between the Jordan and the Mediterranean. One startling fact underscores Israel's demographic challenge. In the Israeli Jewish community the fastest-growing segment is the Haredi population, now already 8 percent of the population, according to the 2010 Israel Central Bureau of Statistics report. For the first time, more than half the first graders enrolled in Israeli schools in 2010 were either Haredi or Israeli Arab. These ultra-Orthodox Jews have much lower levels of participation in the workforce and the IDF than their secular and traditional Orthodox fellow citizens and much higher welfare dependency.

For this cohort, Zionism plays little or no role in their education. This can have a dramatic impact over time in their attachment to Israel, particularly since the birthrates of both groups are larger than that of non-Haredi Israeli Jews—including the large number of Orthodox Jews who are devoted Zionists and rising leaders in the Israeli military. With many of Israel's 1.2 million Arabs seeking a non-Jewish state, along with the restive, hostile population of Palestinians in the territories, a demographic nightmare threatens the democratic

Jewish character of the State of Israel. Israel's peace process with the Palestinians is as much an internal challenge as an external threat, because it will ultimately determine the borders of Israel and the degree to which Israel will maintain its Jewish majority.

A major reason former prime minister Ariel Sharon decided to withdraw from Gaza was his recognition of these demographic imperatives. The reality is not changed by the flawed decision to withdraw unilaterally and in the absence of an agreement with responsible Palestinians. With the rapid increase in the Palestinian and Israeli Arab population, Israel cannot remain a democratic Jewish state while at the same time permanently occupying the West Bank, whatever the Jewish historical claim to the land.

The absence of a credible, reliable peace partner that is able to protect its own population and Israel from attack by Hamas has undercut popular support for the peace process. Yet this process is not a gift to the Palestinians. It is a necessity for Israel to have permanent, secure, internationally recognized borders that will keep it a democratic state and a homeland for Jews. The final contours of an accord put forward at the 2000 Camp David Summit would ensure a Jewish majority in a democratic Israel with large parts of the West Bank returned to the Palestinians, the major Jewish settlement blocs remaining as part of Israel, and a land swap in order to balance territory that was conquered in 1967 and will be ceded to a Palestinian state. An international fund would help pay for Palestinian refugees to move out of their camps into a Palestinian state but not to settle in Israel.

The path to peace remains difficult and largely dependent on the Palestinians deciding they can accept the State of Israel as a Jewish homeland, explicitly or implicitly. But Israeli policy must ensure that the world understands that more barriers to peace exist on the Palestinian than the Israeli side. Israel should avoid the provocative steps of expanding settlements in the West Bank or acquiring blocks in the heart of Palestinian East Jerusalem (as opposed to the Jewish sections of East Jerusalem). This will only complicate the two-state solution that is the only way to maintain Israel as a democratic state with a large Jewish majority.

Demographics have changed the politics of Israel as well. The emigration of Sephardic Jews from Arab lands in the 1950s and 1960s, the Ethiopian emigration of the 1990s, and most particularly the million émigrés from the former Soviet Union have enormously enriched Israel. But combined with the higher birthrates of mainstream Orthodox families and secular nationalists, and the broad public disillusionment with having seen unilateral withdrawals from Lebanon and Gaza trigger rocket attacks, Israel has shifted from a left-of-center to a right-of-center country, deeply suspicious of the likelihood of peace with its neighbors, although healthy majorities continue to support a two-state solution to the Palestinian issue. The most revered institution in Israel, the military, is also affected. The officer corps is no longer disproportionately drawn from the secular kibbutz movement. Today a substantial percentage of elite IDF units and rising officers are religious

Zionists and secular nationalists. The officer corps of the elite Golani Brigade is heavily populated by religious nationalists schooled in special preparatory academies, and in this way, as the coauthor of Israel's military code of ethics, Professor Moshe Halbertal, puts it, the religious right affects "Israeli society through the army," which is the nation's "most respected institution."[201]

While most Jews in the West Bank live there to take advantage of comparatively inexpensive housing that was subsidized by the government to draw them there, part of the formal settler movement is infused with a messianic attachment to settle the entire Holy Land of the Bible. At the extreme, a tiny but dangerous group of zealots view any attempt to stop settlements as a violation of religious mandates. In a state that prides itself on the rule of law, with a genuinely independent judiciary, extreme elements of the settler movement are brazenly taking on the state itself, and it is unclear who will prevail. The religious wing of the settler movement, according to the *New York Times*, has clearly grown more radical and has attacked IDF outposts in the West Bank, as well as torched mosques.

The mainstream Yesha Council, the long-standing umbrella group for settlers, is being challenged by a more militant minority that has ousted some more moderate representatives in local elections and elected activist mayors who reject any territorial compromise. The fervor and the political support for the committed settler community has made it difficult for successive Israeli governments, both left and right, to dismantle new outposts or to stop settlement expansion. The political will to take on this outpost movement has been lacking. It will require a courageous Israeli prime minister, when peace is more a reality than it is today, to confront the outpost ideologues directly as Ben Gurion did when he dismantled the Irgun on the right, in part by blowing up their ship carrying arms, the *Altalena*, and the Palmach on the left to mold these political militias into the Israel Defense Forces to defend the state at its founding. But to his credit, in early 2012 Prime Minister Netanyahu took a first step by forcefully acting against the settlers attacking military posts protecting the mainstream settlements, calling them "terrorists" and stating they would be treated the same as Palestinian terrorists.

In a 2008 study, Peace Now estimated that in 2007 Israel nearly doubled its settlement construction in the West Bank compared with 2006, laying foundations for 1,000 buildings, including 2,600 housing units. The figures of this antisettlement peace group are generally reliable because they are based on both aerial photographs and ground observation. For the first five months of 2008, construction in the West Bank was almost two times greater than in the same period in 2007. More than half of the construction is beyond the defensive wall built by Israel to protect against terrorist infiltrators.[202] In any peace agreement, Israel would clearly keep many established settlements beyond the barrier and should do so for necessary strategic depth. But to continue promoting substantial construction outside the barrier severely complicates any eventual peace agreement by cutting into the heart of a future Palestinian state and injecting a Jewish minority that will be even more difficult to remove.

Today, of Israel's some 7.8 million citizens, 75 percent are Jewish (5.8 million), 20 percent Arab (1.6 million), and the balance are of Christian, Baha'I, or other religions. But the CIA World Factbook reports there are 2.5 million Palestinians in the West Bank, including almost 200,000 in East Jerusalem(with 520,000 Jewish settlers in the West Bank), and another 1.6 million Palestinians in Gaza. Together, there are 4 million Palestinians.[203] These figures make a pause in settlement construction imperative in the West Bank, outside of existing boundaries in the large settlement blocks, to give the Obama administration room for diplomatic maneuver before it is too late to construct a viable, peaceful Palestinian state. It also makes it imperative that all soldiers be inculcated with the concept of civilian control over the military and obedience to the chain of command. Peace with the Palestinians is in Israel's national security interest, if for no other reason than the brute figures of demography. Without a two-state peace settlement, Israel's status as a democracy with a substantial Jewish majority could be at risk within this century.

5

Israel and the New Challenge of Delegitimization

A GLOBAL FORCE OF THE TWENTY-FIRST CENTURY with particular impact on the State of Israel and world Jewry is the rise of a new form of anti-Semitism. It simultaneously seeks to discredit and delegitimize Israel as a state for the Jewish people and targets Diaspora Jews as surrogates for Israel.

Anti-Semitism is a highly charged allegation and must be used with great care. Is there in fact a new form of anti-Semitism, more than sixty years after the Holocaust and the founding of the modern Jewish state? Historian Yehuda Bauer of Yad Vashem, in a speech at the Prague Holocaust Era Assets Conference in June 2009, argued that there was "no new anti-Semitism, only new propaganda of old anti-Semitism."

I disagree. I believe the reality is far more complex. The anti-Semitism of the early part of this century is not the religion-based, stereotyped anti-Semitism of European history that led to degradation, violence, pogroms, and ultimately, together with the Nazi racial theories, the Holocaust. On the whole, the modern Catholic Church since the Second Vatican Council has done an admirable job of fostering reconciliation with Jews and educating its communicants in a new way to relate to Judaism.

Anti-Semitism in the twenty-first century has three manifestations, only the first of which is a lingering traditional anti-Semitism, mainly visible on the right wing of European society and promptly repudiated by European leaders and institutions. There also is undoubtedly an underlying current of unreconstructed anti-Semitism in some parts of post-Holocaust Central and Eastern European anti-Semitism without significant numbers of Jews.

Muslim-based anti-Zionism arose in the twentieth century out of a rise of Arab nationalism and the total rejection of a Jewish state on what the Muslims considered Arab land. Violent attacks in Palestine began before the international community confirmed the creation of Israel at the United Nations in 1947, and escalated to open and repeated warfare by Arab states thereafter.

The refusal to accept the legitimacy of Israel has gradually receded among the Arab states at a formal level through peace treaties with Egypt and Jordan, and then the 2002 Saudi peace initiative spread to Arab and Islamic organizations, from the twenty-two-nation Arab League to the fifty-six-nation Organization of the Islamic Conference (except Iran), as they hesitantly offered to recognize Israel under certain conditions. But at the same time, many of these states and some Palestinians have adopted strategies to undermine the legitimacy of a Jewish state, and worse, Iran and Islamic terrorist groups have pledged to destroy Israel and to target Jews outside Israel.

Of more recent vintage is a third kind, generally espoused by left-wing activists and academics primarily in the U.S. and Europe, who deny that they are anti-Semitic at all. They do not target Jews in the Diaspora but aim at ending the Israeli occupation of Palestinian territories. Where this crosses the line from legitimate criticism of Israeli policies, to which any nation is subject, to anti-Semitism is expressing the criticism in ways that undermine the legitimacy of a Jewish state of Israel. In the twenty-first century it is impossible to oppose the reality of the State of Israel, created by the United Nations as a Jewish state, without being anti-Semitic, because Israel and the Jewish people are so intimately intertwined.

European Anti-Semitism

Hatred of Jews has been a part of European history for over a thousand years, although the actual term *anti-Semitism* is relatively modern, ascribed to the German writer, and politician and avowed anti-Semite, William Marr, who used it in the 1870s "to describe hatred of Jews based on so-called 'scientific racial nationalist grounds.'"[1] The historical basis in Europe is the charge of deicide, that Jews were responsible for the crucifixion of Jesus and are therefore to be permanently punished. In 1095, when most of Europe had adopted Christianity, Pope Urban II launched the First Crusade to expel Muslims from Jerusalem and the Holy Land. The Crusaders engaged in a violent, vicious anti-Jewish rampage along the way. And when they arrived in Jerusalem in 1099, they massacred Jews in the Holy City. The Second (1145–1149) and the Third Crusade (1189–1192), led by King Richard I, Richard the Lionhearted, admired by every schoolchild in the U.S. and Europe, likewise committed mass atrocities.

In 1144 in Norwich, England, the death of a boy, rumored falsely to have been crucified by Jews, led to further falsehoods that Jews had used his blood to bake the matzo used during Passover. For centuries this "blood libel" circulated in Europe and even now is used in anti-Semitic propaganda in Europe and the Arab world.[2] Even in the Medieval and Renaissance centers of international commerce and high civilization, Jews were limited to distinct areas and barred from others, from the original ghetto in Venice to tolerant Holland as late as the seventeenth century. Jews were expelled from England in the thirteenth century, France in the fourteenth century. When the Spanish drove out the Muslims in 1492, one of the first acts of Ferdinand and Isabella, revered in Spain to this day, was to drive out those Jews who refused to convert and suspect those who did through the Inquisition. Many fled to Portugal, where they were shortly expelled again, and others found safety in Turkey and other countries in Europe.

In the Middle Ages, Jews were falsely accused of causing the Black Death and castigated for being money changers and peddlers, when these were often the only occupations open to them. The Hapsburgs expelled the Jews from Vienna in the seventeenth century, and Jews were the target of vicious pogroms in Eastern Europe and Russia, down to the twentieth century. In many European countries Jews were forced to wear distinctive clothing or badges long before the Nazis took power in modern Germany.

In 1903, *The Protocols of the Elders of Zion* was forged by the Russian secret police to foment hatred against the Jews by inventing a totally fictitious cabal of Jews who seek to rule. Not only is it still circulated in our time, especially in the Arab world,[3] but in 2009, Moscow's chief prosecutor refused the request by a human rights group to ban the sale of the book or at least require a clear notice that the text is fake. The prosecutor based his decision on a recommendation by the Russian Academy of Sciences' Psychology Institute that the book did not break Russian law.[4]

The French Revolution attempted to abolish discrimination based on religion or ethnic origin in the 1789 Declaration of the Rights of Man, guaranteeing freedom of religion. European Jews gained equal legal status through Napoleon's victories throughout the Continent, but anti-Semitism was never far beneath the surface, even in Europe's most advanced countries where Jews were more integrated. Napoleon himself had ambivalent views about Jews, genuinely seeking their liberation as individuals, but also seeking their assimilation, by conversion or intermarriage. He wrote his interior minister in 1806 of the need to "reduce, if not destroy, the tendency of Jewish people to practice a very great number of activities that are harmful to civilization and to public order in all the countries of the world. . . . Once part of their youth will take its place in our armies, they will cease to have Jewish interests and sentiments; their interests and sentiments will be French."[5]

Napoleon created a Sanhedrin of elected representatives of the Jewish people to answer questions about their loyalty to France, and he created the Consistories to interface with the government, an institution that exists to this day in France and Belgium. But outside of Napoleon's grasp, his efforts on behalf of making Jews equal citizens met with great resistance, from Prussia to Russia to Austria, where Chancellor Metternich feared "the Jews will believe [Napoleon] to be their promised Messiah."[6]

Anti-Semitism reasserted itself in France at the end of the century when an Alsatian Jew serving that same French Army, Captain Alfred Dreyfus, was falsely convicted of espionage and treason and publicly humiliated, then imprisoned until he became a cause célèbre, thanks to the polemics of the great writer Emile Zola, and finally reinstated as a major in the French army in 1906. Theodor Herzl, a young reporter who covered the Dreyfus case for a Viennese newspaper, became the father of modern Zionism when he concluded from these events that Jews would be secure only within their own state.

Eventually, anti-Semitism exploded into barbarism on an industrial scale with the rise of Nazism, in a country where only a few years before, in the Weimar Republic, Jews had attained prominent positions in public life and were fully integrated into the German economy, if not German society.

The Shoah caused deep reflection across Europe and within the Catholic Church. Israel was formally recognized by the United Nations as a place of Jewish refuge. The Second Ecumenical Council of the Vatican convened in 1962 by Pope John XXIII removed anti-Jewish references in the Catholic liturgy and declared that the Jews, then and now, could not collectively be held responsible for the death of Jesus. Four Catholic bishops who later became pontiffs, including the current Pope Benedict XVI, participated in Vatican II.

Catholic-Jewish dialogues, particularly in the U.S., led by the United States Conference of Catholic Bishops, with the National Council of Synagogues, the Orthodox Union, and the Rabbinical Council of America, as well as with secular groups such as the Anti-Defamation League, have helped create an atmosphere of mutual respect and understanding. Pope John Paul II became the first pope to make an official visit to a synagogue and in 2000 traveled to Israel where he placed a message in the Western Wall bemoaning the "behavior of those who, in the course of history, have caused these children of yours to suffer." In 1993, the Vatican and the State of Israel opened diplomatic relations.

But Europe is still wrestling with its old demons, though in less virulent form. There remain troubling reminders that European anti-Semitism is never far from the surface. Consider a recent statement by a member of the board of the German Bundesbank, Thilo Sarrazin, in the context of negative statements against Muslims for overwhelming Germany and creating a nation of what he called "dunces," because of what he alleged were the Muslims' low IQs. He added that Jews share a "certain gene."[7] Or the statement by trade commissioner of the European Union, Karel De Gucht, who declared that "there is indeed, a religion, I can hardly describe it differently, among most Jews that they are right. So it is not easy to have a rational discussion with moderate Jews about what is happening in the Middle East."[8]

I saw the old form of anti-Semitism in late May 2009 when I was in Austria for a preparatory meeting for the June 2009 Prague Holocaust conference. Despite the Austrian government's significant efforts to get their countrymen to face up to the nation's shameful wartime history through mandatory Holocaust education, the Freedom Party of Austria won almost 20 percent of the vote in the October 2008 parliamentary elections on an anti-immigrant and anti-Muslim platform.

Its leader for years was the notorious anti-Semite Jörg Haider, whose party ran on the slogan "The West in Christian Hands."[9] He died at the wheel of his speeding car that year, but the party's parliamentary leader, Martin Graf, attacked Ariel Muzicant, president of the Vienna Jewish community, by linking him to "the violent leftist mob on the streets."[10] Graf also invited a Holocaust denier to be given special recognition in the parliament and campaigned on a pledge to bar Israel from the European Union. Parliamentary president Barbara Prammer shared with me her deep concern about Graf, lamenting that the scourge of anti-Semitism and right-wing extremism had not been removed. The "new phenomenon" of anti-Semitism and right-wing extremism indicated the need for more education. In the end Graf was not censured by the Austrian parliament.

In Brussels, the Great Synagogue, where Fran and I worshiped, was bombed. Its Rabbi was physically attacked on the streets of Europe's capital. A close friend in Antwerp told me he now takes off his kipoh (skullcap) in some parts of town after young Muslim boys forced him off a sidewalk. Many of the children of our friends in Antwerp and in Brussels have left and made Aliyah to Israel.

The Israeli Dimension in Europe

It is increasingly difficult to distinguish between anti-Israeli sentiments and anti-Semitic attitudes in parts of Europe. Public opinion is much less positive toward Jews in general and Israel in particular. More than one-third of Europeans (twice U.S. levels) subscribe to general negative Jewish stereotypes (for example,, the time-worn canard that Jews have too much power in business and in international financial markets). Over 40 percent feel that Jews talk too much about the Holocaust. About a quarter say that their opinion of Jews is influenced by Israeli actions, and a majority of those declare those actions have a negative effect on their views.

Compared to surveys taken in 2005, there has been a dramatic increase in the likelihood of non-Jewish Europeans questioning the loyalty of their Jewish fellow citizens because of Israel. There has also been a shift in opinion regarding the cause of violence directed against European Jews, with more claiming that it arises from "anti-Jewish feeling" rather than "anti-Israel sentiment."[11] A 2005 poll in Britain's conservative Daily Telegraph indicated that the public considered Israel one of the least attractive countries in the world.

These feelings have all too often translated into anti-Semitic attacks by extremists and angry, alienated youth. In France there was a notable rise in attacks against individual Jews and Jewish communal property, and in 2006 the murder of a Jewish youth, Ilan Halimi, by a Muslim gang in Paris was a punctuation mark of the rise of violence. The police chief in Berlin reported a doubling of neo-Nazi attacks over the course of 2006. The Hate Crime Survey by a respected international organization, Human Rights First, found that in Eastern Europe and Russia, "extreme nationalist political groups have adopted the language of 19th century anti-Semitism."[12]

Nonviolent but still pernicious, the UK University and College Union, representing 120,000 instructors in British colleges, voted in May 2007 to reconsider future exchanges with Israeli academic institutions to protest Israel's treatment of Palestinians, a view shared by substantial elements of the academic community across Europe. Unison, the union representing more than one million British public service workers, has also considered, but ultimately did not take, punitive action against Israel.

Since the outbreak of the Second Intifada in 2000, there has been a steady rise in anti-Semitic incidents in Britain,[13] prompting a parliamentary inquiry initiated in 2007 by then prime minister Tony Blair. Entitled The New Anti-Semitism, the resulting report by the blue-ribbon committee headed by Denis MacShane makes chilling reading. It found a pattern of fear among British Jews, with synagogues attacked, Jewish schoolboys jostled on public transport, rabbis punched and knifed, and private security perceived as a necessity at Jewish weddings and community events.

Fueled by Islamist and far-left activists and militant students on British campuses, Jewish students were reported to have been blocked from expressing their views. The report concluded: "The old anti- Semitism and anti-Zionism have morphed into something more dangerous. Anti-Semitism today is officially sanctioned state ideology in a new crusade to eradicate Jewishness from the region whence it came and to weaken and undermine all the humanist values of rule of law, tolerance, and respect for core rights such as free expression that Jews have fought for over time."[14]

Trying to explain this distressing reality, François Zimeray, France's ambassador for human rights, put forward what I found a cogent analysis. He told me the French as well as others in Europe want to put the Holocaust behind them and help settle their own guilt by portraying Israel negatively—and the Israeli occupation of the West Bank provides the opportunity. "If the victims can be shown to do the same things they [the non-Jewish Europeans] had done," then the Europeans may not be so guilty after all, Zimeray said. He also found a further aspect: The French and other Europeans have done such a poor job of integrating Arabs and other Muslims that when pro-Palestinian feelings emerge as condemnation of Israel, this diverts the local Muslim population from their own governments' failure to integrate them fully into their adopted society in Europe.

Israel's unpopularity in Europe largely stems from stilted European conceptions of Israel's conduct toward the Palestinians. In 2003, the European Commission's Euro barometer survey found 59 percent of respondents ranked Israel first among all nations as a threat to peace—ahead of Iran, North Korea, and Syria. And 74 percent of those reached the same conclusion in Anne Frank's Holland.[15] It is important to recognize that in its formative decades, Israel was the darling of the European left. At that distant time, Israel was seen as the weaker party, besieged on all sides by strong Arab enemies. After Israel triumphed in the 1967 Six Day War and narrowly won the 1973 Yom Kippur War, the occupation of the Palestinian territories intensified, and Israeli parties of the right began reviving long-held territorial claims as far as the Jordan River.

Then much of European society saw the Palestinians as the victims, replacing the Israelis of another era. Israel's continued occupation and settlement have only reinforced this view. Israeli settlements began under Labor-led governments as security tripwires along the Jordan River. But their expansion to other parts of the West Bank became official policy in the Begin government, when Ariel Sharon was installed as housing minister with a remit to settle "Judea and Samaria."

Fashioning a strategy to address this in Europe is difficult because European Jews have neither the critical mass nor the comfort level to engage in overt action of the caliber practiced by American Jewish organizations in the U.S. There is more deference to the state, and the business community is less willing than American businessmen to confront a sitting government. There are Jewish organizations in major European countries, such as the UK, France, Belgium, and Germany, but their power is limited by the small number of Jewish citizens. In Brussels, Europe's informal capital, there is also a plethora of Jewish groups that purport to act across the continent: the World Jewish Congress, the European Jewish Congress, the European Center for Jewish Students, and the Conference of European Rabbis. But there is no umbrella group to coordinate their activities like the Conference of Presidents of Major American Jewish Organizations.

On issues of overt anti-Semitism they have begun to exercise their voice. Moshe Kantor, president of the European Jewish Congress, demanded and received an apology from EU commissioner De Gucht.[16] Stephen Kramer, secretary of the Council of Jews in Germany, accused Bundesbank board member Thilo Sarrazin of racial profiling and anti-Semitism, leading to a condemnation by Chancellor Angela Merkel and his resignation.[17] But these European Jewish groups rarely engage in political issues involving Israel, do not actively lobby the EU or the member-state governments, and generally keep a low profile on issues other than overt anti-Semitism.

Coordination among these groups is essential to reach European leaders in support of Israel and in combating anti-Semitism, from the classical European radical right and left and from a small radical minority of Muslims. European Jewish communities should open interfaith dialogue with moderate Muslims and their religious leaders, and Jews especially should be seen in the vanguard of those combating discrimination against European Muslims and advancing their economic well-being. Jews and Muslims alike are often the target of attacks by populist politicians and should make common cause. Attacks against Muslims, like the one made by Sarrazin, should be denounced by the European Jewish leadership just as forcefully as those against Jews. This can have the collateral advantage of developing trust between European Muslim leaders and their Jewish counterparts.

With the Muslim population growing as the numbers of the European Jewish community decline, political power is shifting. The Muslim population is over 900,000 in the Netherlands, including the mayor of Rotterdam. The Center for Information and Documentation on Israel (CIDI) tries to serve as an AIPAC equivalent there, but there are only 50,000 Dutch Jews. There are similar imbalances throughout Europe.[18] For example, Belgium has 638,000 Muslims, or 6 percent of the population, and only 30,000 Jews; France 4.7 million, or 7.5 percent of the population, compared to 480,000 Jews; Germany 4.1 million, or 5 percent of the total population, compared to 119,000 Jews; and the United Kingdom 2.8 million, or 4.6 percent of the population, compared to 290,000 Jews.

A friend in Brussels recalled that after the 1967 War, his father took him to a pro-Israel demonstration in the heart of the city, where all the leading politicians competed to speak fervently in support of Israel. More recently at the very same place following the Gaza War, leading Belgian politicians spoke at a pro-Palestinian rally.

A new group called ELNET (European Leadership Network) is trying to change this. Organized by Ra'anan Eliaz in Israel and Steve Rosen, formerly of AIPAC, it is encouraging Jewish political activism, notably in France. The network does not endorse candidates or donate money but encourages citizens to support candidates sensitive to Israel and Jewish issues and to become more politically engaged.

Moreover, creating a European think tank in Berlin is under serious consideration. It would be modeled on the Washington Institute for Near East Policy, which was established by American supporters of Israel and has built a reputation for objective analysis, serving as a forum for serious discussion of Middle East issues among scholars and officials from Israel, Arab nations, and the U.S. This could improve the public tone of the European discussion on Middle East and Israeli issues.

A Latin American Perspective: Argentina

I got a view of the challenges facing Jews in the largest Latin American Jewish community, and the sixth largest in the world, during meetings in December 2010 in Buenos Aires with Jewish leaders and with Argentine foreign minister Hector Timerman, himself a Jew. (He is the son of the journalist Jacobo Timerman, imprisoned by the Argentine military junta in the 1970's, an ordeal he described in his book Prisoner Without a Name, Cell Without a Number. He credited inquiries by human rights organizations and officials of the Carter administration, led by President Carter himself, with saving his life by focusing public attention on him.) Depending on how they are counted, Argentina has approximately 180,000 Jews,[19] most in Buenos Aires. This vibrant and politically engaged community has 110 synagogues, Jewish sports clubs, Jewish day schools for each grade level, with around two thousand student; Hillel chapters, offices for groups such as the World Jewish Congress, and a political umbrella group— DAIA—for 140 separate Jewish institutions, headed by Aldo Donzis.

Jewish philanthropy helped create a shelter for abused Jewish children after the Argentine financial crisis in 2001, which devastated the Jewish community at every level and also enabled it to reach out to the unaffiliated half of the community by providing after-school meals and Jewish education for public schoolchildren. To combat assimilation—the intermarriage rate is about 50 percent—the community is taking many of the same steps as American Jews. Eduardo Elsztain, a leading Jewish philanthropist, who is close to the president of Argentina, helps sponsor one thousand Argentine young adults on Birthright each year, and the program has teamed with Hillel to follow up afterward.

There are 2.5 million Argentines of Arab descent, but only half are Muslim, and relations with the Jewish community have been good until recently. Anti-Semitic graffiti disfigured Jewish facilities after the 2008–2009 Gaza War, Jews wearing kipot were roughed up on public buses, and Jewish cemeteries were defaced. The Argentine government acted forcefully against these actions, but their link to events in the Middle East is unmistakable.

Anti-Semitism and reactions against Israel are synonymous. The link between anti-Zionism and anti-Semitism was tragically brought home by the 1992 bombing of the Israeli Embassy in Buenos Aires and the 1994 bombing of the city's Jewish community center, AMIA. My wife Fran and I were deeply moved while visiting the reconstructed AMIA building, with its magnificent Agam memorial sculpture, a tribute to the resiliency of the Argentine Jewish community.

Argentina's Jewish leaders see another ominous and distinctive threat to the Jews of South America: an unholy alliance linking Iran with Hugo Chavez in Venezuela and President Evo Morales in Bolivia. Furthermore, with Brazil developing ties to Iran, there is a rising threat that Latin American nations may no longer follow Washington as they did at Israel's founding and become less friendly to Israel and less accommodating to their own Jewish communities. Argentina followed Brazil, which became the first Latin American country to support the Palestinian's bid for a unilateral declaration in the UN, recognizing the state of Palestine within 1967 borders.

The Gaza War gave Chavez an excuse for severing diplomatic relations with Israel, accusing it of genocide, and further criticizing Venezuela's 15,000 Jews for failing to sympathize with Palestinians in Gaza, while stressing their own Holocaust.[20] A TV figure close to Chavez blamed demonstrations against him on two students he said had "Jewish last names."[21] On a pro-government website, a commentator demanded that citizens "publicly challenge every Jew that you find in the street, shopping center or park" and called for a boycott of Jewish-owned businesses, seizures of Jewish-owned property, and a demonstration at Caracas's largest synagogue. No sooner said than done. On January 30, 2009, the Tifereth Israel congregation in Caracas was attacked by thugs who spray-painted "Jews get out" on the walls and confiscated a membership registry.[22] The following month an explosive device was thrown at a Jewish community center.

Diaspora communities throughout Latin America have been targets of anti-Gaza outbursts that reanimate anti-Semitism as criticism of Israel. Demonstrations erupted against Jews in Bolivia and Argentina. Press reports noted that in Venezuela, Bolivia, and Argentina, "Jews . . . are concerned about the growing anti-Semitic tone of the protestors, who frequently equate Israel with Nazi Germany, a theme increasingly evident on placards that juxtapose the Star of David with the swastika and in some public pronouncements."[23] Bolivia's Morales followed Chavez's lead and expelled the Israeli ambassador over the Gaza War, and there have been anti-Israel demonstrations with anti-Jewish content in several Bolivian cities.

The American Story

The public ethic of the United States has always been one of religious tolerance and openness. The founding documents of the U.S., the Declaration of Independence, that "all men are created equal," and the Constitutional ban on religious tests for office, created a different environment for the persecuted Jews of Europe (if not for the African American slaves of the Founders themselves and for women).

George Washington's 1790 welcoming message to the Jewish community of Rhode Island, in which he declared that the "Government of the United States . . . gives to bigotry no sanction, to persecution no assistance, was an early manifestation of how central religious tolerance was to the founding and operation of the country. The relationship between Jews and non-Jewish America was often very warm. When members of a Philadelphia synagogue sent a message of sympathy to President Lincoln on the death of his young son, Lincoln's moving response referred to the special place of Jews in America.

Yet the promise of the founding documents was not always fulfilled for Jews, just as it was not initially for African Americans or women. In 1862, the same year President Abraham Lincoln signed a law passed by Congress to permit rabbis to serve as chaplains on the battlefields of the Civil War, his most famous general, Ulysses S. Grant, issued General Order Number 11 expelling all Jews in his military district, the Department of the Tennessee, on suspicions Jewish merchants were undermining the boycott of the South. Grant revoked the order only because of President Lincoln's strong objection.[24] Grant spent much of the rest of his public life atoning for his action.

There have been periods of anti-Semitism in the United States. My hometown of Atlanta was the site of one of the more infamous incidents—the 1913 Leo Frank case, in which a Jewish businessman, falsely accused of murdering a teenage girl, Mary Phagan, was convicted in a trial sensationalizing his Jewish background. After Governor John Slaton of Georgia reviewed the evidence, he questioned Frank's guilt and courageously commuted his death sentence to life in prison. An angry mob seized Frank from his prison cell and hanged him. A few other Jews had been lynched, but Frank's lynching was the most widely publicized and the last on American soil.[25] It was a searing memory for the Atlanta Jewish community when I was growing up there. It was not until 1986 that the Georgia State Board of Pardons and Paroles gave Leo Frank a posthumous full pardon.

The Leo Frank trial had nationwide reverberations. The Anti-Defamation League (ADL) was founded in 1913 in direct response, to combat ant-Semitism and the defamation of American Jews. It remains today the premier organization for that purpose, but likewise stands against any injustice based on religion, race, or national origin.

During the Depression and World War II, public opinion polls indicated that some 40 percent of the population held anti-Semitic views, and the Reverend Charles Coughlin took to the airwaves with coarse anti-Semitic rants. This chilled the American Jewish community's demands that Franklin Delano Roosevelt's wartime administration deal more forcefully with the massacre of Europe's Jews. The president vacillated to the point of inaction despite reports of the ongoing Holocaust and eyewitness evidence from inside the Warsaw Ghetto brought to Washington by a brave Polish diplomat, Jan Karski. He told me that FDR impassively told him, as he poured out his heart to the president, to repeat his story to his confidante, Supreme Court justice Felix Frankfurter, a Jew. The great justice listened and retorted: "Mr. Karski, I am not saying you are lying, but I choose not to believe you."[26]

With many Americans, especially those of German and Irish extraction, initially opposed joining what they disdained as "Europe's quarrels," Roosevelt was acutely aware of the political danger of making World War II into a war about the Jews. His argument was that America would save the Jews by winning the war. He never issued a public warning that he was aware of the genocide and would punish those who perpetrated it.

In fact the fate of Europe's Jews was effectively sealed at the 1938 Evian Conference, called by the United States, in which the U.S., Canada, and other Western nations refused to relax immigration quotas to permit increased Jewish emigration. It signaled to Hitler that the world would not lift a finger to help the Jews. Secretary of State Cordell Hull hid his wife's Jewish ancestry, a fact some historians claim led to his indifference to the fate of European Jewry. Most blatant was Assistant Secretary of State Breckinridge Long, who headed the visa division starting in 1940 and reversed policies that had slightly liberalized immigration, making it virtually impossible for Jewish refugees to enter the U.S.

FDR's secretary of the Treasury, Henry Morgenthau Jr., his close friend and country neighbor from a distinguished New York Jewish family, forced the president to establish a War Refugee Board in 1944 by presenting him with a study by his department originally entitled *Report to the Secretary on the Acquiescence of This Government in the Murder of the Jews*. The Board Morgenthau chaired helped save tens of thousands of Jews. Nevertheless, throughout his tenure, FDR remained an icon in the American Jewish community; Jews in those days joked that they believed in three things: Diese Welt (This World), *Yenna Welt* (The World to Come), and Roosevelt!

Even well after the war, anti-Semitism persisted with formal and informal quotas at major American banks, universities, medical and law schools, and law firms. This discrimination was not limited to Jews and applied even more stringently to African Americans and women. My 1967 Harvard Law School class had only twenty-five women out of over five hundred students. I faced it myself when interviewing with law firms in Atlanta: when many major law firms refused to hire me because of my religion. Powell, Goldstein, Frazer & Murphy, founded in the early 1920s by a Jewish lawyer and his non-Jewish colleagues, was a welcome exception. I spent twenty years there in Atlanta and Washington. Most major Atlanta law firms did not begin to hire Jewish associates on a regular basis for several more years. Nor was this limited to Atlanta. Several Wall Street firms in the early 1960s had only token Jewish lawyers, if any. While I was in law school at Harvard in the 1960s, their representatives interviewed prospective associates at the Law Review and consciously refused even to interview members with Jewish names.

It took the Civil Rights Acts of the 1960s, aimed primarily at achieving equality for African Americans but banning discrimination in a wide variety of areas based on religion and gender, for Jews to become widely accepted into America's establishment institutions.

In today's America, there is little hint of old-fashioned anti-Semitism, although militant neo-Nazi groups occasionally flair up. President Nixon's tapes reveal a president with profoundly ant-Semitic attitudes and timeworn caricatures—"Jews are just a very aggressive and abrasive and obnoxious personality."[27] But he was able to separate his prejudices from his support for Israel.

More recently, in March 2010, Congressman Eric Cantor, now the Republican majority leader in the House of Representatives from Virginia and a Jew, was threatened and his Richmond office shot at by a lone anti-Semite. Glenn Beck, the conservative talk show host, has criticized his liberal nemesis George Soros, in terms that raise old Jewish stereotypes, although Beck is a strong supporter of Israel. And the venerable Helen Thomas, the longtime White House correspondent of Lebanese extraction, was chased from her job after declaring that the Middle East impasse could be broken if Jews would "get the hell out of Palestine" and go back to Germany and Poland, where, she said, they belong.

But these are all exceptions to the marked decline in anti-Semitism, probably best demonstrated by the frequency with which non-Jewish parents welcome Jewish spouses with no more difficulty (and probably less) than Jewish parents welcome their new non-Jewish sons- or daughters-in-law. While there remain bastions of exclusivity such as private country clubs, Jews have become fully enmeshed in all aspects of society. There is no greater example of this change than in the Ivy League, the eight prestigious northeast colleges, where Jewish quotas were not formally removed until the early 1960s.[28] Today, not only do Jewish students make up a large proportion of their student bodies, three-quarters of the Ivy League schools have been led recently (or are currently being led) by Jewish presidents.

The U.S. Congress also has a disproportionate number of Jewish members, some from states with small Jewish populations. In one recent Congress both senators from the state of Wisconsin were Jewish, despite the fact that less than 0.5 per- cent of Wisconsin's population is Jewish. In Minnesota (with only 0.9 percent of its population Jewish), one of its two U.S. Senate seats had been held continuously by a Jewish member for more than three decades; during that time the Senate seat has been passed among four different Jewish politicians from both major parties. In the 2012 U.S. Senate, there were twelve Jewish senators out of one hundred, far higher than the 2 percent of the population made up by Jews.

Congressional recesses are organized not just around Christian holidays but Jewish holidays as well. In short, Jews in America face no serious threat of classical anti-Semitism, but they are wise to keep up their guard and respond forcefully to occasional outbursts.

One remaining lair of anti-Semitism is the Internet, where some websites, especially the blogosphere, raised the specter of old-fashioned anti-Semitism in connection with the global financial crisis. One conspiracy theory that gained traction was the utterly false notion that immediately prior to the September 2008 collapse of Lehman Brothers as much as $400 billion was transferred out of the New York investment bank to banks in Israel. But there were no anti-Semitic reverberations in the mainstream media from the Great Recession, not even after Bernard Madoff admitted to running history's greatest Wall Street fraud.

Progress in Europe

What has changed since the Holocaust is the willingness of leaders to come down hard on anti-Semitism. In the winter of 2010, Prime Minister Stephen Harper of Canada, addressing an Ottawa conference, Combating Anti-Semitism, called it a "particularly dangerous form of hatred [that] is now in resurgence through-out the world. . . . Jews today in many parts of the world and many different settings are increasingly subjected to vandalism, threats, slurs, and just plain, old fashioned lies . . . [including] our universities, where Jewish students [are] under attack."[29]

To their credit, and with leadership from President Sarkozy, France added anti-Semitism to its list of hate crimes following an attack by Muslim youths on a young French Jew in the suburbs of Paris. After the celebrated fashion designer John Galliano insulted Jews in a bar in his Paris *quartier* of the Marais, Dior quickly fired him and a French court fined him. The Lithuanian government firmly condemned a group of young men in 2011 in the city of Kaunas who loudly proclaimed that Hitler should have finished his job against the Jews.

It is easy to identify Jewish synagogues and schools throughout Europe by ubiquitous cement barriers and heavily armed police stationed to protect Jews from attacks. This sad symbol of lingering anti-Semitism is nevertheless rec-ognition of what governments are willing to do to protect Jewish citizens and their property.

Many countries are also beginning to understand that Muslim attacks against their Jewish communities are a surrogate for broader assaults on their own Euro-pean societies. In the UK, then prime minister Blair responded to the MacShane report with a series of measures, including instructions to the Foreign Office to protest Arab states that allow anti-Jewish broadcasts, as well as instituting tough new guidelines for the police to investigate anti-Semitic attacks and for universi-ties to counter anti-Jewish ideology on campus.

More broadly, the European Union produced a directive outlawing Internet hate speech; the forty-seven-nation Council of Europe launched a lengthy in-quiry into combating anti-Semitism in Europe; and the European Parliament hosted a World Jewish Congress conference on anti-Semitism in Europe. The Organization for Security and Cooperation in Europe (OSCE) placed anti-

Semitism on its agenda, leading to a 2004 declaration in Berlin decrying the "new forms and expression" of anti-Semitism as a threat to democracy and security. Recognizing how anti-Israel sentiment and anti-Semitism merge, the OSCE declaration stated that "international developments or political issues, including those in Israel or elsewhere in the Middle East, never justify anti-Semitism." The European Union has developed a working definition of anti-Semitism recognizing that it can include activities against the State of Israel—"A certain perception of Jews, which may be expressed as hatred toward Jews. Rhetorical and physical manifestations of anti-Semitism are directed toward Jewish individuals and/or their property, toward Jewish community institutions and religious facilities. In addition, such activities could also target the State of Israel, conceived as a Jewish collectivity."[30]

Holocaust denial is also treated by a number of European organizations and countries as a manifestation of anti-Semitism, from the OSCE to the Parliamentary Assembly of the Council of Europe and the European Court of Human Rights. In 2004, the European Parliament, the main legislative arm of the European Union, passed a resolution calling for action against racism, xenophobia, and anti-Semitism. Some twenty countries, mostly in Europe and led by Germany, have made both anti-Semitism and Holocaust denial a criminal offense. And in 2004, the UN General Assembly recognized anti-Semitism as one of the forms of intolerance and discrimination.

As head of the U.S. delegation at the Prague conference on Holocaust Era Assets, I helped negotiate the June 2009 Terezin Declaration by forty-six countries, strongly rebuking Holocaust denial and calling on the international community to strengthen monitoring of and combat anti-Semitism. David Harris, head of the American Jewish Committee, told me that at no time in his extensive experience had he seen such an array of senior European officials committed to combating anti-Semitism and generally supportive of Israel: then UK prime minister Gordon Brown, President Nicolas Sarkozy of France, Chancellor Angela Merkel of Germany, and then Prime Minister Silvio Berlusconi of Italy.[31]

Muslims, Jews, and Israel

In Muslim countries, for centuries, Jews were a protected minority and like Christians were designated as *dhimmi*, or "protected people"; the Jewish and Christian religions were tolerated, although adherents were regarded as infidels for rejecting Islam. While subject to special taxes and more limited legal and social rights than the Muslim majority, in actual practice they were generally treated better than Jews in Christian lands.[32] While some blamed Jews for the death of the Prophet Mohammed, the indiscriminate killing and expulsion of Jews that occurred in Europe were not widely practiced in Arab Muslim countries. When the Muslims conquered the Land of Israel in 638, a large and vibrant Jewish community remained, in contrast to the massacre of Jews by the Christian Crusaders when Jerusalem was captured some four hundred years later. Maimonides, the great twelfth-century Jewish scholar and physician, flourished in Egypt. The Golden Age of Spain for Jews occurred under Muslim not Christian control.[33] The forced conversions and expulsions from the Iberian Peninsula were triggered by the uniting of the empires of the Catholic monarchs, Isabella and Ferdinand, following their vanquishing the Muslims. In 1492, Ottoman Turkey took in Jews fleeing the Spanish Inquisition, and throughout the European Holocaust, the Turkish Republic protected Jews.

But in the early part of the twentieth century, as Jews migrated in increasing numbers to Palestine, there was a violent reaction by the resident Arab population. It was one thing to tolerate Jews as a small minority in Arab nations, but quite another for Jews to become a majority and stake a claim to their own sovereign statehood in what Arabs considered their own land. In the 1920s there were violent riots against Jewish communities in places such as Hebron, in which scores of Jews were killed. These riots solidified into the Arab Revolt of 1936–1939. During World War II, the grand mufti of Jerusalem, Haj Amin al-Husseini, lived in Berlin; was a close friend of Heinrich Himmler, one the architects of "the final solution"; met Adolf Hitler on November 30, 1941; publicly supported the Nazi campaign against European Jewry; praised the dictator's efforts at "solving the Jewish problem"; and promoted his own plan to expel Jews from Palestine on the Nazi Oriental radio service.[34]

World War II stimulated Arab nationalist feelings in a number of Arab states to rid themselves of Western colonial rule, and the war intensified feelings against their own Jewish communities, as they saw competition in Palestine between the Jewish and Arab populations. European-type pogroms broke out in the 1940s, killing hundreds of Jews in Iraq, Libya, and Syria. By the early 1950s centuries of Jewish life ended, as some 800,000 Jews fled to Israel, their assets confiscated.[35]

Following World War II, the locus of anti-Semitism shifted decisively from Europe to the Middle East and from Christianity to Islam. Israel's creation changed the equation in much of the Arab world: Anti-Zionism and anti-Semitism were often conflated.

The subject of Islamic anti-Semitism must be treated with care, but also with honesty. It is important not to paint with such a broad brush as to assume that all the world's one and one-half billion Muslims, almost one in four people in the world, are anti-Semitic. Islam is the world's second-largest and fastest-growing religion.

The 1.6 billion Muslims are widely dispersed geographically, with forty-nine countries having Muslim majorities. Over 60 percent live in the Asia-Pacific region, with over 1 billion Muslim adherents, and Indonesia is the largest Muslim majority nation. There are large Muslim communities in China, the Balkans, and

Russia and a growing population in Europe,[36] with over 15 million living in the twenty-seven nations of the European Union.[37]

There are more Muslims in Germany than in Lebanon, more in China than in Egypt. A vast majority of Muslims are Sunni, between 87 and 90 percent, with only about 10 to 13 percent Shiite.[38] Iran is the largest majority Shiite nation. As indicated by their dispersion, they defy easy categorization. Even with the 2011 Arab uprisings, the Sunni-Shiite divide remains wide. Tiny Bahrain became a crucible for this division when the Shiite majority, long discriminated against by the two-hundred-year ruling Sunni family, withdrew its opposition party from the parliament and took to the streets in protest, leading Saudi Arabia, separated from Bahrain by only a fifteen-mile causeway, to inject troops. Bahrain has cracked down on even moderate Shiite professionals, including the arrest of doctors treating demonstrators injured by the security police. There have been student attacks with rocks and Molotov cocktails against the Saudi Embassy in Tehran, evoking the attacks against the U.S. shortly after the 1979 Iranian Revolution, through which I lived in the Carter White House. One Middle East expert, David Ottaway, described this as the beginning of a "political and religious cold war."[39]

The year 1928 was a watershed in the Arab world, fusing the Muslim religion with political and social goals with the founding of the Muslim Brotherhood in Ismailia, Egypt, by Hassan al-Banna, originally to oppose British colonial rule and to supplant it with an Islamic state founded upon strict sharia law. Although it was subject to repeated Egyptian government crackdowns after Egypt gained its independence due to fears it was plotting assassinations, it remained the most organized and disciplined opposition. It was never legalized, although tolerated, until the 2011 Arab Spring. Its progeny have sprouted throughout the Middle East, from Jordan to the Gaza Strip.

But for the Muslim Arabs in the Middle East, the creation of the Jewish state of Israel in 1947 was *the* seminal event. The dialogue changed: European states and the Soviet Union, the seat of old-fashioned anti-Semitism, joined the United States in backing the creation of a Jewish state. The Arabs rejected the UN vote and declared war. The 1948 War of Independence was the first of eight wars involving Israel and the Arab Muslim world, the others being the 1956 Sinai campaign; the 1967 Six Day War; the 1968–1970 War of Attrition, with regular Fedayeen attacks inspired by Egyptian president Nasser; the 1973 Yom Kippur War; the 1982 Lebanon War against the PLO; the 2006 Lebanon War against Hezbollah; and the 2008–2009 Gaza conflict. The rallying cry in the Arab world was to "drive the Jews into the sea."

The formation of the Palestine Liberation Organization (PLO) in 1964 brought a new secular Muslim organization into the battle, combining hatred of the Jewish state with Jews everywhere as its surrogates, and the Western countries supporting Israel. The PLO charter formally rejected the 1947 UN resolution creating a Jewish and Arab state out of the British Mandate and stated that

"Armed struggle is the only way to liberate Palestine" (Article 9). Under the leadership of Yasser Arafat, who took control in 1969, all Israelis and Diaspora Jews, men, women, and children, were considered fair game. A wave of violence initiated or inspired by the PLO included the 1970 bombing of European airlines bound for Israel, airline hijackings, and attacks against Israeli school buses, killing twenty-one children in a 1970 attack in Ma'alot; the 1972 Munich attack against the Israeli Olympic team by Black September; the 1976 hijacking of an Israeli civilian aircraft at Entebbe; the 1978 Coastal Road Massacre killing twenty-one Israeli civilians; the attempted assassination and grave wounding of the Israeli ambassador to the UK, Shlomo Argov, in London in 1982; and the 1985 murder of the wheelchair-bound Leon Klinghoffer on the Italian cruise ship *Achille Lauro*.[40]

Other Islamic terrorist groups destroyed the Israeli Embassy in Buenos Aires in 1992 and the city's Jewish community center, AMIA, in 1994; attacked the Israeli Embassy in Mauritania in 2009; and blew up the car of the leader of the Ankara Jewish community in 1994, whom my wife Fran and I had just met during the Clinton administration (he miraculously survived).

In 1987, the PLO launched the First Intifada, a popular Palestinian uprising against Israeli control of the West Bank and Gaza, which lasted until 1993. Fran and I were in Israel when the Intifada began and were warned at our hotel that it would be unsafe to visit the Western Wall (Kotel). But at Fran's insistence we went anyway. The Second Intifada broke out in 2000 after Yasser Arafat rejected a peace offer by Israeli prime minister Ehud Barak, with President Clinton at Camp David, and following Ariel Sharon's attempt to visit the Temple Mount.

Another dimension was added by the Iranian Revolution of 1979, in which for the first time a nation-state joined fundamentalist Islam with active support for terrorism. Iran supported groups such as Hamas and Hezbollah that continued armed struggle after Arafat and the PLO had at least formally foresworn violence. The charters of these groups demonstrate the confluence of anti-Zionism and anti-Semitism. Hamas (Islamic Resistance Movement), a Palestinian radical group, took over where the PLO left off, but with a religious dimension that made compromise more difficult than for the secular PLO and Fatah, its political arm.

Inspired and financially supported by the Iranian government, Hamas was founded in 1987 as a spin-off from the Egyptian Muslim Brotherhood. Hamas identified itself as the Muslim Brotherhood in Palestine, and its 1988 charter pledged to "liberate" Palestine from Israeli control. But unlike the secular PLO, its goal was to establish an Islamic state in Israel, the West Bank, and Gaza, not only pitting Hamas against Israel but also committing it to a "very great and very serious" struggle against Jews, based on supposed secret societies and events going back to the French Revolution. The Hamas charter cites Islamic religious texts to justify killing Jews and to validate their view that the conflict with Israel was an irreconcilable struggle between Jews and Muslims, and Judaism and Islam, between "truth and falsehood."[41]

Hezbollah, a Shiite Muslim terrorist group, emerged during the 1982 Lebanese civil war and also fused Islamic fundamentalism and terrorism; its forces were trained and organized by the Iranian Revolutionary Guard Corps. Its 1985 manifesto sought Israel's "final obliteration." Like Hamas, it explicitly targeted Jews and Judaism, not just Israel. As recently as 2009, Hezbollah pressured a private English-language school in Lebanon to drop excerpts from *The Diary of Anne Frank*. In 1992, Hezbollah declared, "It is an open war until the elimination of Israel and until the death of the last Jew on earth." They have put their words into action, as Argentine prosecutors hold Hezbollah and Iran, which strongly backs them, responsible for the 1994 AMIA bombing in Buenos Aires, killing eighty-five people and wounding another two hundred.[42]

Hassan Nasrallah, the leader of Hezbollah, has said that because there is such a concentration of Jews in Israel, "it will save us the trouble of going after them worldwide." For those radical jihadists not intent on destroying the entire Jewish people, the goal is to eliminate Jews from Israel and the Middle East, just as Hitler set out to make all of Europe *Judenfrei*.[43]

Al-Qaeda, a radical Sunni group, evolved out of the Afghan mujahedeen, who were supported by the Carter and Reagan administrations as a way of ending the Soviet military invasion of Afghanistan. But it took them another step forward in their jihadist goals when Osama bin Laden, one of the mujahedeen leaders, expanded the Islamic fight around the world through a global network of affiliates. While Israel and Palestine have not been central to their goals, they envision the removal of all foreign influences and the establishment of an Islamic caliphate. They view the U.S.-Israeli partnership as part of a Christian-Jewish alliance conspiring to destroy Islam, which they argue gives them their religious justification to kill civilians, not just Christians and Jews but even Muslims who support the West.

The U.S. was drawn into the war on terrorism as early as 1983, with the bombing of the Marine barracks in Beirut during the Lebanese civil war, killing 241 American military personnel, on the very day that my friend and colleague U.S. ambassador Reginald Bartholomew arrived to assume his post. It led to the withdrawal of the international peacekeeping force and of U.S. troops from Lebanon. While there was a division of opinion about whether Iran was the direct culprit, it was more likely Hezbollah, supported by Iran.[44] The next year, in 1984, Ambassador Bartholomew was almost killed when a truck bomb got into the U.S. Embassy compound and exploded, collapsing a wall and a large book-case directly on top of him. In 1996, the Khobar Towers, housing U.S. military personnel in Saudi Arabia, was bombed—either by al-Qaeda, Iran, or Hezbollah—also leading to the withdrawal of American troops.[45]

Long before the al-Qaeda attacks on the World Trade Center and Pentagon, Americans were targets. On August 8, 1998, eight years to the day after American troops were sent to Saudi Arabia, al-Qaeda attacked U.S. embassies in Dar es Salaam, Tanzania, and Nairobi, Kenya, killing hundreds of people, including twelve American diplomats.[46]6 I accompanied Secretary of State Madeleine Albright to Dover Air Force Base, Delaware, to honor the American flag-draped coffins of the victims. In 2000, it was the American destroyer U.S.S. *Cole*, bombed by al-Qaeda in Yemen, killing seventeen American sailors and wounding forty others. And the 2004 bombing of the Madrid train and 2005 bus and subway bombings in London were also al-Qaeda products.

But Jews and Israel have never been far out of range. The 2008 Mumbai massacre of 180 civilians in luxury Indian hotels was another manifestation of radical Islamic rage with an unmistakable anti-Semitic codicil. Lashkar-e-Taiba, created and sponsored by the Pakistan intelligence service to drive India out of Kashmir, turned its focus to destabilizing India by attacking two major hotels frequented by Westerners (including friends of mine in each). The militants targeted wealthy Indians but also assaulted the Chabad Lubavitch House[47] as a perceived representative of Israel; and murdered young American-born rabbi, Gavriel Holtzberg, his pregnant wife, Rivka, and visitors from Israel. One of the terrorists told Indian TV during the siege that he was incensed by the recent visit of an Israeli general to Kashmir. The broader message was that, just like the attacks in Buenos Aires, Islamic terrorists conflate all Jews with Israel and Israel with all Jews.[48]

Menachem Milson, a well-known Israeli scholar of Arabic literature and one of the founders of MEMRI, a respected group that monitors the Arab press, gave a bone-chilling presentation in 2010 in my office of excerpts from a decade of Arab and Iranian television programs illustrating the treatment not just of Israel but of all Jews, by Muslim clerics and teachers of young Muslim children.[49] In the vile accusations by the clerics, Jews are called "dogs and monkeys," "treacherous" and hateful people responsible for all the ills of the world and not just of Palestinians.

There were two strains to these Arab press attacks. First was the use of verses from the Koran and its commentaries, alleging that Jews tried to poison the Prophet Mohammed and were infidels who hid behind "rocks and trees." The second adapted the old European anti-Semitic blood libel to accuse the Jews of using the blood of young Arab boys in Passover services.

The conflation of anti-Zionism with anti-Semitism has long been a staple of Arab propaganda. In 1972, Saudi King Faisal said that Jews "have a certain day on which they mix the blood of non-Jews into their bread and eat it."[50] In 1983, the defense minister of Syria repeated this blood libel in his book, and the Palestinian observer to the UN Human Rights Commission has asserted that Israelis infected three hundred Palestinian children with HIV by injecting the virus during the Intifada. Malaysian prime minister Mahathir Mohamad received a standing ovation at an Islamic conference of fifty-seven states in

2003 for declaring that "the Jews rule the world by proxy. They get others to die for them."[51]

This rhetoric came as no surprise to me. When I was undersecretary of state representing the U.S. at a summit meeting of the Asia-Pacific Economic Cooperation (APEC) in 1997, Mahathir blamed the dramatic fall of Thailand's currency, which triggered the Asian financial crisis, on George Soros, an American financier and Hungarian-born Jew. I publicly contradicted his unfounded assertion. Throughout the Arab world there were false allegations that it was Israel and Jews—not Osama bin Laden—who planned the 9/11 attacks that brought down the World Trade Center and killed almost three thousand Americans. In 2010, a TV series in Turkey conveyed a scandalous set of allegations about brutal Israeli practices against Palestinian children.

A more recent manifestation of this obsession surfaced during the 2009 campaign of the then cultural minister of Egypt, Farouk Hosny, to become head of the United Nations Educational, Scientific, and Cultural Organization (UNESCO). He had stated that he would personally burn any Israeli books he found at the famous Alexandria Library, and he had been alleged to play a role in protecting two of the terrorists who shot Leon Klinghoffer on the *Achille Lauro*, boasting of aiding their escape from Italy.[52] When this came to light and cost Hosny his election, the Egyptian government and press blamed the result on Western prejudice and an "international Jewish conspiracy." One newspaper headline read: "America, Europe and the Jewish Lobby Brought Down Farouk Hosny," and the Egyptian foreign minister at the time, Ahmed Aboul Gheit, criticized "international Judaism and Western powers." Hosny himself contended there "was a group of the world's Jews who had a major influence in the elections who were a serious threat to Egypt taking this position."[53]

Holocaust denial is another weapon used to discredit and delegitimize Israel and foment anti-Semitism. Iranian president Ahmadinejad has taken this to great lengths, hosting a Tehran conference of Holocaust deniers and using his annual addresses to the UN General Assembly to cast doubt about the Shoah. He does this, and many in the Arab world do likewise, either denying it outright or diminishing its gravity, because this undercuts the idea of Israel as a haven for persecuted Jews.

Ironically, Israelis dislike the linkage to the Holocaust for a very different reason, believing it undercuts the historic connection of the Jewish people to the land of Israel. But it is no coincidence that the world community came together in a unique post-Holocaust moment in 1947 to create a Jewish state. This does not denigrate the historical claim of Jews to the Holy Land, which is well established by historians, and by the remarkable archaeological finds since the rebirth of the Third Jewish Commonwealth.

Educational institutions in some Muslim countries also foster militancy. In Pakistan and Afghanistan, where the state is so weak that the *only* effective institutions are Islamic religious institutions, the madrassa has become the mainstream educational institution. Virtually no textbooks or maps produced in the Arab world include the State of Israel. Either through official channels or via wealthy individuals and foundations, Saudi Arabia has spent as much as $75 billion during the past thirty years exporting fundamentalist Wahhabi doctrine, via textbooks and lesson plans.[54] In Wahhabi-oriented schools across the world, a first grader is taught that Judaism and Christianity are false; a sixth grader is instructed that if Muslims are united in a fight against Jews, they will be as victorious as they were against the Christian Crusaders; an eighth grader is taught that the "apes are Jews . . . while the swine are Christians"; and a tenth-grade text teaches that Jews are responsible for many of the world's wars and asserts the authenticity of *The Protocols of the Elders of Zion.*

Following the identification of the large number of radicals of Saudi Arabian origin involved in the 9/11 attacks, Riyadh organized a royal commission to review educational materials, and though the commission's report in 2004 provided some powerful criticism of the texts, not much was changed. The material from the lesson plans just described all comes from the 2008 version of the *reformed* curriculum.

In 2006, when I was vice chairman of Freedom House, the organization's Center for Religious Freedom obtained and published a copy of the curriculum taught at the Islamic Saudi Academy in suburban Washington, D.C. Prince Turki al-Faisal, the Saudi ambassador, invited us to his office. He agreed such material was "unacceptable" and promised that the Islamic school under his embassy's patronage in Northern Virginia would remove the offending language in the next school year, and that he would investigate the use of such curriculum inside Saudi Arabia. But in 2009 the hateful lessons were still being taught, and some in Virginia demanded that the school be closed down.[55]

Positive Steps in the Arab World

In 1977, when I served as chief domestic adviser to President Carter, I negotiated, with Carter's strong support, an agreement between the Business Roundtable, then chaired by Irving Shapiro, the CEO of DuPont, and a number of Jewish groups, including the American Jewish Congress, the American Jewish Committee, and B'Nai Brith, that led to congressional passage of the anti-boycott laws of 1977. This law prohibited American companies from participating in the Arab boycott of Israel, with stiff penalties, the first time such a blow was struck was to prohibit support for Arab efforts to deny the legitimacy of the State of Israel. The late congressman Abe Rosenthal (D-NY) was the chief sponsor in the U.S. Congress. (Ironically, in July 2011, Israel passed a controversial law making it a crime for Israelis to promote a boycott of Israeli products produced in West Bank settlements, which some Israelis contend punishes free speech.)

Despite all the attacks on the legitimacy of Israel and Jews, there is a positive change in parts of the Arab world. It took the hard-won victories in the numerous wars, together with a nuclear weapons capability, to convince many Arab states that, like it or not, Israel was in the Middle East to stay. Then followed a number of negotiations brokered by successive American secretaries of state and presidents, and Anwar Sadat's dramatic visit to Jerusalem in 1977, a gesture of peace for which he paid with his life.

The United Nations overturned the notorious 1975 General Assembly resolution declaring that Zionism was a form of racism—the only resolution in UN history to be revoked.[56] A long process ended Israel's diplomatic isolation, and the Arab boycott declined.[57]

The Oslo Accords, concluded after secret negotiations under Norwegian auspices, and whose signing I watched on September 13, 1993, on the White House lawn, marked a major step toward supporting Israel's legitimacy. For the first time, the Palestinians committed to a peaceful resolution of their dispute with Israel and promised to change the PLO charter calling for Israel's destruction, and they did so.

As a result, the Clinton administration could engage directly with the PLO, and I was given the lead to negotiate economic relationships between Israel and the Palestinians. Between 1997 and 2000, I frequently met Arafat, as well as then Israeli prime ministers Netanyahu and Barak. We made real progress in increasing the number of Palestinians able to work daily in Israel, opening the airport in Gaza, and creating an industrial zone in Gaza that permitted companies based there, using as little as 10 percent Israeli content, to export duty free to the U.S.

Arafat frequently told me about the trust he had in "my friend Rabin." While we will never know if Arafat could have moved from a revolutionary to a true statesman and nation builder had Rabin lived, making the hard compromises necessary for peace, I believe the one bullet from an Israeli extremist that killed Rabin profoundly changed the prospects for peace in the region. But only weeks before the 2000 Camp David Summit between President Clinton and Prime Minister Barak, when I met Arafat in his compound in Ramallah, he warned me: "Tell President Clinton not to invite me to Camp David. I am not ready to go."

Other tangible landmarks undergird Israel's legitimacy and its incorporation in the body of nations, such as its acceptance after decades of exclusion in 2000 by the U.N.'s European regional bloc, where the real work is done. In 2005, Dan Gillerman, Israel's UN ambassador, was elected vice president of the sixtieth UN General Assembly, enabling him to play a role in resolving the 2006 Israel-Lebanon conflict. The last Israeli to hold that position had been Abba Eban in 1952. Another step toward Israel's full incorporation into the body of nations was the

2010 invitation for Israel to join the elite Paris-based Organization for Economic Co-operation and Development (OECD), the organization of major industrial democracies in the world, in which I took a leading role during the Clinton administration, when Israel's entry seemed an unrealistic dream.

In 2002, still smarting from the number of Saudi nationals involved in the 9/11 attacks, Saudi Arabia launched the Arab Peace Initiative at the Beirut Summit of the Arab League, by then crown prince, now king, Abdullah. It was a potentially dramatic breakthrough proposing a plan to end the Arab-Israeli conflict and normalize relations between the entire Arab world and Israel, in exchange for Israel's total withdrawal to pre-1967 lines, including East Jerusalem, and a "just solution" of the Palestinian refugee situation, based on UN Resolution 194. This resolution calls for any refugees "wishing to return to their homes and live at peace with their neighbors" to be able to do so or to obtain compensation. The Arab League has adopted this plan on several occasions, including at the 2007 Arab League Summit.

The plan has obvious unacceptable provisions, but there has never been a formal Israeli response, despite former prime minister Ehud Olmert's remark that it represented a "new way of thinking, the willingness to recognize Israel as an established fact and to debate the conditions of the future solution . . . a step that I can't help but appreciate." In 2009, President Shimon Peres recognized the initiative as a U-turn in the attitude of the Arab states toward peace with Israel, while also registering concerns about its terms.

It is difficult to know if the Arab Peace Initiative genuinely reflects a different attitude toward Israel by mainstream Arab governments or is simply designed to show the U.S. and the West a different face. Nor is it possible to know if there is any flexibility regarding the clearly unacceptable terms of the proposal. But this cannot be determined without a formal Israeli response. I believe even now that Israel should test the willingness of the Arab states to sit down and negotiate and should recognize formally the stated intention of the Arab League to make peace, which is a long way from the three "nos" of the 1967 Khartoum Summit, after Israel's victory in the Six Day War: No formal peace treaty; no direct negotiations; no de jure recognition.[58]

The Saudis also hosted an interfaith dialogue, including Jewish religious figures, to discuss mutual tolerance. And another positive straw in the wind was the 2011 conference organized by young Moroccan college students at Al Akhawayn University in the Atlas Mountains, a day before Ahmadinejad's latest UN Holocaust denial, which brought together Holocaust survivors, leaders of the Moroccan Jewish community, and world-class Holocaust scholars such as Dr. Michael Berenbaum to discuss how to teach the Holocaust in all its dimensions and to pay homage to Morocco's wartime king, Mohammed V, grandfather of the current king, who protected the large Jewish community from the Nazi demands. It was the first such conference ever held in a Muslim country. Elmehdi Boudra, the young university student who organized the conference, said, "What upsets me about this subject is some people's claim that the Holocaust never took place. It is simply absurd to hear such claims in light of the historical evidence the world has today."[59]

While the 2011 Arab upheavals have made the Muslim Brotherhood the most powerful political force in the Arab Middle East, it is likely that a Brotherhood-dominated government will at least keep the formalities of the 1979 Egypt-Israel Peace Treaty. But they are more likely to be forceful champions of Palestinians receiving the same full democratic rights they hope to obtain from the fruits of their revolutions than the rulers they deposed. A 2011 attack on the Israeli embassy by soccer hooligans six months after the Mubarak regime was toppled was disturbing, but even more so was the Army's lack of response, perhaps to placate Muslim political parties, until the last moment, when President Obama intervened at Prime Minister Netanyahu's urgent request, and Egyptian commandos rescued the remaining Israelis.

Egypt, while by no means a fundamentalist nation, is deeply religious. An April 2011 poll by the respected Pew Research Center found that, by 54 percent to 32 percent, Egyptians support annulling the peace treaty with Israel, over two-thirds have a very favorable or mostly favorable view of the Muslim Brotherhood, and similar percentages of Egyptians want religious parties to play a role in their future democratic government.[60] More democracy in Egypt and elsewhere in the Arab world is likely to produce more antagonism, not less, toward Israel, at least until a final settlement on the Palestinian issue.

The International Community and More Subtle Forms of Delegitimization

While traditional anti-Semitism has abated and Arab rulers have grudgingly accepted Israel as a reality, more subtle efforts are being employed to undermine Israel's legitimacy as a Jewish state far beyond the Arab world. This delegitimization is a tool in the hands of Palestinians and their allies in the West to pressure Israel to change its policies toward the Palestinians and to weaken its bargaining power. This is a more challenging campaign than the empty threats by Iranian leaders to wipe Israel off the face of the earth. It has spread widely throughout the Western democracies and is heavily based on the Israeli occupation. The campaign employs evocative words such as *apartheid*. Some of the support for this effort derives from the notion that a Jewish state is somehow improper, an anachronism in the multicultural twenty-first century.

This campaign of delegitimization relies on casting Palestinians as the victims of supposed Israeli aggression, trying to change the perception the world had before the 1967 War. Now Palestinians are trying to become David to Israel's Goliath, even appropriating symbols that equate Israeli treatment of Palestinians as the equivalent of the Nazi liquidation of the Jews in the Holocaust.

Pat Oliphant, a Pulitzer Prize-winning cartoonist whose work is widely syndicated in the U.S., has used images of jackbooted Israeli troops hovering over Palestinians. These types of cartoon stereotypes regularly appear in the Egyptian press.

At times, loose talk by those who are in no way anti-Semitic and support Israel can unwittingly be misused by those looking for any excuse to try to undermine Israel's legitimacy, such as UK prime minister David Cameron's describing Gaza as a "prison" as a result of Israel's blockade against Hamas, on his first trip there. Trade unions in Scandinavia have threatened to boycott Israeli products. In the Western democracies, this campaign of delegitimization often comes from the left, which paints Israel as an aggressor and projects its humanitarian impulses on the Palestinians without looking deeply at the nature of the threat facing Israel. It equates Israel with apartheid South Africa, or even the Nazi oppression of Jews during the Holocaust, and calls for boycotts, divestment, and UN votes for sanctions that were so effective in helping to bring down South Africa's apartheid regime. This takes many forms: organized efforts on college campuses, often inspired by Arab students, such as Israeli Apartheid Week around the world[61]; arguments by left-wing intellectuals that a Jewish state is itself racist and discriminatory (even though Jewish states existed in antiquity, and in modern times the UN General Assembly specifically partitioned the territory of the British Mandate into a Jewish and an Arab state); union boycotts of shipping Israeli goods; disinvestment threats by American churches; cancellation of concerts by international artists; and the silencing and removal of Israeli speakers from international forums and even universities that claim to be fortresses of free speech.

Israeli ambassador Michael Oren, a distinguished historian, was drowned out by students during a speech on the Middle East peace process at the University of California, Irvine, in 2010. I participated in a 2010 debate at New York University, organized by Intelligence Squared, in which former Israeli ambassador to the U.S. Itamar Rabinovich and I were paired against a Palestinian-American, Professor Rashid Khalidi of Columbia University, and Roger Cohen, an International Herald Tribune columnist, on the provocative question of whether the U.S. should end its "special relationship with Israel." The combination of an energized pro-Palestinian group of young people, who packed the large NYU auditorium; apathy by unorganized pro-Israel students; and the better understanding by the Palestinian contingent of the peculiar voting rules led them to "win" the debate.

Yale University decided to close its Initiative for the Interdisciplinary Study of Anti-Semitism, allegedly because it failed to meet the school's standards of scholarship and campus interest. Professor Walter Reich, a member of the initiative's board, believes the decision was triggered by a conference the Initiative sponsored "regarding the fastest growing and most virulent manifestation of contemporary anti-Semitism—the anti-Semitism in the Arab/Muslim world."

Whatever the actual reason for the decision, the right reaction to any criticism should have been to improve the program rather than end it..[62]

A divestment movement was launched at a 2002 conference at the University of California at Berkeley. On some campuses, most violently at San Francisco State, but with lesser forms of harassment at others, Jewish students have been targeted and intimidated as surrogates for Israel. Some twenty leading American universities faced calls to drop Israeli companies and companies that deal with Israel from their endowment funds. One of the most publicized campaigns occurred at Harvard while Lawrence Summers, my colleague in the Clinton administration, was its president. Summers forthrightly rejected the divestment demands, noting that any effort to "single out Israel among all nations as the lone country where it is inappropriate [to invest] . . . is anti-Semitic in effect if not intent."[63]

Thus far all U.S. universities have followed Harvard's lead and refused to join divestment movements against Israel. A number of college presidents signed a 2002 public statement reporting that "students who are Jewish or supporters of Israel's right to exist have received death threats and threats of violence. Property connected to Jewish organizations has been defaced and destroyed. These practices and others directed against any person, group or cause, will not be tolerated on campuses." While some religious denominations—such as the U.S. Presbyterian Church, the United Church of Christ, and the World Council of Churches—have passed divestment resolutions, the vast majority have resisted such calls.

The Line Between Legitimate Criticism and Anti-Semitism

There is a clear line between legitimate criticism of Israeli policies, however harsh or misplaced they may be, and anti-Zionism and anti-Semitism. That line is determined by the nature of the criticism: Is it couched in terms and imagery meant to delegitimize the Jewish state, or is it simply trying to change the policies of the government of Israel? It is, therefore, essential that Jews and Israeli officials not try to rebut critics of government policy by dismissing even stern criticism of government policies as anti-Semitism or anti-Zionism. That would debase the terms for time when they are genuinely justified.

However, it is essential to point out misstatements about Israel in order to arm Jewish students and adults and the general public, with facts to counter false allegations, such as the noxious notion that Israel was created out of European Holocaust guilt that helped dump Jewish refugees onto Palestinian land. The historic connection of the Jewish people to Israel traces back thousands of years to two previous Jewish states destroyed by foreign enemies, but the modern Aliyah began long before World War II. It dates from the late nineteenth century, when Jews began returning to their ancient homeland. They built cities such as Haifa and Tel Aviv, which were already thriving by the 1920s. They drained malarial marshland and developed fallow desert purchased outright from absentee Ottoman owners who had long ago abandoned it.

Washington Post columnist Richard Cohen has noted: "Google 'Israel and apartheid' and you will see that the two are linked in cyberspace." The inference is obvious: "Israel is a state where political and civil rights are withheld on the basis of race and race alone. This is not the case."[64] The term apartheid, he argued, was a formal policy by a minority white government in South Africa disenfranchising its own black majority. Israeli Arabs have legitimate grievances about unequal public services but have full voting rights, participate in the national health care program, and receive free public education. Israel's treatment of West Bank Arabs is also a legitimate basis for debate, but it does not fit any definition of apartheid, since they are not citizens of Israel and have no interest in becoming citizens, unlike the blacks in South Africa. Moreover, it is clear that in any peace agreement, Israel will withdraw from large areas of the West Bank and leave the Palestinians to govern themselves, as they already have in Gaza, for better or worse.

Much of the impetus for the delegitimization campaign is centered in the United Nations General Assembly's Palestinian Rights Committee and the Palestinian Rights Division of the UN Secretariat. There is no other ethnic or national group that has such a preferred designation at the United Nations. Richard Schifter, a former U.S. assistant secretary of state for human rights, has created and leads the American Jewish International Relations Institute, an organization that monitors and combats this trend by working with members of the U.S. Congress and with nations at the UN itself. He notes the effort to delegitimize the Jewish state began under UN auspices more than thirty-five years ago with the slogan "Zionism is Racism" and "the creation of a voting coalition led by Fidel Castro and Muammar Qaddafi that exists to this very day."[65]

Between 1972 and 2006, the U.S. vetoed forty-one UN Security Council resolutions directed against Israel, far more than were proposed against any other member of the United Nations. The most egregious international body trying to delegitimize Israel is the United Nations Human Rights Council (UNHRC), formerly the UN Commission on Human Rights (UNCHR)—a misnomer because of the outrageous human rights violators among its membership. The George W. Bush administration withdrew U.S. participation, but the Obama administration reengaged in hopes of nudging it in a more constructive direction, after UNCHR instituted some reforms and recast itself as the Human Rights Council in 2005–2006. But the council still spends a disproportionate amount of its time and effort on Israel and ignores such regimes as Cuba, Sudan, and Zimbabwe. In its August 2008 meeting, the body "directed three quarters of its indictments of individual states against Israel, and two percent against the military dictatorship in Burma."[66]

According to UN Watch, the UN Human Rights Council employs several tactics to demonize Israel: placing Israel on the agenda as item 7 at every meeting to ensure Israel is always a focal point; excluding Israel from its rightful place in the UN's Asia group, requiring it to finally join the Western group after decades of trying; convening emergency sessions on Israel; and bringing highly politicized "experts" to talk about 9/11 conspiracy theories that Jews and Israel secretly plotted the attacks.

In 2001, the U.N. World Conference against Racism, Racial Discrimination, Xenophobia, and Related Intolerance in Durbin, South Africa, was hijacked by rancorous attacks organized by Palestinian groups and supported by many international NGOs. A follow-up conference eight years later was only marginally better, despite a boycott by many nations, including the U.S., Germany, the Netherlands, Canada, Italy, Australia, New Zealand, and Israel.

Another arrow in the quiver of those seeking to delegitimize Israel is the Palestinian "law-fare" campaign, which has included filing criminal complaints in national courts in Europe against current and former Israeli officials. European universal war crime laws are being used against Israeli officials and to conflate Diaspora Jews with Israel. It is UK legal actions initiated by Palestinian supporters that prevents Tzipi Livni, foreign minister during the Gaza War, and Israeli defense minister Ehud Barak from traveling to England, because of allegations they participated in "war crimes" as a result of their roles in the 2008–2009 Gaza War. The legal campaign also included a 2004 advisory opinion obtained from the International Court of Justice in The Hague holding that the Israeli security barrier and Israeli settlements violated international law, although they were not "grave breaches" or "war crimes."

The "Jewish Lobby"

In the English-speaking Diaspora, the issue of where to draw the line between legitimate, if ill- considered, criticism and anti-Semitism has surfaced in two widely discussed books. The first is by Professors Stephen Walt of Harvard and John Mearsheimer of the University of Chicago, who virtually question the legitimacy of the Jewish state and asserted in an article preceding their book, *The Israel Lobby and U.S. Foreign Policy*,[67] that Israel was born out of "moral crimes" against the Palestinians.

They charged that an Israeli lobby advances Israel's interests at the expense of America. Of this lobby's many alleged wrongs, they state that along with the help of highly placed neoconservative Jews, its members led the Bush administration into the ill-advised invasion of Iraq—not Vice President Cheney, Secretary of Defense Rumsfeld, or President George W. Bush himself. The central thesis espoused by Walt and Mearsheimer is that the Israeli lobby is principally responsible for maintaining the substantial aid Washington provides Israel every year and for ensuring that Washington supports Israel unconditionally. Both, according to the authors, are not in the national interest of the U.S.

Painfully for me, the second book, *Palestine: Peace Not Apartheid*, is by former president Jimmy Carter.[68] He alleges that the American Israel Public Affairs Committee (AIPAC) controls American foreign policy and asserts in the very title of his book that the conduct of Israel's occupation of the Palestinian territories amounts to apartheid. President Carter's harsh criticisms and the unbalanced manner in which he has viewed the Middle East since leaving the White House are deeply and painfully troubling. But I disagree as strongly with his characterization and his recent views toward Israel and its Arab neighbors, as I do with many in the Jewish community who label him an anti-Semite or anti-Israel.

Equally I disagree with my former Harvard law professor and friend Alan Dershowitz, who accuses Carter of changing his views because of Arab monetary gifts to the Carter Presidential Center. Jimmy Carter is incorruptible. His views stem largely from the perception by many on the political left of the treatment of Palestinians during the occupation, which he puts into the context of human rights and civil rights based on his own history as a Southerner who grew up with segregation and the consequent mistreatment of African Americans, without placing the Middle East confrontation in a context of threats to Israel's security.

Such a claim against President Carter neglects his groundbreaking work for world Jewry while in office, including the first anti-Arab boycott law; helping to save Natan Sharansky from possible execution by publicly denying Soviet charges that Sharansky was a U.S. spy; focusing attention on the Jewish journalist Jacobo Timerman, imprisoned in Argentina by the military junta, leading to his release to Israel; openly supporting Soviet dissidents and the Jewish Refusnik movement, as well as greater Jewish emigration from the Soviet Union; creating the U.S. Holocaust Memorial Museum; brokering the first peace between Israel and an Arab neighbor in the Camp David Accords and the Israel-Egypt peace treaty, neither of which could have been achieved without the confidence of Begin and Sadat; steadfastly supporting military and economic funding for Israel; and placing a vast number of Jews in key positions in the White House and throughout the government.

But the fact that someone of his stature, who continues to support a secure Israeli state, would be so strongly critical of Israeli policies toward the Palestinians is cause for concern. I told him that his use of the loaded term apartheid to describe the Israeli occupation was unjustified and historically inaccurate when applied to the Palestinian territories, in comparison to South Africa where the white minority government denied its own black citizens any pretense of civil rights. President Carter's standing in the Jewish community has suffered greatly as a result; many forget his other accomplishments for Israel and the Jewish people.

Senior Israeli leaders have used the term apartheid themselves. They have spoken of the consequences of Israel's trying to control the Palestinian territories permanently. In a 2007 interview with the newspaper Haaretz, then prime minister Ehud Olmert tried to rally Israeli public opinion to support the territorial concessions and bluntly warned: "If the day comes when the two-state solution collapses and we face a South African–style struggle for equal rights . . ., as soon as that happens, the State of Israel is finished." He further noted that "the Jewish organizations, which were our power base in America, will be the first to come out against us because they will say they cannot support a state that does not support democracy and equal rights for all of its residents."[69]

Even more bluntly, Defense Minister Ehud Barak warned his country at a joint 2010 event in Herzliya with Palestinian Authority Prime Minister Salam Fayyad that a failure to make peace with the Palestinians would leave either a state without a Jewish majority or an "apartheid" regime.[70] This underscores how highly charged Israel's policies toward the Palestinians have become.

Natan Sharansky, after his release from a Soviet prison as a Refusnik, went on to become a cabinet minister in several Israeli governments, and currently heads the Jewish Agency. He has developed an incisive test for distinguishing proper criticism of Israeli policies from anti-Semitism. He calls it "the three Ds":

1. Is the Jewish state being demonized by having its actions blown out of proportion, for example, by falsely comparing Israelis to Nazis and Palestinian refugee camps to Auschwitz?
2. Is there a *double* standard, in which Jews of the Jewish state are treated differently from other countries, for example, being singled out by the U.N. Human Rights Council for human rights abuses while Iran, China, Syria, Sudan, and Zimbabwe are left untouched?
3. *Delegitimization*: Is the attack an effort to deny the legitimacy of the Jewish state? Using Sharansky's tests, a critic of Israel or its policies can be seriously wrong without being anti-Semitic.

President Carter calls Israel's security fence an "imprisonment wall" aimed at appropriating Palestinian territory and "imposing a system of . . . apartheid." This is simply not the case. When I was undersecretary of state in the Clinton administration, I made half a dozen trips between 1997 and 2000 to promote economic aspects of the peace process. About 100,000 Palestinian workers were going in and out of Israel every day, as well as 20,000 Palestinian business people permitted to travel into Israel by car with special VIP passes—and no wall.

Construction began only during the Second Intifada as a defensive matter when terrorists were regularly murdering Israeli civilians. It is also critical to clarify serious historical misstatements, such as President Carter's assertion that the international community allowed Jews to "take" Palestinian land when the country was founded; or that the first militants in the region were "Jewish militants" in 1939 with the formation of "the Stern Gang"—ignoring twenty years of Arab violence against Jews, including the 1929 massacre of Hebron's Jewish community and the Arab Revolt of 1936–1939.

It is also important to make clear that the charge of excessive Jewish power over America's policies in the Middle East is both untrue and dangerous. Having been on the receiving end as a former senior U.S. official, I can attest that Jews of various views and persuasions organize to lobby for causes important to the Jewish community, just as business and labor organizations, NGOs of every stripe, from left to right, lobby for their issues with ferocity. But that lobby is itself diffuse, from conservative to liberal groups, from the Zionist Organization of America (ZOA) to J Street, with vastly different ideas of what is best for Israel and U.S.-Israel relations. Even Walt and Mearsheimer define the Israel lobby as a "loose coalition of individuals and organizations [working] to shape U.S. foreign policy in a pro-Israel direction."

They include mainstream groups, such as the American Jewish Committee, the Anti-Defamation League, the Conference of Presidents of Major American Jewish Organizations, AIPAC, Christians United for Israel, and dovish groups, such as the Israel Policy Forum, Tikkun, and Americans for Peace Now. There is little that unites them, except their basic goal: security for the Jewish state. There remains a great gulf among these groups on what policies best promote it.

The cacophony of groups diversified further in 2008 when a new political group, J Street, was formed to support Israel but act as a counterweight to AIPAC's influence on U.S. policy in the Middle East, by taking dovish positions on the Middle East peace process and openly criticizing Israeli policy and conduct toward the Palestinians. It would be difficult to reconcile AIPAC and J Street by categorizing them as part of a *single* Israel lobby.

The American Jewish community is hardly monolithic. Most of the major Jewish organizations have supported Israel's position in the peace process even when the Obama administration harshly criticized Israel's settlement policy. But there are conflicting voices, such as J Street, that speak for many liberal American Jews in supporting the Obama administration and opposing Israel's settlement policy. The founder of J Street, Jeremy Ben-Ami has repeatedly made the distinction between support for Israel and support for the Israeli government's policies, declaring, "People are tired of being told that you are either with us or against us."

As recently as the spring of 2011, there was a vigorous debate over J Street's decision, which I believe was misguided, to oppose the Obama administration's veto of a 2011 UN resolution to condemn Israeli settlements. This led Congressman Gary Ackerman (D-NY), a staunch supporter of Israel, but also someone who had been supportive of J Street, to disassociate himself from the organization, stating that J Street's actions, showed the "befuddled choice of an organization so open-minded about what constitutes support for Israel that its brains have fallen out."[71] And the Knesset, just as wrongly, held a hearing before its Immigration, Absorption, and Diaspora Affairs Committee, to declare J Street "anti-Israeli" for giving support to Palestinian arguments that Israel has been "villainous" in its conduct toward the Palestinians.[72] While I disagree with some of J Street's policies, it is important to have a pro-Zionist liberal group to help keep potentially disaffected liberal Jews, particularly young people, within the pro-Israel tent. And I have urged the Israeli Embassy in Washington to reach out to J Street, which they have done, rather than shun them, as they did initially.

The majority of American Jews supports the president, supports a two-state solution, and does not feel well represented by organizations that demand obedient acquiescence to every wish of the Israeli government. In March 2010, after a diplomatic embarrassment over settlements, a poll found little change in American Jewish support for President Obama's handling of relations with Israel—55 percent approved compared with 54 percent in 2009, although his disapproval rating among Jews rose 5 percent to 37 percent.[73] Even the May 2011 confrontation with Prime Minister Netanyahu in the Oval Office, over the president's proposal for the parties to negotiate on the basis of the pre-1967 borders, with agreed land swaps, did not precipitously lower the president's standing in the Jewish community, according to a Gallup poll.

Much of AIPAC's work is what one scholar, Walter Russell Mead, calls "straightforward pork-barrel politics . . . involving foreign aid and arms deals." He concludes that Walt and Mearsheimer "never show that the legislative victories represent real control over critical matters of national policy either in the United States or the Middle East."[74] Walt and Mearsheimer argue that Jewish campaign finance is the critical source of power for the Israel lobby. American Jews are generous political contributors, far out of proportion to their share of the population, to the campaigns of candidates who share their views on a range of issues, of which Israel is only one.

But significantly, Mead points out, the total amount of "pro-Israel" money in any election is often dwarfed by money that flows from other sources. For instance, in Hillary Clinton's 2006 Senate campaign, the now secretary of state received more than $300,000 in supposedly "pro-Israel" money. But that was far overshadowed by what Mead describes as the millions she received from the "pro-women," "pro–real estate," and "pro–law firm" lobbies, which contributed far more.[75]

Indeed, the influence of American Jews is counterbalanced by other groups seeking to influence American policy: corporations with close ties to their Arab suppliers, business groups, and academics and think tanks stressing the national security interests of closer U.S. relations to the Arab world. Decisions with respect to Israel and the Middle East are not dominated by Jews, who make up 2 percent of the U.S. population, but are made by the clash of conflicting domestic interests and international considerations. Walt and Mearsheimer are naïve about the interplay of domestic politics and foreign policy.

The bottom line from my personal experience is that Washington is a tough town where groups go after each other and rarely give any quarter. But because Israel is so prominent in the news, and the stakes in the Middle East are so important to America's national security, pro-Israel groups stand out from others that seek to counteract their influence, often represented by lobbyists for competing interests. As long as pro-Israel groups argue that America's interests are served as they lobby for Israel, there is no legitimate basis for charges of dual loyalty, nor should they be cowed by such criticism. It is a price worth paying for being an integral part of the policy debate in Washington.

Fundamentally, U.S. support for Israel derives not from lobbying campaigns by Jewish organizations but from the American people's broad support and sympathy for Israel as a democratic state in what had been a sea of dictatorships; because it is pro-American and embodies Western values—a major part of which were, at their outset, Jewish values; and because for many it is the Holy Land they revere for religious reasons, seeing Israel as the safe custodian for Christian holy places. After September 11, 2001, the American public sized up Israel as an ally against Islamic terrorists. Without this bedrock support, no amount of lobbying would be successful. A Gallup poll on American attitudes toward Israel, in February 2010, showed the highest level of support in almost twenty years: more than six in ten Americans (63 percent) for Israel, with only 15 percent siding with the Palestinians.[76]

Even with this bedrock of support, the stilted picture of supposed unstinting, unapologetic official American support for Israel is belied by both recent and more distant history. *Every* administration since Israel's creation has staked out policy positions and taken actions that at times have been at odds with Israeli policy. Although President Truman bravely recognized Israel as a Jewish state over the opposition of his revered secretary of state, George Marshall, he imposed an arms embargo during the critical period of Israel's War of Independence. President Eisenhower forced an Israeli withdrawal from the Suez Canal in 1956 after a tripartite invasion with Britain and France. The George H.W. Bush administration took a strong stance against Israeli settlements and withheld loan guarantees to protest new ones. In 1978, President Carter sold $9 billion in advanced F-15 fighter jets to Saudi Arabia and fifty F-5 jets to Egypt, balanced with the sale of seventy-five F-16s to Israel, leading to a major confrontation with AIPAC, which the Carter administration narrowly won in Congress. In 1981, the Reagan administration sold $29 billion in airborne warning and control systems (AWACS) planes and KE-3 refueling aircraft to Saudi Arabia as part of the largest foreign arms sale to date, eliciting a comment of "profound regret" from Israeli prime minister Begin. Even the George W. Bush administration—which conventional wisdom suggests gave Israel carte blanche—balanced its $30 billion ten-year military assistance program for Israel in 2008 with a $20 billion arms package to Saudi Arabia and other Gulf states. It also turned a cold shoulder to Prime Minister Ehud Olmert's request for flyover rights in Iraqi airspace and bunker-busting bombs that could have facilitated an Israeli air attack on Iran's nuclear sites.

At the outset of the Obama administration in 2009, the president called for a settlement freeze and urged that Israel cease all building outside the 1949 armistice Green Line, including East Jerusalem. Prime Minister Netanyahu eventually agreed to a ten-month freeze, not including Jerusalem. But an announcement of new housing units in Jerusalem during the visit of Vice President Joe Biden incensed the White House. And there are differences between the two countries over the circumstances and timing of a possible military attack on Iran's nuclear facilities. Yet, still the Obama administration has strengthened military and intelligence cooperation, raised military aid to Israel to $3 billion a year, added another $200 million for Israel's Iron Dome antimissile system, and quietly approved the bunker-busting bombs in 2009.[77]

No administration has given Israel all it wants or has agreed with every Israeli policy. As the *Washington Post* noted, "the past few years alone has seen the U.S. government promote a Palestinian election [that Israel] opposed; refuse it weapons it might have used for an attack on Iran's nuclear facilities; and adopt a policy of direct negotiations with a regime that denies the Holocaust and that promises to wipe Israel off the map. Two Israeli governments have been forced from office since the early 1990s after open clashes with Washington over matters such as settlement construction in the occupied territories."[78]

Finally, Israel is not the sole focus of attention for the majority of U.S. Jews. Some surveys indicate that roughly one-quarter of American Jews feel little attachment to Israel, less than 40 percent feel "a lot," and only one-third feel that supporting Israel is actually part of being Jewish. Senator John Kerry received some 75 percent of the American Jewish vote against President Bush in the 2004 presidential election, despite the president's image as one of America's most unabashedly pro-Israel presidents, largely because American Jews are generally liberal and vote on the basis of domestic social issues and not just Israel. In 2008, Barack Obama received similar support from Jewish voters against the Republican nominee, Senator John McCain, a steadfast supporter of Israel for decades.

Nevertheless, it would be inaccurate to understate the influence of the organized Jewish community and AIPAC, the most recognizable pro-Israel organization. The Conference of Presidents of Major American Jewish Organizations has effectively coordinated the energies of fifty-two national Jewish organizations. For a significant portion of the American Jewish public, but by no means all, support for Israel is a key condition of supporting a candidate, an initial litmus test before other issues are taken into account. The energy level and commitment to strengthen U.S. support for Israel are driven by a belief that American national interests are served by a strong Israel. There is also an emotional pull to not repeat the general silence of American Jews during the Holocaust. And AIPAC has been remarkably successful in its stated mission; two-thirds of the U.S. Congress can usually be expected to attend the annual AIPAC policy conferences in Washington. The U.S. president and secretary of state speak almost every year. Still, AIPAC's ability to mobilize its members is impressive but not dispositive.

Several recent events have shown that in some national security and law enforcement circles, Israel's influence in the U.S. is viewed with suspicion. In 2005, two former AIPAC officials, Steven Rosen and Keith Weissman, were indicted for conspiring to disclose national security secrets. Both operated openly in dealing with the U.S. government and were not accused of transferring any classified information to Israel. But the 1917 Espionage Act, under which they were charged, had never been used to prosecute private citizens, and a Defense Department official pleaded guilty to providing them with classified information. In Washington there is a constant exchange of information between government officials and journalists, lobbyists, think-tank representatives, and others trying to keep up with the latest policy developments. President Obama's attorney general, Eric Holder, dropped the case after he took office. Rosen attributed his indictment to the FBI's sense that "Jews are more loyal to Israel than to America." Although the Rosen case is troubling and should never have been brought, I disagree with Rosen's charge on the basis of my experience in government working with the FBI and do not believe it is accurate.

This is a very different situation from the case of Jonathan Pollard, imprisoned during the Reagan era. Pollard was an employee of the Defense Department, not a private citizen, with access to highly classified information. He was paid by an Israeli intelligence agency to provide sensitive information to Israel. Given the severity of his life sentence, there are many in the American Jewish community who sympathize with Pollard, but I am not one of them. Pollard did incalculable damage to his country, to Israel's standing with the U.S. national security and intelligence communities, and to American Jews, who for years had difficulty obtaining employment in sensitive positions in the intelligence community because of Pollard and his Israeli spymasters.

The 2009 case of a Washington-based scientist, Stewart Nozette, who did classified work for NASA and the Defense Department while earning over $200,000 from the government-owned Israel Aircraft Industries, adds to the dossier of alleged Israeli spying in the United States, even though the Israeli government is not mentioned in any of the charges. Nozette was arrested following a sting operation in which FBI agents posing as operatives for Israel's Mossad persuaded him to accept cash in exchange for secrets. There is videotape of him telling the FBI officers that he believed they were Israeli agents and that he always assumed he had been working with them.

The proper response by Nozette, or any current or former U.S. government official with access to classified materials, is to reject sharing information with Israeli or any other foreign agents, let alone accept payment for doing so.[79]

I see this as neither an anti-Israel or anti-Semitic action but as part of the concern, rightly or wrongly, within the U.S. intelligence community, and widely shared by American policy makers, that Israel conducts a pervasive spying campaign in the U.S.

One further element in American attitudes toward Israel is a disproportionate scrutiny that amounts to a double standard. There are two examples, neither amounting to anti-Semitism but both demonstrating the difficulty for Israel to behave like any other state without creating repercussions. In recent years, several prominent Israeli companies have had difficulty acquiring American high-technology companies. Any acquisition by a foreign corporation of a U.S. asset that may have an impact on national security must be reviewed by an interagency U.S. governmental body chaired by the Treasury Department. The Defense and Justice Departments (including the FBI) have often opposed Israeli purchases of sensitive high-tech U.S. companies. This seems odd given the close military relationship between the two governments and their extensive sharing of intelligence.

There is a lingering concern that Israel may transfer some of that technology to China, even though the budding Jerusalem-Beijing military relationship was curtailed by Israel years ago because of U.S. objections. Especially troubling was one explanation given to me by two senior officials in two different departments in the George W. Bush administration, both strong supporters of Israel. They asserted that there was deep anxiety over what they felt was aggressive Israeli spying in the United States, which they believed was counterproductive and unnecessary given the high degree of intelligence sharing with Israel. Although the allegations were strongly denied by the Israeli Embassy, the very fact that they were voiced to me by two officials in whom I have great confidence is troubling. More recently, a former senior intelligence official told me that while there is close intelligence sharing with Israel, that Israel engages in counter-intelligence to verify the accuracy of what the U.S. shares with them.

Another matter reveals special scrutiny accorded Israel outside the realm of national security. In 2009, Freedom House, the oldest and I believe most balanced human rights group in the United States, issued its annual ranking of press freedom in nations around the world. I was its vice-chairman at the time. Israel had been downgraded from the first category, "free press," to the second category of "partly free" press, lumped with countries such as Egypt that have a state-controlled press. Countries in the third category are considered to have no free press at all. Freedom House has no animus toward Israel, quite the contrary.

An official at Freedom House told me that the downgrading principally involved Israel's restrictions on the free passage of journalists into and out of Gaza during its attack there to end rocket fire into Israel. I responded that many countries, including the U.S., restrict press coverage during a war and that the three-week Gaza War should not be cause for damaging Israeli's reputation in this way—even more when one considers that some of the most vocal critics of the Gaza invasion were members of the Israeli press. He agreed with me that "Israel does have one of the world's most vibrant . . . presses." But the ranking stood.

In 2010, Freedom House moved Israel back into the "free press" category, where it remains. But my colleague in the organization explained that even before the Gaza War, Israel "historically ranked near the cusp between "free" and "partly free" because of military censorship, some controls on Arab journalists, and other issues related to the ongoing conflict. He added that countries are rated on the basis of their actions and not government intentions, and Israel was not the only country whose score was affected by reporting of and access to local conflicts. He added: "We spent more time discussing and going over the analysis of Israel than any other country by far."

Other American-based human rights NGOs, such as Amnesty International and Human Rights Watch, have been harshly critical of Israel's occupation of the West Bank, and Gaza before its 2005 withdrawal. This makes the recent complaint by Robert Bernstein, the founder of Human Rights Watch and its active chairman for twenty years, all the more important. Writing in the New York Times, he repeatedly castigated his own organization for "issuing reports on the Israeli-Arab conflict that are helping those who wish to turn Israel into a pariah state." When he was head of the organization, he wrote that Human Rights Watch focused on drawing "a sharp line between the democratic and non- democratic worlds, in an effort to create clarity in human rights." Now he felt the organization had cast aside the distinction between open and closed societies. Bernstein noted that Israel has some eighty human rights groups of its own, a vibrant press, an in- dependent judiciary, a democratically elected government, and "probably more journalists per capita than any other country in the world." Yet he continued, "in recent years, Human Rights Watch has written far more condemnations of Israel for violations of international law than of any other country in the region." His most damning criticism of the organization he once headed was that it "lost critical perspective on a conflict in which Israel has been repeatedly attacked by Hamas and Hezbollah, organizations that go after Israeli citizens and use their own people as human shields."[80]

Support for Israel in the United States and Beyond: The Repercussions of Gaza and Lebanon

Warning signals for Israel have arisen in the United States that were largely dormant prior to the Gaza War, and they seem to have emerged with force. Israel needs to pay heed. On April 27, 2009, a poll conducted by James Zogby, a respected Arab American pollster, for the British Broadcasting Corporation's *Doha Debates*, found that substantial majorities of Americans who voted in the 2008 presidential elections believed that resolution of the Palestinian-Israeli conflict was important; that the conflict negatively affected U.S. interests in the Middle East; that both Israelis and Palestinians were entitled to equal rights; and that there should be a Palestinian state. While favorable attitudes toward Israel remained strong, the Zogby poll found that pluralities of Americans believe that the Obama administration should move away from President Bush's virtually unconditional support of Israel, that President Obama should steer a middle course between Israel and the Palestinians, and that he should "get tough" with Israel on settlements.

The poll found a surprisingly deep partisan divide. For example, three-quarters of Senator John McCain's supporters believed that the interests of the U.S. and Israel are identical, and nearly as many believe the U.S. is strengthened by its support of Israel. But the Obama voters strongly disagreed. More than half disagreed that the interests of the two countries are identical, and half actually held that the U.S. is weakened by its support for Israel. Only about 20 percent believed that the U.S. is strengthened by the close partnership. Some of this divergence arises from McCain's strong support among Evangelical Christians, who are also staunch supporters of Israel for theological reasons. But it is a troubling sign that Obama voters would hold such unsympathetic views, because they were largely younger voters and represented the base of Obama's margin of victory.

Israel is a sovereign state and must determine for itself when to engage in conflict. The second Lebanon War has been roundly criticized in Israel, even by the official investigation conducted by its own Winograd Commission. By contrast the Gaza War was widely supported, following months of Hamas rockets from Gaza falling unceasingly and increasingly deeply into Israel, attacks that no sovereign state could accept.

Both conflicts militarily weakened radical groups bent on Israel's destruction. But both also gave Hamas and Hezbollah significant political capital. Hezbollah is a stronger political force in Lebanon, winning more seats in the 2009 elections than ever before, although not enough to form a government. Hamas initially captured the imagination of the Arab masses, although in Gaza itself, its support appears to have been eroded by war and economic failure, until Israel's 2011 exchange with Hamas of over one thousand prisoners for Gilad Shalit.

Nevertheless, the Gaza War provided grounds for anti-Israel and anti-Semitic activities, although anti-Semites will always find excuses to act. But when Israel engages in conflicts out of clear self-defense, the potential for their impact abroad must also be considered. Pro-western Arab leaders, including President Abbas, either publicly or privately supported Israel's efforts to crush Hamas, some even going so far as to criticize Hamas before the invasion. But throughout the Arab world the populace was bludgeoned by hourly pictures of Gaza horrors brought into their living rooms by the provocative coverage of Al Jazeera, the Arab satellite television network. With few exceptions, ordinary Arabs condemned Israel and challenged the pro-Western regimes that had never sympathized with Hamas.

ADL's Abraham Foxman has told me that Islamic radicals conflate Israel and the Jewish Diaspora with attacks against Jewish institutions, "crossing lines I have never seen before."[81] In Europe, Latin America, and the U.S., there have been outbursts of anti-Semitism. The European Jewish Congress reported that in the first three months of 2009, following the Gaza War, the number of anti-Semitic incidents in Europe exceeded the total for the entire year of 2008.[82]

The UN Goldstone Report

One of the gravest blows to Israel's reputation as a result of the conduct of the Gaza War was the report by a U.N. fact-finding mission established in April 2009 by the UN Human Rights Council and headed by Richard Goldstone, a distinguished South African jurist and a Jew. The report discriminates against Israel in the way it is treated, in comparison with other nations. It also raises profound questions about whether the rules of war that were developed for nation-states can be applied equally to asymmetrical conflicts, especially when irregular combatants embed themselves among the civilian population for protection. Israel faces this problem whenever it fights against Hamas, Hezbollah, and Islamic Jihad, just like the U.S. and its allies in Iraq and Afghanistan facing sectarian militias or the Taliban.

Judge Goldstone's reputation provided a patina of respectability to what otherwise could have been dismissed as just another errant mission by the notoriously anti-Israel UN Human Rights Council. He has served on the board of governors of the Hebrew University of Jerusalem, was president of World ORT, and has been associated with Brandeis University in the United States. He was a member of the Constitutional Court of South Africa, the nation's highest court, and a former prosecutor of the international criminal tribunals for the former Yugoslavia and Rwanda, where he distinguished himself.[83]

The Human Rights Council resolution that led to the Goldstone Commission lacked balance from the outset. It sent a commission to "investigate all violations of international human rights law and international humanitarian law by the occupying power, Israel, against the Palestinian people." It further loaded the dice by referring in advance of the mission to the "massive ongoing Israeli military operation in the occupied Palestinian territory, particularly in the occupied Gaza Strip . . . and to the "Israeli siege [that] . . . constitutes collective punishment of Palestinian civilians . . . and leads to the systematic destruction of the cultural heritage of the Palestinian people." Goldstone has told me that he insisted on broadening the mandate to include possible war crimes by Hamas, and while he was told by the Council that his mandate could include possible Hamas war crimes, it was never formally expanded.

The 575-page report found that both Israel and Hamas committed war crimes and crimes against humanity, although the press focused on Israel and not Hamas. This is logical, since Israel is a democratic nation-state, while Hamas is a self-declared terrorist organization. Still, three-fourths of the content is focused on the Israeli response to Hamas's rocket attacks on Israel's civilian population, rather than the preceding years of rocket attacks. As for Israel, the report concluded that it (a) intentionally targeted Palestinian civilians and caused between 1,387 and 1,417 civilian deaths; (b) used Palestinians as human shields during combat and destroyed the foundations of Gaza's civilian life such as food production and the water system, and (c) employed disproportionate force in "a deliberately disproportionate attack designed to punish, humiliate and terrorize a civilian population."[84] These findings represented a devastating and unfair attack on an Israeli army rigorously trained to limit civilian casualties.

The Council voted twenty-five to six to support the findings, but eleven nations including almost all the major democracies abstained, and five cast no vote at all, including Britain and France. The vote was nevertheless sufficient to send the matter to the UN Security Council, but there it was blocked by the U.S. The Obama administration condemned the report as deeply flawed and unbalanced in its focus on Israel, especially, as U.S. ambassador Susan Rice declared, since it had originated with a long history of focusing on Israel, "to the exclusion of credible sustained treatment of the world's most egregious instances of human rights abuses in places like Sudan or Zimbabwe or Burma."[85]

In addressing the Goldstone Report it is important to take a clear view of reality. Israel, like all countries, is subject to a body of international human rights treaties and international law and custom. Any nation that intentionally targets a civilian population would be guilty of war crimes. But this is where law ends and politics begins. A number of eminent legal scholars have taken the Goldstone Report to task for faulty assumptions on the laws of war, incomplete fact finding, and the question of whether Israel's occupation of the Palestinian territories is in fact a violation of international law.[86]

The report also deemphasized important statistics: Between April 2001 and the end of 2008, Israel was hit by 4,246 rockets and 4,180 mortar shells fired from Gaza by Hamas, killing fourteen Israeli civilians and wounding more than four hundred, and spreading fear among thousands in the southern part of the country.[87] The report completely ignores Israel's numerous diplomatic efforts to stop the rockets by making contact with Hamas through the European Union and Egypt. As for the finding of disproportionate force being deliberately deployed, Israeli President Shimon Peres has publicly asserted that before bombing buildings, Israel made thousands of telephone calls to Palestinians asking them to evacuate sites targeted as suspected Hamas locations.

In dealing with the question of whether individual human rights violations by Israeli soldiers amounted to war crimes, the Goldstone Commission lost a great opportunity to suggest a revision of the laws of war. Had the report focused on how a nation can conduct war against terrorist groups that shelter themselves among the civilian population inside schools, hospitals, and other public buildings in the clear knowledge that attacks are bound to lead to civilian casualties, it would have taken a major step in clarifying and perhaps even resolving one of the great moral dilemmas that has emerged from the asymmetrical warfare that characterizes our new century. A closer examination might have led to far different conclusions about Israeli conduct.

International law has not caught up with the evolution of modern warfare, which does not generally pit traditional states against each other, but rather non-state terrorist organizations that are often supported by governments, such as Iran and Syria. But they operate on their own, like the Taliban, Hamas, and Hezbollah as well as al-Qaeda and its affiliates across the Middle East.

The U.S. and its allies fighting the Taliban and al-Qaeda in Yemen, Afghanistan, and Pakistan make every effort to reduce the number of civilian casualties, but the appropriate use of Predator drones that kill their militants inevitably kill some innocent civilians. This is not a war crime. Even in past conventional wars, tremendous collateral damage was visited upon millions of civilians in the allied bombings of German and Japanese cities during World War II, culminating in the firebombing of Dresden and the atomic bombs dropped on Japan, then more recently in the Bush administration's "shock and awe" campaign in Iraq, ostensibly designed to inflict maximum bomb damage to electrical and other infrastructure but also killing civilians in still uncounted numbers. None should be considered war crimes.

Nor has there been any war during which individual soldiers in the heat of battle do not commit human rights violations. One of the most widely known and controversial involved Lieutenant William Calley, who was tried, convicted, and punished for his role as commanding officer in the 1968 My Lai Massacre of civilian men, women, and children during the Vietnam War. But this did not make the civilian or military leadership responsible for Calley's actions.

Terrible things can happen in the unbearable stress of battle, especially against an unseen enemy. Some such events probably occurred during the fierce fighting in Gaza, and a handful of Israeli soldiers have been court-martialed. But the Goldstone Report produced scant evidence of a pattern extending throughout the IDF that could be condemned as orders that amounted to war crimes.

Indeed, eighteen months after the report was issued, Judge Goldstone remarkably recanted a central part of its criticism in a lengthy article he published in the *Washington Post* in March of 2011, declaring that he no longer believed that Israel had intentionally targeted civilians.[88] While partly blaming Israel for refusing to cooperate with his commission, he indicated that the report by the UN committee of independent experts that followed up his commission's recommendations found that "Israel has dedicated significant resources to investigate over 400 allegations of operational misconduct in Gaza." But Hamas, he wrote, had conducted no investigation into the years of rocket and mortar attacks against Israel.

Moreover, Goldstone conceded that Israel's own military investigation—which was recognized by the UN committee—indicated that "civilians were not intentionally targeted as a matter of policy." Judge Goldstone also conceded that the UN Human Rights Council had a historic bias against Israel. He also stressed that for the first time, a UN body had found Hamas guilty of illegal activities, and he had hoped that "in the face of a clear finding that its members were committing serious war crimes, Hamas would curtail its attacks. Sadly, that has not been the case. Hundreds more rockets and mortar rounds have been directed at civilian targets in southern Israel."

The statement by this distinguished judge setting the record straight is important and courageous, but the damage was done. Moreover, the members of his own commission criticized him for changing his views.[89] He made clear to me he was stung by Israel's refusal to cooperate with his commission, which he felt would have provided Israel an opportunity to rebut Hamas's contentions. Israel also lost opportunities to mitigate the damage to its reputation, first by not participating in the commission's investigation, presenting its own evidence of Hamas rocket attacks over the years and the substantial efforts Israel made to avoid civilian casualties, trying to shape its conclusions, and then by not conducting its own civilian review as it did after the 2006 Lebanon War.

That investigation, conducted by a commission under former Tel Aviv district judge Eliyahu Winograd, was charged by the Israeli government to study and report on the Lebanon War—including mistakes made by Israeli commanders as well as soldiers. It is a model of accountability and self-examination that could have followed the Gaza War. Given the fact that the IDF produced its own extensive report in July 2009, the Israeli government could have instituted civilian review and included extensive interviews with combat soldiers and their officers.

There is a lesson here for countries apart from Israel. The United States and its NATO allies are now and no doubt soon again will be fighting asymmetrical wars against violent non-state actors that insidiously seek cover in civilian populations. New rules of war must be developed to reach a contemporary definition of what constitutes genuine crimes against humanity, as future wars are unlikely to be between major nation-states.

Arab governments have long used the Palestinian conflict to divert public attention from the lack of economic growth, from the actions of their own opaque and autocratic regimes, and from inadequate public services they provide. This worked until the recent uprisings across the Arab landscape, but now economic opportunity and individual freedom compete with, but do not supplant, the

Palestinian issue among the newly empowered Arab publics. Indeed, they tie their desire for freedom and democracy to that claimed by the Palestinians.

The continued expansion of settlements makes it more difficult for Israel to rally world opinion against proliferating anti-Semitic and delegitimizing attacks. There is a difference between asserting a right to build on contested territory and doing so at this sensitive time. Prime Minister Netanyahu recognized this in agreeing to an unprecedented ten-month moratorium on West Bank settlement activity, to which the Palestinians did not respond until the ninth month. But his inability to persuade his own cabinet to agree to the Obama administration's request for a simple three-month extension, even with lavish offers of additional military assistance, complicated the ability of the U.S. to combat political attacks against Israel. Clearly the Palestinians remain recalcitrant. But if so, it will then be easier for Israel and the U.S. to point publicly to the real source of the impasse.

The legality of Israel's settlements in the territory it captured after the Six Day War in 1967 can be endlessly debated. On one side, the Fourth Geneva Convention of 1949 holds that a country capturing territory in war cannot make changes such as settling its own people on the land or building a defensive wall that includes the conquered territory. This view is supported by a 2004 advisory opinion of the International Court of Justice. Others, including the Israeli Supreme Court, argue that the annexation of the West Bank by Jordan overrode the UN resolution of 1947 partitioning what was the British Mandate of Palestine between the state of Israel and an Arab state yet to be formed. In 1988, Jordan's King Hussein renounced all claims to the West Bank. Egypt never incorporated Gaza into its territory prior to the Six Day War, even though it controlled the territory and held that its status was subject to negotiation in an ultimate peace treaty.

This tangled history tends to support the argument that the Geneva Convention does not apply. But all these are purely legal—even legalistic—arguments. The political fact is that the U.S. and virtually every other country in the world do not accept Israeli sovereignty over the West Bank or East Jerusalem, although it is clear, as recognized by President George W. Bush and by President Obama in his 2011 AIPAC speech, that significant parts of the territories with major settlement blocks, and the Jewish neighborhoods of East Jerusalem, would become part of Israel in any peace agreement.

It is important not to overreact. Israel is a sovereign state, and its actions must be subject to the same scrutiny and criticism—neither more nor less, and no matter how disagreeable—as any other nation. But its settlement policy, more than any other factor, has led to a growing isolation and has unwittingly provided ammunition to those seeking to undermine Israel's legitimacy. The expansion of settlements and the increased encroachment upon land where Palestinians actually live isolates Israel and compounds its leaders' difficulty in rallying world opinion against unjust attacks.

There are serious consequences to world opinion when radical settlers poison Palestinian olive trees and deface mosques, Palestinians feel pressured to leave neighborhoods in East Jerusalem, and armed outposts sprout on West Bank hilltops in violation of Israel's own laws. While there may be only several hundred radical settlers, they cause disproportionate damage to Israel's image. Israel's own national police chief, Yohanan Danino, considers them a "major threat" than can "produce an escalation" and has created a special police unit to track their activities, while Benny Begin, son of the late prime minister and a minister in the Netanyahu government, calls them "scoundrels."[90]

A United States senator who is a strong defender of Israel shared his frustration with the Israel government's unwillingness to deal with the settler movement. I also met with an ambassador in Washington from a friendly Arab country, deeply committed to the peace process, who has spent significant amounts of time in Israel. He despaired that moderates in his region are undercut because the peace process is stalled, in no small part because of Palestinian intransigence. He believed that a pause in settlement activity could unblock the peace process as well as facilitate Arab compliance with sanctions against Iran.

Clearly, there are security justifications for maintaining some control over parts of the contested territories in any peace agreement, as President Obama has made clear, and a political necessity for large blocs of settlements to remain under Israel's control. But these can be accommodated with territorial swaps. What is crucial is to remove a weapon from those who would delegitimize Israel by clearly defining the boundaries of existing settlements and building only up, not out; dismantling illegal outposts under Israel's own laws, and denying them any electricity or water; preventing new building in heavily Palestinian areas; swiftly punishing settlers who destroy Palestinian property; and publicly laying out Israel's own peace proposals.

Israel no longer is the victimized underdog in the eyes of much of the world; its very success as a nation has transferred that role to the Palestinians, and they have exploited it skillfully. The answer is not for Israel to play the weak partner, for its economic strength, military might, and technological prowess are its greatest protection. Rather, it is essential to use its strengths to be generous in its attitude toward those Palestinians who want peace, even while acting firmly toward those who promote violence.

For the first time in two millennia, Jews are no longer flotsam and jetsam, subject to the whim and caprice of despotic rulers and violently anti-Jewish populations. After two thousand years of exile, a strong sovereign Jewish state flourishes. Many of its most severe challenges also threaten the U.S., the West, and even moderate Arab leaders. Diaspora Jews are more integrated into their societies than ever before in recorded Jewish history. Despite all the lingering, albeit weakened, vestiges of the centuries-old, European-based anti-Semitism; despite the shift in the locus of a new anti-Semitism to the Muslim world since the founding of the Jewish state of Israel; despite the efforts, some violent, some subtle, to attack the legitimacy of Israel as a Jewish homeland, I am optimistic. Israel is more firmly embedded in the globalized economic world than ever. But it risks a return to diplomatic isolation without a peace accord with the Palestinians.

The last missing link is peace with the Palestinians. Israel lives in an Arab sea. The Arab and Muslim worlds must come to terms with a Jewish state in their midst, and when they do it will dramatically change public opinion in Israel. But at the same time, Israel must be seen to do all it can to come to terms with the Palestinians at its doorstep and to demonstrate to the world that if there is a lack of progress, it is due to Palestinian intransigence and unwillingness to accept generous terms of peace—as they have already been offered and failed to accept, by then prime minister Barak to Yasser Arafat at Camp David in 2000, again in 2001 at Taba, and in 2008 by then prime minister Ehud Olmert to Palestinian president Mahmoud Abbas.Israel cannot make peace alone and still faces hostility from sections of the Palestinian population as well as others in the Arab world. But it should do all it can to ease the plight of the average Palestinian and to stop further encroachment on territories where Palestinians live and earn their livelihood.

There also has to be a clear understanding among Israel's leaders that the surest way to undercut the pernicious efforts to undermine Israel's legitimacy is to recognize unequivocally the legitimacy of the Palestinian's right to a state. They must take every possible step consistent with their country's security to make it clear to the world that Israel will make the compromises necessary to achieve a contiguous Palestinian state if the Palestinians do everything possible to ensure Israel's safety against radical elements in their own community and in the region.

Too many Israelis and American Jewish figures view the status quo as acceptable, because Israel's economy is strong, because, thankfully, there is virtually no terrorism inside Israel, and because there are genuine risks in peace. But the dividends of peace are too often forgotten, and if they were better recognized and understood, they could embolden Israel to make the tough compromises necessary for peace and put the onus on the Palestinian side to negotiate seriously. Peace would make it easier for rising new global powers to develop closer ties with Israel.

Peace would accelerate Israel's acceptance in a globalized world. Peace would strengthen pro-Western, modernizing Arab states and weaken the appeal of radical Islamic states and terrorist groups. Peace would enhance Jewish identity in the Diaspora. Peace would be the strongest antidote to the effort to undermine Israel's legitimacy as a Jewish state and would help ensure a durable, democratic state with a Jewish majority. And if peace proves unachievable in the short term, it should be clearly seen that the responsibility rests with the Palestinians and the Arab states, not with Israel.

6

The Future of the U.S-Israeli Relationship

I N A WORLD WHERE ISRAEL has many relationships but no dependable ally except the United States, its relationship to the U.S. will remain essential to Israel's long-term security.

There is no precedent in history for a mighty nation like the U.S. to lavish as much support, over such a long a period, on such a small one. Israel receives more American military assistance than any other country and some of Washington's most sophisticated arms. Until the Clinton administration, when Israel decided on its own initiative to phase out U.S. economic assistance (which I negotiated with then finance minister Yaacov Neeman), it was also America's leading foreign aid recipient.

Israel's interests in the United Nations are defended by the U.S. veto in the UN Security Council, more than forty times between 1972 and 2011, often the only nation supporting Israel.[1] The U.S. shares real-time intelligence more closely with Israel than any other nation except Britain, Canada, and Australia—more than with Germany and other European allies. By all accounts, the Israeli-U.S. military relationship has never been better, more coordinated, and more intimate. More broadly than arms, financial aid, and intelligence sharing, America's Middle East agenda is significantly driven by Israel's security concerns, at times clashing with national security interests in the twenty-two countries that make up the Arab Middle East.

Why does such a small state receive such remarkable support from a global superpower? Five pillars undergird this support: the American public, the American Jewish community, the U.S. Congress, foreign policy elites, and the American president.

American Public Support

Support for Israel among the general American public remains strong in public opinion polls, withstanding criticism of conduct during the Gaza war. As noted in chapter 5, the 2010 Gallup poll taken a year after Israel's forces stopped most rocket attacks from Gaza showed 63 percent supporting Israel—a twenty-year-high—compared to only 15 percent for the Palestinians. This overwhelmingly favorable proportion extended to general views polled by Gallup through all age groups, and only one-quarter of those who did not favor Israel described themselves as genuinely hostile. By contrast, the same Gallup survey found only 20 percent of Americans hold a favorable view of the Palestinian Authority, with 70 percent negative. This is remarkable, given the press reports of Israel's conduct in the Gaza War. One year later, in February 2011, Gallup found the proportions virtually unchanged in favor of Israel.

The State of Israel is the Holy Land for the generally religious American populace, particularly Evangelical Christians. Israel is also seen as sharing democratic values with the U.S., was a staunch ally of the U.S. throughout the Cold War, and continues to make common cause with the U.S. in combating radical Islamic terrorists, which Americans see as a prime national security threat. The American people recognize Israel's strategic value, so domestic political support and American foreign policy toward Israel are closely connected.

The American Jewish Community

Support within the American Jewish community is also a key ingredient, although it would have limited impact without the solid base of general public support. Jews make up only 2 percent of the American population, overwhelmingly support Israel as a Jewish state, and are highly sensitive to its security. The diversity of views within the American Jewish community toward specific Israeli policies, but there is no divergence on the importance of maintaining a strong, secure Jewish state after the experience of the Holocaust, only differences on the best way to achieve it.

As Zionist sentiment for a Jewish State in Israel began to surface in the period between the two world wars, Louis Brandeis brilliantly articulated for American Jews the relationship between their country, their religion, and Zionism: "To be a good American, we must be better Jews; and to be better Jews we must be better Zionists."[2]

But attachment to Zionism was hardly universal. Among Reform Jews, in particular, Zionist sentiment was weak, and there is doubt about the wisdom of a Jewish state in some Orthodox circles. Even after the creation of the Jewish state in 1948, the emotional ties of American Jews were tenuous. The striking

Israeli victory in the 1967 Six Day War created a pride among American Jews and an emotional connection that has intensified over the decades. Now Israel is a focal point of American Jewish identity, a virtual secular religion for Jews of all persuasions. The intensity of support among the Jewish leadership in America is remarkable. Across the length and breadth of the United States, synagogues and temples display ubiquitous signs: "We Support Israel." The Jewish community is highly organized politically; contributes a disproportionate number of political candidates relative to the size of the community; has among the highest voting turnout of any cohort in the country; and can be decisive in states such as Florida, California, New York, and a number of northeastern states.

The community is overwhelmingly liberal and Democratic, contrary to the general proposition that conservatism rises with incomes. As Milton Himmelfarb once crudely quipped, "Jews earn like Episcopalians and vote like Puerto Ricans."[3] This is because of a shared memory of the exodus from Egypt, freed from slavery; because of a shared memory of being an oppressed minority; and because of the values of the Jewish prophets, who stressed feeding the hungry, clothing the naked, and letting the oppressed go free. Maimonides developed a hierarchy of charity, the highest level being donations that are anonymous and provide assistance to people so they can help themselves.

In the 2004 presidential elections, 75 percent voted for Senator John Kerry over President George W. Bush, even though Mr. Bush was viewed by Israelis as one of the most supportive American presidents since the founding of the state. The leadership of the major American Jewish organizations almost always lines up behind Israeli policy, although their followers in the broader Jewish public are more diverse and selective, especially on the issue of West Bank settlements and advancing the peace process with the Palestinians. While Jewish voters generally support President Obama on most issues—indeed his strongest supporters among any ethnic group of white voters—they disapprove of his handling of the Israeli-Palestinian issue by 67 to 28 percent.[4] But these low numbers from a 2010 poll have improved recently with the President's strong actions against Iran and his recent speeches at the United Nations in 2011 and at AIPAC in both 2011 and 2012.

It is critically important that Israel never become a partisan wedge issue. And that is now a risk, particularly over the rift on Israel's settlement policies. If there was one dark cloud for Israel in the Gallup polls showing almost historically high support, it is a potential partisan divide. Since 2001, there has been a 25 percent boost in sympathy for Israel among Republicans to an astounding 85 percent and an 18 percent increase among independents to 60 per cent; during that decade, support among Democrats has remained basically flat at 48 percent.[5]

I believe this arises from human rights concerns involving Palestinians, who now are viewed by many liberals as underdogs, under pressure from the Israeli army and from expanded settlements on what they believe is their land. The congressional mood on settlements is changing among some Democrats, while Republicans unequivocally support their expansion. John Kerry, chairman of the Senate Foreign Relations Committee, supported the Obama policy on expanding settlements, while Democratic representative Gary Ackerman of New York, an unwavering champion of Israel, warned that "having children can't be an excuse for expanding a settlement. Neither side should be expanding beyond its perimeters or attacking the other side."[6]

The increasing use of Israel as a partisan political issue is becoming particularly heated with the upcoming 2012 presidential campaign. There are close ideological ties between Prime Minister Netanyahu's Likud Party and the conservative wing of the Republican Party, which dominates the U.S. House of Representatives. The Christian Right, which is a key constituency of the Republican base, supports expanded settlements in the West Bank so Israel can control the entire Holy Land, oblivious of the Palestinians who live there, in part to herald what they believe will then be a new messianic era. If the Palestinians pursue statehood through the UN, the likelihood is high that Congress will cut off much of the $600 million in annual funding, except for U.S. training of the Palestinian police.

Texas governor Rick Perry has delivered a stinging rebuke of President Obama's Israel policies as a staple of his now-ended presidential campaign, calling them "naïve, arrogant, misguided and dangerous"; has called for moving the U.S. Embassy from Tel Aviv to Jerusalem; and supported continued construction of settlements.[7] Former Massachusetts governor Mitt Romney, the leading Republican presidential candidate, has charged that President Obama has "thrown Israel under the bus." It has become a staple of the Republican presidential primary battles to charge President Obama with being insufficiently supportive of Israel taking possible military action against Iran's nuclear program.

The president received a stinging rebuff from a heavily Jewish and traditionally Democratic district of New York City, which sent to Congress a Republican whose special election campaign in the summer of 2011 was keyed to his support for Israel and opposition to President Obama's Middle East policies, adding further partisan political fire to the Republican effort to woo traditionally Jewish Democratic voters.[8]

There is a National Jewish Democratic Council (which I helped create over twenty-five years ago with Mort Mandel of Cleveland) and a competing Republican Jewish Coalition in Washington.

United States Congress

The United States Congress has long provided Israel's most consistent base of support within the American government and a check on executive branch actions toward Israel. In today's polarized political atmosphere in Washington, unstinting support for Israel is one of the few things on which Democrats and Republicans in Congress can agree. Resolutions supporting Israel are approved by overwhelming bipartisan majorities and are often used to rebuke a president seeming to tilt against Israel. Unlike the presidency and the executive branch, which must balance broader foreign policy concerns in its dealings with Israel, Members of Congress have a focus largely on domestic issues. Prime Minister Netanyahu's 2011 public standoff before the world's press with the president, in his own Oval Office, sharply criticizing the president's proposal that peace negotiations should be based on pre-1967 borders, with agreed land swaps to take into account realities on the ground, are actions few other allies, certainly ones so dependent on U.S. support, would have taken. But the prime minister was emboldened to do so because of certain support from Congress for his position. He followed his confrontation with the president by successfully taking his case against the president's peace proposal to a joint session of Congress, where he received a rapturous reception, with more standing ovations than presidents normally receive in their annual State of the Union addresses. The Senate majority leader of the president's own Democratic Party, Harry Reid, was one of the chief cheerleaders as the prime minister pummeled the president's policies.

This won the prime minister political points at home at Obama's expense and among members of Congress from both parties.[9] But it was a Pyrrhic victory because it has the potential to erode the relationship that is the bedrock of Israel's international support. The Obama policy against new settlement construction has general support among many Jewish members of Congress. A poll by J Street, the liberal-oriented pro-Israel group, found that 60 percent of American Jews opposed settlement expansion, 72 percent supported U.S. pressure on Israel and its Arab neighbors for a peace agreement, and 57 percent supported pressure on Israel alone. While the poll reinforced J Street's own positions, it is worth considering as a data point.

Prime Minister Netanyahu's support in Congress is so strong that the Obama administration actually asked him to intervene to help ensure that Congress would not block $50 million in new aid to the Palestinian Authority after the Hamas-Fatah pact.[10]

Israel is one of the most favored destinations for congressional visits abroad during recess periods. During the August 2011 break, a bipartisan delegation of more than eighty members of the House of Representatives visited Israel and the West Bank, under the auspices of the American Israel Education Foundation, a charitable organization affiliated with AIPAC.[11]

President Obama's September 2011 speech to the UN General Assembly has been called by Howard Kohr, the head of AIPAC, one of the most pro-Israel speeches ever given by an American president. Gone were his 2009 calls for settlement freezes or reiterations of his May 2011 call for negotiations based on pre-1967 borders, with agreed land swaps. For now the power of Israel in the U.S.

Congress has helped change the direction of the peace process. But in fairness, no administration has done more, despite differences over settlement policy, than the Obama administration to provide military aid to bolster Israel's security.

The American Presidency

Because the president of the United States has unique constitutional powers in foreign and national security policy as commander in chief, the American presidency is also an indispensable institution in the Israel relationship. Unlike Congress, which sees the Middle East largely through domestic political eyes, American presidents must consider many factors, including the views of the Arab world. While American presidents have uniformly supported the existence of a secure Jewish state, each has acted over the objections of Israel's American supporters and Israel itself. The administration of every American president since the 1967 War has to a greater or lesser degree supported the exchange of land for peace embedded in UN Resolutions 242 and 338.

Likewise, they opposed settlement expansion, some more vociferously (Carter, George H.W. Bush, and Obama) than others (Reagan, Clinton, and George W. Bush). But even the most supportive presidents have balanced support for Israel against the need to maintain strong alliances with pro-Western Arab nations. Carter sold fighters to Saudi Arabia, despite strong opposition from AIPAC; Reagan overcame similar opposition in selling AWACS surveillance planes to the Saudis. Bush and Obama balanced massive arms sales to Israel with a large deal for Saudi Arabia and the Gulf states. And George W. Bush reined in Israel's tactical options for attacking Iran's nuclear facilities.

Foreign Policy Elites

A last leg of the relationship is the foreign policy elites in the research foundations, think tanks, and nongovernmental organizations that help shape American policy. These cover the gamut from the Middle East Policy Forum, supported by Exxon, to the Middle East Institute, which has a more pro-Arab tilt, but they are overwhelmed by a multiplicity of institutions and scholars who are supportive of Israel. Many of the leading scholars drawn to Middle East studies are Jewish or have strong pro-Israel leanings, although they may have different prescriptions for how U.S.-Israel policy should be conducted. Major think tanks devoted to Israel-Arab issues were founded by American Jews, such as the Washington Institute for Near East Policy by Barbara and Larry Weinberg; the Center for Middle East Peace by S. Daniel Abrahams; and the Saban Center for

Middle East Policy at the Brookings Institution, initiated by the Egyptian-born Israeli American Haim Saban.

One dimension often ignored in this special relationship is Israel's contribution to U.S. security interests. While America's relative weight may seem one-sided, the relationship is definitely a two-way street. Israel provides concrete benefits to the United States. During the Cold War, Israel was the most reliable ally in a region where many of the Arab states were aligned with the Soviet Union, and it helped retard the spread of Soviet power. Israel has helped the U.S. on many occasions when it was not directly in its own security interest—for example, in repelling the PLO's 1970 Black September attack on the Jordanian monarchy. During the first Gulf War, with Scud missiles landing from Iraq, Israel refrained from retaliating at the request of President George H. W. Bush in order to avoid splintering America's Arab alliance against Saddam Hussein.

Israel continues to share real-time intelligence on terrorism aimed at the U.S. and the West and not just terrorism directed at Israel. General George F. Keegan, the former head of U.S Air Force intelligence, said that he could not have obtained the same intelligence he received from Israel even from "five CIAs." He indicated that between 1974 and 1990, Israel received over $18 billion in U.S. military assistance, but, according to his calculations, the U.S. received between $50 and $80 billion in intelligence, research and development savings, and Soviet weaponry captured and transferred to the U.S.

U.S. Senator Daniel Inouye (D-Hawaii) stated that Israeli information on Soviet arms saved the U.S. billions of dollars. Israeli arms purchases from Boeing and General Dynamics support U.S. jobs—some estimate as many as 50,000—since the great majority of Israel's U.S. military aid must be spent in America.[12] With U.S. assistance, Israel developed the world's first land-based antimissile system, the Arrow, fully sharing its technology to aid in the development of a similar American system.

The U.S. and Israel frequently conduct mutually beneficial joint military exercises. Israel also shares cutting-edge defense technology, such as Israeli-made armor and medical battlefield expertise that has saved the lives of American soldiers in Iraq and Afghanistan, and has aided the capture of al-Qaeda leadership in Iraq. Israel developed and provides unmanned aerial drones to the U.S. Customs and Border Protection on the Mexican border. The microchip technology helps make U.S. passports more secure. And inside Israel itself, the U.S. maintains a large stock of military supplies for use in the region.

These benefits were recently summarized in a report for the Washington Institute for Near East Policy by Robert Blackwill and Walter Slocombe, senior officials respectively in the Bush and Clinton administrations, stressing the ways in which Israel is a strategic asset of the U.S., including Israel's counter-nuclear proliferation actions, such as the 1981 bombing of Iraq's Ostrak nuclear facility and the 2007 bombing of Syria's nuclear facility at al-Kibar; exchanges of military and intelligence information; counterterrorism cooperation; collaboration on missile defense and cyber defense; and America's use of Israeli technology, such as drone unmanned aerial systems used to track down terrorists in Afghanistan and special armored vehicles that help protect American troops from roadside bombs in Iraq and Afghanistan.[13]

Divergent Views and Clouds on the U.S.-Israel Relationship

No bilateral relationship remains static and unchanged by events, and several major differences can potentially strain America's special relationship with Israel—differences over nuclear proliferation policies; whether progress in the Middle East peace process between Israel and the Palestinians is linked to broader U.S. strategic interests in the region; intelligence sharing; and internal challenges to Israel's robust democracy, a key basis for the special relationship.

There is a potential divergent view on nuclear arms. President Obama is pushing hard for nuclear disarmament worldwide and to limit the spread of nuclear arms in the Middle East. For decades, Arab governments have pressed for the Middle East to become a nuclear-free zone, which really means crippling or even scrapping Israel's nuclear capability, which they lack. At the Nuclear Non-Proliferation Treaty review at the United Nations in May 2010, the U.S. joined Russia, the UK, France, and China in an appeal against all nuclear weapons in the region, and the final communiqué singled out Israel with no reference to Iran—let alone to Pakistan and India, the two confirmed nuclear powers nearby.[14]

Under Secretary of State Ellen Tauscher told the UN conference that it would be hard to imagine negotiating "any kind of [nuclear] free zone in the absence of a comprehensive peace plan that is running on a parallel track."[15]

The U.S. has entered into a civilian nuclear treaty with India and provides massive assistance to help Pakistan fight the Taliban, so Israel can point to these two nations, neither of which has foresworn nuclear weapons or signed the Non-Proliferation Treaty. Only Israel can determine if and when it should sign the treaty, but the risks are obvious when Iran is developing its own nuclear weapons capability, and Israel's nuclear deterrent substantially bolsters its regional position. If Israel were to place its nuclear program under the auspices of UN inspectors, given the general hostility of the UN toward Israel, it would be taking an enormous security risk while Iran is driving toward nuclear capability.

More significant is the divergent views of Israel and the U.S. on the best way to stop Iran from developing a nuclear weapon. Both countries share a common concern about the dire threat, and Israel has fully supported the American strategy of increasingly tough sanctions against Iran, most recently targeting the Iranian central bank.

Israel and the U.S. are closely coordinating on missile defense systems in Israel and in the Middle East, to defend against any Iranian missile attack. The Stuxnet computer virus attack that disabled about 20 percent of Iran's centrifuges at Natanz, by getting them to spin out of control while appearing to Iran's controllers to be operating properly, was apparently coordinated with the U.S. Iran's centrifuges were based on a design by A. Q. Khan, a Pakistani metallurgist, who stole the design from the Dutch, for whom he had been working. Khan took the design for the so-called P-1 centrifuge to Pakistan and then sold it to Iran, Libya, and North Korea. The effectiveness of the computer worm was tested in nuclear centrifuges Israel built at Dimona to duplicate those used by Iran. The virus temporarily set back Iran's uranium enrichment program and is considered the most "sophisticated cyber weapon ever deployed." The German company Siemens, which supplied computer controllers to Iran, evidently cooperated with the U.S. to identify their vulnerabilities, which Stuxnet then exploited.[16] The CIA has been involved in trying to derail Iran's nuclear program by covertly inserting sabotaged parts into Iran's nuclear supply chain and encouraging Iran's nuclear scientists to defect.[17]

Moreover, the president and secretary of state have forcefully responded to Iran's threat to close the strategic Strait of Hormuz and to keep U.S. warships out of the Persian Gulf, leaving no doubt that military retaliation would be taken, since these strategic areas are international and not under Iran's control.

President Obama made clear in his 2012 AIPAC speech that he is committed to prevent Iran from acquiring nuclear weapons, by military force if necessary, rather than a containment policy after Iran acquires a nuclear weapon. But Israel wants to prevent Iran from acquiring a "nuclear capability", and has a shorter timetable for military action that the U.S.

The U.S. believes that economic sanctions should be given more time to work, while Israel doubts they will be successfully. Secretary of Defense Leon Panetta sought but failed to get an agreement from Prime Minister Netanyahu of prior notice of any Israeli decision to attack Iran's nuclear facilities, just as Israel has sought but failed to obtain U.S. support for an attack, and additional bunker-busting bombs to carry it out.

But if Iran proceeds with its nuclear program, oblivious to the costs, there may be a point at which Israel will feel more compelled to take military action than the U.S. Israel puts a faster timeline on a possible Iranian nuclear device than the U.S. Although both countries believe an actual nuclear weapon is a few years off, Israeli experts have told me they may have only until the spring of 2012 to attack the centrifuges now being moved from Natanz to the underground facility at Qom, while the U.S., with more military capability near Iran's borders, has more breathing space.

There is American unease over the wave of assassinations, some of which almost certainly emanate from the Mossad, which have killed five of Iran's top nuclear scientists going back to January 2010, most recently on January 11, 2012, and wounded a sixth, who now heads Iran's nuclear program, as well as an unexplained explosion in November 2011 at an Iranian missile base, killing a top Iranian general. Some U.S. experts on Iran believe Iran itself may be behind the killings, given how brazen they are in broad daylight, and the common use of motorcyclists who attach the bombs to moving cars, with no culprits ever located,[18] suggesting some of the nuclear scientists were sympathetic to the domestic opposition.

The most recent attack elicited an unusually strong condemnation from the White House and top State and Defense officials, with Secretary of Defense Panetta stating, "That's not what the United States does."[19] In fact, there is a long-standing executive order banning assassinations. The growing Obama administration fear is that this wave of assassinations may stiffen the resolve of Iran. My view is they are far preferable to an airstrike by Israel or the U.S. on Iran's nuclear sites, and they hold far fewer threats to Israel and the U.S. than an overt attack, both from Iran and the international community. Iran's own history of assassinations, most recently its foiled attempt to kill the Saudi ambassador to the U.S. in a Washington restaurant, gives it less international standing to complain.

The purpose of all the actions to disrupt Iran's nuclear program is to get Iran to obey UN Security Council resolutions, refrain from destabilizing the Middle East with nuclear weapons, and return to the negotiating table. But the hour of decision is near when Israel will need to make one of its most profound decisions since its founding: Does it openly attack Iran's nuclear facilities, and what reaction will it elicit from Washington, its ally?

Linkage or Not?

A second divergence in policy between the U.S. and Israeli governments is over the concept of linking a peaceful resolution of the Israeli-Palestinian conflict to stability in the Middle East and curbing Iran's nuclear ambitions. The Obama administration strongly believes in "linkage," as it is called in diplomatic jargon—that Israel's progress in the peace process with the Palestinians is directly linked with America's broad interests in the region of strengthening moderate regimes, reaching out to the new Islamic parties, and maintaining an international coalition against Iran's nuclear ambitions. Israel rejects linkage, believing resolution of the Palestinian issue is unrelated to other national security threats in the Middle East.

Israel's former ambassador to the U.S. Sallai Meridor, like many close to Netanyahu, argued passionately to me: "To think that what happens here [in Israel] has a major impact on the state of affairs in Afghanistan, Pakistan, and Iraq is, in my view, quite far from accurate."[20]

Netanyahu, in a 2010 address to AIPAC in Washington, expressed the Israeli view in more sweeping rhetoric: "Militant Islam does not hate the West because of Israel. It hates Israel because of the West—because it sees Israel as an outpost of freedom and democracy that prevents them from overrunning the Middle East."[21]

Two leading experts on the Middle East, one American, one Israeli, who do not support Prime Minister Netanyahu's policies in many areas, support Netanyahu's views on linkage. Aaron David Miller, who spent twenty years as a senior Middle East negotiator, strongly opposes the notion that a solution would, "like some magic potion," solve U.S. problems in the region. "In a broken, angry region with so many problems, it stretches the bounds of credulity to the breaking point to argue that settling the Arab-Israeli conflict is the most critical issue, or that its resolution would somehow guarantee Middle East stability," he said.[22]

Professor Shlomo Avineri, one of Israel's most eminent political thinkers and director general of the Foreign Ministry in the first Yitzhak Rabin government, believes that linkage is a "mantra" on which Arab countries have for decades blamed their domestic failures, and that the growth of Islamic radicalism, the 9/11 attack, and Iran's nuclear program would have happened nevertheless. The Bush administration's fateful decision to invade Iraq, which has colored much of the attitude of the Muslim world toward the U.S., was likewise totally disconnected from the Israeli-Palestinian standoff.

The Obama administration is equally adamant that linkage does exist. It sees the Iranian nuclear threat and the fight against terrorism as one side of the coin and the solution to Palestinian statehood as the other side.

Like its predecessors, the Obama administration is deeply committed to Israel's security. It has shown this in continuing high levels of military and economic assistance and cooperation; sharing intelligence; blocking the referral of the Goldstone Report to the UN Security Council; vetoing a 2011 UN resolution condemning Israeli settlements; taking on the Iranian nuclear program that is Israel's gravest threat; and battling against the Palestinian bid for statehood at the UN in isolation from almost all of America's close European allies. But the administration has also concluded that advancing the peace process is important not only to Israel and the Palestinians but also to the national security interests of the United States.

This has always been one reason that so many American administrations have made such extraordinary efforts to achieve peace in the region. A constant in American policy has been securing a stable oil supply in the Middle East and strengthening pro-Western Muslim regimes, initially against the Soviet Union and now against radical groups and regimes, and trying to guide the revolutions of the Arab Spring in a positive direction.

The Israeli government does not seem to appreciate the change in attitude that has accompanied the enormous American effort that has gone into the spreading war against al-Qaeda and other radical groups. The high degree of risk to American soldiers, the diversion of American energies, and the huge financial commitment this has entailed have given great urgency to resolving the stalemate between Israel and the Palestinians. While Israelis may believe that their recent relative immunity to terrorist attack means the status quo can endure, many Americans do not.

But that should not obscure a fundamental difference of views between Israel and the United States. Israelis believe there is little or no relationship between their conflict with the Palestinians and the broader American-led campaign against terrorism. They correctly point out that if the Israeli conflict were magically ended tomorrow, it is unimaginable that al-Qaeda and its allies would end their terrorism against the West and pro-Western Arab states. Put this way, the Israelis are right. But as the conflict in Afghanistan lingers into its tenth year; as the process of extricating the American military from Iraq was completed at the end of 2011, with significant instability and violence in its wake; as Pakistan fights for its life as a sovereign state with massive American assistance, even while Joint Chiefs of Staff chairman Admiral Mike Mullen cites evidence that its security services (ISI) support the terrorist Haqqani network that kills American troops and attacked the U.S. Embassy in Afghanistan, the Obama administration believes that the Israeli-Palestinian conflict provides Iran, al-Qaeda, and other radical Islamic groups with a rallying cry to recruit new jihadists. This is not because the Palestinian issue is of central importance to the terrorists, but because the terrorists realize that the Palestinian cause is central to much of the Muslim world.

Linkage was stated most graphically by General David H. Petraeus, a genuine American hero, whose strategy of troop surge and championing of the "Sunni Awakening" helped turn the tide in Iraq, who went on to command allied forces in Afghanistan, and most recently to become CIA director. In testimony before the Senate Armed Services Committee in March of 2010, Petraeus said that lack of progress on Middle East peace as well as the continuing conflict itself "foments anti-American sentiment due to a perception of U.S. favoritism toward Israel." He added that Arab anger at the situation limits U.S. strength and effectiveness across the Middle East—then his area of responsibility—and weakens moderate Arab regimes. "Meanwhile, al-Qaeda and other militant groups exploit that anger to mobilize support," said Petraeus. He also stressed that "a credible U.S. effort on Arab-Israeli issues" would undercut the militant policies of Israel's own archenemy, Iran.[23]

General James Jones, Obama's then-national security adviser , told J Street that " Israeli security and peace are inseparable, and that "If I could advise the President to solve one problem among the many problems this (the Palestinian issue) would be it. This is the epicenter where we should focus our efforts."

The belief in linkage is a major reason for the Obama administration's public ire when new settlement activity in East Jerusalem was announced without warning during Vice President Joseph Biden's visit to Jerusalem in March 2010—to his intense personal embarrassment at what looked like a deliberate provocation, whether or not it actually was. (Granted, similar irritation should have been expressed by Washington about the unwillingness of the Palestinians to enter direct negotiations, or the refusal of Arab governments to agree to the president's direct request for such confidence-building measures as granting civilian over flight rights to El Al.)

Vice President Biden, who ranks among Israel's strongest supporters in Washington, told Israeli officials following the announcement of new housing construction in East Jerusalem, "What you are doing here undermines the security of our troops who are fighting in Iraq, Afghanistan and Pakistan. That endangers us and endangers regional peace."[24]

Secretary of State Hillary Clinton articulated this view of linkage at an AIPAC conference: "Behind these terrorist organizations and their rockets we see the destabilizing influence of Iran. Now, reaching a two-state solution will not end all these threats, but failure to do so gives the extremist foes a pretext to spread violence, instability and hatred."[25] President Obama himself has said that the U.S. has a "vital national security interest" in settling the Israeli-Palestinian conflict because "when conflict breaks out . . . that ends up costing us significantly in terms of both blood and treasure."[26]

The dynamic between Washington and Jerusalem has been changed by America's need to develop and maintain Arab cooperation for its tough stand against Iran, to shore up the moderate Arab regimes in their battle against Islamic terrorists, and to strengthen the newly emerging Islamic democratic forces from the Arab Spring, who can take either a moderate or radical course in the years ahead.

Even after the Arab Spring, there is a strong desire on the part of key, pro-Western Arab states to solve the conflict to strengthen their hand against Iran and deny it a further argument to radicalize the region. At the same time, Iran and its allies want to block peace with Israel. At the Doha Summit in January 2009, Iran's supporters, Qatar and Mauritania, announced they were severing ties with Israel. Iran's supreme leader Khamenei equated those moderate Arab leaders who maintain ties to Israel (many of whom have been deposed in the Arab revolutions) with "Jews at the time of the Prophet Muhammad, who were considered his enemies."

My views on linkage are somewhere between the two viewpoints. The Israeli-Palestinian issue is not the central feature in developments following the Arab Spring, the great internal struggle for supremacy between moderate and militant elements in the Arab countries, or the Iranian nuclear threat. But just as certainly, progress in resolving the Israeli-Palestinian conflict would help the

U.S. rally support of key Arab governments to support tough action against Iran's budding nuclear program; to strengthen moderate governments in the region; to establish a beachhead in reaching out to the new Islamic forces in the area; and to undercut the ability of radical groups such as al-Qaeda to use the Israeli-Palestinian conflict as a recruiting device for young militants. The Bush administration's fateful decision to invade Iraq, which has colored much of the attitude of the Muslim world toward the U.S., was likewise totally disconnected from the Israeli-Palestinian standoff.

But for me, the debate over linkage misses a more fundamental point. A genuine peace process between the Israel and the Palestinians is not a compromise to give the U.S. nor a gift to the Palestinians. It is essential to Israel's security and its status as a democratic, Jewish State.

Would progress in the Israeli-Palestinian peace process cause Iran to stop its nuclear program? No. Would it lead the new Islamic forces to embrace Israel? No. Would it cause al-Qaeda, Hezbollah, and Hamas to lay down their arms? No. But tangible movement toward a resolution of the dispute would strengthen the hand of the U.S. and moderates in the region, and it would deny terrorists a powerful recruiting tool and instrument to rally Arab public opinion against the U.S., the West, and Israel.

Israel and the United States must work together to bridge their differences on linkage and strengthen the pro-Western elements that remain in the region. Nothing would be more important in ensuring Israel's long-term security.

Some in the American Jewish community and in Israel advanced various critiques of President Obama's 2009 Cairo speech to the Muslim world because they favor the expansion of settlements, or they believe Obama created a moral equivalence between the suffering of the Palestinians and the Jews, or because they wanted more emphasis on democracy and human rights in the Muslim world. Others criticize Obama for not mentioning the Jews who fled from Arab states after 1948. A broader critique, particularly in Israel, was the objection to Obama's tracing Israel's creation to the Holocaust rather than the Jews' historical connection to the Holy Land. Whatever their validity, some of these criticisms miss the broader point of his historic speech. One was to recognize the errors of Western colonial rule and of the U.S. and the West in toppling Iran's elected government in 1953. Another was to confront the Arab world with the enduring relationship between the U.S. and Israel, with the permanence of Israel, and with the evils of Holocaust denial and anti-Semitism, together with his own strong condemnation of violence and his determination to forge peace in the region.

The most important aim of Obama's rhetorical and diplomatic outreach was to create a bond with tens of millions of Muslims who may be more likely to follow Washington's lead, particularly if the administration can help resolve the Palestinian-Israeli dispute. If that happens, it would ultimately be to Israel's benefit. The absence of progress in the peace process in the two years since the Cairo speech has reduced the standing of the U.S. and President Obama in the Arab world to Israel's detriment, although this not should not fall predominantly on the shoulders of Israel.

Settlements

Curbing the growth of settlements would put relations with Washington on a sounder footing and help ensure Israel's own future as a democratic state with a Jewish majority. Tip O'Neill, former speaker of the U.S. House of Representatives, famously proclaimed that "All politics is local." While any Israeli government must be mindful of the pro-settlement parties in its coalition, this domestic political imperative should not put so much at risk: straining relations with America; isolating Israel in world public opinion; providing fuel for those who seek to undermine Israel's legitimacy; complicating the ability to forge a coalition against Iran; and, most significantly, imperiling Israel's ability to remain a Jewish majority state. Yet, that is the course Israel seems bent on following—at least in the absence of a credible Palestinian peace partner.

Clearly, the Obama administration made a critical error in its early months in office by publicly demanding a complete freeze on settlements without first engaging the new Netanyahu government in discussions that would have taken into account the domestic political problems posed by the governing coalition's conservative and pro-settlement members. The administration has since worked hard to bridge the differences. The Netanyahu government agreed to impose a ten-month building moratorium, the first of its kind ever proposed; Jerusalem was excluded, with the understanding that no new permits would be issued for the city during that period. But Abbas did not seriously engage in negotiations until the very end of the period.

The original U.S. request set a high bar for the demands by the Palestinian side; they could hardly accept less than what the Obama administration sought. The Palestinians seized on the Israelis' refusal to accept a complete freeze or even to agree to Obama's request for a three-month extension of the moratorium. This was their excuse to delay resuming negotiations on the tough compromises necessary for any peace agreement.

Still, this initial error does not change the basic argument against further expansion of the settlements. The Obama administration's determined pressure against expansion is grounded in the idea of linkage.

In the 2003 Road Map, Israel bound itself to freeze settlement activity, but the Jewish population of the West Bank—even excluding significant Jewish building activity in East Jerusalem—has increased significantly, so that the Israel Central Bureau of Statistics and the CIA World Factbook estimate that in 2011 there were well over 300,000 Israeli Jews living in some 120 authorized settlements and around 100 outposts, illegal under Israeli law. No new bids for government construction were issued after November of 2008, but government-backed construction in the West Bank accounts for less than half of new building. As a show of support in mid-August of 2009, four members of the Israeli Cabinet visited unauthorized Jewish outposts even though they are illegal under Israel's own laws. Combine this with an aggressive settler movement, with militant factions flouting even Israeli military limits on their activity, and an extremely volatile element complicates relations between the U.S. and Israel.

Settlement expansion can undermine a sense of shared purpose and values. Israel's respect for the rule of law is a pillar of its support in the U.S. The Israeli Supreme Court has ruled that settlements in the territories occupied by Israel following the 1967 war do not violate either Israeli or international law, nor does the wall erected against the infiltration of Palestinian terrorists. In 2007, the Israeli Supreme Court ruled that this barrier, which has saved countless Israeli lives, must be rerouted to take less agricultural land away from the Palestinian village of Bilin. For five years, local Palestinians and their Israeli supporters have held weekly protests against the barrier in this area. In January 2011, a Palestinian woman protestor died from the effects of tear gas fired by Israeli forces—but still the court's ruling had not been carried out to give the villagers more access to their land.[27]

Outposts are constructed deeper and faster in the West Bank than the political will to dismantle them, contrary to Israel's own laws, Supreme Court decisions, and pledges to the U.S.[28] There is no sign of a decision to remove all of those built after 2001, as stipulated by the Quartet's Road Map during the George W. Bush administration and agreed to by Israel. A settler at one outpost threw down the gauntlet: "There is no way that Judea and Samaria (the West Bank) will be given to the Arabs."[29]

Former U.S. ambassador to Israel Daniel Kurtzer has detailed the extent to which Israel has acted in contravention of its own laws. In October 1979, the Israeli Supreme Court ruled in the Elon Moreh case that the state could not seize private Palestinian land to build settlements without a specific security justification and an elaborate cabinet-level decision, not simply to clear the way for expanded Israeli civilian settlements. In fact, Ambassador Kurtzer found that since the mid-1990s, Israeli governments have adhered to the policy of not authorizing any new settlements. But this has not stopped settler activists from establishing outposts against Israeli law.

A 2005 report by Talya Sasson, a Justice Ministry official, asked by then prime minister Ariel Sharon to investigate the outpost activity, delivered a searing indictment. She noted that settlers repeatedly made unauthorized claims to land, then hauled trailers to each site and occupied them. Israeli authorities with whom the settlers had developed connections would link the temporary shelters to the electricity grid, pave roads, and gradually develop infrastructure for more permanent settlements. So the Israeli government has indirectly supported outposts through infrastructure development, illegal under its own laws.[30]

On August 2, 2011, the Israeli Supreme Court issued a landmark decision in a case brought by Palestinians and Peace Now, ordering the government to remove a flagship outpost at Migron consisting of a group of some sixty mobile homes placed on private Palestinian land on a hilltop north of Jerusalem in the West Bank. This was the first ruling requiring the eviction of the outposts by a certain date. This strong blow for the rule of law carries legal and political ramifications, since around eighty of the ninety-nine unauthorized outposts in the West Bank are built in whole or in part on private Palestinian land. The effort to remove the three hundred settlers at Migron is likely to cause a firestorm in the West Bank settlement movement, a key constituency of the Netanyahu government. This is a test of whether Israel's commitment to the rule of law extends to settlement activity in the West Bank.[31]

At the conclusion of the 2007 Annapolis conference with President Bush and Palestinian president Abbas, when there was hope for the peace process, Prime Minister Olmert grimly proclaimed, "If the day comes when the two-state solution collapses, and we face a South African–style struggle for equal rights, also for the Palestinians in the territories, then, as soon as that happens, the State of Israel is finished." Recognizing the impact on American opinion, he said that "the Jewish organizations, which were our power base in America, will come out against us because they will say they cannot support a state that does not support democracy and equal voting rights for all its residents."[32]

Shortly before leaving office facing a criminal investigation, Prime Minister Olmert said that if Israel truly wanted peace with the Palestinians, it would have to withdraw from most of the West Bank as well as East Jerusalem, and exchange the same amount of Israeli territory for any occupied land it sought to keep. Olmert had also served as mayor of Jerusalem and publicly conceded that he had been "unwilling to look at reality in all its depth" for more than thirty-five years and therefore had changed his mind. Holding onto all the Arab quarters of East Jerusalem, he warned, would bring 270,000 Palestinians inside Israel's security barrier and increase the risk of terrorist attacks. "A decision has to be made," Olmert declared. "This decision is a difficult, terrible decision that contradicts our natural instincts, our innermost desires, our collective memories, the prayers of the Jewish people for two thousand years."[33]

Israeli president Shimon Peres has also suggested his own sensible compromise for East Jerusalem, similar to that of former prime ministers Barak and Olmert: There would be continued Israeli building in the overwhelmingly Jewish neighborhoods of Jerusalem erected after the Six Day War, but not in the Arab neighborhoods. This distinction has never been adopted.

Let me be clear: I do not believe settlements are the chief impediment to a final resolution of the Palestinian problem. The major obstacle remains the unwillingness of the Palestinians and parts of the Arab world to come finally and fully to terms with the reality of a Jewish state in their midst—within any boundaries. An April 2010 poll by An-Najah University in the West Bank indicated that 67 percent of the residents of the West Bank and Gaza oppose the creation of a Palestinian state limited to the 1967 borders (which in any peace agreement would be redrawn to encompass in Israel the large settlement blocs). And 77 percent rejected making Jerusalem the capital to be shared by an eventual Palestinian state and Israel. Yet, this is the absolute maximum to which Israel could ever agree.[34] Moreover, the Palestinian leadership has repeatedly refused generous offers from Israel, reinforcing Abba Eban's old adage that the Palestinians "never miss an opportunity to miss an opportunity."

Examples also abound of the apparent unwillingness of the Palestinian people, even in the West Bank let alone by Hamas in Gaza, to abandon the glorification of terrorists and look to the future. The Palestinian town of El Bireh has named a square for Dalal Mughrabi, the woman who in 1978 helped hijack a bus in which thirty-seven Israelis were killed. Only a short distance from the Ramallah office of Palestinian Prime Minister Fayyad, where I had many meetings with Yasser Arafat during the Clinton administration, a main street was named for Yahya Ayyash, the notorious "Engineer"—a Hamas bomb maker responsible for the deaths of dozens of Israelis, who was killed by a booby-trapped Israeli cell phone.

If these sentiments ever change, I believe Israeli attitudes likewise will change, as they did following then Egyptian president Anwar Sadat's bold trip to Jerusalem to declare "No more wars." But Israeli opinion has been hardened by the absence of a credible peace partner and above all by the rain of Hamas rockets after Israel withdrew completely from Gaza. In the meantime, Israel must reiterate Prime Minister Netanyahu's acceptance of a two-state solution within defensible borders, as well as demonstrate that commitment by preventing any action by Israeli citizens that would further complicate a solution—principally the expansion of settlements outward on new land that would create new "facts on the ground." Let the Palestinians and not the Israelis be seen as obstructionists, and the diplomatic climate would change. If the Palestinians continue to be unwilling to engage in negotiations, the burden of any impasse in the peace process should rest on them and not on Israel.

Halting the growth of settlement on more disputed land is not a gift to the Palestinians, it is an imperative for Israel. President Shimon Peres, who has participated at the highest levels of government for virtually all of Israel's six-plus decades, warned that continued expansion of settlements and the impasse on the peace process meant that "We're about to crash into the wall. We're galloping at full speed towards a situation where Israel will cease to exist as a Jewish State" and might become a bi-national state, losing its distinctively Jewish character.[35] Israel should not allow Palestinian intransigence to lead it to take self-defeating actions that preclude a two-state solution.

Prime Minister Netanyahu may be coming to this realization himself. He said in August 2011 that if the Palestinians accept Israel as a Jewish state and back off from their UN effort at statehood, he was ready to use the pre-1967 lines as a starting point for negotiations, with agreed land swaps, the very position he severely chastised President Obama for proposing in May of 2011.[36]

And yet, as if nothing changed, another round of two thousand homes was announced in November 2011 in a Jewish neighborhood in Jerusalem and in two West Bank settlements, Efrat and Maale Adumim, just as the Quartet was again trying to get negotiations going, drawing a rebuke from the administration.[37] I believe that development in Jewish areas of Jerusalem is reasonable and—if they do not expand the boundaries of the major settlement blocs that will stay with Israel in any final agreement—acceptable. But the timing of the announcements complicates efforts to resume negotiations and is unnecessarily provocative when the U.S. is working hard to derail UN statehood for the Palestinians.

The State of Israeli Democracy

One of the bedrocks of the intimate U.S.-Israel relationship is Israel's vibrant democracy in a Middle East sea of autocracy. A series of internal events has the potential to undermine American public and Jewish support in the U.S. and the Diaspora.

One is the radicalization of a small fraction of the settler movement, who have torched and defaced mosques, not only in the West Bank but also in Israeli Arab villages, and burned Palestinian olive trees. They have even attacked an Israeli Army base, lighting fires and destroying army vehicles, and occupied another army post, all as part of a campaign they call "price tag," settling scores for both Palestinian violence against settlers and against Israeli security forces for dismantling illegal Jewish outposts in the West Bank.

Fortunately, the mainstream settler leadership has condemned the actions of the radicals, saying they had caused "great harm" to the settler movement.[38] The Israeli government has come down hard on them. Defense Minister Ehud Barak has called them "criminals." President Shimon Peres and the chief rabbis of Israel visited a mosque that had been burned, showing solidarity with the imam of the mosque.[39] Brigadier General Nitzan Alon, then the commander of the IDF's Judea and Samaria Division, expressed concern about the increased violence by radical settlers, which he called "Jewish terrorism," and said, "We should do more to stop it." To prevent more attacks against Palestinian olive trees, the army is shortening the harvest season and providing more protection.[40]

Prime Minister Netanyahu acted forcefully, stating that Israeli radicals would be treated the same way as Palestinian militants, with administrative detention for long periods of time without charges, and trials in military courts.[41]

In addition, suspected Jewish radicals would be banned from the West Bank, and soldiers would be authorized to arrest them.[42]

Radical settlers are not the only challenge to Israel's vibrant democracy. There is a growing concern by Israeli journalists that their press freedom is being stifled. In November 2011, five hundred journalists convened in Tel Aviv to protest the government's action to take a long-established left-leaning Israeli-Palestinian radio station off the air and, more broadly, to oppose the government-backed libel legislation that could limit investigative journalism, a lifeblood of a free society. The bill allows a government official or anyone who felt falsely libeled by the press to get an award, even if he could not prove he suffered any harm, and requires that before an article be written, the person being targeted must be given the chance to fully comment. The senior columnist for Maariv, Ben Caspit, called this the "Putinization of Israel," adding "I never dreamed that I would see such things." Bloggers feel they would be particularly endangered, given the rapidity with which they place things on the Internet. One, Shuki Galili, said that "Journalist Theodor Herzl [the founder of modern Zionism] must be turning in his grave."[43]

These concerns by Israeli journalists have already taken a toll. Freedom House's 2011 report on freedom of the press mentions Israel as one of several countries where there is a robust press and gives Israel its top ranking on the Freedom Index, but where there are threats to media freedom. Reporters Without Borders in their 2010 report puts Israel in the "notable problems" category (the U.S. is ranked "satisfactory" rather than "good," the top category).

Another concern is a series of Likud Party bills that would restrict the activities of Israeli nongovernmental organizations (NGOs), including Peace Now and the human rights group B'Tselem, by limiting and heavily taxing their contributions from foreign governments, such as the EU. Foreign Minister Avigdor Lieberman called some of the groups affected by the legislation "collaborators in terror."[44] While these may be modified or never pass at all, some are supported by the prime minister and bespeak a mindset that is disquieting and will upset many Americans, including American Jews, who look to Israel to be a model democracy in a difficult neighborhood. It is hardly worth alienating supporters of Israel by such legislation. The normally pro-Israel editorial page of the Washington Post puts it bluntly: "Those who, like Mr. Netanyahu, worry about the 'delegitimization" of Israel will only advance that cause if they are seen to erode the country's democratic freedom."[45]

An even more sensitive issue has arisen at the same time that could also drive a wedge between Israel and many Diaspora Jews: the status of women. This is an odd issue, because one would be hard-pressed to find a country in which women have a more prominent role: the chief justice of the Israeli supreme court; mandatory military service, with women in combat roles; the leader of the principle party in opposition; a former prime minister; full participation in all areas of business and professional life.

At the founding of the state, David Ben Gurion, a secular Jew like most of the Zionist leadership, reached an agreement in which the Orthodox rabbinate would have control over religious matters, such as marriage, divorce, and conversion. Since then there has been a live-and-let-live situation. While strict control over conversions has meant that most Diaspora Jews converted in their countries will not have them recognized in Israel if they move there (make Aliyah), and while many secular Israeli Jews rankle at Orthodox weddings, and a small percentage even go to Cyprus to get a civil marriage, these issues have been contained. Likewise, the restriction on women having to use a separate part of the Western Wall to pray has generally been manageable, with only occasional flare-ups.

But with the growth of the ultra-Orthodox population (Haredi), approaching one million in a population of 7.8 million, over 20 percent of the primary school population, and increasing rapidly due to very high birthrates, with increasing dominance in Jerusalem; with political parties representing their interests and obtaining large subsidies for their yeshivas; and with most men out of the workforce and exempt from military service, studying the Torah full time (although some are beginning to serve in the military and trying to acquire work skills), the possibility of a secular versus Haredi battle splitting Israeli society and alienating many Diaspora Jews is increasing. The controversies are spilling into more and more areas of public life.

Several recent incidents have put the matter out front: Female soldiers were asked to leave an event entirely during dancing at a Simchat Torah celebration. The annual parade celebrating the 1967 reunification of Jerusalem has separated marchers and onlookers by gender. In Ashdod, a female singer was dropped from the cast when Orthodox subscribers objected to having to hear a woman's voice. Women are required to sit at the back of public Egged buses that serve Haredi neighborhoods to separate men and women, despite an Israeli Supreme Court decision banning the enforcement of separate seating; when the Jerusalem police commander had the temerity to enforce the Supreme Court decision, posters depicted him as Hitler.[46] The wife of a prominent Israeli official told me of her fear of entering a Haredi neighborhood during a festival celebration, until her husband was recognized.

A women's health care conference barred women from speaking from the podium, leading a number of speakers to cancel. Haredi men spit on an eight-year-old girl they felt was immodestly dressed. The chief rabbi of the air force resigned when the army decided not to excuse Haredi soldiers from attending an event with female singers. And particularly galling for many secular Israelis was an incident in which the Haredi acting health minister refused to present

Professor Channa Maayan with the ministry's prize for her work on hereditary diseases found particularly in Jews, insisting a male colleague accept the award on her behalf.[47]

This has resulted from the increasing rigidity and fundamentalism of the Haredi leadership on matters that were ignored in the past. Their views on a Jewish state are different from those of the mainstream Orthodox, pro-Zionist leadership of Rabbi Avraham Burg and his National Religious Party, which formed the backbone of coalition governments for the first decades of the state.

As these gender issues have burst onto the front page of the *New York Times* and into a column by a major *Washington Post* columnist, Ruth Marcus, they present what seems to be a different Israel than many have idealized. This reportedly led Secretary of State Hillary Clinton, a longtime strong supporter of Israel, to liken the separate seating of women and men in public buses to the Rosa Parks incident. This courageous African American woman was arrested in 1955 for refusing to give up her seat to a white rider in a racially segregated bus in Montgomery, Alabama, sparking the civil rights movement. Secretary Clinton's comparison elicited a sharp retort from Israeli government officials.[48]

And former president Bill Clinton mused that the influx of Russian Jews had created an obstacle to peace,[49] while there is an undercurrent in other circles that somehow Russian Jews brought with them a history of living under autocracy that itself has changed the nature of Israeli democracy.

It is important to keep a sense of perspective. The fundamentalist movement of the Orthodox establishment and the growth of the Haredi in Israel are part of a similar direction in the Christian movement in the United States and in parts of the Muslim world, as a revolt against modernity, and what is perceived as the undermining of traditions and family values in a globalized digital world.

Israel made a decision at its birth as a modern state to allow greater religious participation in the state than the U.S. or other liberal democracies, having the Shabbat as an official day of rest, observing the laws of kashrut for food served at state institutions and events, and exempting Orthodox men from military service. These principles go back to the founding of the state, and are proper and necessary to accommodate the observant part of the Jewish people in a Jewish state.

The separate seating on buses, however distressing, is limited to only those few buses going into Haredi neighborhoods and is subject to a Supreme Court ruling. The press, while legitimately concerned about changes in libel law, is remarkably free and openly critical of government, in a state constantly under attack. The military is strictly under civilian control and not religious domination.[50] NGOs will continue to have freedom to act, when all is said and done. Democracies such as France legally prevent Muslim women from wearing a burqa, and Switzerland had banned construction of minarets on mosques, neither of which Israel has ever considered enacting.

The immigration of Russian Jews has been a great boon to Israel in terms of talent, energy, and commitment to the State of Israel. There is little question that a significant percentage have a more conservative political bent and distrust of the peace process, and together with rocket attacks from Hamas following the Gaza pullout and the absence of what many in Israel believe to be a credible peace partner, Russian Jews have helped tilt Israel from a center-left to a center-right nation.

Foreign Minister Lieberman, a Moldovan by birth, has made troubling statements about loyalty oaths for Israeli Arabs and transferring them to a Palestinian state as part of a final status agreement. There may well be compelling national security reasons for Israel to refrain from criticizing the recent Russian elections, widely condemned abroad and within Russia as fraudulent, given Russia's strategic importance on issues such as Iran's nuclear program. But it does not put Israeli democracy in the best light when Mr. Lieberman, after meeting in Moscow with Prime Minister Vladimir Putin, declares the Russian elections "absolutely fair, free, and democratic."[51] But Mr. Lieberman does not necessarily represent the views of all Russian émigrés.

There is no reason to believe they threaten Israeli democracy, and they have participated fully in Israel's political life. Over time, like other immigrant groups from Eastern Europe, the Arab states, and Ethiopia who came to Israel from countries with no democratic tradition, Russian Jews will increasingly adopt Israel's democratic norms.

Still these divisive issues cannot be ignored. Just as Ben Gurion reached a historic agreement with the Orthodox leadership that has served the state well, it is essential that today's leadership strike a twenty-first century understanding, or the issues, particularly of women's roles, will have a corrosive impact on Israel's democracy. The Orthodox rabbinate should maintain the control they were given by Ben Gurion over social and family issues but exercise it judiciously. If the Haredi do not wish to listen to women singing, they should not be forced to do so. State institutions, such as the Army, have been and should remain sensitive to Orthodox concerns. But the Haredi should not seek to change the fundamental basis of equality of men and women in service, nor insist on separate seating for public transportation or to limit the ability of women to fully and equally participate in national celebratory events. Antidemocratic calls such as those in 2010 from the chief rabbi of Sefad, Shmuel Eliyahu, urging Jewish residents to refuse to rent or sell to Israeli Arabs or other non-Jews, should be swiftly rebutted by the Israeli government.[52]

Israel must not be seen as going in a fundamentalist religious direction or it risks losing support among many circles in the United States and in the American and Diaspora communities worldwide.

The most corrosive threat to Israel's democratic values is the steps that necessarily must be taken to control violence in the Palestinian territories. There is no alternative to vigorous Israeli military intrusion in the West Bank to protect existing settlements and Israeli citizens from terrorist attacks. This will be essential until there is a two-state solution with defined borders that leave the large settlement blocs under Israeli sovereignty, along with clear and enforceable security guarantees to prevent a Palestinian state from being a launching pad for rocket attacks and terrorists, as suggested by former general and deputy defense minister Ephraim Sneh—a demilitarized Palestinian state; a credible security force along the Jordan River; a defense treaty with the Palestinians and Jordan; and continued U.S. support for Israel's military superiority.[53]

But there is a cost to this necessary intrusion into the lives of the majority of Palestinians prepared to accept a two-state solution. Now the U.S.-trained Palestinian forces control about 40 percent of the West Bank, with Israeli forces controlling the balance of Palestinian territory. But even the Palestinian-controlled territory, where most Palestinians live, is subject to regular nightly raids.[54] Israel cannot negotiate peace with itself, but the faster it can extricate itself from occupying an unwilling population, the stronger Israel's democracy will be.

The Economist Intelligence Unit's 2011 Democracy Index gives Israel a ranking of "flawed democracy," their second-highest category, with the U.S. ranked as a "full democracy." This is highly unfair in my opinion, given Israel's active and engaged electorate, the transparency of its decision-making process, the accountability of the government to its citizens, and the robust and diverse press reporting (even with the concerns mentioned). But it is worth reflecting on the need for Israel to address any misperceptions.

Are the Palestinians Ready to Govern a State?

Israel and the U.S. differ on whether the Palestinians are ready to govern their own state and able to root out terrorists and prevent the area from becoming a launching pad for rockets and a base for suicide bombers.

Israel agrees with the United States that the Palestinian government in the West Bank has made important progress in building a credible security force but doubts it is strong enough to ensure Israel's security without Israeli intelligence support and military presence.

Moshe Yalon, a minister in the Netanyahu government and former IDF chief of staff, has voiced the predominant government position: "The belief in land for peace has failed. We gave land in return for terror in Judea and Samaria [West Bank] and land in return for rockets in Gaza."[55] But the Obama administration believes the Palestinians are ready, that Prime Minister Salam Fayyad is building the institutions of statehood, and that the progress of the Palestinian police, trained by the American military at bases in Jordan, augers well for a Palestinian state controlling its borders and rooting out terrorists.

There are several ways for a Palestinian state to be created. One is a unilateral declaration, with borders, the fate of refugees, and the location of its capital to be negotiated later. Salam Fayyad has begun to build the infrastructure of government; I know him well and am confident in him as a man of peace, and Israelis have no reason to be surprised by his target dates. In 2010 he told a conference in Israel that the Palestinians would be ready to establish a state in the following year.[56] An American-educated Palestinian Christian who spent almost a decade working at the World Bank in Washington, Fayyad is incorruptible and the first Palestinian leader genuinely committed to peace with Israel. He has launched a large tree-planting program in the West Bank, near the cities of Bethlehem and Qalqilya, to lay claim to Palestinian land. There is a historic parallel—the remarkable program that the Jewish National Fund began under the British Mandate to restore the environment, to bring Jews back to the land, and to lay claim to what became the State of Israel. The planting continued and now totals about one-quarter of a million trees that have transformed the land of Israel. Every American family with even faint Zionist sentiments can recall the metal blue boxes with a slot for coins "to plant a tree in Israel" and larger donations for trees planted in the Promised Land in memory of those who never lived to see it. The Palestinians have learned a lesson, and some call their program "treefare." The Palestinian Authority is using tree plantings to establish facts on the ground.

The Palestinian Ministry of Agriculture is focusing on sites near settlements such as Efrat, which not coincidentally is the largest settlement bloc of the militant Gush Etzion, just south of Jerusalem. The trees would block Efrat's expansion onto land claimed by the Palestinians. The Palestinian Authority's tree-planting campaign is aided by the Olive Tree Campaign of the Joint Advocacy Initiative of the East Jerusalem YMCA and the YMCA of Palestine, which solicits volunteers online for what they call a program of "civil international solidarity with Palestinians."[57] The YMCA network has launched a campaign to plant 50,000 trees and has planted several thousand in fields near Nablus and Ramallah and in the Jerusalem area. An Israeli group called Rabbis for Human Rights, headed by an American-born Reform rabbi, Arik Ascherman, has planted more than 50,000 trees in Palestinian territories, largely funded by donations from American Jews.[58]

By far the most ambitious program was announced in 2009: The United Nations Development Program and the Palestinian Authority's Ministry of Agriculture undertook a five-year Green Palestine initiative to plant five million olive, almond, peach, and apricot trees in the West Bank and Gaza. But when the Jewish National Fund itself donated 3,000 trees from its nurseries in Israel to the planned Palestinian city of Rawabi near Ramallah, nationalist Israeli politicians objected.[59]

The "tree war" continued when Prime Minister Netanyahu went to a West Bank settlement bloc to plant a tree, symbolizing Israel's intention to keep the major settlement blocs in any peace agreement, such as Maale Adumim and Ariel.

More significant, Fayyad's concrete steps to build the institutions of statehood are having results. The Palestinian Authority's police force displays increasing capability and willingness to take on Hamas in the West Bank.[60] Their progress surprised even the Israeli military and prompted it to withdraw from places such as Jenin, once a Hamas hotbed. Fayyad is also trying to improve the justice system, schools, and physical infrastructure. Aided by the Netanyahu government's removal of many Israeli checkpoints, the West Bank economy grew by 7 percent in 2009, avoiding the Great Recession that slowed most of the world. The IMF estimates that the West Bank economy grew by 9 percent in the first half of 2010, while the economy of Gaza, boosted by Israel's relaxation of import restrictions, expanded by 16 percent.[61] And GDP growth in the West Bank in 2011 approached 10 percent.

Foreign investment is slowly beginning to come to the West Bank. Qatar's cellular phone company injected $700 million and created thousands of jobs; the Palestine Investment Fund and the U.S. government's Overseas Private Investment Corporation (OPIC) provided $16 million in loan guarantees. The Palestine Fund was created after the 1993 Oslo Accords and now has assets of $800 million. The fund invests in housing and infrastructure, has established a private equity fund for the small and medium-sized businesses that employ about 85 percent of Palestinians,[62] and is planning a "techno park" as a base for technology companies.[63]

Fayyad was simultaneously plowing ahead with a new and unfortunate strategy, calling for a boycott of Israeli goods produced in the territories; the Palestinian Authority went a step further by making it a criminal offense for a Palestinian to work in an Israeli settlement. This economic warfare is legally unenforceable under the Israeli control, but it underscores the Palestinians' level of frustration and is counterproductive: Between 25,000 and 30,000 Palestinians work in the settlements. The Israeli press has described this focus on nonviolent protests against the occupation as a "White Intifada."[64]

In 2010, Fatah held its first party congress in twenty years and its first ever in the Palestinian territories. To replace the aging Arafat generation of exiles, it elected a younger and more pragmatic generation of leaders who grew up in the territories, strengthening the domestic political base of Abbas and Fayyad with a more united party to confront Hamas and enter into negotiations with Israel.

But with all his nation-building work and his credibility with Israel, the U.S., and the Europeans, Fayyad's future has been left uncertain by an agreement between Hamas and Fatah on April 27, 2011, to establish an interim unity government, promoted by the interim Egyptian government, seeking to show more aggressive support of Palestine against Israel. One of the many negative results of the agreement is that Fayyad will likely be removed on the demand of Hamas, depriving the Palestinians of their most credible leader. His fate remains unclear.[65]

The deal—and its uncertain outcome—underscores Fatah's weakness. React-ing to the Egyptian-brokered deal, Netanyahu declared that "the Palestinian Authority has to choose between peace with Israel and peace with Hamas," and President Peres called the agreement a "fatal match" that "will allow terrorists" to make decisions on Israel's security.[66] Fatah's negotiator, Azzam al-Ahmad, said he had chosen reconciliation with Hamas to send a message of internal political unity to Palestinian youth and a message everywhere that the Israeli oc-cupation must end. They were pressured by demonstrations inspired by the Arab Spring demanding a united front.[67]

But on a practical level, Hamas and Fatah's Palestinian Authority are at log-gerheads over the most fundamental issues, throwing into doubt the long-term viability of their pact. Hamas wants to achieve by violence an Islamic Palestinian state in all of pre-1948 British mandatory Palestine, while Fatah seeks a negoti-ated two-state solution with a secular Palestinian state along pre-1967 lines. They even disagree on the push by Abbas for UN recognition of statehood, with Hamas concerned this would lead to a peaceful resolution, with two states, just as Israel gained support for statehood from the United Nations in 1947.

The Palestinian Authority is continuing to share intelligence on the where-abouts of Hamas figures with Israel, although they are no longer arresting them.[68] While the Palestinian Authority has repeatedly turned down past gener-ous offers in 2000 at Camp David, in 2001 at Taba, and in 2008 from then prime minister Olmert, the Netanyahu government has done little to support the more peaceful Palestinian party at the expense of the most radical forces, thus denying the moderates credibility to tell their people that statehood would come more rapidly at the negotiating table than from the barrel of a gun. Even the thousand person prisoner exchange for Gilad Shalit was done entirely through Hamas, strengthening their hand at the expense of Abbas.

Although President Obama pledged support for a Palestinian state in his 2010 address to the UN General Assembly, in 2011, he pledged to veto recognition in the Security Council, as Israel urged, arguing that only bilateral negotiations could produce a two-state solution. He has worked hard and successfully to block action on the Abbas statehood petition at the UN Security Council.

In this position, he has strong American public support, as an April 2011 poll indicates 51 percent of Americans opposed the unilateral declaration of a Pales-tinian state outside a negotiated peace deal with Israel.[69]

The Palestinians may still seek support in the UN General Assembly, where the U.S. veto does not apply, under the Uniting for Peace precedent used by the U.S. to gain support for military action against North Korea in the Korean War. Even this is problematic, since the administration got the Quartet (U.S., EU, UN, Russia) to issue a proclamation on the day Abbas handed his application for UN membership to the UN Secretary General, calling for a renewal of negotiations, with specific timetables for each side to submit detailed peace plans.

Even if the UN General Assembly acted favorably, there would be no recognized borders a Palestinian state could control; Israeli troops would remain in place, as would Jewish settlements; and the Palestinian government would not control its own airspace or travel into, out of, or even *within* its territory. Moreover, two competing Palestinian governments in the West Bank and Gaza would thoroughly blur the nature and powers of the supposed new state.

But recognition of a Palestinian state, even in a stunted form by more than one hundred member nations of the UN General Assembly, would change the international diplomatic context and, above all, the negotiating dynamic with Israel and the world. Governments would establish diplomatic missions and demand access to what they will designate as embassies. Israeli actions challenged by the Palestinian state would become internationalized and could be considered subject to sanctions against a fellow UN member—above all the continued presence of settlements and the Israel Defense Forces that protect them on what the Palestinians claim, with UN backing, as their sovereign territory.

Intelligence exchanges between the Palestinian police and Israel may be compromised, along with Israeli antiterrorist actions. Israeli military tribunals would be undercut in their trials of Palestinian crimes against Israeli settlers. Palestinians would seek redress in their own rudimentary court system and would almost certainly seek to bring suits against Israel in the International Criminal Court, putting Israel on the defensive.

While the Fatah leaders claim that recognition will strengthen their hand in negotiations, it is more likely to do the opposite by escalating levels of confrontation and giving Hamas a major voice in a new Palestinian government and, possibly, ultimate control. Rather than making difficult concessions on Palestinian refugees, the status of Jerusalem, and security to reach an agreement, going to the United Nations represents an easy way out. Instead of the negotiated land for peace formula that produced the landmark 1979 treaty with Egypt and the 1994 Jordan-Israel treaty, the UN ploy, as Charles Krauthammer put it well, would be "land without peace," with no reciprocal recognition as a Jewish State or agreed borders.[70]

Netanyahu has warned of retaliation, and he may be forced into taking measures to head off the Palestinians' momentum, especially if Palestinian demonstrators surround and attack even illegal outposts, where armed and militant settlers have left no doubt that they will shoot to kill any invaders. It would be far better to forestall a UN by having a forthcoming Israeli government peace plan within the timeline set by the Quartet.

A second alternative is maintaining the status quo. For many Israelis, this is the easiest option and, in the short term, the least threatening. Thanks to the security barrier and efforts against Hamas by both the IDF and Palestinian Authority, terrorism is dramatically down inside Israel. There were no deaths from terrorist attacks in 2009 and 2010, but a bomb struck a bus in Jerusalem, and a family of settlers in the West Bank were brutally killed in 2011. This led Netanyahu to respond by supporting more settlement expansion. The economy has rebounded, and foreign investment and tourists continue to pour into Israel

Why take risks for peace? This becomes an even more tempting option after the Fatah-Hamas agreement, which holds the possibility of an election within a year that may expand Hamas's power into the West Bank, and the upheavals in the Arab world, with all their uncertainties. Still, it remains in Israel's essential long-term interest to remove the burden of controlling 2.5 million Palestinians in the West Bank, let alone another 1.5 million Gazans.[71] Even if peace proves impossible in the short term, everything must be done to separate the two peoples in the West Bank, without Israeli settlements further encroaching on Palestinian private land.

A third alternative is the announcement of an American plan or blueprint for peace. One senior administration official has stated: "Incrementalism hasn't worked. As a global power with global responsibilities, we have to do something. . . . [The plan would] take on the absolute requirements of Palestinian security and the requirements of Palestinian sovereignty in a way that makes sense."[72] President Obama's speech of May 19, 2011, indicating that Palestinian-Israeli negotiations should be based on Israel's 1967 border, with agreed land swaps, represented a compromise. The president's special Middle East negotiator, George Mitchell, pressed for a full-blown American plan to achieve this and resigned shortly after his advice was disregarded. Dennis Ross, an experienced Middle East hand in the National Security Council, disagreed and argued that the United States should not commit itself to specific parameters. He has now left the administration. In the end, President Obama recognized that putting an American plan on the table was too risky because it would be rejected out of hand by both sides. If Washington published such a plan and it went nowhere, what next?

The best approach remains a negotiated settlement between the two sides, with the U.S. as mediator, producing proposals to help overcome differences. The imponderable is that if the reconciliation holds between Fatah and Hamas, the Palestinians will likely delay negotiations in the hope of receiving a public mandate in a 2012 election. Progress has been made in the peace process only when both sides wanted it and when the U.S. could help both sides compromise seemingly irreconcilable positions.

The U.S. has played a major diplomatic role since Secretary of State Henry Kissinger helped broker the partial withdrawal of Israeli forces from the Egyptian Sinai in the 1970's. It continued at Camp David under two presidents, Carter and Clinton. This would permit the U.S. to lay out possible solutions and would also give Israel a greater hand in shaping the final agreement.

The Quartet agreed to the U.S. position, which Israel also accepted, that negotiations should initially focus on two key issues: (1) security guarantees to protect

Israel against future attack and (2) borders for both states. Much discussion on this has already occurred privately between the Palestinian and Israeli governments. The status of Jerusalem and the Palestinian refugees should be the last issues, taken up only in a later phase. This is far better than a sweeping American proposal that tried to define all these upfront and would be dead on arrival.

The Quartet proposal got nowhere until King Abdullah of Jordan intervened and invited the parties to negotiate in Amman on the basis of the Quartet's concept. Both sides have at least submitted detailed responses, which is the first time there have been any significant negotiations in the last three years.

The Jordanian-brokered negotiations give Prime Minister Netanyahu the opportunity to take the offensive with a two-state proposal based on President Obama's May 2011 parameters—pre-1967 borders with mutually negotiated land swaps to allow major settlement blocs to remain in the redrawn borders of Israel. The Prime Minister has given indications he may be prepared to embrace this concept, with appropriate security guarantees and a commitment from the Palestinians that at the end of the day they will accept a Jewish state.

This approach was supported in the spring of 2011 by major Israeli figures, including the former heads of the Mossad and Shin Bet. They met with Abbas to emphasize their position.

If the Palestinians seriously negotiate on borders, Netanyahu may need to form a broad-based unity government to break the veto of his more conservative coalition partners. This would require the Kadima Party and the Labor Party to cast aside their own short-term political considerations and support him. With the turmoil in the Arab Middle East and the certainty of strong UN General Assembly support for a Palestinian state, if the matter is ever put to a vote, it is an hour of maximum risk for Israel. Domestic Israeli politics therefore need to be cast aside.

It is entirely possible that even a bold Israeli initiative on borders will not be acceptable to the Palestinians. But it would shift the ball to the Palestinians' court, forcing the hand of both Fatah and Hamas. It might also divide the two Palestinian factions, casting a sharp light on their different approaches. And it could shore up support in Europe and within the U.S. administration.

Through one path or another, it is inevitable that the Palestinians will obtain statehood sooner rather than later. It is essential that Israel play a constructive role in ensuring the terms of Palestinian statehood meet Israel's bottom-line needs.

The U.S. must recognize that the risk premium for Israel to make major concessions has increased with the Arab Spring's bringing in Islamic-influenced governments in key countries such as Egypt, more hostile to Israel, and with the Hamas-Fatah pact. Evacuating most of the West Bank entails far greater risks than the unilateral Gaza withdrawal under Ariel Sharon, exposing Israel's major cities and industrial facilities to rocket attacks from just across the new boundaries. What if Hamas attacked a multilateral force overseeing a peace agreement in the West Bank? Would a UN force do any better in preventing a new Palestinian state from smuggling in rockets than their abysmal record in Lebanon, where following the 2006 Lebanon War, Hezbollah has built an arsenal of 40,000 rockets and missiles?

Despite Fayyad's progress in creating the nascent institutions of statehood, and the success of the U.S. training efforts, there remain huge risks to relying solely on Palestinian police and security forces to defend what would be Israel's redrawn boundaries against radicals. While the agreement between Hamas and Fatah leaves each security service in charge of its own territories, Fatah's security service may not continue to cooperate in arresting Hamas terrorists or sharing intelligence with Israel. Addressing such security concerns is critical for gaining popular support among Israelis for any peace agreement after it is reached by those in authority.

When we met at the World Economic Forum in Davos, Switzerland, early in 2011, Fayyad spoke to me with great urgency in light of the upheavals in the region. He said it would send a very important psychological signal for the IDF to withdraw from all major West Bank cities as they already have from several, including Jenin. The fact that Israeli troops keep "coming back into large cities from which they have nominally withdrawn" has had a serious impact on the Palestinian public's view of the chances for statehood, he said, and stopping this would demonstrate progress toward statehood. He emphasized that intelligence sharing "at historic levels of quality" had proven the ability of the Palestinian police to deal with security threats to Israel.

This is not the view of the Israeli government. When I raised Fayyad's request with a senior official in the Netanyahu government, he said Fayyad was not correctly assessing the capacity and the willingness of his security forces to fight terrorism. While the Palestinian Authority forces were good at law and order, I was told, they had not reached that level in confronting terrorism, even when Israel provided the intelligence. Israel is sensitive to incursions and keeps them to a bare minimum, the official noted, but the IDF feels it must be able to enter any area in the West Bank to root out terrorists. This will become an even greater Israeli imperative with Hamas's increased influence over decisions in a new Palestinian government that will be less likely to mount active campaigns against the Hamas terrorist network in the West Bank.

When I met Fayyad at the 2012 World Economic Forum in Davos, he seemed resigned that the Iranian nuclear crisis had sidelined the Middle East peace process. At a plenary session in which he and Israeli president Shimon Peres were the only two speakers, he was sober, reserved, and constructive, in sharp contrast to the histrionics of Turkish prime minister Erdogan in the same location in 2009, when he walked off the stage he shared with president Peres.

To provide assurance to Israel of America's full support in any two-state solution, several things are essential. The U.S. and Israel must closely coordinate policy following the Middle East political earthquake. If Hamas wins the 2012 elections, the U.S. must make tough decisions about the level of engagement with the new government and whether to continue its large assistance program to the Palestinians.

To bolster Israel to combat its own rejectionists, the U.S. by word and deed must make clear its unshakable commitment to Israel's security. President Obama sent an April 2010 letter to Alan Solow, then chairman of the Conference of Presidents of Major American Jewish Organizations, providing a number of reassurances on the "special relationship," including shared values, shared security threats, the "unshakeable" commitment to Israel's security, and the need for negotiated settlement with the Palestinians, and that the U.S. "alliance with Israel serves our national security interests."[73] President Obama followed this up with a 2011 UN General Assembly speech that AIPAC applauded. He told the world audience that "America's commitment to Israel's security is unshakeable, and our friendship with Israel is deep and enduring. And so we believe that any lasting peace must acknowledge the very real security concerns that Israel faces every single day. Let's be honest: Israel is surrounded by neighbors that have waged repeated wars against it. Israel's citizens have been killed by rockets fired at their homes and suicide bombs on their buses. Israel's children come of age knowing that throughout the region, other children are taught to hate them. Israel, a small country of less than eight million people, looks out at a world where leaders of much larger nations threaten to wipe them off of the map. The Jewish people carry the burden of centuries of exile, persecution, and the fresh memory of knowing that six million people were killed simply because of who they were. . . . These facts cannot be denied. The Jewish people have forged a successful state in their historic homeland. Israel deserves recognition. It deserves normal relations with its neighbors. And friends of the Palestinians do them no favors by ignoring this truth, just as friends of Israel must recognize the need to pursue a two-state solution with a secure Israel next to an independent Palestine."

This speech was seminal, by recognizing the long-standing attachment of the Jewish people to "their historic homeland" rather than relating it to the Holocaust alone, as the president's 2009 Cairo speech was seen by critics as implying. The speech demonstrates a keen sense of Jewish history. It avoids any notion of equal suffering between Israelis and Palestinians. And it addresses Israel's security needs in any peace agreement.[74] The president's 2012 AIPAC speech forcefully reiterated these points.

Another demonstration of America's commitment was to be a unique joint defense exercise, called Austere Challenge 12, to strengthen Israel's defense systems and coordinate them better with U.S. forces. It was postponed in early 2012 because of tensions with Iran over its nuclear program. But it is precisely because of the assurance Israelis need that the U.S. will help defend against any Iranian attack, as well as any provocations from its immediate neighbors, that this joint exercise should be rescheduled as soon as possible.[75]

It is more critical than ever for President Obama to share his sentiments and commitments directly with the Israeli people, by making his first presidential visit and speaking from his heart, as he did to the Muslim world in Cairo in 2009. No Israeli government can be expected to make far-reaching concessions and take the risks for peace without a high level of trust by the Israeli people and their government in the president of the United States. Much of the Israeli public concern has evaporated with the president's 2011 UN speech, but seeing is believing, and Israelis need to see President Obama in the flesh and take his measure.[76]

Final Thoughts

The Future of the Jews

EVEN WITH ALL THE CHALLENGES, the future of the Jewish people, in their own state and the Diaspora, is more secure against their enemies than at any time in their 3,500-year history. There has never been a time when it is better to be Jewish, either in the Diaspora or in the State of Israel, and when Jews are better able to face the great challenges of the future.

What is unique compared to any other time in Jewish history is the combination of a Jewish Diaspora firmly embedded in the mainstream of their countries, and protected by a rule of law, and a Jewish sovereign state far stronger, far better able to defend itself against all foes, than the two previous Jewish commonwealths of the First and Second Temple periods of antiquity.

Even with efforts to delegitimize Israel as a Jewish state, and with its diplomatic isolation over settlements and policies toward the Palestinians, Israel is firmly accepted in institutions such as the group of industrial democracies, the OECD, the International Red Cross network, and a regional bureau of the United Nations, all of which would have been unimaginable only a few years before. Differences with the U.S. over particular Middle East policies cannot obscure the sound grounding in public and political support of the unique and special alliance between the world's greatest democracy and one of its smallest.

Positive Developments

Many of the Global Forces of the twenty-first century I have discussed present challenges that the State of Israel and the Jewish people share with other peoples and nations, even though some impact Jews inside and outside Israel with special particularity—globalization; the battle for the direction of the 1.6 billion people in the Muslim world; and nontraditional security issues such as nuclear proliferation, environmental crises, and cyberwarfare.

The Jewish people also are especially well-positioned to deal with many of these Global Forces. An example is Globalization, the phenomenon of vast amounts of capital, goods, services, data and people moving across national boundaries at dramatic speeds unrivaled in history. Digital technology and the Internet are the backbone of globalization, diffusing knowledge and information around the globe, with an impact on people and nations every bit as revolutionary as Gutenberg's invention of the printing press in the mid-fifteenth century.

For sure, there are down sides to globalization. It places a premium on knowledge and skills that lead to income inequality within and between nations. Islamic militants and terrorists use the Internet to recruit, fund, and direct terrorist activities. Cyberattacks are compromising corporate technology and government secrets and can imperil the operation of inadequately protected computers which operate the vital infrastructure systems of nations, from power grids to water supplies to essential financial services.[1] U.S. corporations and key government agencies are constantly bombarded by cyberattacks; China is testing cyberattack capabilities in military exercises which could be used to shut done vital systems in the U.S[2]; and Israel is not immune. In early 2012, the Web sites of the Tel Aviv Stock Exchange and El Al Airlines were disrupted by cyberattacks.[3] There is the risk of a new, potent form of warfare, cyberwar, with attacks by nations difficult to trace. Already, Russia has used cyberattacks against Estonian Websites in 2007 and in its 2008 war against Georgia.

But Israel is a world class, high tech powerhouse, as able to effectively use cyberwar as any nation, except the United States. The 2001 Stuxnet computer "worm," widely believed to emanate from Israel, damaged up to one-tenth of Iran's nuclear centrifuges.

In a more positive way, globalization is an unalloyed positive for the Jewish people and for Israel. The key to success in our globalized world is a passion for education, adaptability, and entrepreneurship. These are traits that Jews have acquired in order to survive and thrive over the millennia. Jews have been able to incorporate the best of the cultures in the countries to which they were forced to flee, and to enrich those societies by their own contributions.

Even more broadly, a globalized world is an interdependent world, in which most nations have an unparalled stake in each other's prosperity. Products incorporate components from all over the globe, and there is no such thing as a purely American, European, Japanese, or Chinese product. Supply chains span the world to supply multinational corporations based in every major continent. Financial services and capital spans national boundaries. In this interdependent world, the Jewish people and the State of Israel, are deeply embedded and an essential part of its success.

There are other positive developments; one that is particularly surprising: energy security. As a result of discoveries of large deposits of natural gas off Israel's shore, Israel's dependence upon Egyptian natural gas through a pipeline that has been blown-up several times since the Egyptian revolution, may decline markedly over time. Israel can also reduce its dependence upon imported oil and coal, and could attract large amounts of foreign investment to convert the natural gas to LNG for export.

Also the choke-hold the Arab Middle East has over oil production should decline over the next several decades. Alternate energy sources like biofuels, wind, and solar will become more prevalent around the world, although still a small part of world energy needs, Conservation measures will take hold because of rising energy prices, like improved fuel efficiency standards for vehicles, better insulation for homes and businesses, and new lighting technologies, LEDs.

At the same time the U.S. is at the cusp of a profound shift in its energy picture. The Marcellus shale rock formation from New York State to the mid-Atlantic region holds enormous quantities of clean burning natural gas. Europe has large quantities, as well. Heavy oil deposits will also make the U.S. more self-reliant. And the Western Hemisphere, not the Persian Gulf, will become the prime source of U.S. energy imports, from tar sands in Canada to massive offshore energy in Brazil.

Because Israel's security and global peace are so heavily dependent upon the United States, the direction the U.S. takes in the twenty-first century will have major impacts on Israel and on the quality of the world our children and grandchildren will inhabit. For sure, Israel also strengthens U.S. national security in many ways not often appreciated. But the U.S. is Israel's major arms supplier; Israel's major defender in the United Nations, having vetoed over 40 anti-Israel resolutions in the past several decades; shares real-time intelligence with Israel, exceeded by few other nations in the world; and the U.S. is leading the battle to break the back of Islamic terrorism, which threatens Israel as well as broader Western interests, with hundreds of billions of dollars of U.S. taxpayer support, large contingents of soldiers, thousands of whom have given their lives or have life-long scars of war, and drone technology, initially developed in Israel.

The Implications of the Shift in Power from the West to the East and South

There is clearly a shift of power and influence from the United States, Israel's only real ally, and Europe, with which it shares democratic, free-market values, to the emerging nations of Asia and Latin America, with tiny Jewish populations and no shared history. The rise of the U.S. as a world power after World War I and II had a profoundly positive impact on global stability, prosperity, and freedom, as well as on Jews and Israel. The U.S. has been the ballast for maintaining world order during all of Israel's six decades.

For the first time in its history, although still the most powerful nation, the U.S. is not the ascendant power. The relative advantage the U.S. enjoyed immediately after the collapse of Communism has narrowed and will continue to erode over time, as the emerging giants of China, India, and Brazil, along with other resurgent nations like South Korea, Turkey, Indonesia, and South Africa, assert themselves. A multi-polar world exists in which the U.S. must work closely with other key countries to meet a host of global challenges. The U.S. has created a new institution, the G20, as the major source of global economic coordination, effectively replacing the G7 industrial democracies.

The Great Recession of 2008–2009, from which the U.S. is just recovering, and in which Europe remains mired, has punctuated the shift in economic power. The "Washington Consensus" of frugal fiscal and monetary policy, free market democracy, with light regulation, investments in education and infrastructure, which the U.S. successfully sold as the model for the developing world, lies in tatters, because America did not follow its own principles.

The U.S. has created a deep hole for itself. Median family incomes have stagnated for decades, and were lower in 2009 than a decade before. Income inequality has hit untenable levels, with the top 10 percent of American earners having garnered almost all the increased income over the past several decades. A new measure by the U.S. Census Bureau found 100 million Americans, one in three, are in poverty (50 million) or near poverty (51 million), nearly half living in suburbs.[4]

Our education system has declined from first to twelfth in percentage of college graduates, and math and reading scores for young American students are near the bottom rung of industrialized nations. For a country that has prided itself on upward mobility, the U.S. has less intergenerational economic mobility than most other advanced nations.[5] The nation's infrastructure of roads, bridges, water systems, and rail lines are crumbling. American manufacturing firms have shed workers so rapidly in the past ten years, relying upon production abroad, that one expert has found all of the gains of the past 70 years has been lost, one of three factory jobs.[6] Even the vaunted American family is in distress, with a majority of mothers younger than 30 having children out of wedlock.[7]

America's fiscal picture is bleak, with the U.S. public sector deficits at 10 percent of GDP, over a trillion dollars annually for the past three years, more than twice the levels of even the Eurozone countries. By U.S. calculations total debt to GDP is 60 percent, but by the measurement of the International Monetary Fund, U.S. gross public debt in 2011 was at 100 percent of America's gross domestic product.[8] And in 2011, each American household's share of the national debt approached two years of median household income.[9]

Nothing dramatizes the shifting of economic power from the West to the East and South more than the fact that 2012 will be the first year in modern history in which more than half of global growth will come from developing countries, almost 40 percent from China alone.[10]

But America is not a beached whale. I have long believed not to ever bet against the United States and its resilience! It remains the strongest country in the world. With only 4.5 percent of the world population it is the world's largest economy, representing over twenty of global GDP, has the world's best universities, and is the fountain of innovation in a Digital Era. A sustainable economic recovery is finally beginning, with over 2 million new jobs likely to be created in 2012, and unemployment likely to drop below 8 percent, although still high by historical levels. American companies have over $2 trillion in cash waiting to be invested as the clouds over the economic future begin to clear. Of the Fortune Global 500 largest companies, over 300 are either European or American.[11] Importantly, the United States has a better demographic profile than virtually any advanced industrial democracy, and is aging at a less rapid rate than even China, with its one child policy, significantly because of Hispanic immigration and solid birthrates.

I firmly believe there is a bipartisan consensus that will manifest itself after the 2012 presidential election, regardless of the winner, to reduce the U.S. government deficits by $4 trillion over the next ten years. Most significant, the United States is the preeminent military power in the world, uniquely able to project air, sea, and ground power around the globe. U.S. military personnel are stationed in 135 countries, train scores of foreign military forces, and thus has 11 aircraft carrier strike groups—no other state operates even one. The American military budget is greater than those of the next 14 nations. American military strength adds immeasurably to Israel's national security.

While there is no Pax Americana, the American dollar will remain the world's principal reserve currency for the foreseeable future, with significant advantages to the United States, and the English language is more dominant than ever as the medium of commercial, financial, and academic communication around the globe.

It was always unrealistic to expect American dominance as the world's sole superpower. We live in a multipolar world in which the U.S. must work with others as never before to shape a prosperous, free, and safer world. The most important bilateral relationship for the U.S. has become the one with China. The emergence of China as a global power is one of the most important Global Forces of this century, and the way it is managed will be crucial to world stability and to Israel's interests. China is a key country in dealing with North Korea's nuclear threat and in the negotiations with Iran over its nuclear program.

There are few global challenges that can be successfully met without American and Chinese cooperation, and yet it is a relationship between two countries with vastly cultures, economic and governance models, and security concerns. Yet like Siamese twins the U.S. and China are bound together by shared economic imperatives. In 1985, bilateral trade was $7.7 billion and there were only 10,000 visas issued to their respective citizens for visits; by 2011 two-way trade leaped to $440 billion and three million visas were issued. Chinese has become one of the most popular foreign languages in American universities, and English is the dominant foreign language taught in China.

For all of China's amazing progress, it has the largest number of people in poverty in the world, a per capita income that places it in the bottom rung of nations; an imperative to create millions of new jobs each year for the more than 20 million Chinese coming from the countryside to urban areas; and an aging society.

From Israel's perspective, while Judaism is not one of the recognized religions, and China votes consistently with the Arab bloc in the UN, China has no history of anti-Semitism, maintains a healthy relationship with Israel, including growing two way trade, and needs Israel's high tech products and technology.

Israel needs to broaden its relationships with all of the BRIC countries—Brazil, Russia, India, and China—and renew the outreach to developing nations in Africa and Asia, as it did in its formative years.

And likewise, Israel and its supporters in the U.S. must recognize that the face of America is dramatically changing, and by mid-century, the majority of the country will be composed of today's minorities, Asian, Hispanic, and African-Americans, with little connection to Jews and to Israel. Efforts like the American Jewish Committee's Project Interchange to bring tomorrow's leaders in those communities to Israel should be dramatically expanded.

The Battle for the Direction of the Muslim World: the Arab Spring

The one area in which the U.S. has indisputably lost influence is in the Arab Middle East, the very area Israel needs it the most. The Arab Spring is as profound a global development as the collapse of Communism and the end of the Soviet Empire was in the late twentieth century. From Israel's perspective, the Arab Spring has the prospect of becoming the Arab Winter, as it has empowered Islamic forces, even the more moderate variations, who have more animus toward Israel than the leaders the revolutions displaced. An underlying message of the Arab Spring is a revolt against centuries of perceived dominance by foreign powers, whether by the Ottoman Empire, Western colonial powers in the late nineteenth and early twentieth centuries, or the U.S. in the latter part of the twentieth century and into the twenty-first. They will want to chart their own course.

If there is a silver lining for Israel and the Jewish people in the Arab Spring, it is that over time, if the Arab Middle East can genuinely develop democratic values—and that is a big "if"—this will ultimately unleash the creative abilities of the Muslim peoples of the area and embed them in a globalized society, with a stake in a stable, prosperous world. In addition, managing the turmoil of the transition from decades of autocracy, and the burning desire of the Arab peoples for jobs and a better way of life, will preoccupy the new Islamic leaders, who will be expected to deliver economic opportunity, rather than foreign adventures against Israel or a move toward fundamentalism and radicalism.

The direction Egypt takes will have the most impact on its Arab neighbors, Israel, and the U.S. But in the end, I hope that the Muslim Brotherhood-led government will recognize they cannot deliver services for their people without Western assistance. Egypt swallowed its post-revolutionary pride to seek a loan from the Washington-based International Monetary Fund.

And for all the loss of influence the U.S. will suffer from the Arab Spring, there is no competing force to fill the vacuum, with Russia no substitute for the Soviet Union, and China largely interested in the Middle East for oil rather than political power. The U.S. has already reached out to the new Islamic-dominated governments, who in the end will need Western investment. Turkey, whose relations with Israel are severely strained, but not broken, will be the emerging power most aggressive in extending its influence in the wake of the Arab Spring, serving itself as a model with its moderate Islamic rule, booming economy, and strong army. But even with Turkey's more Eastern tilt in light of its rejection for membership in the European Union, Turkey is a NATO member, cannot afford to alienate the U.S., is not an Arab country, and carries its own baggage as the successor to the Ottoman Turkish Empire.[12] Turkey recently agreed to accept an American anti-missile system aimed at Iran.

As unsettled as the Middle East is, there are positive developments. The twenty-two member Arab League led opposition to ousting Libya's Quaddafi, supporting NATO military attacks against his regime, and are taking a strong stand against Iran's only ally in the region, Syria's President Bashar al-Assad, calling for his resignation. Assad, not Israel, was condemned in early 2012 by an overwhelming vote in the UN General Assembly. His inevitable fall will badly undercut Iran, which is already out of step with democratic impulses released by the Arab revolutions.

Iran: The Gravest Threat

No country has been more intertwined with Jewish history than Iran, and its predecessors, the Babylonian and Persian Empires, for almost 3000 years. So it is today. The Babylonians ruled much of the known world in the sixth century BCE, when they conquered Israel, destroyed the First Temple and the First Jewish Commonwealth in 586 BCE, and took the Jews in slavery to Babylon. The Persians conquered Babylonia, and Cyrus the Great freed the Jews and permitted them to return to Israel, rebuild the Temple and have a substantial amount of religious and political freedom. But a substantial percentage stayed in what became Persia, and created a continuous Jewish culture and presence. For many religious Jews the Babylonian Talmud remains more authoritative than the Jerusalem Talmud, At the birth of Israel's independence in 1948 there were between 100,000 to 150,000 Jews in Iran.

U.S. and Israeli history intersected in 1953, when the CIA engineered a coup against a popularly elected government and re-installed the Shah of Iran to his throne. The Shah protected the Jews of Iran and established close military relations with Israel. When the 1979 Iranian Revolution deposed the Shah and replaced him with the militant theocratic leadership of Ayatollah Khomeini and his followers, Israeli, American, and Jewish history abruptly and profoundly changed, and I was witness to it. Iranian Jews living in the U.S. came to see me in the Carter White House to plead for President Carter's intervention. By the tens of thousands, Jews fled Iran fearing for their lives, only to be turned back by U.S. Embassies in Europe.

This evoked the history of the Holocaust era, where the Roosevelt administration barred Jews struggling the escape Hitler's grasp from entering the United States. I was determined this would not be repeated. With the assistance of the President's White House counsel, Robert Lipshutz, we were able to get President Carter to create a new visa status to permit over 50,000 Iranian Jews, Christians, and members of the Baha'i faith to enter the U.S. as "temporary" visitors, but who would not be required to return to revolutionary Iran until the Shah was returned to his throne. Los Angeles has the largest contingent of Iranian Jews, while several thousand Jews still live in Iran.

Militant Iran has been a major problem for American and Israeli governments ever since. The hostage crisis helped defeat President Carter. The Iran-Contra Affair bedeviled President Reagan. The Iraq War under President George W. Bush led Iran to help militant Shiite clerics fight the American troops and their roadside bombs killed and wounded thousands of U.S. soldiers. And now, the Iranian nuclear program, begun as a civilian program under the Shah, along with Iran's support for terrorism, impacts both the Israeli government and the Obama administration.

Iran is the greatest security threat to Israel at multiple levels. It is the prime state sponsor of terrorism aimed at Israel. It provides a substantial amount of the budget of Hamas in Gaza, and sends thousands of missiles through Syria to Hezbollah in Lebanon, some of which have the range to strike deep in the heart of Israel. Iran also supplied the roadside bombs in Iraq, which killed and wounded thousands of American soldiers, and used its influence with radical Shiite parties to block an agreement with the Iraqi government for the long-term presence of American troops in Iraq, which would have also helped Israel by giving the U.S. foot soldiers close to Iran's borders. Moreover, Iran is intent on blocking any progress in the Middle East peace process, through its leverage with Hamas and Islamic Jihad.

But the gravest threat, which some in Israel call an existential threat, is that Iran would acquire a nuclear weapon, and given the professed desire of its President Mahmoud Ahmadinejad to wipe Israel from the face of the earth, might use it. A nuclear-armed Iran would have enormously negative effects on Israel, Arab states in the region, on the balance of power in the Middle East, and on the future of the nuclear non-proliferation regime.

Iran would be further emboldened to support terrorist groups against Israel and the U.S., or to take other radical actions like closing the Straits of Hormuz, through which a substantial part of the world's oil flows daily, knowing it had a nuclear umbrella to protect itself against retaliation. Iran would instantly become the strongest power in the region, next to Israel, tilting the balance of power even more unfavorably against the West and Israel than the Arab Spring has already done.

The Nuclear Non-Proliferation Treaty, already on tenuous grounds, would be fatally undermined. Arab states like Saudi Arabia and Egypt would press forward with nuclear weapons programs as a counterbalance. It could share its nuclear weapons capability with the terrorist groups it supports. Equally grave, if a state can ignore four UN Security Council sanction resolutions, withstand withering economic sanctions from the U.S. and EU, and still acquire nuclear weapons, the entire system of global governance of nuclear weapons, backed up by the International Atomic Energy Agency (IAEA), would be eviscerated.

The United States and Israel share similar goals with respect to Iran's nuclear program, and their positions were better coordinated as a result of the March 2012 Washington meeting between Prime Minister Netanyahu and President Obama. The President made it clear he does not support a containment policy, assuming Iran will acquire a nuclear weapon, but rather policy to prevent Iran from acquiring a nuclear weapon, in the last resort by military means. Still critically important differences remain. The stakes are so high that Iran could be the most divisive issue between the two allies in decades.

For one thing, there is a fundamental difference on the basic intelligence. Israel believes Iran has made a decision to acquire a nuclear weapon and is taking steps to make it a reality. But the consensus view of the sixteen U.S. intelligence agencies is that while Iran may be seeking to become "nuclear weapons capable," it has not yet made a decision to build a bomb. This has been consistently repeated in their 2007, 2010, and 2012 findings, backed-up by testimony from Secretary of Defense Leon Panetta, General Martin Dempsey, chairman of the Joint Chiefs of Staff, and director of national intelligence James Clapper.[13] The position of the U.S. intelligence agencies may be partly leaning over backward to avoid making the wrong call, as they catastrophically did in finding that Iraq's Sadaam Hussein had weapons of mass destruction.

The U.S. intelligence estimates are hard to square with steps the Iranians have taken that no country seeking only a civilian nuclear capacity would ever undertake—enriching uranium to higher levels that can be easily raised to weapons grade; burying centrifuges that enrich uranium deep underground to avoid an attack; consistently refusing to cooperate with the IAEA in answering basic questions about their program and opening up all their nuclear facilities to IAEA inspection; keeping secret their newest plant at Fordow, near Qum; acquiring materials used only for a nuclear weapon, and performing computer simulations of nuclear explosions; developing medium and long-range missiles capable of delivering a nuclear payload to Israel, the Persian Gulf, and as far away as Eastern Europe.

Indeed, there is an unprecedented situation in which a UN body, the IAEA, has gone further than the U.S. intelligence agencies in finding that Iran is taking actions consistent with a nuclear weapons program. Director General Yukiya Amano said blunt that his agency had "serious concerns regarding possible military dimensions to Iran's nuclear program."[14]

A second major difference between Israel and the U.S. over Iran's nuclear program is on the best way to derail it. The U.S. believes that economic sanctions, together with negotiations, can bring Iran to its senses, while Israel doubts they will work.

In fact, the sanctions now imposed on Iran are without precedent since World War II in their severity and breadth, and will be further enhanced when the EU stops purchasing oil from Iran on July 1, 2012. If the U.S. can persuade some of Iran's key Asian customers—China, India, South Korea, and Japan—to reduce or eliminate their purchases of Iranian oil, which Saudi Arabia has pledged to replace; if all Iranian banks can be expelled from the Brussels-based SWIFT data transmission system; and if the U.S. follows through on sanctions against the Central Bank of Iran, the pressure on Iran will be intensified.

Already sanctions have had a devastating economic impact, although they have not slowed down Iran's nuclear program: inflation if officially 20 percent is likely closer to 30 percent; unemployment is at double digit levels; the price of basic commodities has skyrocketed; and Iran's currency has lost 40 percent of its value compared to the dollar in unofficial markets.[15]

There are severe internal political divisions within Iran, between Supreme Leader Ayatollah Ruhollah Khamenei, President Ahmadinejad, and other prominent political leaders, within the Revolutionary Guard, and within the clerical establishment itself.[16]

Under pressure, Iran has agreed in early March 2012 to resume long-delayed negotiations under the auspices of the Five plus One formula (the five members of the UN Security Council and Germany). Iran announced at the same time that it was prepared to open a key military base to IAEA inspectors, if other agreements could be reached.[17] And Khamenei has said that nuclear weapons are a "sin" under Islamic law. They may be stalling for time while they continue to build-up more enriched uranium, and hope to forestall a military attack until they have safely. But this should become evident shortly, and if they are bluffing, will clear the way for more forceful actions.

The third difference, and the one that could trigger serious differences in the U.S.-Israel relationship between Israel, is how to determine the red-line and timing for military action. For Israel, the red line is when Iran becomes "nuclear capable"—when it has all the components for a nuclear weapon and can quickly put them together into a nuclear weapon when it wishes. For the U.S. the key is when Iran is actually putting the pieces together. This key difference is driven by several factors. For Israel, once in Defense Minister Ehud Barak's terms, Iran has achieved a "zone of immunity," by placing its centrifuges deep underground, Israel must act or lose the opportunity to do so. For Israel, with less sophisticated bunker-busting bombs and longer distances to reach targets in Iran, the timeline is the end of Spring 2012. For the U.S., with the most modern bunker-busting bombs and military assets closer to Iran, a military strike could be postponed for at least a year, to give the last round of sanctions a chance to work. There would be telltale signs if Iran crosses the line, since it will have to expel the IAEA inspectors, in order to reconfigure its centrifuges to enrich uranium to weapons grade.

The Obama administration has grave concerns about the fall-out from a military action, and wants to postpone it until all other measures have been tried. This is particularly the case when Israeli Defense Minister Barak has indicated that even a successful strike, which itself is problematic, would only set back Iran's program by some three years. The fall-out include a dramatic run-up of crude oil and gasoline prices, which could imperil the budding U.S. economic recovery; rally Arab support for Iran when it is now isolated and out-of-step with the democratic impulses of the Arab Spring; retaliate against Israel through its Hezbollah and Hamas surrogates, and against U.S. assets in the region; undercut the EU's sanctions efforts, which are far stronger than as a former U.S. Ambassador to the EU, I could have ever envisaged; and strengthen the Iranian regime at home, now struggling to maintain public support, particularly among the middle class.

President Obama has made it clear in his private meeting with Prime Minister Netanyahu and in public statements that he opposes Israel using military force at this time, although recognizing Israel has the right to defend itself. With all of the downsides, and while talks have now commenced, if Israel attacks Iran it would severely strain relations with the administration.

My view is that it is unacceptable and dangerous to the U.S., Europe, the region, and to Israel for a radical regime like Iran's to acquire nuclear weapons, and that the military option must remain on the table. But the fall-out from an attack, particularly from Israel, is so grave, that every option should be exhausted before exercising the military option. If every option short of military steps have failed, it would give greater credence to an eventual military attack.

There is one part of the Israeli equation that cannot be ignored, and that is the Holocaust component. Prime Minister Netanyahu is haunted by the notion of a second Holocaust in our era, this time a nuclear Holocaust from Iran. It is fine to point out that Iran's leaders would have to take leave of their senses to try to mount such an attack, which if it were successful, would kill hundreds of thousands of Palestinians, as well, and create a nuclear fallout over the whole region. But when the President of a country combines rhetoric to destroy Israel, and that is combined with a nuclear program which at the least seeks to be "nuclear capable," American policymakers must recognize the modern historical context. Hitler's threats against the Jews were ignored until it was too late, even by many Jews.

Israel should not feel that it must choose between its special relationship with its only ally and its own self-defense. For Israel not to attack, it must have what Amos Yadlin, former chief of Israeli military intelligence calls a "zone of trust," that the U.S. would act, if all else has failed. I believe that trust would be well placed.[18] To avoid having Iran cause a rift between Israel and the U.S. it is essential that policy be closely coordinated, with each side appreciating the national security interests of the other.

Even if the current crisis with Iran can be averted by a compromise on Iran's nuclear program, for the foreseeable future Iran, a large nation with an educated citizenry, a strong scientific, nuclear, and military capability, and a zealous, militant Islamic leadership, firmly entrenched by fear and force, will continue to seek regional hegemony, this must be forcefully met at every level by the United States, the Western and Asian democracies, and every country that benefits from global stability and growth.

Internal Challenges: The Diaspora

I believe the Jewish people and Israel can handle all external threats, In the Diaspora anti-Semitism has markedly declined and when it rears its head, is promptly condemned—although it will never be completely eradicated, as dramatized by a 2012 study by an official German government commission, showing 20 percent of Germans still harbor anti-Semitic beliefs, despite decades of education.[19]

The most profound challenge facing the Jewish people, and where I have the most concern, is not the ability to surmount external enemies but the ability to overcome internal challenges, threatening the fabric of the Jewish people through assimilation in the Diaspora, and sharp divisions within Israel about how its people see its future as a Jewish state—the need for Israel to be at peace with itself.

The period since the end of World War II has been unequaled in the long history of the Jewish Diaspora. There has never been a time in recorded Jewish history when Jews in the Diaspora were as free, were as protected, and have made the scope of contributions they are now making in every field of endeavor to their home countries and to the world—artistic, cultural, scientific, medical, legal, governmental, academic, business, finance, and philanthropy.

Jews have survived millennia of degradation, discrimination, marginalization, and violence. Jews in the Diaspora must now show they can survive and thrive with prosperity, full acceptance and integration into the broader community.

The Jewish community in the U.S., and in much of the Diaspora, is like a company with two divisions of equal weight, one healthy and thriving, the other bankrupt and threatening the future of the entire enterprise. There is a significant core of Diaspora Jews, roughly one-half of the total Jewish population, who are deeply involved in Jewish religious and secular life, devoted to the State of Israel, and committed to passing along their Jewish heritage to their children and grandchildren.

But the demographics of the Diaspora are disastrous in the United States and even more so in Europe and Latin America. The combination of birthrates far below the level necessary to have a stable population; intermarriage rates at 50 percent and climbing, with low levels of conversion by the non-Jewish spouse; and general disaffiliation creates a cloud over the future strength of the Diaspora.

For the first time in Jewish history, Jews outside of Israel will be Jews by choice. They must see Judaism as relevant to their lives, time-honored traditions as enriching and meaningful in a fast-moving Digital Era, and Jewish culture and religious practices as fulfilling. In the decades to follow, Diaspora Jews will have to run even faster to stay identified and relevant as the general population, particularly in the United States, continues to grow; must stress Jewish education, particularly full-time day school education; will have to urgently reach out to the peripherally identified Jews to keep them part of the Jewish community; and must make non-Jewish spouses feel completely accepted in Jewish institutions so that the children of mixed marriages are raised as Jews.

A recent report from the Brandeis University Steinhardt Social Research Institute offers some hope. Despite declining membership and funding for central Jewish institutions, like the federation movement, new startup organizations like Birthright Israel, are thriving; intermarried couples are being more successfully engaged; there has been an "explosion in the availability and quality of Jewish education"; and there may be as many as 6.5 million American, claiming Jewish identity or who are children of parents raising them as Jews- still a tiny percentage of the American public, but more than the 5 million generally assumed.[20]

Because Diaspora identity is so tightly bound-up with the State of Israel, the course that Israel follows in the decades ahead will have a powerful impact on the degree of Jewish identity in the Diaspora

Israel at Peace with Itself

The Jewish people throughout history have always exhibited sharp divisions over fundamental issues such as the role of Judaism in their lives, divisions sharpened by their dispersion to the four corners of the world and their absorption of the cultural traditions of the countries in which they sought refuge. The difference today is that those divisions are thrown together in a sovereign state, with Jews from diverse parts of the globe with starkly different perspectives, from which a consensus must be reached for the state to properly function. A common language, common experience in the army, common threats faced daily, pride in common artistic and scientific accomplishments, and a common commitment to defend the largest Jewish community in the world after millennia of suffering have provided the glue to hold this diverse Jewish population together. But now inescapable choices must be made that threaten the common fabric woven since 1948.

Israelis look outside their country and observe a great battle within the Muslim world. But Israel has its own deep divisions, less evident to the outside world, but very real and serious. More than sixty years after the creation of the state there is no internal consensus about borders, its relationship with its fellow Israeli Arab citizens, and its ultimate goals with regard to its Palestinian neighbors and the Arab nations of the region. Even the role of religion in the civil society of the Jewish state is a conundrum. The time has come when Israel will be required to provide answers to these questions; they can no longer be postponed.

In starkest terms, the question is whether a majority of Israelis, out of a combination of religious zealotry and legitimate security concerns, insist on a "Greater Israel" that encompasses most, if not all, of the West Bank. This would mean Israel will eventually find itself going it alone in contravention to the views of even friendly countries including the U.S.

I hope and believe Israel will be guided by different considerations—the many practical difficulties of controlling a large, hostile Palestinian population; the recognition that peace with the Palestinians would bolster moderate Arab states against their own radicals; and the realization of Israel's founding vision of a secure, democratic state with a Jewish majority. Achieving these cannot be accomplished without a willing and effective Palestinian partner, but Israel's own policy should not undermine the possibility that one day the right peace partner will emerge.

Polls have long shown that the overwhelming majority of Israelis would accept a two-state solution if it genuinely produced peace and security. One Israeli expert believes only about 15 percent of the Israeli public would reject any deal on religious or ideological grounds.[21] But the fractured Israeli political system of proportional representation and party lists rewards single-interest and splinter parties and gives that rejectionist minority a disproportionate voice in government. Ideology, animated by fervor and determination, often trumps pragmatism and compromise.

Especially troubling is the radicalization of a small, messianic segment of the settler movement that openly defies the authority of the government and the army, builds outposts illegal under Israel's own laws, torches mosques, burns the Koran, poisons Palestinian olive trees, and even attacks Israel's own soldiers protecting the vast majority of peaceful West Bank settlers.[22]

These zealots, and the mainstream settler movement, should remember that one of the most frequently emphasized portions of the Bible, stated repeatedly more than a dozen times, is the fair treatment of the *ger*, the "stranger," harking back to the time when Jews were mistreated as strangers in Egypt. Judges are admonished by Moses, in one of his last discourses, that when the Israelites enter the Promised Land, "Hear out your fellow man, and decide justly between any man and a fellow Israelite or a stranger."[23] Now that a major segment of Palestinian leadership is at last willing to live at peace with a Jewish state, it would be wise to reflect on ancient teachings. This is exactly what the Israeli Supreme Court has done in its decisions limiting the ability to take land on which Palestinians live.

As Israeli politics have shifted to the right after the unilateral Gaza withdrawal produced not peace but Hamas rockets, there has been an ideological change in the nation's most revered institution, the IDF. From its founding, a disproportionate percentage of its officer corps came from the generally liberal, secular kibbutz movement. In the past twenty years there has been an infusion of religious young people, some siding with the settler movement and even defending it in uniform. In respected brigades some soldiers speak darkly of refusing to remove West Bank settlers if ordered to do so by civil authorities, because of commands from their rabbis, although this bravado has yet to be tested. These questions must be settled by Israelis, here and now. They have every right to be skeptical of the Arabs' willingness to accept a Jewish state in the Middle East, but crucial decisions also rest with the Israelis, who must decide the size, shape, and character of their own Jewish state.

Another crucial decision must be made by the Jewish majority: How will it deal with its own Arab minority? Will the majority effectively conclude that Arab residents are a dangerous fifth column threatening Israel's security? Or will it agree to best efforts to provide equal services and integration into Israeli society? This is not an easy decision. In America it took a Civil War, almost eighty years after the creation of the United States, for African Americans to be freed from slavery, and another century after that to achieve basic civil rights of unencumbered voting and equal access to public accommodation and housing as a matter of law. Americans were dealing with a minority that was intensely loyal to the United States, had fought its wars in unequal circumstances, wanted nothing more than full equality as Americans, and achieved their goals by peaceful means and with a remarkable leader, Martin Luther King Jr., nowhere to be found in the Israeli Arab or Palestinian leadership. Israel faces a much more complex situation of divided loyalties that may intensify when pro-Palestinian sympathies find a concrete object in a Palestinian state.

A vast majority of Israeli Arabs want to remain within the State of Israel (although they do not want to accept it as a Jewish state), even if given the choice of eventually moving to a Palestinian state. Some Israeli Arabs openly supported their Palestinian brethren during the 2008–2009 Gaza War. Like the Palestinians, the Israeli Arabs commemorate what they call Nakba ("catastrophe") Day, a day of mourning marking the anniversary of Israeli independence while their Jewish neighbors are celebrating it. This is extraordinary conduct for the citizens of any state.

But the solution is not loyalty oaths to a Jewish state. Loyalty oaths ask more of the Israeli Arabs than the U.S. or most other countries ask of their citizens. Nor is their transfer to a Palestinian state remotely feasible or desirable. Rather, it is better to treat them as full partners in the Jewish state by improving their lot, delivering equal state services, and ending hiring and other informal methods of discrimination. A recent survey indicates they would respond positively, as nearly 53 percent of Israeli Arabs say they are proud to be Israelis.[24]

With all the stresses of daily life, external threats, and mounting political uncertainty among Israel's Arab neighbors, Israel's tolerance for internal dissent is precious to the character of the state, and to continued enthusiastic support from the Diaspora. Yet leaders of some of Israel's most prominent human rights groups are facing an increasingly hostile environment in their own country, as dissent from government policy is increasingly equated with opposing the state itself. Groups such as the Association for Civil Rights in Israel were sharply criticized for publishing *Breaking the Silence*, which includes accounts by anonymous Israeli soldiers of human rights violations during the Gaza War. Israeli demonstrators were detained for long periods after protesting the eviction of Palestinian families from East Jerusalem neighborhoods to allow Israelis to displace them. The New Israel Fund, which sends some $30 million a year to Israeli groups promoting democracy and Israeli Arab rights, was attacked by a nationalist group, Im Tirtzu (Theodor Herzl's famous statement, "If you will it, it is no dream"), on billboards portraying the fund's president, an ardent American Zionist named Naomi Chazan, with horns.[25] A vibrant civil society must be able to spread dissenting views, however unpopular, as a fundamental basis for democracy.

Bills introduced in the Knesset have sought to limit and tax foreign government funding of Israeli NGOs deemed "political"; punish calls for boycotts of products from Jewish settlements in the West Bank; and challenge investigative reporting by increasing compensation for inaccurate reporting on public figures. These types of measures should be opposed, as undemocratic.

All the twenty-first-century global forces will touch world Jewry and Israel— some simply for citizens of the world, others with particular resonance to Jews. But these challenges pale in comparison to decisions Israel must make about its own future. This is the essence of finally regaining sovereignty in a Jewish state after two thousand years of powerlessness in exile. The War of Independence and all those that followed were waged to preserve that sovereign right. But it is not absolute. In the twenty-first century, every nation's ability to exercise its sovereign authority is constrained by international norms and institutions as well as by global economic, military, and diplomatic realities. No state is totally free simply to act as it wishes, Israel included.

What sustains my optimism is history. Jews have survived under the most unimaginably difficult circumstances for three millennia. The resilience of the Jewish people has enabled them to endure calamities that would have long ago eliminated other peoples—the destruction of the symbols of sovereignty in the First (586 BCE) and Second (70 CE) Temples; repeated pogroms, expulsions, and massacres throughout Europe, culminating in the Shoah; and a state of war waged by most of the Arab world against the Third Jewish Commonwealth since its formation in 1948. Through all of this, the Jewish people have survived and thrived, while the empires that conquered, dispersed, or threatened us are in the dustbin of history.

In the twenty-first century, a Jewish state of Israel has become a major player on the world scene, raising its head unashamedly high among the nations. The modern State of Israel has enabled the Jewish people to emerge from the shadows of history; to cast aside centuries of living at the caprice of rulers and hostile populations; to serve as an example of democratic nation building; to become a center of the technologies that will be the keys to the twenty-first-century's prosperity and security. Young Israelis in generation after generation have proudly accepted mandatory military service with years thereafter of reserve duty (milium), often volunteering for the most dangerous brigades and assignments. Israel is better positioned than the great majority of countries to meet this century's global challenges directly and with optimism.

For all of the flaws in its political system, with multiple small parties, the Israeli government remains sensitive to public opinion. This has been shown most recently by the reaction to the social protests of the summer of 2011. The Netanyahu government promptly responded by establishing a blue ribbon commission headed by respected Tel Aviv University economist Manuel Trajtenberg, which proposed within eight weeks an $8 billion five-year program aimed at dealing with Israel's significant income inequalities, starting the construction of hundreds of thousands of apartments, increasing housing subsidies for the needy, increasing taxes on the wealthy, and supplying free public education for children beginning at age three. This would be financed by reductions in the defense budget. Prime Minister Netanyahu has embraced these recommendations. Few countries, democratic or autocratic, could have responded with such alacrity.

In just over six decades, Jews from scores of countries in every part of the world have fulfilled the Prophet Jeremiah's vision of reuniting exiles 2,500 years ago after the destruction of the First Temple: "I . . . will gather them from the uttermost parts of the world; the blind and lame among them; woman with child and woman in travail; a great company shall come back there."[26]

We live in an information age when a people's greatest asset is not their country's natural wealth but their own human resources. The words of the quintessential American author, the humorist Mark Twain, said at the end of the nineteenth century, apply today: "The Jews have the best average brain of any people in the world. The Jews are the only race who work wholly with their brains and never with their hands. . . . They are peculiarly and conspicuously the world's intellectual aristocracy."[27]

The Jewish people and the State of Israel will overcome actual threats and internal challenges, but Jewish destiny demands Jewish unity and Jewish identification. The Jewish people must now deal with the challenges within.

Three things enabled the Jewish people not only to survive but also to thrive during the millennia of wandering. One was a deep, abiding attachment to the Holy Land; even when dispersed to the four corners of the globe, Jews maintained their unbroken longing to return, even under the most trying circumstances. Second was an attachment to the Torah of Moses, the Mishnah of the third century of our era and the Talmud in the sixth and seventh centuries, and the Jewish traditions and holiday celebrations that flowed from it. And third is an almost mystical sense of peoplehood, a spirit that attaches Jews to each other in whatever place or circumstance they meet.

It is the common responsibility of the Jewish people to ensure that the fierce and challenging global forces of the new century strengthen, not weaken, the State of Israel, Jewish religious and cultural traditions, and the unique sense of Jewish peoplehood. All have taken the Jewish people through an unbroken history of three millennia, and will propel world Jewry forward in the twenty-first century and thereafter.

Notes

Chapter 1

1. Francis Fukuyama, "The End of History?," *The National Interest*, 1989; quote from his 1992 book, *The End of History and the Last Mind*.

2. National Intelligence Council, *Global Trends 2025: A Transformed World*, NIC, 2008.

3. Richard Haass, "The Age of Non-Polarity," *Foreign Affairs*, May/June 2008.

4. David Franklin, "The World in 2010," *The Economist*, January 2010.

5. Alcatel-Lucent Presentation, February 3, 2009.

6. Tony Hayward, group president BP, World Economic Forum, Davos, Switzerland, January 28, 2010.

7. Remarks of Ilham Aliyev, President of Azerbaijan, World Economic Forum, January 28, 2010, Davos, Switzerland.

8. Paul Kedrosky, *Bloomberg*, October 24, 2010, based on 2010 IMF World Economic Outlook.

9. Speech by David Rubenstein, co-founder of The Carlyle Group, World Economic Forum, January 27, 2011, Davos, Switzerland.

10. Walter Russell Mead, *God and Gold: Britain, America, and the Making of the Modern World*, New York: Knopf, 2007.

11. Samuel Berg, "Obama Doctrine: Vol. 1," *Washington Post*, May 30, 2010.

12. World Bank World Development Report 2010, "Development and Climate Change."

13. "Energy in the Developing World: Power to the People," *The Economist*, September 4, 2010.

14. "Special Report on China," *The Economist*, June 25, 2011.

15. Stephen Green, chairman of HSBC Bank, *The Economist*, The World in 2010, January 2010.

16. Report of World Steel Association, *New York Times*, February 7, 2010.

17. Blain Harden, "A Crisis Looms as Economy Slowly Melts," *Washington Post*, February 4, 2010.

18. Editorial, "Back in Business," *Washington Post*, May 11, 2011.

19. Ted C. Fishman, "Graying Nation, Shifting Powers," *International Herald Tribune*, October 16–17, 2010.

20. Conversation with William Johnson, CEO of H.J. Heinz, Atlanta, Georgia, November 3, 2010.

21. David Barboza, "China's Sprint for the Gold," *New York Times*, November 15, 2009.

22. Xu Kuangdi, Presentation at the United Parcel Service Board Meeting, Shanghai, August 2008.

23. Robert Hormats, under secretary of state for economic, energy, and agricultural affairs, speech at the World Economic Forum, Davos, Switzerland, January 28, 2010.

24. Arian Eunjung Cha, "Chinese Banks Find Their Credit in High Demand," *Washington Post*, January 2, 2010.

25. David Barboza, "Blackstone's Deal Is a Nod to China's Currency and New Wealth," *New York Times*, November 10, 2009.

26. Liz Alderman, "China Looks to Europe for Deals and Friends," *New York Times*, November 2, 2010.

27. This group includes Brunei, Burma, Cambodia, Indonesia, Laos, Malaysia, Philippines, Singapore, Thailand, and Vietnam.

28. Ariana Eunjung Cha, "Taiwan, China Negotiating a Landmark Free Trade Agreement," *Washington Post*, February 21, 2009.

29. Michael Wines, "Australia Nourishing China's Economic Engine," *New York Times*, June 3, 2009.

30. Andrew E. Kramer, "New Natural Gas Pipeline from Central Asia Feeds China," *New York Times*, December 15, 2009.

31. China Statistics, *China Today*.

32. Keith Bradsher, "Chinese Firms Take Commanding Lead in Production of Renewable Energy," *International Herald Tribune*, February 1, 2010.

33. Asia Society report, cited in Richard McGregor, "Chinese Poised to Amass Over $1,000bn of Foreign Assets," *Financial Times*, May 5, 2011.

34. President Hu, quoted in "A Special Report on China and America," *The Economist*, October 24, 2009.

35. Sam Dillon, "Foreign Languages Fade in Class—Except Chinese," *New York Times*, January 21, 2010.

36. John Pomfret, "As China Rises, so Does Its Influence on the Hill," *Washington Post*, January 9, 2010.

37. Andrew Higgins, "China Showcasing Its Softer Side," *Washington Post*, December 2, 2009.

38. "Special Report on China," *The Economist*, June 25, 2011.

39. Robert J. Samuelson, "China's $2.4 Trillion Slush Fund," *Washington Post*, January 25, 2010.

40. Keith Bradsher, "China Benefits as U.S. Solar Industry Withers," *New York Times*, September 2, 2011.

41. See, for example, C. Fred Bergsten, "A Partnership of Equals," *Foreign Affairs*, July/August, 2008, pages 57–69.

42. "Facing Up to China," *The Economist*, February 6, 2010.

43. China Watch, *China Daily*, March 25, 2011.

44. Yu Bin, director general of macroeconomic research for the State Council's research center, quoted in Keith B. Richburg, "China Says Its Era of Rapid Growth Is Over," *Washington Post*, December 16, 2011.

45. Professor Jeffrey Wasserstrom, University of California, Irvine, at the John Fisher Zeidman Lecture, Washington, D.C., March 25, 2011.

46. Michael Wines and Sharon LaFraniere, "New Census Finds China's Population Growth Has Slowed," *New York Times*, April 29, 2011.

47. Barbara Beck, "Peak Labour," *The Economist*, The World in 2010, January 2010.

48. Michael Wines and Sharon LaFraniere, "New Census Finds China's Population Growth Has Slowed," *New York Times*, April 29, 2011.

49. "Special Report on China," *The Economist*, June 25, 2011.

50. Sharon LaFraniere and Michael Wines, "Protest Over Chemical Plant Shows Greater Pressure on China from Citizens," *New York Times*, August 16, 2011.

51. Keith B. Richburg, "China Says Its Era of Rapid Growth Is Over," *Washington Post*, December 16, 2011.

52. Editorial, "What Do China's Workers Want?" *New York Times*, June 13, 2010.

53. "Beyond a Boom," *Newsweek*, June 20, 2010.

54. Andrew Jacobs, "Village Revolts Over Inequities of Chinese Life," *New York Times*, December 15, 2011.

55. Mark Landler and Edward Wong, "China Says Clinton Harms Relations with Criticism of Internet Censorship," *New York Times*, January 23, 2010.

56. Edward Wong, "After a 10-Month Ban, Western China Is Online," *New York Times*, May 15, 2010.

57. Katherine Halle and Geoff Dyson, "Veterans Urge End to China Censorship," *Financial Times*, October 13, 2010.

58. Keith B. Richburg, "China Tightens Control of Microblogs," *Washington Post*, October 5, 2011.

59. Andrew Jacobs, "Beijing Tells Cafes to Track Clients Who Surf Internet," *International Herald Tribune*, July 26, 2011.

60. Editorial, "China and the W.T.O." *New York Times*, August 14, 2009.

61. Pam Woodall, "The Dragon Still Roars," *The Economist*, The World in 2010, January 2010.

62. Anand Giridharadas, "Time Warps in the Climate Clash," *New York Times*, December 20, 2009.

63. See *The Economist*, "China Buys Up the World" and "Being Eaten by the Dragon," November 13, 2010.

64. Michael Wines and Sharon LaFraniere, "New Census Finds China's Population Growth Has Slowed," *New York Times*, April 29, 2011.

65. *The Economist*, "Special Report on China," June 25, 2011.

66. Ariana Eunjung Cha, "In China, Despair Mounting Among Migrant Workers," *Washington Post*, March 4, 2009.

67. John Pomfret, "In Historic Turn, Vietnam Casts China as Opponent," *Washington Post*, October 30, 2010.

68. Speech by Minister Mentor Lee Kuan Yew at the U.S.-ASEAN Business Council, Washington, D.C., October 27, 2009.

69. Jackie Calmes, "President Hits His Stride on Foreign, but Familiar, Territory," *New York Times*, November 21, 2011.

70. President Obama's remarks, October 12, 2011, Honolulu, Hawaii.

71. Jim Yardley, "China Intensifies Tug of War with India Over Nepal, with Tibet in the Shadows," *New York Times*, February 18, 2010.

72. James Lamont and Geoff Dyer, "Indians Offer to Help China Shipping," *Financial Times*, February 18, 2010.

73. Mark Landler and Michael Wines, "As China Rises Wary Neighbors Form Alliances," *New York Times*, October 31, 2010.

74. Howard Schneider, "U.S. Grain Helps Put Meat on Chinese Plates," *Washington Post*, May 23, 2011.

75. Keith B. Richburg, "In China, Biden Seeks Closer Economic Ties," *Washington Post*, August 19, 2011.

76. Mike Mullen, "A Step Toward Trust with China," *International Herald Tribune*, July 27, 2011.

77. Yan Xuetong, "How China Can Defeat America," *New York Times*, November 21, 2011.

78. Simon Cox, "An Imperfect Storm," *The Economist*, The World in 2010, January 2010.

79. Thomas L. Friedman, "Do Believe the Hype," *New York Times*, November 3, 2010.

80. Simon Cox, "An Imperfect Storm," *The Economist*, The World in 2010, January 2010.

81. Emily Wax, "India's Space Ambitions Take Off," *Washington Post*, November 4, 2009.

82. Conversation with Kanwal Sibal, former foreign secretary of India, Marrakesh, Morocco, October 17, 2010.

83. Anand Giridharadas, "Land of Gandhi Asserts Itself as a Global Military Power," *New York Times*, September 22, 2008, page A9.

84. "US, India Agree to Widen Ties, Ease Defense Sales," *Associated Press*, July 20, 2009.

85. Glenn Kessler, "US, India Set Up Strategic Dialogue," *Washington Post*, July 21, 2009.

86. Jim Yardley, "Anna Hazare Ends Hunger Strike as Indian Parliament Agrees to His Demands," *New York Times*, August 27, 2011.

87. Alexei Barrionuevo, "Brazil's New Leader Starts in Shadow of Predecessor," *New York Times*, January 1, 2011.

88. Alexei Barrionuevo, "Latin America Shows Its Collective Strategy," *International Herald Tribune*, December 18, 2008; Andrew Grace, "Financial Crisis 'Caused by White Men with Blue Eyes,'" *Independent* (London), March 27, 2009.

89. Mark Landler, "US Drops Bid to Sway Israel on Settlements," *New York Times*, December 8, 2010.

90. Quoted in Leon Aron, "Vladimir Putin Plans His Return," *Washington Post*, October 16, 2010.

91. Speech on March 8, 2010, to Veracity Worldwide in New York City.

92. Ethan Bronner, "Sarkozy Said to Have Called for Replacing Israeli Foreign Minister," *New York Times*, July 1, 2009.

93. Allan Brownfeld, "American Jewish Leaders Accused of Silence in the Face of Growing Racism in Israel," *Washington Report on Middle East Affairs*, May/June 2009, page 54.

94. John Efron, Steven Weitzman, Matthias Lehmann, and Joshua Holo, *The Jews: A History*, 2009, chapter 10, pages 255–256.

95. Ellen Berry, "President Medvedev of Russia Dismisses Georgia's Leader as a Political Corpse," *New York Times*, September 3, 2008.

96. Steve Erlanger, "NATO Acts to Resume Its Relations with Russia," *New York Times*, January 20, 2009.

97. Judy Dempsey, "Despite Crises, Germany Sees Russia as a Land of Opportunity," *New York Times*, October 25, 2008.

98. See, generally, Peter Baker, "US Sees Much to Fear in a Hostile Russia," *New York Times*, August 22, 2008.

99. Peter Fedynsky, "Cheap Oil May Spark Russian Budget Crisis," *Voice of America*, December 15, 2008.

100. Joe Nocera, "Guilty Verdict for a Tycoon and Russia," *New York Times*, January 2, 2011.

101. See, for example, Thom Shanker, "Gas Cut by Kremlin Highlights US Concern Over Russian Intentions," *New York Times*, January 9, 2009.

102. Strobe Talbott, "A Russian 'Reset Button' Based on Inclusion," *Financial Times*, February 24, 2009.

103. Fareed Zakaria, "Levers on Moscow," *Washington Post*, September 1, 2008.

104. Michael Schwirtz, "Parliament Speaker, Ally of Putin, Resigns from Post," *New York Times*, December 18, 2011.

105. Kathy Lally and Will Englund, "In Today's Russia, Democracy Yields to Bureaucracy," *Washington Post*, August 19, 2011.

106. Winston Churchill, BBC Broadcast, London, October 1, 1939.

107. Briefing. "Who Runs the World?" *The Economist*, July 5, 2008, page 8.

108. Seth Mydans, "Inflation Delivers a Blow to Vietnam's Spirits," *New York Times*, August 24, 2009.

109. U.S. Census Bureau, International Statistics.

110. Neil MacFarquhar and Ethan Bronner, "U.N. Faults Israel on Flotilla Raid, not on Blockade," *New York Times*, September 2, 2011.

111. "G-7 Will Be Overtaken by Emerging Economies in 2032, PriceWaterhouse Says," www .bloomberg.com/news/2011-01-07/g-7-economy-will-be-overtaken-by-emerging-markets-in-two -decades-pwc-says.html.

112. Ministry of Foreign Affairs, "Japan-Israel Relations," 2010.

113. Michael Schuman, "Why Detroit Is Not Too Big to Fail," *Time*, December 19, 2008; see also Paul Krugman, *The Return of Depression Economics and the Crisis of 2008*, New York: Norton, 2009.

114. Hugh Pym, BBC News, "Japan: Debt, Demographics and Deflation," November 30, 2010.

115. "Japan's Demographic Time Bomb," *Bangkok Post*, July 25, 2011.

116. Hugh Pym, BBC News, "Japan: Debt, Demographics and Deflation," November 30, 2010.

117. Charles Sizemore, "Japan's Demographic Challenge," March 22, 2009, with comment by H.S. Dent, June 5, 2009, www.marketskeptics.com/2009/06.

118. Eurostat data, 2011.

119. UN Department of Environment and Social Affairs, World Population Project, "Demographics of Europe," October 12, 2011.

120. Official statement of the delegation of the EU to Israel.

121. European Commission, Directorate General for Trade; IMF, World Economic and Financial Survey, "Navigating Stormy Waters," October 2011.

122. Gail Collins, "Waiting for Somebody," *New York Times*, September 30, 2010.

123. Poll cited in Joel Achenbach, "An Alarm Bell for an America in Decline?" *Washington Post*, August 11, 2011.

124. David Broder, "New Task for a Budget Straight Talker," *Washington Post*, March 16, 2008.

125. Quoted in David E. Sanger, "A Red-Ink Decade," *New York Times*, February 2, 2010.

126. Ian Bremmer, "State Capitalism Comes of Age," *Foreign Affairs*, May/June 2009.

127. David Pilling and Ralph Atkins, "A Quest for Other Ways," *Financial Times*, March 16, 2009.

128. David Pilling and Ralph Atkins, "A Quest for Other Ways," *Financial Times*, March 16, 2009.

129. Michel E. Porter and Mark R. Kramer, "Shared Value," *Harvard Business Review*, January/ February 2011.

130. The Coca-Cola Company, "Our Commitment to Making a Positive Difference in the World," 2009/2010 Sustainability Review.

131. Howard Schneider and Mary Beth Sheridan, "U.S., China Complete 'Milestone' Agreement," *Washington Post*, May 11, 2011.

132. David Barboza, "China Urges New Reserve to Replace the Dollar," *New York Times*, March 24, 2009.

133. Michael Wines, "China Leader Asks US to Guarantee Debt Holding," *New York Times*, March 14, 2009.

134. Lally Weymouth Interview of Noriel Roubini, "I Am Not Dr. Doom," *Washington Post*, April 27, 2009.

135. Sebastian Mallaby, "Beijing's Would-Be Houdinis," *Washington Post*, May 26, 2009.

136. Sebastian Mallaby, "Beijing's Would-Be Houdinis," *Washington Post*, May 26, 2009.

137. Shai Oster, "Malaysia, China, Consider Ending Trade in Dollars," *Wall Street Journal*, June 4, 2009.

138. See also "Crying for Freedom," *The Economist*, January 14, 2010, reporting on the Freedom House report.

139. "Crying for Freedom," *The Economist*, January 14, 2010.

140. Kathrin Hille, "Chinese Missile Tilts Power in the Pacific," *Financial Times*, December 29, 2010.

141. FT.com, December 28, 2010.

142. Michael Wines and Edward Wong, "China's Push on Military Is Beginning to Bear Fruit," *New York Times*, January 6, 2011.

143. NPR Report, January 6, 2011.

144. Elisabeth Bumiller, "U.S. Official Warns about China's Military Buildup," *New York Times*, August 25, 2011.

145. William Wan, "China Tests Its First Aircraft Carrier," *Washington Post*, August 11, 2011.

146. Piers Brendon, "Like Rome Before the Fall? Not Yet," *New York Times*, February 25, 2010.

147. Editorial, "Back in Business," *Washington Post*, May 11, 2011.

148. Schumpeter, "Declining by Degree," *The Economist*, September 4, 2010.

149. McKinsey Global Institute, "Growth and Renewal in the United States: Retooling America's Economic Engine," February 2011.

150. See the Israel Democracy Institute, Policy Paper Number 49, 2004, by Avi Ben-Bassat and Momi Dahan.

151. International Energy Agency, "2011 Key World Energy Statistics," citing 2009 data.

152. Michael Wines, "China Takes a Loss to Get Ahead in the Business of Fresh Water," *New York Times*, October 26, 2011.

153. Conversation with Kanwal Sibal, former foreign secretary of India, Marrakesh, Morocco, October 17, 2010.

Chapter 2

1. Nick Bunkley and David Jolly, "Disruptions Spread in Global Carmaking," *New York Times*, March 25, 2011.

2. Pascal Lamy, director general of the World Trade Organization, World Economic Forum, Davos, Switzerland, January 29, 2011.

3. Ethan Bronner, "Issues Stand Before Israel in Joining Elite Group," *New York Times*, January 20, 2010.

4. See Katie Hafner, "Paul Baran, Internet Pioneer, Dies at 84," *New York Times*, March 28, 2011; Wikipedia, "Digital Revolution"; Wikipedia, "Information Age."

5. John Markoff, "To Enhance Chip Speed, Intel Enters 3rd Dimension," *New York Times*, May 5, 2011.

6. Kevin Johnson, CEO, Juniper Networks, World Economic Forum, Davos, Switzerland, January 26, 2011.

7. National Cable & Telecommunications Association, "History of Cable Television," NCTA.com.

8. Paul Vitello, "Lead Us to Tweet, and Forgive the Trespassers," *New York Times*, July 5, 2009.

9. Michael Schwartz, "Tale of Botched Traffic Operation Increases Russians' Mistrust of Moscow Police," *New York Times*, March 11, 2010.

10. Keith B.Richburg, "Chinese Scandals Raise Public Ire," *Washington Post*, January 1, 2011.

11. Anand Giridharadas, "Africa's Gift to Silicon Valley: How to Track a Crisis," *New York Times*, March 14, 2010.

12. World Economic Forum Annual Meeting 2010, "Redesigning with Technology Pioneers," January 28, 2010, Davos, Switzerland.

13. William J. Broad, "Laser Advances Raise Fears of Terrorist Nuclear Ability," *New York Times*, August 21, 2011.

14. Peter Finn and Mary Beth Sheridan, "Package Bombs Linked to al-Qaeda," *Washington Post*, October 31, 2010.

15. Matt Richtel, "Egypt Halts Most Internet and Cell Services, and Scale of Shutdown Surprises Experts," *New York Times*, January 29, 2011.

16. Joby Warrick, "Iran Said to Be Aiding Syrian Crackdown," *Washington Post*, May 29, 2011.

17. I have drawn heavily from an excellent article by Mary Beth Sheridan, "Autocratic Regimes Take Fight to Cyberspace," *Washington Post*, May 22, 2011.

18. Nick Bilton, "Phony Virus Protector Found to Infect Macs," *International Herald Tribune*, May 27, 2011.

19. World Economic Forum 2010, "The Information Age and Human Behavior I and II," January 28, 2010.

20. Jan Hoffman, "A Girl's Nude Photo, and Altered Lives," *New York Times*, March 26, 2011; Jan Hoffman, "States Struggle with Minors' Sexting," *New York Times*, March 26, 2011; Tamar Lewin, "Rethinking Sex Offender Laws for Youth Sexting," *New York Times*, March 20, 2011.

21. Wikipedia, "Wikileaks."

22. Noam Cohen and Brian Stelter, "Airstrike Video Brings Notice to a Web Site," *New York Times*, April 7, 2010.

23. Bob Herbert, "Losing Our Way," *New York Times*, March 26, 2011.

24. World Economic Forum Annual Meeting 2010, "Who Is the New Consumer?" Davos, Switzerland, January 27, 2010.

25. Sam Dillon, "Many Countries Pass US on Education, Global Expert Says," *International Herald Tribune*, March 11, 2010, citing a study by Andreas Scheicher of the OECD.

26. Jeffrey Garten, "The Dangers of Turning Inward," *Wall Street Journal*, February 28, 2009.

27. Nelson D. Schwartz, "Unemployment Surges Around the World, Threatening Stability," *New York Times*, February 15, 2009.

28. Martin Fackler, "In Japan, a Robust Yen Undermines the Markets," *New York Times*, October 28, 2008.

29. Joby Warrick, "CIA Adds Economy to Threat Update," *Washington Post*, February 26, 2009.

30. Jeffrey Garten, "The Dangers of Turning Inward," *Wall Street Journal*, March 2, 2009.

31. Jeffrey Garten, "The Dangers of Turning Inward," *Wall Street Journal*, March 2, 2009.

32. Philip Stephens, "The World Confronts a Choice Between Chaos and Order," *Financial Times*, November 20, 2008.

33. United Nations, "Peacekeeping Fact Sheet," November 30, 2011, www.un.org/en.

34. Joby Warrick, "Assad's Chemical Arsenal Stirs Fear," *Washington Post*, August 29, 2011.

35. Philip Stephens, "India Faces a Choice: Is It a Big Power or a Giant Power?" *Financial Times*, March 20, 2009.

36. "Gloom, but Not Doom," *New York Times*, December 4, 2008 (citing *Global Trends 2025*).

37. Amitai Etzioni, "Tomorrow's Institutions Today," *Foreign Affairs*, May/June, 2009.

38. Arab Human Development Report 2009, "Challenges to Human Security in the Arab Countries," United Nations Development Programme, Regional Bureaus for Arab States.

39. "Special Report: The Arab World," *The Economist*, July 25, 2009.

40. See Jacob Berkman, "Madoff Scandal Rocks Jewish Philanthropic World," *Jewish Journal*, December 16, 2008.

41. Wikipedia, "United Nations Commission on Human Rights."

42. Stella Korin-Lieber, "Braverman: Globalization Greatest Danger not Iran," *Israel Business Arena*, January 21, 2008.

43. Moti Bassok, "Income Gaps in Israel Higher Than in any EU Country," *Haaretz*, October 18, 2010 (citing a 2010 report from Israel's Central Bureau of Statistics); according to Israel's Central Bureau of Statistics, average per capita income after taxes among Israel's top 20 percent of earners is 7.5 times the bottom 20 percent; the average gap in the EU is 4.9 times.

44. National Insurance Institute Report, November 2009, reported in *The Jerusalem Report*, December 7, 2009.

45. Dan Senor and Saul Singer, "Start-Up Nation: The Story of Israel's Economic Miracle," Council on Foreign Relations, 2009.

46. See Taglit-Birthright Israel, "Did You Know? 62 Facts About Israel," a compilation of 62 facts about Israel on Israel's 62nd anniversary as a country, 2010.

47. Amnon Rubenstein, "Red Tape Mania: Worse Than the Arab Boycott," *Jerusalem Post*, January 30, 2008.

48. Amnon Rubenstein, "Red Tape Mania: Worse Than the Arab Boycott," *Jerusalem Post*, January 30, 2008.

Chapter 3

1. John Efron, Steven Weitzman, Matthias Lehmann, Joshua Holo, *The Jews: A History*, Upper Saddle River, NJ: Pearson, 2009; see chapter Six, "Under the Crescent," page 120.

2. Susilo Bambang Yudhoyono, president of Indonesia, World Economic Forum, Davos, Switzerland, January 27, 2011.

3. Barry Merkin, "Population Levels, Trends and Policies in the Arab Region: Challenges and Opportunities," Arab Human Development Report, United Nations Development Program, 2010.

4. U.S. Code Congressional and Administrative News, 98th Congress, Second Session, 1984, October 19, vol. 2, par. 3077, 98 STAT. 2707.

5. Jewish Virtual Library, "Fedayeen."

6. Wikipedia, "Munich Massacre"; Mitchell Bard, "The Munich Massacre," Jewish Virtual Library.

7. BBC on This Day, "1984: U.S. Embassy Blast Kills 20."

8. See Jo Becker, "Beirut Bank Seen as a Hub of Hezbollah's Financing," *New York Times*, December 14, 2011.

9. Wikipedia, "Hamas," extensive sources.

10. Wikipedia, "al-Qaeda."

11. See Bill Roggio and Alexander Mayer, "Senior al Qaeda and Taliban Leaders Killed in U.S. Airstrikes in Pakistan, 2004–2011," The Long War Journal, updated on November 17, 2011; Pam Benson, "U.S. Official: Al Qaeda's Number 2 Has Been Killed," CNN, August 27, 2011.

12. Briefing by UPS officials at UPS Board Meeting following the discovery on October 29, 2010, of a bomb on a UPS cargo plane originating in Yemen and found in East Midlands Airport, UK, October, 2010; Vikram Dodd, Richard Norton-Taylor, and Paul Harris, *The Guardian*, November 20, 2010.

13. Eric Schmitt and Thom Shanker, "Al Qaeda Trying to Harness Toxin for Bombs, U.S. Officials Fear," *New York Times*, August 13, 2011.

14. Al Jazeera blog, 2011.

15. "On the Brink: Weak States and U.S. National Security," A Report of the Commission on Weak States and U.S. National Security, Sponsored by the Center for Global Development, Stuart E. Eizenstat and John Edward Porter, cochairs, Jeremy M. Weinstein, project director.

16. See Saad Eddin Ibrahim, "An Outreach to Muslims," *Washington Post*, December 20, 2008.

17. Susilo Bambang Yudhoyono, president of Indonesia, World Economic Forum, Davos, Switzerland, January 27, 2011.

18. Kareem Fahim, "Syria's Solidarity with Islamists Ends at Home," *New York Times*, September 4, 2010.

19. See Wikipedia, "The Clash of Civilizations."

20. James Blitz, "FT Poll Shows Support for Burka Ban," *Financial Times*, March 2, 2010.

21. Matthew Weaver, "Angela Merkel: German Multiculturalism Has 'Utterly Failed,'" *The Guardian*, October 17, 2010.

22. Enayat Najafizada and Rod Norland, "Afghans Avenge Koran Burning; Protest Kills 12," *New York Times*, April 2, 2011; Lizette Alvarez and Don Van Natta, Jr., "Pastor Who Burned Koran Seeks Retribution for Deaths," *New York Times*, April 2, 2011.

23. David Ignatius, "A Short Fuse in Pakistan," *Washington Post*, April 10, 2009.

24. Scott Shane, "In Pakistan, Standing Up to Extremists," *Washington Post*, March 6, 2011.

25. Jane Perlez, "For Pakistan, Attack Exposes Security Flaws," *New York Times*, March 4, 2009; see also, Jane Perlez and Pir Zubair Shah, "Porous Pakistan Border Could Hinder US," *New York Times*, May 4, 2009.

26. Sabrina Tavernise, "Pakistan's Islamic Schools Fill Void, Fuel Militancy," *New York Times*, May 3, 2009.

27. Pamela Constable, "Splintered Taliban Thwarts Afghan Peace," *Washington Post*, April 3, 2009, page A8.

28. Peter Behr, Helene Cooper, and Mark Mazzetti, May 1, 2011.

29. Griff Witte, "Being Pro-U.S. in Pakistan Is a Dangerous Proposition," *Washington Post*, June 25, 2011.

30. Jane Perlez, "Pakistan Pulls Closer to a Reluctant China," *New York Times*, October 6, 2011.

31. Carlotta Gall, "Pakistan Faces a Divide of Age on Muslim Law," *New York Times*, January 11, 2011.

32. Jim Hoagland, "Behind the Afghan Strategy," *Washington Post*, March 22, 2009.

33. "Taliban Proposes Holding Talks with the U.S. in Qatar," *Washington Post*, January 4, 2012.

34. Karen DeYoung and Peter Finn, "Karzai Supports U.S.-Taliban Talks," *Washington Post*, January 5, 2012.

35. Karen Bruilliard and Haq Nawaz Khan, "Militant Groups in Pakistan Unite," *Washington Post*, January 4, 2012.

36. Karen Bruilliard and Haq Nawaz Khan, "Pakistan's Tribal-Belt Initiative Lauded," *Washington Post*, August 18, 2011.

37. David Ignatius, "Listening in Kabul," *Washington Post*, April 7, 2009; Jim Hoagland, "Behind the Afghan Strategy," *Washington Post*, March 22, 2009.

38. Cited in Helene Cooper, "Dreaming of Splitting the Taliban," *New York Times*, March 8, 2009.

39. Henry A. Kissinger, "How to Exit Afghanistan," *Washington Post*, June 8, 2011.

40. Michael Slackman, "Hard Line Force Extends Grip Over Splintered Iran," *New York Times*, July 20, 2009.

41. Robert Worth, "In Iran, Harsh Talk as Election Nears," *New York Times*, June 7, 2009.

42. Farnaz Fassihi, "Iranians Stage Major Demonstrations," *Wall Street Journal*, November 5, 2009.

43. Thomas Erdbrink, "Iran Election in Dispute as 2 Candidates Claim Victory," *Washington Post*, June 3, 2009.

44. Clifford Krauss, "Iran's President to Lead Next OPEC Meeting," *New York Times*, May 20, 2011.

45. Neil MacFarquhar, "Iranian Calls Israel Racist at Meeting in Geneva," *New York Times*, April 21, 2009, page A4.

46. Ernesto Londono, "Iran Looks to Foil U.S. Deal with Afghans," *Washington Post*, January 5, 2012.

47. Thomas Erdbrink and Joby Warrick, "Iran Fears the Worst as West Steps Up Pressure," *Washington Post*, January 5, 2012.

48. Joby Warrick and Steven Mufson, "Iranian Warning Aimed at U.S. Ships," *Washington Post*, January 4, 2012; Thomas Erdbrink, "Iran Seeks to Bar Foreign Ships from Gulf," *Washington Post*, January 5, 2012.

49. Joby Warrick, "Iran Seeks Closer Ties in Latin America," *Washington Post*, January 2, 2012.

50. Jack Healy and Michael S. Schmidt, "Iraqi Insurgents Take Up Politics, Raising Tensions," *New York Times*, January 6, 2012.

51. Vincent Romani, Crown Center for Middle East Studies, Brandeis University, 2010.

52. NPR report, November 22, 2010.

53. Donna Abu-Nasr, "Saudi King to Attend UN Interfaith Dialogue," *Associated Press*, October 26, 2008.

54. Catherine Lyons, "Saudi Prince Nayef Named as Successor," *Global Post*, October 28, 2011.

55. Tim Arango, "Iraq Crushing Youths' Efforts to Be Heard," *New York Times*, April 14, 2011.

56. Joel Greenberg, "Motorcade of Jordan's King Said to Be Attacked," *Washington Post*, June 14, 2011.

57. Tom Perry, "Latest Egypt Vote Brings Islamists Closer to Win," Reuters, January 6, 2012.

58. Conversation of January 6, 2012, with Mostafa Terrab, CEO of OCP; remarks of Moroccan Prime Minister Abdelilah Benkirane, World Economic Forum, January 26, 2012, Davos, Switzerland.

59. Anthony Shadid, "A Veteran Islamist Imagines a Democratic Future for the New Tunisia," *New York Times*, October 20, 2011.

60. Ethan Bronner, "Threat by Turkish Premier Raises Tensions with Israel," *New York Times*, September 10, 2011.

61. Craig Whitlock, "U.S.-Turkey Deal Paves Way for Radar Near Iran," *Washington Post*, September 15, 2011.

62. Dan Bilefsky and Sebnem Arsu, "Turkey's Glow Dims as Press Faces Charges," *New York Times*, January 5, 2012.

63. Neil MacFarquhar, "Radicals' Turn to Democracy Alarms Egypt," *New York Times*, April 2, 2011.

64. Ali Gomaa, "In Egypt's Democracy, Room for Islam," *New York Times*, April 2, 2011.

65. David D. Kirkpatrick and Heba Afify, "Protestors Pull Down Wall Outside Israeli Embassy in Cairo," *New York Times*, September 10, 2011.

66. Rod Nordland and David D. Kirkpatrick, "Islamists' Growing Sway Raises Questions for Libya," *New York Times*, September 15, 2011.

67. See Bobby Ghosh, "The Rise of Moderate Islam," *Time*, July 21, 2011.

68. Jeffrey Goldberg, "Danger: Falling Tyrants," *The Atlantic*, June 2011.

69. Editorial, "Keeping the Arab Spring Alive," *Washington Post*, December 17, 2011.

70. Samuel P. Huntington, "The Clash of Civilizations?" *Foreign Affairs*, Summer 1993.

71. Editorial, "A New Middle East Policy," *Washington Post*, May 21, 2011.

72. See her interview with Jeffrey Goldberg, "Danger: Falling Tyrants," *The Atlantic*, June 2011, page 50.

73. Elisabeth Bumiller, "Gates Meets with Ruler of Emirates on Iran," *New York Times*, March 12, 2010.

74. Thomas Erdbrink, "Iran Opposition Renews Calls for Demonstration," *Washington Post*, February 14, 2011.

75. Michael Slackman, "In Beirut Vote, Signs for US," *New York Times*, June 9, 2009.

76. Isabel Kershner, "Egypt's Upheaval Hardens Israel's Stance on Peace," *New York Times*, February 3, 2011.

77. Daniel Epstein, "Israeli Companies Outsourcing to Palestinians," Associated Press, *Buenos Aires Herald*, December 27, 2010.

78. Wikipedia, "Palestinian Authority Security Forces Training Program," Wikipedia.org/wiki/Keith Dayton.

79. Yaakov Katz, "Quietly Taking Over," *The Jerusalem Post*, October 22, 2010.

80. Editorial, "Palestinian Security Forces," Voice of America, March 28, 2009.

81. Ethan Bronner, "U.S. Helps Palestinians Build Forces for Security, *New York Times*, February 26, 2009.

82. Ethan Bronner, "West Bank: Actor Activist Killed," *New York Times*, April 28, 2009.

83. Isabel Kershner, "Abbas Rejects Calling Israel a Jewish State," *New York Times*, April 28, 2009.

84. National Committee for the Heads of the Arab Local Authorities in Israel, "The Future Vision of the Palestinian Arabs in Israel," 2006.

85. Robert Wright, "A UN Plan for Israel," *New York Times*, December 14, 2010.

86. See Yonatan Silverman, "The Big Lie Called Nakba Day," *American Thinker*, July 28, 2011.

87. See Fareed Zakaria, "Israel's Arabs Within," *Washington Post*, February 16, 2009.

88. Ethan Bronner, "Desert's Sand and Rocks Become Precious Resources in West Bank Dispute," *New York Times*, March 7, 2009.

89. Editorial, "A Return to Negotiations," *Washington Post*, January 3, 2012.

Chapter 4

1. Arms Control Association, "Nuclear Weapons: Who Has What at a Glance," October 2007.

2. Peter Baker, "With Arms Treaty, a Challenge Remains," *New York Times*, April 8, 2010; Neil MacFarquhar, "Iran Angrily Defends Nuclear Program," *New York Times*, May 4, 2010.

3. Salman Masood, "Pakistan May Investigate Nuclear Scientist's Ties to Iran," *New York Times*, March 23, 2010.

4. William Broad, "Laser Advances Raise Fears of Terrorist Nuclear Ability," *New York Times*, August 21, 2011.

5. Henry A. Kissinger, "Obama's Foreign Policy Challenge," *Washington Post*, April 22, 2009.

6. Thom Shanker and David Sanger, "Pakistan Is Rapidly Adding Nuclear Arms, U.S. Says," *New York Times*, May 18, 2009.

7. Steven Lee Myers and Choe Sang-Hun, "North Korea Agrees to Suspend Its Nuclear Program," *New York Times*, March 1, 2012.

8. James L. Lindsay and Rahy Takeyh, "After Iran Gets the Bomb," *Foreign Affairs*, March/April 2010; see summary by the authors, "How Containment Could Mean War," *Washington Post*, March 4, 2010.

9. See Gideon Rachman, "A Nuclear Iran? Decision Time Is Here," *Financial Times*, February 24, 2009.

10. Quoted in David E. Sanger, "Rethinking the Unthinkable," *New York Times*, March 14, 2010.

11. Richard Cohen, "Dangerous Behavior from Iran," *Washington Post*, October 18, 2011.

12. Ali Larijani, quoted in Ray Takeyh, "Why Tehran Seeks the Bomb," *Washington Post*, December 9, 2011.

13. Thomas Erdbrink, "Iran's First Nuclear Power Plant Set for Tests Before Launch," *Washington Post*, February 23, 2009.

14. Colin Freeman and Philip Sherwell, "Iranian Fatwa Approves Use of Nuclear Weapons," *The Telegraph* (UK), January 7, 2009.

15. David Sanger and William Broad, "Allies' Clocks Tick Differently on Iran," *New York Times*, March 15, 2009.

16. IAEA report summarized in Editorial, "Running Out of Time," *Washington Post*, November 20, 2011; Ronen Bergman, "Will Israel Attack Iran?" *New York Times Magazine*, January 29, 2012, and Ronen Berman, "For Israel, Decision Time Looms on Striking Iran," *International Herald Tribune*, January 28–29, 2012.

17. Stephen Rademaker and Blaine Misztal, "Iran's Growing Stockpile," *Washington Post*, November 8, 2011.

18. Nazila Fathi, "Iran Opens First Plant to Produce Atomic Fuel," *New York Times*, April 10, 2009.

19. David E. Sanger, "U.S. Rejected Aid for Israeli Raid on Nuclear Site," *New York Times*, January 11, 2009.

20. Cited in Editorial, "Truth from Vienna," *Washington Post*, February 20, 2010.

21. David E. Sanger, "U.S. Rejected Aid for Israeli Raid on Nuclear Site," *New York Times*, January 11, 2009; William Broad, "Atomic Agency Views Iran's Stepped Up Enrichment of Uranium as a Violation," *New York Times*, February 12, 2010; Michael Slackman, "Iran Boasts It Can Make Fuel for Nuclear Bomb," *New York Times*, February 12, 2010.

22. Daniel Dombey, "Increase in Secrecy Adds to Fears Over Iran's Nuclear Ambitions," *Financial Times*, February 25, 2009.

23. David E. Sanger, "Iran Trumpets Nuclear Ability at a 2d Plant," *New York Times*, January 9, 2012.

24. Ehud Barak's comments at the World Economic Forum, January 27, 2012, Davos, Switzerland.

25. David E. Sanger and William J. Broad, "U.N. Agency Says Iran Data Points to A-Bomb Work," *New York Times*, November 8, 2011.

26. Barbara Slavin, "How Reliable Is Intelligence on Iran's Nuclear Program?" Iran Task Force, Atlantic Council, September 2011.

27. Joby Warrick, "IAEA Says Foreign Expertise Has Brought Iran to the Threshold of Nuclear Capability," *Washington Post*, November 6, 2011.

28. Joby Warrick, "IAEA Says Foreign Expertise Has Brought Iran to Threshold of Nuclear Capability," *Washington Post*, November 6, 2011.

29. Clapper testimony cited in Patrick B. Pexton, "Getting Ahead of the Facts on Iran," *Washington Post*, December 9, 2011.

30. Conversation, New York City, January 9, 2012.

31. Dan Bilefsky, "China Delays Report Suggesting North Korea Violated Sanction," *New York Times*, May 15, 2011.

32. Associated Press, "Iran Unveils Underground Missile Silos," *International Herald Tribune*, June 28, 2011.

33. Nazila Fathi and William J. Broad, "Iran Launches Satellite as U.S. Takes Wary Note," *New York Times*, February 4, 2009; Thomas Erdbrink and Joby Warrick, "Iran Reports Launching Its Own Satellite," *Washington Post*, February 4, 2009.

34. Joby Warrick, "Iran Using Front Companies to Get Bomb Parts from U.S.," *Washington Post*, January 11, 2009.

35. Conversation with General Michael Hayden, New York City, January 9, 2012.

36. William J. Broad and David E. Sanger, "As Nuclear Conference Opens, U.S. Is Pushing to Deter a Mideast Arms Race," *New York Times*, May 3, 2010.

37. "Obama Offer Is Denounced by Ayatollah," *New York Times*, March 22, 2010.

38. *CIA World Factbook*, 2007; *Oil & Gas Journal 2010*, cited in Wikipedia, "International Ranking of Iran."

39. Guy Dinmore, Najmeh Bozorgmehr, and Alex Barker, "EU Trio Targets Tougher List of Iran Sanctions," *Financial Times*, February 26, 2009; Thomas Erdbrink and Mary Beth Sheridan, "Ahmadinejad Claims Progress in Iranian Nuclear Program," *Washington Post*, April 8, 2009.

40. Daniel Dombey, "Atomic Agitation," *Financial Times*, January 7, 2010.

41. Isabel Kershner, "Israeli Ex-Spy Predicts Delay for Iran's Nuclear Ambitions," *New York Times*, January 8, 2011.

42. Editorial, "Tehran's Ambitions," *New York Times*, September 17, 2011.

43. Michael Makovsky and Blaise Misztal, "Obama Shifts Toward Containment," *Washington Post*, December 9, 2011.

44. Carol E. Lee and Jay Solomon, "Obama Sharpens Tone on Iran," *Wall Street Journal*, March 3–4, 2012.

45. Conversation with General Michael Hayden, New York City, January 9, 2012.

46. Michael Makovsky and Blaise Misztal, "Obama Shifts Toward Containment," *Washington Post*, December 9, 2011.

47. *Der Spiegel*, November 2008.

48. Elisabeth Bumiller, "Israel Expresses Impatience Over U.S. Effort Toward Iran," *International Herald Tribune*, July 28, 2009.

49. Conversation with General Michael Hayden, New York City, January 9, 2012.

50. David Sanger and William Broad, "Allies' Clocks Tick Differently on Iran," *New York Times*, March 15, 2009.

51. Quoted in Roger Cohen, "Realpolitik for Iran," *New York Times*, April 14, 2009.

52. David E. Sanger, "U.S. Rejected Aid for Israeli Raid on Nuclear Site," *New York Times*, January 11, 2009.

53. Jonathan Ferziger and David Lerman, "Israeli Army Chief Says Nation Needs to be Ready to Strike Iran," *Bloomberg News*, February 2, 2012.

54. Robert O. Freedman, "Countdown on Tehran," *Baltimore Jewish Times*, April 24, 2009.

55. Peter Baker, "Obama Suggests U.S. May Rethink Antimissile Plan," *New York Times*, March 3, 2009; Ron Kampeas, JTA News and Features, "As Bibi Plans for U.S. Trip, Pre-Game Warm-up Ensues," *Washington Jewish Week*, May 14, 2009.

56. James L. Lindsay and Rahy Takeyh, "After Iran Gets the Bomb," *Foreign Affairs*, March/April 2010.

57. Conversation with General Michael Hayden, New York City, January 9, 2012.

58. See Ronen Bergman, "The Secret War with Iran," *Free Press*, 2008, summarized in an op-ed article; Ronen Bergman, "Israel's Secret War with Iran," *Wall Street Journal*, May 16–17, 2009.

59. Adla Massoud, "U.S. allies in 'rivalry' with Iran," *Al Jazeera* (Qatar), April 29, 2009.

60. Ethan Bronner, "Israel Faces Difficult Task in Shifting Policy Away from Palestinians and Toward Iran," *New York Times*, May 4, 2009.

61. Associated Press, "Israel PM Seen Set for Palestinian State," *Newsday* (NY), May 17, 2009.

62. David E. Sanger, James Glanz, and Jo Becker, "From Arabs and Israelis, Sharp Distress Over a Nuclear Iran," *New York Times*, November 30, 2010.

63. Ethan Bronner, "Israel Faces Difficult Task in Shifting Policy Away from Palestinians and Toward Iran," *New York Times*, May 4, 2009.

64. Associated Press, "Israel PM Seen Set for Palestinian State," *Newsday* (NY), May 17, 2009.

65. *Wall Street Journal* editorial, "Wishing Upon Iran," February 27, 2012.

66. Secretary of Defense Leon Panetta's statement of February 16, 2012, quoted in Carol E. Lee and Jay Solomon, "Obama Sharpens Tone on Iran," *Wall Street Journal*, March 3–4; see also Frederick W. Kagan and Maseh Zarif, "America's Iranian Self-Deception," *Wall Street Journal*, February 27, 2012.

67. Salman Masood, "Pakistan May Investigate Nuclear Scientists' Ties to Iran," *Pittsburgh Post-Gazette*, March 23, 2010; "A Win for Nonproliferation," *Time Magazine*, December 13, 2010.

68. Mary Beth Sheridan and Scott Wilson, "Obama Presses for Unity on Iran," *Washington Post*, April 13, 2010.

69. George P. Shultz, William J. Perry, Henry A. Kissinger, and Sam Nunn, "A World Free of Nuclear Weapons," *Wall Street Journal*, January 4, 2007.

70. Arms Control Association, "Nuclear Weapons: Who Has What at a Glance," October 2007.

71. David Sanger, "In Coming Years, U.S. to Face Choice on a New Class of Weapons for Swift Strike," *New York Times*, April 23, 2010.

72. Anne Applebaum, "Yes, We Can . . . Disarm?" *Washington Post*, April 7, 2009.

73. William J. Broad, "Buffet's Donation Helps U.N. Atomic Agency Create a Global Nuclear Fuel Bank," *New York Times*, December 4, 2010.

74. Eric Schmitt and Thom Shanker, "U.S. Adapts Cold-War Idea to Fight Terrorists," *New York Times*, March 18, 2008.

75. Andrew C. Revoking, "At Conference on the Risks to Earth, Few Are Optimistic," *New York Times*, August 24, 2008.

76. World Economic Forum Annual Meeting 2010, "Securing Cyberspace," Davos, Switzerland, January 30, 2010.

77. These insights are garnered from a February 12, 2012 briefing of a board of directors on which I sit.

78. Ellen Nakashima, "Security Firm Identifies Extensive Cyber Spying," *Washington Post*, August 3, 2011.

79. World Economic Forum, "Industries under Cybersiege," Davos, Switzerland, January 29, 2011.

80. David Ignatius, "Building a Cyber Defense," *Washington Post*, August 14, 2011.

81. "An Anonymous Foe," *The Economist*, June 18, 2011; Editorial, "The Cloud Darkens," *New York Times*, June 30, 2011.

82. Medius Research, "China, Cyber Espionage and U.S. National Security," 2010, prepared for Patriot Majority, www.scribd.com/doc/33788819/China.

83. "Briefing Cyberwar," *The Economist*, July 3, 2010.

84. Mark McDonald, "In Cyberattack, Virus Infects 40 Web Sites in South Korea," *New York Times*, March 5, 2011.

85. Thom Shanker, "In Blunt Report to Congress, U.S. Accuses China and Russia of Internet Spying," *New York Times*, November 4, 2011; Ellen Nakashima, "U.S. Cyber-Spying Report Points to China and Russia," *Washington Post*, November 4, 2011.

86. David Sanger, "Iran Fights Malware Attacking Computer," *New York Times*, September 26, 2010.

87. David Sanger, "Iran Fights Malware Attacking Computers," *New York Times*, September 26, 2010.

88. David Sanger, John Markoff, and Thom Shanker, "U.S. Steps Up Effort on Digital Defenses," *New York Times*, April 28, 2009.

89. Editorial, "The Cloud Darkens," *New York Times*, June 30, 2011.

90. Helene Cooper, "U.S. Calls for Global Cyber Security Strategy," *New York Times*, May 17, 2011.

91. David Ignatius, "Building a Cyber-Defense," *Washington Post*, August 14, 2011.

92. John Markoff, "Vast Spy System Loots Computers in 103 Countries," *New York Times*, March 29, 2009.

93. Sabrina Tavernise and Wagar Gillani, "Frustrated Generation Wages Jihad in Pakistan," *New York Times*, February 28, 2010.

94. Speeches of Deputy Secretary of Defense William J. Lynn III, Stratcom Cyber Symposium, Omaha, Nebraska, May 16, 2011, and at the National Defense University, Washington, D.C., July 14, 2011.

95. Siobhan Gorman, August Cole, and Yochi Dreazen, "Computer Species Breach Fighter Jet Project," *Wall Street Journal*, April 21, 2009.

96. Speeches of Deputy Secretary of Defense William J. Lynn III, Stratcom Cyber Symposium, Omaha, Nebraska, May 16, 2011, and at the National Defense University, Washington, D.C., July 14, 2011.

97. William J. Lynn III, "Defending a New Domain: The Pentagon's Cyberstrategy," *Foreign Affairs*, 89(5), 2010

98. NPR Report, January 4, 2011.

99. Ellen Nakashima and Craig Whitlock, "Air Force's New Tool: 'We Can See Everything,'" *Washington Post*, January 2, 2011.

100. David Ignatius, "Transforming U.S. Military Might into 21st-century Weapons," *Washington Post*, January 2, 2011.

101. Sharon LaFraniere, "China to Scan Text Messages to Spot 'Unhealthy Content,'" *New York Times*, January 20, 2010.

102. Editorial, "Enabling China," *International Herald Tribune*, July 26, 2011.

103. Editorial, "Enabling China," *International Herald Tribune*, July 26, 2011.

104. John Markoff, "Report Looks at How China Meddled with the Internet," citing the annual 2010 report of the United States-China Economic and Security Revision, *New York Times*, November 18, 2010.

105. Mark Landler, "U.S. Hopes Exponents of Internet Services Will Help Open Closed Societies," *New York Times*, March 8, 2010.

106. James Glanz and John Markoff, "U.S. Underwrites Internet Detour around Censors," *New York Times*, June 12, 2011.

107. Mark Landler, "U.S. Hopes Exponents of Internet Services Will Help Open Closed Societies," *New York Times*, March 8, 2010.

108. World Economic Forum Annual Meeting 2010, "Securing Cyberspace," Davos, Switzerland, January 30, 2010.

109. Ellen Nakashima, "NSA Chief Faces Questions About New Cyber-Command," *Washington Post*, April 15, 2010.

110. David E. Sanger and Elisabeth Bumiller, "Pentagon to Consider Cyber-Attack Acts of War," *New York Times*, June 1, 2011.

111. David E. Sanger and Elisabeth Bumiller, "Pentagon to Consider Cyber-Attack Acts of War," *New York Times*, June 1, 2011.

112. Paul Sagan, Akamai, World Economic Forum, Davos, Switzerland, January 29, 2011.

113. Juliet Eilperin, "Emissions Linked to End of 2,000-Year Arctic Trend," *Washington Post*, September 4, 2009.

114. Jim Hoagland, "Preparing for a Sea Change," *Washington Post*, July 5, 2009.

115. International Institute for Sustainable Development, *Trade, Aid, and Security*, 2007.

116. Report of David Lobell, Justin Costa-Roberts, and Wolfram Schlenker, in *Science* magazine, which also notes that extra CO_2 emissions act as a fertilizer, encouraging plant growth and offsetting some of the losses from rising temperatures, cited in Justin Gillis, "Global Warming Reduces Expected Yields of Harvests in Some Countries, Study Says," *New York Times*, May 6, 2011.

117. See Justin Gillis, "A Warming Planet Struggles to Feed Itself," *New York Times*, June 5, 2011, for an excellent analysis.

118. John M. Broder, "Climate Change: A Battle on Many Fronts," *International Herald Tribune*, January 25, 2012.

119. Juliet Eilperin, "Firms Start to See Climate Changes as Barrier to Profit," *Washington Post*, September 21, 2009.

120. David Fahrenthold and Juliet Eilperin, "White House Is Prepared to Set First National Limits on Greenhouse Gases," *Washington Post*, September 16, 2009.

121. Ehud Zion Waldocks, "Jewish Environmentalists Launch Campaign to Combat Climate Change," *Jerusalem Post*, October 22, 2009.

122. "Water: Our Thirsty World," *National Geographic*, April 2010.

123. Arab Development Report, page 3.

124. World Economic Forum 2010, "Rebuilding Water Management," Davos, Switzerland, January 30, 2010.

125. "Don't make the Desert Bloom," *The Economist*, June 7, 2008.

126. "Don't make the Desert Bloom," *The Economist*, June 7, 2008.

127. Joseph W. Dellapenna, "Designing Legal Structures of Water Management Need to Fulfill the Israeli-Palestinian Declaration of Principles," *The Palestine Yearbook of International Law* (1992/1994), pages 63–103.

128. Jan Mouawad, "China's Rapid Growth Shifts the Geopolitics of Oil," *New York Times*, March 20, 2010.

129. John Kerry and Lindsey Graham, "Yes We Can (Pass Climate Change Legislation)," *New York Times*, October 10, 2009.

130. Edward Schumacher-Matos, "Closing In on Hugo Chavez," *Washington Post*, February 14, 2009.

131. Roula Khalaf and Lionel Barber, "A Long Way Down," *Financial Times*, October 20, 2008.

132. "Energy Inefficient," *New York Times*, January 19, 2009.

133. Elisabeth Rosenthal and Felicity Barringer, "Green Promise Seen in Switch to LED Lighting," *New York Times*, May 30, 2009.

134. I benefited from the expertise of Yossie Hollander, chairman of OneEnergyPolicy.org and an Israeli-born high-tech pioneer, who helped revolutionize the software industry in Israel and now focuses on alternative energy, at meetings on September 22, 2011, and January 20, 2012.

135. Steve Lohr, "Highway to the Unknown," *New York Times*, May 20, 2009.

136. Elisabeth Rosenthal, "Seeing Oil's Limits, Gulf States Invest Heavily in Clean Energy," *New York Times*, January 13, 2009.

137. Citing Nick Robins, energy and climate change analyst at HSBC in London, cited in John M. Broder, "Climate Change: A Battle on Many Fronts," *International Herald Tribune*, January 25, 2012.

138. Jonathan Starkey, "Wind Projects at a Standstill," *Washington Post*, July 11, 2009.

139. Stephen Lacey, "Solar Stunner: America Is a $1.9 Billion Exporter of Solar Products," Renewable Energy World.com, August 29, 2011.

140. Daniel Yergin, "Oil's New World Order," *Washington Post*, October 28, 2010.

141. Simon Romero, "New Fields Bring Americas to Top of U.S. Companies' List," *New York Times*, September 20, 2011.

142. Daniel Yergin, "Oil's New World Order," *Washington Post*, October 28, 2010.

143. John Deutch, "An Energy Trove to Tap with Care," *Washington Post*, August 19, 2011.

144. National Petroleum Council.

145. John Deutch, "An Energy Trove to Tap with Care," *Washington Post*, August 19, 2011; David Brooks, "Shale Gas Revolution," *New York Times*, November 4, 2011.

146. Ian Urbina, "New Report by Agency Lowers Estimates of Natural Gas in U.S.," New York times, January 29, 2012.

147. Sylvia Pfeifer, Pilita Clark, and Ed Crooks, "Opponents Try to Stifle the Shale Gas Revolution," *Financial Times*, May 21, 2011.

148. Jad Mouawad, "China's Rapid Growth Shifts the Geopolitics of Oil," *New York Times*, March 20, 2010.

149. Robert J. Samuelson, "The Bias Against Oil and Gas," *Washington Post*, May 4, 2009.

150. Nicholas Eberstadt, "5 Myths About Global Population," *Washington Post*, November 6, 2011.

151. "Strength in Numbers," GlobalFirepower.com, 2011.

152. Rosner's Domain, "Migrating Israelis, Numbers and Difficulties," *The Jerusalem Post*, July 7, 2011.

153. Nicholas Eberstadt, "The Demographic Future," *Foreign Affairs*, November/December 2010.

154. Michael Hodin, executive director of Global Coalition on Aging and adjunct senior fellow, speech at The Council on Foreign Relations in Washington, D.C., April 20, 2011.

155. Adele Hayutin, "Population Aging Will Reshape Global Economics and Geopolitics," Stanford Center on Longevity, 2010.

156. Carol Morello and Dan Balz, "California Population Burgeons," *Washington Post*, March 9, 2011.

157. Peter Slevin, "Republican Party Looks to Rebuild Support Among Hispanics," *Washington Post*, February 21, 2010.

158. David S. Broder, "The Coming Latino Effect," *Washington Post*, April 4, 2010.

159. Speech by Muhtar Kent, chairman and CEO of Coca-Cola, New York City, December 8, 2010.

160. Presentation by Professor Jeffrey A. Rosensweig, Goizueta Business School, Emory University, Kiwanis Club, Atlanta, Georgia, November 30, 2010.

161. David Brooks, "Relax, We'll Be Fine," *New York Times*, April 6, 2010.

162. Judy Dempsey, "Germany's Green Party Elects First Ethnic Turk as Leader," *New York Times*, November 17, 2008.

163. Conversation with former Austrian chancellor Wolfgang Schuessel, 2010, Vienna.

164. Fouad Ajami, "Strangers in the Land," *New York Times*, July 29, 2009 (reviewing Christopher Caldwell, *Reflections on the Revolution in Europe: Immigration, Islam and the West*, New York: Doubleday, 2009).

165. Michael Kimmelman, "In Dresden, Cultural Beauty Meets Ugly Bigotry," *New York Times*, August 15, 2009.

166. Arieh O'Sullivan, "Israel Sells More Drone Technology to UK," *Bloomberg News*, April 16, 2010.

167. *CIA World Factbook*, 2011.

168. 2007 Pew Research Center study.

169. 2007 Pew Research Center study.

170. Pew Research Center, "Muslim Americans: Middle Class and Mostly Mainstream," May 22, 2007.

171. Tara Bahrampour and Michelle Boorstein, "Muslims Express Optimism," *Washington Post*, August 3, 2011.

172. Population Reference Bureau, August 2009, *USA Today*, August 28–30, 2009.

173. Speech by James Wolfensohn, former president of the World Bank, 2009 Presidential Conference, Jerusalem.

174. Israel Central Bureau of Statistics, North American Jewish Databank, 2010; Jewish Virtual Library, "The Jewish Population of the World," 2010.

175. United Nations Study, "World Population to Reach 10 billion by 2100 if Fertility in all Countries Converges to Replacement Levels," press release, May 3, 2011.

176. Dr. James Vaupel, Max Plank Institute, Germany, CNN Interview, March 25, 2010.

177. SimpleToRemember, Judaism Online, "World Jewish Population," compiled by Ner LeElef.

178. Jewish People Policy Planning Institute, Annual Assessment, 2008; Jewish Virtual Library, "The Jewish Population of the World," 2010.

179. Hillel: The Foundation for Jewish Campus Life study; provided by Josh Blumenthal, North Carolina Hillel, Chapel Hill, October 29, 2007.

180. Sue Fishkoff, "Red, White, and Kosher," *New York Times*, July 4, 2010.

181. Ann Levin, "It's Kosher to Be Kosher Again," *Los Angeles Times*, December 15, 1990.

182. Carla Rivera, "Jewish Day Schools Facing an Economic Crisis," *Los Angeles Times*, May 18, 2009.

183. Hillel: The Foundation for Jewish Campus Life study; provided by Josh Blumenthal, North Carolina Hillel, Chapel Hill, October 29, 2007.

184. Adherents.com; Bob Mims, "Virtual Shabbat CD Released to Rebuild Eroding Ranks of Practicing Jews," *Salt Lake City Tribune*, October 3, 1999.

185. Gary Tobin, *Opening the Gates*, San Francisco: Jossey-Bass, 1999, page 2 (citing Council of Jewish Federations 1992 report).

186. Ed Case, "Birthright Israel Trips and Intermarriage," *Interfaith Family*, October 27, 2009.

187. Carla Rivera, "Jewish Day Schools Facing an Economic Crisis," *Los Angeles Times*, May 18, 2009.

188. Gary A. Tobin and Arych Weinberg, "A Study of Jewish Foundations," Institute for Jewish and Community Research, San Francisco, 2007.

189. See Gary Tobin, Jeffrey Solomon, and Alexander Karp, "Mega-Gifts in American Philanthropy: General and Jewish Giving Patterns Between 1995–2000," Institute for Jewish and Community Research, San Francisco, 2003.

190. Conversation with Barry Shrage, November 16, 2007.

191. Barry Shrage, "A Community without Barriers to Entry and with a Vision of Jewish Life as High as Sinai," speech, March 31, 2004.

192. National Public Radio, Ira Flatow show, "Technology Friday," May 21, 2010.

193. See Gary Tobin's important book *Opening the Gates*, San Francisco: Jossey-Bass, 1999; his untimely passing in 2009 deprived the Jewish community of an important voice on a variety of challenges facing American and world Jewry.

194. Gary Tobin, *Opening the Gates*, San Francisco: Jossey-Bass, 1999, page 174.

195. Gary Tobin, *Opening the Gates*, San Francisco: Jossey-Bass, 1999, page 8.

196. Gary Tobin, *Opening the Gates*, San Francisco: Jossey-Bass, 1999, page 11.

197. Barry Shrage, "A Community without Barriers to Entry and with a Vision of Jewish Life as High as Sinai," speech, March 31, 2004.

198. Sarna quoted in Barry Shrage, "A Community without Barriers to Entry and with a Vision of Jewish Life as High as Sinai," speech, March 31, 2004. See also, Jonathan Sarna, *American Judaism: A History*, New Haven: Yale University Press, 2005, page 374.

199. Richard Jackson, director and senior fellow, Global Aging Initiative, Center for Strategic and International Studies, told me this at an April 20, 2011, conference sponsored by the Council on Foreign Relations in Washington, in which I also spoke.

200. See Howard Schneider, "Nazareth Hopes Pope's Visit Will Boost Tourism," *Washington Post*, May 4, 2009.

201. Quoted in Ethan Bronner, "A Religious War in Israel's Army," *New York Times*, March 22, 2009.

202. Jay Bookman, "Israeli Settlement Growth Endangers Israel," *Atlanta Journal-Constitution*, February 17, 2009.

203. See Eugene Rogan, "Refugees for Settlers Is the Way Forward for Israel," *Financial Times*, March 29, 2010 (citing different figures from the Central Intelligence Agency, namely 177,000 Israelis in East Jerusalem and 187,000 in the West Bank, as well as 224,000 Palestinian refugees in camps in Lebanon and 126,000 in Syria).

Chapter 5

1. See, generally, Kenneth S. Stern, "Anti-Semitism Today: How It Is the Same, How It Is Different, and How to Fight It," *American Jewish Committee*, December 2006.

2. Laurie Goodstein, "A Phrase with Roots in Anti-Semitism," *New York Times*, January 13, 2011.

3. See, generally, John Efron, Steven Weitzman, Matthias Lehmann, and Joshua Holo, *The Jews: A History*, chapter 7, "Under the Cross," Upper Saddle River, NJ: Pearson Prentice Hall, 2009.

4. "Moscow Prosecutor Refuses to Ban *Protocols of the Elders of Zion*, One of the Most Infamous Fake Antisemitic Books," March 3, 2009, The Coordination Forum for Countering Antisemitism, Yearly Evaluation, 2010.

5. John Efron, Steven Weitzmann, Matthias Lehmann, and Joshua Holo, *The Jews: A History*, chapter 10, "The State of the Jews, Jews and the State," Upper Saddle River, NJ: Pearson Prentice Hall, 2009.

6. Wikipedia, "Napoleon and the Jews."

7. Michael Woodhead, "'All Jews Share a Certain Gene': German Banker Sparks Outrage with 'Stupid' Comments," MailOnline, August 30, 2010.

8. Statement of September 2, 2010, to a Belgian radio station; "De Gucht 'Regrets' Remarks About Jews," EuropeanVoice.com, September 3, 2010; "EU Trade Chief Apologizes for Saying You Can't Have a 'Rational Conversation about Middle East with Jews,'" MailOnline, Reuters, Mail Foreign Service, September 4, 2010.

9. Conversations with Dr. Ariel Muzicant, president of the Jewish Community of Vienna; Hannah Lessing, secretary general of the Austrian National Fund and of the General Settlement Fund; and John Conway, U.S. ambassador and acting charge d'affaires to Austria, in Vienna, Austria, all on May 28, 2009.

10. Dr. Barbara Serloth, Klubsekretär, quoted in parliamentary documents of May 27, 2009.

11. Gabriel Miland, "Shocking Increase in Anti-Semitism," *The Express* (UK), July 18, 2007.

12. Human Rights First, *Anti-Semitism: 2007 Hate Crime Survey*.

13. "The PM and a Ban on Hate Groups," *Evening Standard* (London), July 4, 2007.

14. Denis MacShane, "The New Anti-Semitism," *Washington Post*, September 4, 2007.

15. Stuart E. Eizenstat, *Imperfect Justice: Looted Assets, Slave Labor, and the Unfinished Business of World War II*, page 369, paperback edition, 2004.

16. Haaretz.com, "EU Trade Chief Apologizes for Blaming Jews for Blocking Mideast Peace," March 9, 2010.

17. Michael Woodhead, "'All Jews Share a Certain Gene': German Banker Sparks Outrage with 'Stupid" Comments," MailOnline, August 30, 2010.

18. Michael Woodhead, "'All Jews Share a Certain Gene': German Banker Sparks Outrage with 'Stupid" Comments," MailOnline, August 30, 2010.

19. Pew Research Center report, "The Future of the Global Muslim Population, January 27, 2011; Jewish Virtual Library, "The Jewish Population of the World," 2010.

20. Wikipedia, "History of the Jews of Argentina."

21. "Officers Charged in Synagogue Attack," *New York Times*, March 27, 2009.

22. Edward Schumacher Matos, "Closing in on Hugo Chavez," *Washington Post*, February 14, 2009.

23. "Mr. Chavez vs. the Jews: With George W. Bush Gone, Venezuela's Strongman Has Found New Enemies," *Washington Post*, February 12, 2009.

24. Juan Forero and Joshua Partlow, "Jews in S. America Increasingly Uneasy: Government and Media Seen Fostering Anti-Semitism in Venezuela, Elsewhere," *Washington Post*, February 8, 2009.

25. Hannah Silberman, "Creating Context: Atlanta and the New South," playbill for *Parade*, a play about the Leo Frank trial, Ford's Theatre, September 2011.

26. See "Infamous Lynching," www.americanlynching.com/infamous-old.html.

27. David Engel, "Jan Karski's Mission to the West, 1942–1944," *Holocaust and Genocide Studies*, 5(4), 1990, pages 363–380.

28. Adam Nagourney, "In Tapes, Nixon Rails About Jews and Blacks," *New York Times*, December 11, 2010.

29. John Efron, Steven Weitzmann, Matthias Lehmann, and Joshua Holo, *The Jews: A History*, chapter 15, "Difficult Freedoms," Upper Saddle River, NJ: Pearson Prentice Hall, 2009.

30. "Combating Anti-Semitism," Ottawa, Canada, November 8, 2010.

31. European Monitoring Centre on Racism and Xenophobia, discussion paper, "Working Definition of Anti-Semitism," 2006.

32. Conversation in New York City, May 20, 2009.

33. Bernard Lewis, *The Jews of Islam*, Princeton: Princeton University Press, 1987. See, also, John Efron, Steven Weitzmann, Matthias Lehmann, and Joshua Holo, *The Jews: A History*, chapter 6, "Under the Crescent," Upper Saddle River, NJ: Pearson Prentice Hall, 2009.

34. Howard M. Sachar, *Farewell Espana*, New York: Vintage, 1994.

35. John Efron, Steven Weitzmann, Matthias Lehmann, and Joshua Holo, *The Jews: A History*, chapter 15, "Difficult Freedoms," Upper Saddle River, NJ: Pearson Prentice Hall, 2009.

36. John Efron, Steven Weitzmann, Matthias Lehmann, and Joshua Holo, *The Jews: A History*, chapter 15, "Difficult Freedoms," Upper Saddle River, NJ: Pearson Prentice Hall, 2009.

37. Pew Research Center report, "World Muslim Population," 2010.

38. Wikipedia, "Islam in Europe."

39. Pew Forum on Religion, October 7, 2009.

40. Thomas Erdbrink and Joby Warrick, "Bahrain Crackdown Fuels Tensions in Gulf Region," *Washington Post*, April 23, 2011.

41. Committee for Accuracy in the Middle East Reporting in America, "Yasser Arafat's Timeline of Terror," November 13, 2004.

42. Wikipedia, "Hamas."

43. Wikipedia, "Hezbollah."

44. Clifford D. May, "A World Without Jews," *Moment Magazine*, May/June 2009, page 20.

45. Wikipedia, "1983 Beirut Barracks Bombing."

46. Wikipedia, "Khobar Towers Bombing."

47. Wikipedia, "1998 United States Embassy Bombings."

48. Elaine Sciolino, "Islamic Justice Rising, with a British Flavor," *International Herald Tribune*, November 20, 2008.

49. J.J. Goldberg, "Why the Jews? Debate Erupts Over How to Explain the Mumbai Terror," *The Forward*, December 26, 2008.

50. Menachem Milson, speech at the Sixth and I Street Synagogue, under the auspices of the Foundation for Jewish Studies, Washington, D.C., May 27, 2010.

51. Mitchell C. Bard, "The Treatment of Jews in Arab/Islamic Countries," Myths and Facts Online, 2011.

52. Stuart E. Eizenstat, *Imperfect Justice: Looted Assets, Forced Labor, and the Unfinished Business of World War II*, Public Affairs, paperback edition, 2004, page 368.

53. Steve Erlanger, "Amid Heavy Intrigue, UNESCO Picks New Leader," *International Herald Tribune*, September 24, 2009.

54. Michael Slachman, "Egypt Ponders Failed Drive for UNESCO," *New York Times*, September 28, 2009.

55. Nina Shea, "Jihad K-12," *National Review Online*, March 13, 2009.

56. Sandhya Somashekhar, "Attacks on School's Teachings Drown out Traffic Concerns," *Washington Post*, March 23, 2009.

57. United Nations General Assembly Resolution 3379.

58. *Gale Encyclopedia of the Mideast and North Africa*, "Madrid Conference (1991)."

59. Wikipedia, "Khartoum Resolution."

60. Samuel G. Freedman, "Distinctive Mission for Muslims' Conference: Remembering the Holocaust," *New York Times*, September 24, 2011.

61. Andrew Kohot, Pew Research Center poll, reported on NPR, April 25, 2011.

62. Richard Cohen, "Apartheid? Not Israel," *Washington Post*, March 2, 2010.

63. "Yale University Is Foolishly Shutting Down Nation's Leading Center for the Study of Anti-Semitism," Editorial, *New York Daily News*, June 18, 2011.

64. Lawrence Summers, "The Rising Specter of Anti-Semitism," *Providence Journal-Bulletin*, October 12, 2002.

65. Richard Cohen, "Lie of Apartheid," *Washington Post*, March 4, 2010.

66. See letter of March 21, 2010, to AHIRI Board Members.

67. Ruth Wisse, "Are American Jews Too Powerful? Not Even Close," *Washington Post*, November 4, 2007.

68. Stephen M. Walt and John J. Mearsheimer, *The Israel Lobby and U.S. Foreign Policy*, New York: Farrar, Straus and Giroux, 2007.

69. Jimmy Carter, *Palestine: Peace Not Apartheid*, New York: Simon & Schuster, 2006.

70. Barak Ravid, David Landau, Aluf Benn, and Shumeul Rosner, "Olmert to Haaretz: Two-State Solution, or Israel Is Done For," *Haaretz*, November 29, 1997; see also, Rory McCarthy, "Israel Risks Apartheid-Like Struggle if Two-State Solution Fails, Says Olmert," *The Guardian*, November 30, 2007.

71. Rory McCarthy, "Barak: Make Peace with Palestinians or Face Apartheid," *The Guardian*, February 3, 2010.

72. Ron Kampeas, "Ackerman: 'J Street Ain't It,'" *Jewish Herald-Voice*, February 3, 2011.

73. Janine Zacharia, "U.S. Jewish Group's Israel Stance Debated," *Washington Post*, March 24, 2011.

74. Paul Vitello, "On Israel, US Jews Show Divergent Views, Often Parting from Leaders," *New York Times*, May 6, 2010.

75. Walter Russell Mead, "Jerusalem Syndrome: Decoding the Israel Lobby," reviewing the Walt/Mearsheimer book in *Foreign Affairs*, November/December 2007, page 165.

76. Walter Russell Mead, "Jerusalem Syndrome: Decoding the Israel Lobby," reviewing the Walt/Mearsheimer book in *Foreign Affairs*, November/December 2007, page 165.

77. See Gallup Poll, Princeton, N.J., by Lydia Saad, taken between February 1–3, 2010.

78. Thom Shanker, "U.S. Quietly Supplies Israel with Bunker-Busting Bombs," *New York Times*, September 24, 2011.

79. "Blame the Lobby: The Obama Administration's Latest Failed Nominee Peddles a Conspiracy Theory," *Washington Post*, March 12, 2009.

80. Maria Glod, "Scientist Gave Israelis Secrets, Court Told," *Washington Post*, October 30, 2009; Richard Greenberg, "Exceptionally Disturbing," *Washington Jewish Week*, October 29, 2009.

81. Robert L. Bernstein, "Rights Watchdog, Lost in the Mideast," *New York Times*, October 20, 2009.

82. Discussion with Abraham Foxman of ADL on May 20, 2009, in New York City.

83. Clifford May, "A World without Jews," *Moment Magazine*, May/June 2009.

84. Richard Greenberg, "Goldstone Rebuts Charges of Bias," *Washington Jewish Week*, October 8, 2009.

85. UN Human Rights Council, "United Nations Fact Finding Mission on the Gaza Conflict," released September 15, 2009.

86. E.B. Solomont, "US 'Concerned' with Goldstone Report," *Jerusalem Post*, September 21, 2009.

87. See, for example, Nicholas Rostow, university counsel and vice chancellor for legal affairs, State University of New York, "The Human Rights Council (Goldstone) Report and International Law," Volume 40, *Israel Yearbook on Human Rights 2010*, furnished to me in unpublished form on March 30, 2010; Alan Dershowitz, Harvard Law School, "The Case Against the Goldstone Report: A Study of Evidentiary Bias," 2010; Dori Gold, Jerusalem Center for Public Affairs, "The UN Gaza Report: A Substantive Critique," 2009, www.jcpa.org; M. Halbertal, "The Goldstone Illusion," *The New Republic*, November 7, 2009; T. Norwitz, "An Open Letter to Richard Goldstone," October 19, 2009, www.commentarymagazine.com.

88. Jackson Diehl, "Israel's Gaza Vindication," *Washington Post*, September 21, 2009.

89. Richard Goldstone, "Revisiting Gaza," *Washington Post*, April 3, 2011.

90. See, generally, Ethan Bronner and Jennifer Medina, "Investigator on Gaza Was Guided by His Past," *New York Times*, April 20, 2011; Ethan Bronner and Isabel Kershner, "Head of U.N. Panel Regrets Saying Israel Intentionally Killed Gazans," *New York Times*, April 3, 2011.

91. Ethan Bronner, "Tensions Simmer on West Bank," *New York Times*, September 24, 2011.

Chapter 6

1. U.S. State Department figures, published in Jewish Virtual Library, "U.S. Vetoes of UN Resolutions Critical of Israel," 1972–2011.

2. Citation in the National Museum of American Jewish History, Philadelphia.

3. James Q. Wilson, "Why Don't Jews Like the Christians Who Like them?" *City Magazine*, Winter 2008.

4. Quinnipiac University poll taken April 14–19, 2010.

5. See Lydia Saad, supra, February 24, 2010.

6. Harold Meyerson, "Netanyahu Feels the Heat," *Washington Post*, June 17, 2009.

7. Richard A. Oppel Jr. "Taking on Rivals, Perry Trumpets Support for Israel," *New York Times*, September 21, 2011.

8. Gallup, Lydia Saad, "Solid Majority of Jewish Americans Still Approve of Obama," Princeton, New Jersey, July 5, 2011.

9. Howard Schneider, "Netanyahu's Defiance of U.S. Resonates at Home," *Washington Post*, August 19, 2009.

10. Jennifer Steinhauer and Steven Lee Myers, "House G.O.P. Finds a Growing Bond with Netanyahu," *New York Times*, September 21, 2011.

11. Jennifer Steinhauer, "A Recess Destination with Bipartisan Support: Israel and the West Bank," *New York Times*, August 16, 2011

12. General Keegan, quoted in Dr. Steve Carol, "What Israel Does for the United States," July 29, 2009.

13. 2011 Report for the Washington Institute for Near East Studies by Robert Blackwill and Walter Slocombe, "Israel: A Strategic Asset for the United States," reported in Israel, *Ynetnews*, November 2, 2011.

14. Janine Zacharia and Mary Beth Sheridan, "Israel Angry Over Being Singled Out in Nuclear Plan," *Washington Post*, May 30, 2010; Neil MacFarquhar, "189 Nations Reaffirm Goal of Ban on Nuclear Weapons," *New York Times*, May 29, 2010.

15. World Briefing, "U.S. Joins Call to Make Mideast Free of Atomic Weapons," *New York Times*, May 6, 2010.

16. William J. Broad, John Murkoff, and David E. Sanger, "Israel Tests Called Crucial in Iran Nuclear Setback," *New York Times*, January 16, 2011.

17. Scott Shane, "Iran's Adversaries Said to Step Up Covert Actions, *New York Times*, January 12, 2012.

18. See comments of Karim Sadjadpour, an Iran expert at the Carnegie Endowment for International Peace, quoted in Scott Shane, "Iran Adversaries Said to Step Up Covert Actions," *New York Times*, January 12, 2012.

19. CNN wire staff, "Iran Threatens Israel, U.S. Over Scientist Killing," updated January 15, 2012.

20. Ethan Bronner, "Rift Exposes Larger Split on Mideast," *New York Times*, March 29, 2010.

21. Daniel Dombey and Tobias Buck, "An Unsettled Alliance," *Financial Times*, April 13, 2010.

22. Aaron David Miller, "The False Religion of Mideast Peace and Why I'm No Longer a Believer," *Foreign Policy*, April 2010.

23. See pages 12 and 33 of testimony; also see Mark Landler, "Risk and Opportunities in Fight with Israel," *New York Times*, March 17, 2010, and Stephen M. Walt, "Finding Out Who Israel's Real Friends Are, *Washington Post*, March 21, 2010.

24. Natash Mozgovaya, "Top Obama Aide: U.S. Commitment to Israel is Not a Slogan," *Haaretz*, October 27, 2009.

25. Quoted in Thomas L. Friedman, "Driving Drunk in Jerusalem," *New York Times*, March 4, 2010.

26. Daniel Dombey and Tobias Buck, "An Unsettled Alliance," *Financial Times*, April 13, 2010.

27. Editorial, "The View From Jerusalem," *Wall Street Journal*, April 19, 2010.

28. Isabel Kershner, "Tear Gas Kills a Palestinian Protestor," *New York Times*, January 2, 2011; Joel Greenberg, "Palestinian Woman Dies After Tear-Gassing," *Washington Post*, January 2, 2011.

29. See, for example, Daniel Kurtzer, "Behind the Settlements," American Interest Online, March/April, 2010.

30. Tobias Buck, "Israel Moves to Placate U.S. by Clearing More on 'Outposts,'" *Financial Times*, May 27, 2009.

31. Daniel Kurtzer, "Behind the Settlements," The American Interest, March–April 2010, www.the-american-interest.com/article.cfm?piece=781.

32. Joel Greenberg, "Israeli Supreme Court Orders Largest West Bank Outpost Removed," *Washington Post*, August 2, 2011; Chaim Levinson, "Israel's Supreme Court Orders State to Dismantle Largest West Bank Outpost," Haaretz.com, August, 2, 2011.

33. Barak Ravid, David Landau, Aluf Benn, and Shmuel Rosner, "Olmert to Haaretz: Two-State Solution, or Israel Is Done For," *Haaretz*, November 29, 2011; Rory McCarthy, "Israel Risks Apartheid-Like Struggle if Two-State Solution Fails, Says Olmert, *The Guardian*, November 30, 2007.

34. Ethan Bronner, "Olmert Says Israel Should Pull Out of West Bank," *New York Times*, September 30, 2008.

35. Angus Reid, *Global Monitor*, April 30, 2010.

36. Yossi Verter, "Peres Warns: Israel Is in Danger of Ceasing to Exist as a Jewish State," *Haaretz*, June 17, 2011.

37. Jessica Steinberg, "Netanyahu's New Chess Game," ITA News and Features, *Washington Jewish Week*, August 11, 2011.

38. Joel Greenberg and Joby Warrick, "Israel Building Plan Draws Fresh Rebukes," *Washington Post*, November 2, 2011; Isabel Kershner, "Israel Plans to Speed Up Settlement Growth," *New York Times*, November 2, 2011.

39. Joel Greenberg, "Settlers Suspected in Vandalism at Base," *Washington Post*, September 8, 2011.

40. Isabel Kershner, "A Mosque Is Set on Fire in an Israeli Arab Village," *New York Times*, October 4, 2011.

41. Ethan Bronner, "Israel's West Bank General Warns Against Radicals," *New York Times*, October 12, 2011.

42. Ethan Bronner, "Israel Leader Sets Curbs on Settlers for Violence," *New York Times*, December 15, 2011.

43. Joel Greenberg, "Vandals Set Fire to Mosque in West Bank," *Washington Post*, December 16, 2011.

44. Nathan Jeffay, "Israel Journalists Fear New Media Restrictions," *Forward*, December 9, 2011.

45. Eric Alterman, "Drifting Away from the West," *Forward*, December 16, 2011.

46. Editorial, "Israel's Shot at Stifling Speech: NGOs Should Not Be Undermined," *Washington Post*, November 21, 2011.

47. Ruth Marcus, "In Israel, an Unequal Life for women," *Washington Post*, December 3, 2011. Marcus provoked a firestorm with her column.

48. Ethan Bronner and Isabel Kershner, "Israeli Women Core of Debate on Orthodoxy," *New York Times*, January 15, 2012.

49. See Herb Keinon, "Israeli Officials 'Disappointed' by Clinton's Remarks about Threats to Israeli Democracy," *Jerusalem Post*, December 7, 2011; Phoebe Greenwood, "Israel Furious at Hillary Clinton's Concern for Israeli Democracy," *Telegraph* (UK), December 7, 2011.

50. Remarks of former U.S. president Bill Clinton at the Clinton Global Initiative, New York City, September 21, 2010, reported in Jonathan Lis and Natasha Mozgovaya, "Bill Clinton's 'Russian Immigrants an Obstacle to Peace' Comment Draws Fire in Israel," *Haaretz*, September 22, 2010.

51. Daniel Jonah Goldhagen, "A Model for the Arab World," *Forward*, December 16, 2011.

52. Thomas L. Friedman, "Newt, Mitt, Bibi, and Vladimir," *New York Times*, December 14, 2011.

53. Isabel Kershner, "Ties Between Israel and Arab Allies Fray Over Mosque Burning," *New York Times*, October 7, 2011.

54. Ephraim Sneh, "Bad Borders, Good Neighbors," *New York Times*, January, 2012.

55. Ethan Bronner, "Israel's West Bank General Warns Against Radicals," *New York Times*, October 12, 2011.

56. Quoted in Ethan Bronner, "Rift Exposes Larger Split in Views on Mideast," *New York Times*, March 29, 2010.

57. Tobias Buck, "Palestinians Eye Ban on Goods from Settlements," *Financial Times*, March 16, 2010.

58. http://visitpalestine.webs.com/treeplantingfeb2012.htm.

59. palestinevideo.blogspot.com, December 30, 2010.

60. Barrel Ravid and Avi Issacharuff, "Palestinians: Neighbor's Claim to West Bank Destroys Peace," *Haaretz*, January 24, 2010.

61. Ethan Bronner, "Security and Economic Revival Raise Hopes in the West Bank," *New York Times*, July 17, 2009.

62. Alisa Odenheimer, "West Bank Economy Grows 9% in First Half While Gaza Expands 16%, IMF Says," *Bloomberg*, September 14, 2010.

63. Edmund Sanders, "Selling a Piece of Palestinian Main Street," *Los Angeles Times*, February 15, 2010.

64. "Palestine Investment Fund Plans IT Park in New Development," Ma'an News Agency, February 15, 2010; information supplied on February 26, 2010, by the Palestinian Business Committee for Peace and Reform.

65. See, for example, Shaul Mishal and Doron Mazza, "Preempting a 'White Intifada,'" *Haaretz*, February 22, 2010.

66. Former president Carter has taken a contrary view from mine about the Hamas-Fatah agreement, arguing it will strengthen the prospects of peace by allowing Palestinian president Abbas to negotiate on behalf of all Palestinians. Jimmy Carter, "A Partnership that Could Bring Mideast Peace," *Washington Post*, 2011. But Hamas will ultimately dominate any coalition government, and its intransigence and charter calling for Israel's destruction hardly auger well for peace.

67. Statement of Prime Minister Netanyahu and President Peres, Atlas Shrugs, May 1, 2011.

68. Ethan Bronner and Isabel Kershner, "Rival Factions of Palestinians Reach an Accord," *New York Times*, April 28, 2011.

69. Meeting of August 6, 2011, with Major General Yadlin.

70. Poll from the Israel Project, Bridges for Peace, "Poll: Most Americans Oppose Unilateral Palestinian State," April 14, 2011.

71. Charles Krauthammer, "Land Without Peace," *Washington Post*, September 30, 2011.

72. *CIA World Factbook*, December 20, 2011.

73. David Ignatius, "Obama's Mideast Plan," *Washington Post*, April 7, 2010.

74. AIPAC memo, "Administration Reaffirms Value of U.S.-Israel Alliance," April 23, 2010.

75. "Obama's Speech to the UN General Assembly, as Prepared," *National Journal*, September 21, 2011.

76. Associated Press, "U.S. and Israel Delay Plans for Joint Military Exercise," *International Herald Tribune*, January 17, 2012.

77. Paul Krugman, "How Fares the Dream?" *New York Times*, January 17, 2012.

Final Thoughts

1. Editorial, "Guarding Against Cyberattacks," *Washington Post*, February 13, 2012.

2. Ellen Nakashima, "Report: China is Testing Cyberattack Capabilities," *Washington Post*, March 8, 2012, reporting on an study by the U.S.-China Economic and Security Review Commission.

3. Isabel Kershner, "2 Israeli Web Sites Crippled As Cyberwar Escalates," *New York Times*, January 17, 2012.

4. Jason de Perle, Robert Gebeloff, and Sabrina Tavernise. "Older, Suburban, and Struggling," *New York Times*, November 19, 2011.

5. Paul Krugman, "How Fares the Dream?" *New York Times*, January 17, 2012.

6. Adam Davidson Atlantic Monthly essay, "Making It in America," cited it Thomas L. Friedman, "Average is Over," *New York Times*, January 26, 2012.

7. Jason De Perle and Sabrina Tavernise, "Unwed Mothers Now Majority Before Age 30," *New York Times*, February 8, 2012.

8. Brian Childs, "Fate of the Euro: A Contrarian View," *International Herald Tribune*, January 25, 2012.

9. Steven Rattner, "The Dangerous Notion that Debt Doesn't Matter," *New York Times*, January 25, 2012.

10. Nomura Global Economics, cited in BlackRock presentation, 2012.

11. Nicholas D. Kristoff, "Why is Europe a Dirty Word?" *New York Times*, January 15, 2012.

12. See an excellent analysis of Turkey by Soner Cagaptay, "The Empires Strike Back," *New York Times*, January 15, 2012.

13. James Risen and Mark Mazzetti, "U.S. Agencies See No Move by Iran to Build a Bomb, *New York Times*, February 24, 2012.

14. Scott Wilson and Joby Warrick, "Obama Assures Israel on Iran," *Washington Post*, March 6, 2012.

15. Yasmin Alem and Barbara Slavin Paper, "Iran's Internal Politics: The Supreme Leader Grows Ever Lonelier at the Top," Atlantic Council, Washington, D.C., March 2012.

16. Yasmin Alem and Barbara Slavin, supra).

17. Joby Warrick and Thomas Erdbrink, "U.S. Allies Agree to New Talks with Iran," *Washington Post*, March 6, 2012.

18. Amos Yadlin, "Israel's Last Chance to Strike Iran," *New York Times*, February 29, 2012; see also Yossi Klein Halevi, "Can Israel Trust the United States When It Comes to Iran?" *The New Republic*, March 2, 2012.

19. Melissa Eddy, "Court Keeps Hitler Work From Newsstands," *International Herald Tribune*, January 26, 2012; AP, "Study Shows Persistence of Anti-Semitic Attitudes," *Washington Post*, January 24, 2012.

20. See Leonard Saxe, "Where Policymakers and Researchers Diverge," *Forward*, November 11, 2011, discussing the Brandeis study; see also David Marker, "Only Another Survey Will Do," *Forward*, November 11, 2011, arguing for a new National Jewish Population Survey.

21. Gerald Steinberg, chairman of the Political Science Department at Bar Ilan University, quoted in Ethan Bronner, "It's the Divisions within That Pose the Greater Obstacles to Peace with Foes," *New York Times*, June 7, 2009.

22. Linda Gradstein, "The Price Gets Higher," *The Jerusalem Report*, November 7, 2011.

23. Deuteronomy 1:16 (D'Varim).

24. Israel Survey 2011, in the Israel Democracy Index, Jerusalem.

25. J. J. Goldberg, "Rightists Target New Israel Fund Over Grantees," *The Jewish Daily Forward*, January 31, 2010.

26. Jeremiah 31:1–20.

27. Letter to Joseph Twichell, October 23, 1897.

Index

ADL. *See* Anti-Defamation League

Afghanistan: Koran burning in, 122; United States' commitment to, 122, 278; United States military intervention in, 120

Af-Pak: battles converging in, 120–21; education of militancy in, 241–42; high stakes in, 124; interconnectivity of, 121–23; Obama's strategy with, 124; United States working around government corruption in, 124–25

aging populations, 201–2

Ahmadinejad, Mahmoud, 32, 131; Holocaust denial of, 128–29, 241; Khamenei's power struggle with, 128

AIPAC. *See* American Israel Public Affairs Committee

Albright, Madeleine, 53

Aliyah to Israel, Jewish Diaspora and, 208–9

Alon, Nitzan, 285

alternative energy, 194–96. *See also* green energy

American-Israeli Joint Economic Development Group, 50

American Israel Public Affairs Committee (AIPAC), 253

American Jewish Committee, pro-Israel leaders in Europe, 235

American Jews: in government, 4–5; internal challenges of, 313; Israel and United States

relations supported by, 268–70; Israel loyalty of, 255–57; liberalism of, 255, 269; mythical political power of, 252–56; Obama supported by, 253, 255; Six Day War providing pride for, 269; Zionism views of, 268–69. *See also* Jewish Diaspora

Anon, Kofi, 90

Anonymous, 176–77

Anti-Defamation League (ADL), 231

anti-Semitism: in Arab Spring, 135–36; Arab world's positive improvements with, 242–45; in Argentina, 229–30; "blood libel" and, 222–23, 240; in EU, 222–25; EU progress on, 234–35; in France, 223–24, 234; Gaza War causing, 259–60; Holocaust denial as, 235; international community and, 245–47; Internet and, 100, 233–34, 248; from Israeli-Palestinian dispute, 246; Israel legitimate criticism *vs.*, 247–58; from Madoff scandal, 95; Muslims and, 236–42; new forms of, 221–22; in United Kingdom, 226; in United States, 231–34, 246–47, 258–60

"apartheid," Israeli-Palestinian dispute and, 248–51

APEC. *See* Asia-Pacific Economic Cooperation

AQAP. *See* al-Qaeda in the Arabian Peninsula

Arab Peace Initiative, 244

Arab Spring, 1–2, 55; alternative scenarios arising from, 137–38; anti-Semitism in,